MW00620701

"*Pillars for Freedom* is a book that must be read and studied. It is one of the most important books on conservative values and policies that has ever been written."

Michael R. Pompeo, former Secretary of State,
and former Director of the Central Intelligence Agency

"When he was in his early 20s, Richard Levine single-handedly wrote Ronald Reagan's speech for the recommissioning of the battleship New Jersey. *Pillars for Freedom* exceeds the importance of even that momentous address for it compels our nation to change course. This book is unique in blending religious precepts, philosophy, history, and far-seeing commentary to create a blueprint for our times. *Pillars for Freedom* is a masterstroke."

Dr. John F. Lehman, Jr., former Secretary of the Navy,
and 9/11 Commission member

"*Pillars for Freedom* is a masterful analysis of current, grave, geopolitical challenges, including those posed by the People's Republic of China and Russia's brutal war in Ukraine. This is a book that considers the totality of our times and critically addresses our place in a momentous period in which the future of liberty lies in peril. It is a must read!"

Ambassador Paula J. Dobriansky,
former Under Secretary of State for Global Affairs

"Today, we are in dire need of people to light the way forward. In *Pillars For Freedom*, Richard Levine, using a historical framework, provides compelling insights into key national issues. Reasserting the best features of our heritage is essential to meeting our future with clarity. My hope is that leadership and governance will be channeled to meet Richard's expansive vision for our country."

Admiral William O. Studeman, USN (Ret),
former Deputy Director of Central Intelligence

Pillars for Freedom

Richard B. Levine

An exploration of the pillars of America's national power and the foundations and principles on which they rest

FIDELIS
PUBLISHING

FIDELIS PUBLISHING®

ISBN: 9781956454611
ISBN: 9781956454628 (eBook)

Pillars for Freedom
An Exploration of the Pillars of America's National Power and the Foundations and Principles on Which They Rest

©2023 Richard B Levine, LLC

Manufactured in the United States of America
10 9 8 7 6 5 4 3 2 1

Cover Design by Diana Lawrence
Interior Design by Xcel Graphic

Order at www.faithfultext.com for a significant discount. Email info@fidelispublishing.com to inquire about bulk purchase discounts.

Fidelis Publishing, LLC
Winchester, VA • Nashville, TN
www.fidelispublishing.com

For Terry

The night is nearly over, and the daylight is near, so let us discard the deeds of darkness and put on the armor of light.

Romans 13:12

CONTENTS

FOREWORD

It is almost morning in America. Light is seeping into the horizon.

Our nation has undergone a transformation in this century that has brought great knowledge—but at a cost that must never again be paid. Technology must not become our god. Utopian narratives, which shroud Marxist predations, cannot become our standard.

As a people, we have surmounted the atrocities of 9/11 and have fought for freedom for those who had none. While our nation's intent in Afghanistan and in Iraq was noble, our massive interventions, constrained by onerous rules of engagement, depleted our country's military strength as well as our resolve.

The men and women who comprise America, whose hopes and dreams constitute the mantle that supports our country, have too often been forgotten or have been given short shrift. America's citizenry is the core of the United States; their interests must always come first. This fact is not discerned by the elites who disparage those who are the salt of the earth. In their condescension, our nation's self-professed overclass habitually claim a faculty they do not demonstrate, which is wisdom.

Through a maze of foreign wars in the first two decades of this century, our nation's leadership has too frequently forgotten the discernment expressed by our Founders that America is strong and secure when we lead by our example and not by our intervention through the force of arms. We disregard the wisdom of our Founders at our peril.

America's armed forces must be rebuilt and be rescued from Marxist theories, which are insinuated into our military's ranks by being paraded as progressivism or as critical race theory. In fact, these dogmas are levers that mask an insidious effort to destroy our military's cohesion, thereby undermining deterrence, for such a course will hobble America's ability to project power when required.

As we search for answers in a new century, we must rise as one people, or we will fall as many. We are a nation of countrymen, for each American is our brother or our sister.

Our country must be based on our love for each other and never upon hate. The present time is marred by injuries to our treasured principles and assaults upon our institutions. These pillages are further actualized through intense economic hardships, uncountable protests, and severe international threats. Each of these havocs is due, in large measure, to the stark inadequacies and to the perilous pursuits of the boastful but incompetent administration that now occupies the White House.

Without a sound economy our country will be lost. Therefore, our economy must be secured by concrete restraints on government spending; such reductions must be augmented by the elimination of regulatory overreach. These matters must be addressed immediately.

In the face of a national debt that far exceeds thirty trillion dollars, America must return to sensible frugality. What is thirty trillion dollars? This amount, if laid out in dollar bills, would constitute thirty million individual stacks, with each stack consisting of one million dollars. These towers would each be 358 feet high, which is approximately two-thirds the height of the Washington Monument.

Expenditures built upon waste and apathy never make sense for a family, nor do they make sense for a nation. America must return to our moral core if we are to repair our economy by reducing the size and the scope of government. To do otherwise is to allow runaway spending no boundary, though we know that its derivative is inflation, which constitutes the forfeiture of our nation's future, thereby destroying our children's dreams.

It is time to admit that the root of America's problems is not political but moral. Spending money we do not have, believing that irresponsible actions do not entail tangible costs, and permitting our nation's laws and the solemn oaths taken by public officials to be rendered meaningless, constitute a recipe for national collapse.

We must comprehend that being an American is a privilege; it is also a birthright for many of our citizens. Illegality cannot be a direct steppingstone to citizenship. Contempt for our laws must not be a passport. No nation welcomes more legal immigrants than does the United States. America must be a beacon for those who strive for freedom and for a better life, but our country cannot be a doormat.

Secure borders must be supported by an unceasing enforcement of consequential immigration laws and an application of policies that stress assimilation and reverence for our nation's founding principles. Only with these pieces in place can America be both strong and welcoming. We are a nation, not lines on a map that can be ignored with impunity.

If America should fail, the world will collapse, ushering in a ruinous epoch that may exceed the chaos and the poverty that accompanied the fall of Rome. Only by returning to our Judeo-Christian heritage and by embracing the superlative traditions and means of governance formed by America's Founding Fathers, can our country return to stability and resume its illustrious path.

Our nation's Founders existed as persons of their time and were flawed, for perfection does not exist in our world, and conduct is very often coerced by the age in which we live. Our Founders fought valiantly to redirect the tide of their days to the service of liberty and to set in motion the means, through our Founding Documents, to accomplish what they could not accomplish, the manifestation of freedom for every American, which took the Civil War and the loss of 700,000 lives to compel.

Our planet has always been scourged by slavery, which still exists throughout the world and now surges within America due to our porous southern border, which permits human trafficking. This horrendous situation has been instigated and inflamed by the Biden administration. Today, the number of people enslaved globally is the highest in history. Each and every person held in bondage must be freed. There is no more important pursuit.

America's Founding was not based upon the institutionalization of slavery but its repudiation through the mandated application of our Founding Documents. The patriots who established our Republic formed the most admirable nation to ever exist, for America has accomplished a singular feat in world history: We expanded freedom, despite grievous errors, for every subsequent generation since our Founding. This is our legacy, but it is incomplete.

America must never forget the ravages and the inhumanity of slavery or the detestable treatment of Native Americans that still scars our Republic. Franklin Delano Roosevelt's internment of Japanese Americans, during World War II, must never be excused, though it was errantly legitimized by the Supreme Court in the Korematsu decision of 1944.

Segregation must never be repeated under any guise, though many colleges and universities are attempting to reinstitute this obscenity; it is our obligation to stop this ruinous blight. If we repeat the sins of our past, in service to neo-Marxist ideologies, we will betray the priceless legacies of Frederick Douglass and Martin Luther King.

These great men understood that monuments not only explicate our past, they also mark our progress. We must learn from history, not destroy it, for if we excise or edit the story of our country, we will dismantle avenues for future growth.

I am an Evangelical Christian, having come to know Jesus Christ through Bible study, led by fellow cadets at the United States Military Academy at West Point, almost forty years ago. My fellow cadets cared enough for me to show me not only the way to a better life, but the way to eternal peace and fellowship with God. In their treasured company, I learned that while money is used to establish value, it must never be used to establish worth—for worth resides in the individual and is created by God and not by our labors.

As secretary of state, I kept an open Bible on my desk and read from it every day. From its incomparable wisdom, I sought and attained the tools of leadership and the belief in a better world to come.

I believe it is the break of dawn in America. We must meet it with purpose, with virtue, and with determination, fortified by our knowledge that our nation is a prime force for good. The present darkness must presage a new day.

Our country will persevere through the last remnants of night. We are poised for the resurgence of our nation's spirit. We must heed the call to rebuild America's foundations, so that our children and their posterity may rejoice in a land that must always be a beacon to the entire world.

Pillars for Freedom is a book that must be read and studied. It is one of the most important books on conservative values and policies that has ever been written.

My journey after service in the Trump administration has been enriched by my association with the author of this book. I came to know Richard through an introduction after the publication of his articles on national security and his book on China policy, *America's #1 Adversary*, which he coauthored with Vice Admiral John Poindexter and Robert McFarlane, who served as assistants to the president for national security affairs during the Reagan presidency.

Richard and I worked together on many important policy papers and speeches that I presented within our country and abroad. The chapters on nuclear weapons policy, economic security, and other sections of this book derive, in part, from this work.

At a young age, Richard made outstanding contributions to our nation's security policies, for he served four assistants to the president for national security affairs and three secretaries of the Navy. In the White House, Richard directed America's audacious response in the tanker Ypapanti hostage incident in which an oil tanker, loaded with millions of gallons of crude, threatened grave environmental damage to America's East Coast.

Richard wrote Ronald Reagan's principal defense address, delivered during his first term in office, for the recommissioning of the battleship USS New Jersey on December 28, 1982. Later, Richard would create, with Ambassador Robert Keating, the Food for Progress initiative, which has become one of our nation's most important international food aid programs.

Serving in the Department of the Navy, Richard originated its international program office and its technology transfer and security assistance review board, which exist to this day. Richard received two presidential letters of commendation. While still in his twenties, Richard became our nation's youngest recipient of the Department of the Navy's highest civilian honor, the Distinguished Civilian Service Award.

Life, however, often does not follow an even or predictable course. Richard was gravely disabled in January 1994 but fought back over a course of decades to regain his health. Through his journey, Richard has come to a profound understanding of the juncture of national security policy, world history, religion, and moral philosophy.

I believe his insights as recorded in this book are unequaled and must become a touchstone for the Republican Party. Paramount in Richard's conception of conservatism is that the principles that built our country are for everyone, not just people who are of the same race, religion, creed, background, or economic status.

Spanning five decades, Richard's trek toward truth reaches its zenith in this glorious work. I pray that its many messages touch every American.

The first major product of my collaboration with Richard was my speech of July 26, 2021, concerning the virtues of a conservative, given at The Ronald Reagan Presidential Library and Museum as part of their series titled, "A Time for Choosing."

As follows in this introduction are words taken from that address. I record them for they represent the core of the issues we face.

The American family, the faith we have in God and country, and hard work—fused with moral courage and introspection—built our nation into the greatest force for good the world has ever known. Unless we act now to assert faith and morality, our nation cannot be strong, and if America is not strong, the world will be at the mercy of tyrants and enter an era we dare not imagine.

I am forever grateful I came of age to serve my country during the presidency of Ronald Reagan, whom Richard knew well. Four decades ago, before my appointment to the United States Military Academy at West Point, I studied the life of my future Commander in Chief. Ronald Reagan came to define my conception—and that of my entire class—of what it means to be an American.

Though Ronald Reagan oversaw the rebuilding of America's military, he did so in order that our nation would attain peace through strength. Our fortieth president hated war. He thus set an indelible standard that graduates of West Point must always be soldiers of peace.

Faith has been our nation's strength. Without God's grace, it is immensely difficult for a soldier to lead his brothers and sisters into battle, for the sacrifices that may be demanded exceed any recompense in this world. To those serving in harm's way, it is the certain knowledge of everlasting life after this existence that conveys undaunted courage to the weary and implacable resolve to the reticent.

This is the truth George Washington understood when he commanded a force of farmers, hunters, and merchants to victory over the greatest army and navy in the world. This is the wisdom Ronald Reagan expressed when he defeated the undefeatable—the evil empire that was the Soviet Union—without war, but with a heart full of faith.

We must draw on these immortal examples if we are to meet the grave challenges we now face as a people. To reclaim America, there is no more important resource than the churches, synagogues, mosques, and temples that grace our land. There is no more important need than to hear their voices state: We must return to our moral core, lest all be lost.

When I was elected to Congress, made director of the Central Intelligence Agency, and later confirmed as secretary of state, my thoughts, concerning the challenges I would face, placed before me President Reagan's image, for he exemplified a nobility of spirit, without which no leader can command. President Reagan's statecraft informed what President Trump and I did to curtail Iran's nuclear abilities. It also provided the template for our actions to contain Vladimir Putin.

Unfortunately, what we accomplished has been cast aside by the deep state that is Washington. In their clandestine negotiations with Iran and in their elimination of our sanctions to inhibit Russia from supplying natural gas to Germany, they put our world at risk.

America must restore its character, its leadership, and its exceptionalism. The enunciation of faith is paramount. Our proclamation within the halls of power that God's relationship is with the individual and not the collective is essential. We, as conservatives, need to communicate our belief that everyone is endowed with dignity that must be respected because we all bear the mark of the Creator.

This principle is the means to bring our divided country together without hatred or acrimony. It is also an idea that statists reject. This is their Achilles' heel and is revealed by the actions of privileged elites who applaud what they, themselves, would not do, as they use and take advantage of those they pretend to support.

True conservatism in America declined after the Reagan presidency. The administration of which I was a part brought grit, populism, and disruptive innovation to revivify conservative principles.

Too many times, we have forgotten that our greatest gift to other nations is our example, not our force of arms. At home, we have tarnished our institutions and have compromised our belief in limited government and the necessity of the separation of powers.

We have allowed our courts to legislate, the executive to dictate, and Congress to exceed the bounds of its constitutional authorities. Chicago, New York, and especially Washington symbolize a dysfunction that is grasped by friend and foe alike.

The present crisis cannot be papered over. To move forward, we should not shirk any aspect of our history nor feel ashamed—for we have overcome, we have prevailed, and we have foresworn that which is corruptive of America's most reverent ideals.

Joy and hope must transcend our nation's present deterioration and discord. It is with this understanding and respect for our past that we must once again openly profess our faith, our devotion to our families, and proclaim, unapologetically, the words, "I am an American."

We must not look upon our opponents in anger, for it is both ablative to virtue and corrosive to judgement. James Madison, the father of our Constitution, believed that both openness and boldness, but not rancor, were vital for effective leadership.

Abraham Lincoln did not look upon his many adversaries and detractors in fury, but in righteousness, for it was in righteousness that King David thanked a loving God, who fortified and ennobled him. Psalm 41:12 recites David's gratitude, "Because of my integrity you uphold me and set me in your presence forever."

Today, many politicians state publicly that integrity is priceless. Is this the reason so many demonstrate they cannot afford it?

Virtues are developed through God's grace and are the foundation of our Republic and of all human happiness. Frederick Douglass stated, "The life of the nation is secure only while the nation is honest, truthful, and virtuous." No truer statement has ever been spoken.

The antidote to strife is virtue. America's virtues are not represented by our wealth. *Our virtues are our wealth.* America is strongest when we act according to our Founding Documents, which faith has imbued. We are weakest when we disregard this priceless heritage.

Narratives have replaced reality. Deprecating fictions concerning the establishment of our nation are presented as fact. Rather than seek truth, those who seek power demand subservience to stories propagated by disingenuous elites and spewed by unscrupulous politicians enabled by the internet and social media. The result is a nation separated from truth, but bound by narratives that superficially support the dispossessed, but actually enrich America's new ruling class who believe they are entitled to control the lives of others, though they often have trouble controlling their own.

This politburo of false virtue believes they are smarter than everyone else, but in their arrogance, this wealthy and privileged group betrays itself to be destitute, for no government, no elite, and no authority has ever created prosperity and happiness by making itself lord over men and women born free. Radicals hope to take from us the joy and pride we have in our country. We must not let them.

Where there is no joy or pride, hope is forfeit. Imagine a proud mother of two daughters, born into slavery, who perished establishing a new route for the Underground Railroad: What would this courageous woman not have given to see her children raised in the freedom and opportunities of today, rather than to the life of burden she knew?

Further, imagine a Choctaw warrior in 1918, serving in the American Expeditionary Force during the assault on Forest Farm in France. Aware from his elders' oral histories of the broken treaties and grievous losses suffered by his people, aware that Native Americans could not yet vote in our national elections, this incomparably selfless man nonetheless used his tribe's unique language to confound the German force before him, becoming one of our nation's first code talkers.

This gallant action helped bring victory to an American Army. By his deeds, this Choctaw soldier demonstrated that while the past informs the present, it must never be an obstacle to a better, more vibrant future. We owe it to all Americans who lived and died under the yoke of oppression to celebrate what we have and what we have become.

History is the sum total of actions both good and bad, brave and irresolute; it cannot be parsed and strained to remove parts that are offensive, for to do so is to rob our past of the richness and complexity that built the road to our present day. These two stories, to which the names of many of our forebears may be applied, represent the giants who formed the foundation upon which our nation rests. I ask you to imagine what these two persons would not have given to have been part of the America of today, yet I do not believe either would have given up their place in history if in so doing they would have altered our country's character.

Collapse from within is possible. Race and open borders have become levers for the left to sow societal disunity. Immigration without assimilation, illicit drugs, human trafficking, disputed elections, and inflationary risk have become tools to disassemble our Republic. In what must be an attempt at national suicide, we allow MS-13 assassins to pass through our borders with gang tattoos covering their faces while we are lectured by our media for our obstinacy.

The histories of our heroes should, instead, be taught, so students may comprehend the potential for excellence that exists within every person. Dr. Norman Borlaug, born in 1914, created the green revolution. President Carter wrote that Dr. Borlaug did more than any "individual in history in the battle to end world hunger," for he developed the high-yield wheat and agricultural practices that averted starvation in Mexico, India, Pakistan, China, and Africa.

In destitute villages the world over, Norman Borlaug did not see race, religion, or color. He asked but one question: Do these people have enough food? In so doing, he saved more lives than any person who ever lived. He was the recipient of the Nobel Peace Prize, the Presidential Medal of Freedom, the Congressional Gold Medal, and countless accolades from around the globe, yet his accomplishments are taught infrequently, if at all, in our public schools. This must change.

We dwell on our faults as if they were unique and not ubiquitous to every land that has ever existed. When will we teach our children of America's triumphs? Our country is tearing itself apart and for what?

Anarchy and the elimination of our police cannot but bring us death and fear. Discrimination cannot be fought with more discrimination. And the form of socialism that is now being praised by woke politicians and billionaires will bring our democracy to its knees by culling dissenting opinions while concealing harmful biases in search engines and in social media platforms.

If we do not act to secure our elections, demand voter identification, and end online manipulation, we will be governed by forces beyond our control. Who will benefit? Not America, but an array of global interests that has amassed power and uncountable wealth through their usurpation of the American dream. This is done by selling or commoditizing the engines of our economy.

China has infiltrated Hollywood, academia, our technology companies, and the corporations that control America's media, publishing, and news sources. Our strengths have been turned against us. Communist influence must be eliminated in our country—root and branch. Might is what China understands, and we are showing little of it.

Terrorism and disintegration in the Middle East support the interests of Beijing and Tehran as well as Moscow. For China, terrorism instigated by Iran diverts American military capabilities.

Iran's active nuclear weapons program compounds this danger and has been supported surreptitiously by China for decades. For Iran, its ties to the East constitute an invaluable source of dual-use technology, much of it stolen from the United States and our allies.

President Trump and I recognized that America's relationship with Israel must be unshakable to constrain Iran's objectives and those of its confederates. Before the Trump administration, the status of Jerusalem had been a diplomatic chess piece. It is not. It is the eternal capital of the Jewish people. Our decisive action in moving our embassy to Jerusalem demonstrated determination and in so doing removed an obstacle to the Abraham Accords, which saw four Muslim-majority nations make peace with Israel.

We must recognize that new dangers to freedom appear constantly. Pandemics, genetic engineering, cyberwarfare, power-grid disruptions, and artificial intelligence have the potential to change our world. Vision is the key to meeting these and other challenges.

Ronald Reagan and Mikhail Gorbachev established the foundations for the International Thermonuclear Experimental Reactor program during their summit in 1985. Now being made operational, this project will explore the production of fusion energy. If successful, Ronald Reagan's vision will, in this century, bring the heart of the sun's power to our planet.

Truly clean energy will finally exist in infinite supply. This was imagination. This was exceptionalism. Since we cannot find this type of prescience and grit in our government today, we must take back the Senate and the presidency to create it.

The great poem, "The Ruin," written more than one thousand years ago, records the remnants of Roman Britain, which was built centuries earlier, but lost to time, "This masonry is wondrous; fates broke it; courtyard pavements were smashed; the work of giants is decaying."

This must never be the future of America. Events may have pushed our nation into a furnace, but the Book of Daniel tells us that people of faith cannot be harmed by such a test.

With hands on our hearts, we must turn a glowing furnace into a forge. Within it we will form our "rendezvous with destiny."

We will renew the dream, we will honor the past, and we will chart a brave path forward, for in so doing, we will light the way for the entire world. May this momentous book be our torch.

Michael R. Pompeo   July 19, 2023

PREFACE

In humility, I offer my ideas in these pages as to how our nation should meet our shared future. In his *Poetics*, Aristotle explained that character is revealed when choices are difficult and not easily made. Though we find ourselves besieged through an accumulation of misjudgments and aggravated misdeeds, our present quandary provides us with an unequaled opportunity to demonstrate America's true character—to ourselves and to the world.

The emphasis of this book encompasses national security, its international dimensions, its foundations, and its pillars, but my purpose is more expansive. I seek to demonstrate the nexus between national objectives, domestic goals, and international security policies. Our world becomes more interdependent each day. The separation between domestic concerns and international affairs no longer exists—if it ever did.

As has been demonstrated by Vladimir Putin's illegal and merciless assault against the independent nation of Ukraine, a war half-a-world away can affect Americans directly—in the emptying of our savings and in the quashing of our dreams. Our nation's geostrategic and policy choices directly affect the homeland and the entirety of our citizenry. It is obligatory that we consider not only the consequences of our actions but unintended ramifications, which are often difficult to envision.

Throughout my journey to describe our nation's foundations and pillars of power, I benefited enormously from insights and recommendations offered by former Secretary of State Michael Pompeo, who previously served as the director of the Central Intelligence

Agency. Vice Admiral John Poindexter and William Martin also provided superb advice.

William and I served under John Poindexter on Ronald Reagan's National Security Council staff. John Poindexter, physicist, strategist, and dear friend, possesses an extraordinary mind, which is only equaled by his love for our country. William Martin, who became deputy secretary of energy during the Reagan administration, is one of the world's most incisive experts on energy issues. Through my associations with these three men and other former White House colleagues, issues of conspicuous difficulty became at once possible to be considered. Solutions to matters thought insoluble are thus proposed.

This is a book of ideas; I have not omitted complexity where elaboration is required, for we must seek the resolution of many of America's most difficult problems, not the plying of empty political rhetoric. True answers require honesty, for only this can turn ideas into actions. The pages of this book do not present an easy path, for the path to distinction and preeminence is never painless or undemanding. This book presents important problems of immense scope that cry for answers, which I attempt to provide based upon a lifetime of inquiry, hardship, and service.

Problems are presented in each chapter along with ameliorative actions, which are described both in the text and are highlighted in summary sections throughout the book. In addition, twelve charts are provided to illuminate complex issues. Thus, this book may be read in different ways: It can be read cover-to-cover; the summary sections can be reviewed first, or sections of text can be studied along with the charts, which each cover multiple chapters. Through this varied format, it is my hope that this volume may touch the greatest possible number of readers, for our nation's future depends upon the decisions we make today.

CHAPTER I

TRUTH

We, as men and women, are each ennobled by our Creator's vision that we build an ever more moral, bountiful, and secure union. America is a lantern of liberty for the entire world. Therefore, the candle we keep must never be extinguished.

As Americans, we believe in the power of dreams, made possible by education. We maintain the necessity of limited government, lower taxes, and deficit reductions. We support trade and economic security agreements that always place America's interests first. We uphold that each person is created in the image of God, deserving of respect that must be protected from injustice. These interlocking precepts are the core of America's essence. The foregoing principles comprise the sinews of who we are: They are not subject to barter.

Truth

An immortal truth governs the universe: God can become man, but man can never become God. The first part of this statement is the font of all mercy, for to be Christian is to know humanity's Savior. The second part of the statement is the basis for great evil, for despotism, fascism, Nazism, and communism are all rooted in the belief that man can be as God and, therefore, know no bounds.

The destruction of limits permits evil to masquerade as good and thus deceive, for humankind is born into sin, which precipitates iniquities if the standards we hold are only our own. It is this realization that impelled Thomas Jefferson to set unalienable rights as the basis for our Republic, in the Declaration of Independence, for these rights come from our Creator and not from man and therefore cannot be abridged.

It is the recognition of these rights that separates America's Founding from that of every other nation. It is upon this foundation that the Constitutional Convention in 1787 created a lasting template for liberty. James Madison's genius penned words to express eternal truths that our Founders carved into the Constitution and the Bill of Rights.

These three masterworks are our legacy that reflects the essence of American exceptionalism that we should proclaim, for our nation's place is based upon the rights of the individual and not the prerogatives of the state. We are a lantern of liberty for the entire world. Therefore, the candle we keep must never be abated or extinguished.

Threats

The kleptocratic theocrats who rule Iran and subjugate its people should never be allowed to possess a nuclear weapon. Iran's march and the spread of terrorism must be arrested in the Middle East and in Africa. In 2020, Secretary of State Michael Pompeo presided over peace agreements between Israel and four countries: the United Arab Emirates, Bahrain, Sudan, and Morocco, marking the first time since 1994 that peace was made between an Arab nation and Israel.

Other Muslim countries sought to be part of the Abraham Accords, but the Biden administration deemphasized this grand accomplishment, not wishing to credit the Trump administration as the authors of peace within the Middle East. One of the means to stop Iran and to interdict the spread of terrorism is to resume the hard work that led to these accords, but, deplorably, President Joseph Biden is more concerned with placating extremists, both within and outside America, who support radical Palestinian objectives, including the eradication of the Jewish state of Israel.

Terrorism exists both beyond and inside our borders: Transnational criminal organizations kill more than 100,000 Americans each year through the provision of illegal drugs.[1] These losses match the total numbers of servicemen killed on average each year during World War II, yet we have declared no war on this viperous enemy.

Cartels penetrate our borders, smuggling those they seek to enslave and traffic. The Biden administration, by its actions and by its timorousness in the face of leftists and thugs, has opened the gates, empowering these cartels to cross our borders to murder and to violate the lives of Americans in every state and in every city in our country. How dare President Biden and his administration not defend the lives of American citizens in the face of this rampage?

Ominously, transnational criminal organizations receive support from China and from other belligerent states that see the cartels as an effective tool in the conduct of threshold or liminal warfare, in which state participation may be cloaked or be designed to be publicly disputed. Making common cause with criminal organizations is not China's only crime.

The coronavirus pandemic scarred America and the world. The multitude of Americans who have died now far exceeds one million souls, far more than twice the number of our countrymen killed in the Second World War. This staggering price, however, does not count those who have been crippled or who will die years before

---

[1] https://www.whitehouse.gov/briefing-room/statements-releases/2022/03/01/fact-sheet-addressing-addiction-and-the-overdose-epidemic/

their time due to the medical and the financial ramifications of the pandemic.

Based on a substantial body of evidence, including recent conformations that the first three individuals who fell ill from the virus were scientists at the Wuhan Institute of Virology,[2] I assert that this catastrophe was created by gain-of-function research that may have been directly or indirectly funded by the United States Government, that the release of the virus was covered up by the Chinese Communist Party, and that the lethal spread of SARS-CoV-2 throughout the world was actuated by the People's Republic of China and its president, through the facilitation of the transit of infected persons globally while such travel within China was severely restricted. There must be a reckoning, for if there is none, this obscenity will repeat itself, perhaps involving a pathogen of even stronger virulence. This cannot be permitted to occur.

Russia's assaultive war against Ukraine has devastated the European peace and a cradle of world civilization. We must be on watch, for if China dominates a weakened Russia, a pan-Eurasian colossus could be formed that could be even more dangerous than these irridentist countries are individually.

It is imperative that the principles of American military and energy dominance, coupled with restraint in the use of force that commits our nation to battle, be advanced. These precepts must govern our nation's actions today but are depreciated. It is thus vital that we believe with all our hearts that neither the pandemic wrought by China nor the infamy perpetrated by Vladimir Putin has destroyed our prayers or our hopes for the future but has focused them.

Standards and Questions

America, today, advocates for equality and for opportunity for all people. These objectives can be attained if we insist on advancement

---

[2]https://www.wsj.com/articles/u-s-funded-scientist-among-three-chinese-researchers-who-fell-ill-amid-early-covid-19-outbreak-3f919567?mod=hp_lead_pos11

based upon meritocracies that exalt excellence. Decisions based upon merit must be colorblind, lest such determinations preference one group of Americans over another.

As Americans, we believe in the power of dreams, which must be facilitated through passionate, incisive, and affordable education. We uphold the necessity of lower taxes and the prioritization of deficit reductions. We support trade and economic security agreements that always place America's interests and standards first. These interlocking precepts are the core of our nation: We must commit to always championing these standards in our nation and around the world.

The foregoing principles comprise the sinews of our country; they are not subject to barter. They can never be purchased, for each of us know, in our own heart, that what we do must stand God's judgement, for eternity awaits each of us and cannot be set aside. These are American values, which we must defend.

Inquiry

President Biden, in a rare press conference given on January 19, 2022, asked, "What are Republicans for? What are they for? Name me one thing they're for."[3] Republicans bear an obligation to answer these questions, for President Biden and his administration are bereft of ideas to solve our nation's crises, for they are the authors of many of the calamities we face.

Abraham Lincoln was my party's first president. Along with Martin Luther King, no single person in history fought harder for the freedom of America's children, so they would know lives of happiness and opportunity. Republicans comprehend that prejudice can never be fought with more prejudice.

Treating all persons as individuals is the means to vanquish the injustice that can be perpetrated against people based upon racial, ethnic, religious, or social attributes. The recognition that every

---

[3]https://www.newsweek.com/kevin-mccarthy-responds-joe-biden-days-later-what-republicans-1671993

person is a unique creation of God is the means to defeat all prejudice, which is defined as the application of preconceived judgements that may result in hostility or harm.

Though the traits of duty, honor, wholesomeness, and faith are now repressed due to a stifling political class, they are the heart of America: Their beat is strong for those who have ears to listen. Republicans recognize that freedom is in jeopardy, for liberty is not understood by America's self-anointed ruling class, which bankrolls the Democratic Party to cloak the consummate greed and will for power present in each of these debased groups. These usurpers pocket the hard-earned money of citizens or print it, though inflation is the most regressive tax. America's acquisitive class does not have the time or the patience to learn that the prices of basic goods—food, gas, and shelter—constitute the greatest proportion of wages for working Americans who do not have letters after their names.

Republicans hold that liberty, as promised in our Declaration of Independence, is our birthright. Liberty, however, is only possible if limited government is practiced, for expansive government, through its reckless actions, subverts individual agency and choice, ultimately destroying freedom.

Republicans believe that the free expression of faith and the sanctity of the American family are prerequisites to contentment and to the enrichment of our nation. Any government program that circumscribes faith or hurts American families is never acceptable, yet a cascade of actions against these central institutions is perpetrated by Democratic politicians, intent on substituting the veneration of an all-powerful state for our love of the Lord and the blessings of all those we hold dear.

Republicans proclaim that each life is precious, for each is a gift of God. Republicans assert that every person is deserving of respect, no matter their situation or station, for we each bear the mark that is the imprint of our Creator, who must never be disrespected. Republicans defend the rule of law, which is upheld by community-based sheriffs' departments and police forces that enforce professional standards in their service to all Americans.

Republicans know, as George Washington did, that a strong defense is the surest means to secure peace, for timidity in the face of belligerence invites conflict and with it, the loss of life. Republicans contend that China is an existential threat, whose stated intentions cannot be trusted. Beijing hid the origin of a vicious plague, permitting it to reach every corner of the globe, killing millions and wreaking devastation.

Republicans affirm that we must thwart China's theft of American jobs and intellectual property. Communist China cannot be placated; it must be confronted. We must expose its deceits and its crimes, but this is impossible for an administration that does not believe in American exceptionalism.

Republicans understand that Russia and Iran will remain grievous threats to America and to the world until their present regimes collapse. No arms control negotiations with the president of Russia or with the president of Iran can bear fruit if all their regimes know or recognize is hate and power.

Republicans appreciate that the free market, unbridled by excessive governmental regulation, is the engine for economic growth for America and for all the nations of the world. True advancements and the unleashing of human potential are never accomplished by dictatorial bureaucrats, who fancy themselves the creators of tomorrow, though they cannot manage the present.

Republicans emphasize that our environment must be preserved. American energy dominance is necessary to ensure clean air, clean water, and the vibrancy of our nation's heartland and cities, for abundant power is essential to create the jobs and the prosperity necessary to address environmental concerns.

Republicans stress that we must reinvigorate our schools and learn from history, not destroy it. Republicans maintain that an essential element of humanity is nationhood: Those who seek to upturn it speak of a past that never was and a future that must never be. We must finish the wall.

I would ask President Biden: Have you no capacity, sir, for introspection? You promised to shut down the virus. Not only did you fail utterly, you have damaged our nation in your perfunctory attempts to fulfill your empty rhetoric.

You promised to burnish other nations' respect for America, but you are the architect of the deadly and calamitous retreat from Afghanistan that has both armed and invigorated our country's enemies. American energy dominance is lost, for you put Russia and Saudi Arabia in charge, with predictable results. You did so by empowering the Kremlin by restricting American hydrocarbon production. You next impaired and infuriated Riyad, by delisting the Houthi insurgency in Yemen as a terrorist organization,[4] though it is supported by Iran, the rogue state with which you seek to reestablish a discredited nuclear agreement, which is not a treaty but a malicious farce that will breed instability.

Inflation is rampant, and our economy is in tatters. Love of country demands that we ask the man who occupies the Oval Office: Will you change course, Mr. President, or will you preside over the collapse of our principles and our civil society?

Nature

Diversity in our country now means stultifying homogeneity, for it is too often based on color and not on reverence for the individual. American exceptionalism is a heresy to the left and to the Biden administration, for they envision a future that will be bereft of nations.

Human achievement is not bound by what a free people can accomplish but is restricted by the rigidity of the worldview of those who believe they understand the aspirations and the competencies of persons whom they have never met and do not know. In contrast, we understand that American exceptionalism is based upon the autonomy of the individual.

---

[4]https://www.cnn.com/2021/02/05/politics/us-houthis-terrorist-list/index.html

Our citizens excel in every field of human endeavor: It is they who enrich the world. This is what the communist, the neo-Marxist, and the radical activist can never tolerate: human beings that do not fit within the left's warped and narrow view of what free people can achieve.

A technocratic bureaucracy rarely instigates innovation, rather it serves as an adverse force, entrenching complacency and mediocrity. Innovation may, in certain instances, be spurred by governmental action, but such innovation almost always is bracketed by what can be envisioned by bureaucrats.

The type of innovation that is the hallmark of America is different. Profound innovation, which built our nation, creates not only that which was envisioned but that which is unimagined or unseen. Profound innovation is almost never contemplated by governmental authorities.

When our government directs that we must build just one way or in one direction, it crowds out actions in other domains that could, in fact, be far more fruitful. If our government has proven anything in its centuries of existence, it is that it is not omniscient: It has never outsmarted the intellect of the American people and never will. Left untrammeled by unnecessary regulation and burdensome taxation, it is the dynamism of our people that drives the world forward as our citizens' creativity exceeds the expectations of any collective.

Learning and achievement are the substrates for America's global leadership in the sciences, in technology, and in manufacturing, but the Biden administration has placed our institutions and means of education in jeopardy. A vibrant civil society supports the American worker and farmer and places their interests first; it does this by prioritizing limited government, national sovereignty, and voting integrity. Prudent national security policies instill American military strength, energy dominance, and cybersecurity.

If America is to lead and to prosper in this century and beyond, education, the civil society, and national security must all be unassailable. Understanding and embracing America's Founding and our country's central principles are fundamental to the realization of these crucial objectives.

A Government for the People

The Book of Genesis records, "Come, let us build ourselves a city and a tower with its top in the heavens, and let us make a name for ourselves." This monument to hubris was the Tower of Babel. We cannot let it be replicated. We must forestall the federal government from crowning the tower that is Washington, which venerates its bureaucratic class. What must we do to end this march to oblivion?

Part of the answer is to reform our federal bureaucracies, for they are unbound: They are thus incapable of moderation, which is the prerequisite for good governance. President Eisenhower, whose life was marked by inquiry and by parsimony, reformed the federal bureaucracy; by doing so, government employment rolls were reduced by 212,700 in 1953, which improved efficiency and performance in the period that followed the Korean War.[5]

We need such bold leadership today. Government spends money it does not have because callow politicians appropriate it—after colluding with bureaucrats whose only measure of success is the attainment of power, which is denominated not in what gets done but in how much money is spent.

There is no quest for performance or solvency; neither is there any gratitude expressed to those civil servants who seek to eliminate waste and fraud. The annual federal budget for fiscal year 2022 amounts to approximately six trillion dollars, of which almost one-third will be financed by the assumption of debt.[6] This enormous sum

---

[5]https://ebrary.net/167583/history/personnel_management_eisenhowers_ federal_civil_service_reforms#:~:text=Eisenhower%20undertook%20a%20 major%20reduction%20in%20force.%20Federal,filling%20vacancies%20 caused%20by%20resignation%2C%20retirement%2C%20or%20death.

[6]https://www.thebalancemoney.com/u-s-federal-budget-breakdown-3305789#:~:text=President%20Joe%20Biden%20released%20a%20%246.011%20 trillion%20federal,a%20%241.837%20trillion%20deficit%20for%20Oct.%20 1%2C%202022.

and that for fiscal years 2023 and 2024 could not be obligated nor spent except for the absolute dereliction of the duties of governance.

Unfortunately, these crimes against our people are abetted by a Federal Reserve that has lost its way. Its mission was to control the nation's money supply[7] and interbank interest rates in service of our economy and its stability.[8] The Federal Reserve has unfortunately become the coconspirator of an administration that seeks to buy votes by first stealing from the public. President Biden's preferred mechanisms for such theft are inflation and the assumption of ruinous debt.

To right this ship, the size and the scope of government must be reduced markedly. The Federal Reserve must be made to return to its core missions, as established by law. In the past, problems inherent in the federal bureaucracy were understood by members of both parties. This is no longer the case.

The following words of Franklin Delano Roosevelt may stun today's Democrats. In addressing the president of the National Federation of Federal Employees, during the height of the Great Depression, President Roosevelt wrote,

> Particularly, I want to emphasize my conviction that militant tactics have no place in the functions of any organization of Government employees. Upon employees in the Federal service rests the obligation to serve the whole people, whose interests and welfare require orderliness and continuity in the conduct of Government activities. This obligation is paramount.[9]

These words, written by the Democratic Party's greatest politician, who led America through the Second World War, would be anathema today, for this statement summarizes one element of the crises

---

[7]https://www.stlouisfed.org/on-the-economy/2018/july/federal-reserve-control-supply-money
[8]https://money.usnews.com/investing/term/federal-funds-rate
[9]https://www.presidency.ucsb.edu/documents/letter-the-resolution-federation-federal-employees-against-strikes-federal-service

we face. The following steps must be taken by the next administration, for President Biden has only redoubled these problems.

First, there must be a process. Decisions to reduce federal expenditures, including the size and the scope of the federal workforce, must be made through the application of proven business and analytic tools.

Problems of this magnitude cannot be solved by ad hoc decisions. Formal processes must be instituted without delay to reduce the size of the federal workforce by three percent per year in all non-military departments.

Concomitant with these workforce reductions, total federal spending must be reduced significantly during a new administration's first term, such that expenditures will ultimately be met by the receipt of taxes, which for individuals and for businesses should not be increased but be lowered. This will spur enormous economic growth, enhancing tax receipts, which will portend balanced budgets and, in time, meaningful reductions in our national debt.

Second, our nation's permanent bureaucracy must be apolitical. The president is the executive branch according to the Constitution. The president represents the will of the entire nation. If a permanent bureaucracy is wedded to its own politics, it subverts the intent of the American people, as expressed through national elections. This is not only unacceptable, it threatens our entire democratic process.

A new administration must be able to fire those bureaucrats who are partisan in their actions and duplicitous in their objectives. The Department of Justice would be an excellent place to start, given the litany of its abuses and its infringements upon individual liberty.

Third, a civil servant must truly be the servant of the people, not a lord over them. Bureaucrats rule by regulations or by executive orders, which they frame. Officials may also subvert laws, which may be contorted to suit purposes divergent from the original intent of each statute.

Congress must write laws, free from the impetus for power generated by unelected bureaucrats. Any evisceration of the separation of powers is unacceptable.

Executive orders and presidential decrees are grossly misused. They are not a substitute for lawmaking; executive orders are often short-lived and ineffective, for they can be cancelled at the whim of a subsequent executive. The president should issue executive orders sparingly and never in opposition to established law, for the executive does not make law but enforces it.

President Biden's announcement to wipe away student loan debt is emblematic of his administration's affronts to the rule of law and to the role of Congress as the sole lawmaker. If it had been allowed to stand, this barely veiled parlay to buy votes would have cost American taxpayers over half-a-trillion dollars at a time of perilous inflation. Those who would have been forced to foot this bill include citizens who never had the opportunity to go to college and those who have already repaid their student loans. This unconscionable presidential action is an outrage that must never be allowed to metastasize in an altered form.

Even more damaging is the president's disavowal of established law through his refusal, in opposition to his presidential oath, to execute faithfully the office of the chief executive. The supreme manifestation of this illegal obstinance is President Biden's actions that result in open borders and illegal immigration.

Fourth, the federal hiring process must be freed from surreptitious political appointments that occur by rigging job selection criteria. Excellence, and not anything else, must be the federal government's standard in hiring.

Our purpose must be the creation of a lean government workforce that is apolitical, for civil servants must support the administrations of either party. The president controls approximately 4,000 political positions, which are crucial to every administration, for they enforce the president's policies. Consideration to increasing this number must be undertaken with the utmost care, for our country's solvency demands substantial reductions in the federal workforce—not more political agents who would be associated with one party, only to be removed after the opposing party comes to power.

The federal bureaucracy, after being streamlined, should be marked by actions that evince consistency and deference to the president. The federal workforce must demonstrate service to the citizenry, not hyper-partisanship.

It is easier to remove political bias than to counterbalance it. For a conservative administration, the primary objective should be to remove political activism from the bureaucracy. To attempt to compensate for it by adding to the other side of the ledger would almost certainly not achieve the desired effect, noting that highly entrenched political forces oppose such an equilibrium.

Presidential appointments are the means to effect an administration's policies, which constitute the catalyzing force of the people, as established through national elections. Our country's system of national elections, as enforced by the United States Electoral College, must not be subverted by a clandestine force of unelected partisans who act in opposition to presidential prerogatives.

We must institute rigorous and auditable practices to ensure professionalism in government. Patent acts of partisanship within the scope of governmental duties must be harshly rebuked if such acts are perpetrated by civil servants. It is in both parties' interests to reform government. Democrats do not see this, Republicans must.

Traps

Corrupt politicians engineer fake lures that appear superior to what is real, hoping citizens will succumb to such ploys. These goads whet appetites to pursue that which cannot be attained or that which is detrimental if achieved. Biologist Niko Tinbergen, who was a recipient of the Nobel Prize in Physiology or Medicine in 1973, called unrealizable enticements, supernormal stimuli. They are at the heart of unethical political posturing, which is now the mainstay of the Democratic Party.

Outrageous pandering is pronounced among progressive agents who embrace whatever narrative is most constructive to their realization or their maintenance of power. Political power, combined with obstruction that is abetted by loopholes in our laws, permits unearned wealth to be conveyed to family members of elected officials, who, in turn, enrich the politicians who remain the first cause of such theft.

We face information warfare of a type heretofore unknown. It is propelled by the People's Republic of China, which seeks dominance in this sphere. China, assisted by revolutionary forces within America, is helping engineer something akin to a snare. This trap, in a political sense, is constituted by the corruption of our Republic's government and its supportive institutions by a myriad of influences, such that our nation's evolved traits, which include a free press and democratic institutions, have become maladaptive, thereby presaging the extinction of the society that we have known.

It is through such traps that America's freedoms and means of holding elections have been turned against their prior expressions, so that all roads lead to despair, for all promises are ultimately broken. Our freedoms are being repurposed so that they may be used as bludgeons to destroy our Republic. This threat has its roots in a series of ideas that do not derive from experience or the world in which we live.

At the heart of this pretense is the creation of false realities. These are most properly called hyperreal, for spun or accreted narratives constitute a hall of mirrors inculcated or enabled by the press, social media, and search companies.

Social constructionism posits that reality is the product of many minds' conjuring it into existence. There is substantial support for this conjecture within the academic community; indeed, this thinking is now common within elite institutions. Emblematic of such incantations is the lie that America is replete with systemic racism. This specter has become a modus to transform thought into actuality.

The Biden presidency's deficit spending, which has no peacetime precedent in American history, may be viewed as the product of a newfound Aladdin's Lamp, for the administration seems intent on wishing an incorporeal, utopian reality into existence, even if it bankrupts our nation. Seen through this lens, the aberrant behavior of leftists, as opposed to classical liberals, may be understood.

Intellectual foundations of the present neo-Marxist movement in America, which is infatuated with the mutability of common language, may be traced, in part, to the German philosopher Martin Heidegger, who aspired to be named the philosopher of the Nazi party. It was he who posited the insubstantiality of reality as projected through language, to enable lies to become truths, and repeated errors, achievements. This philosophy has become a major substrate for leftist thought, though it is rooted in fascism.

Reality does not, however, exist in our minds to be whispered into existence by dint of language, which, itself, is deemed by the left to be devoid of shared meaning, thus exposing the internal contradictions of the left's phantasms. Our perceptions of the world are formed by consciousness, but no number of kindred minds make a god. We have much harm to undo if our nation's course is to be corrected.

Monuments

As a society, we must not forswear history; we must also protect what is created as art. Without markers to the past our future cannot be charted, for the certainty of history vanishes when the last witness to it dies.

One hundred years from now, what history might be taught of the impact of slavery in America if all our monuments are demolished? This we cannot know, for as with the Ministry of Truth in George Orwell's *Nineteen Eighty-Four*, our nation's history could be rewritten incessantly to suit ephemeral political imperatives.

By allowing the toppling of the markers of our nation's history, in the form of public sculptures of great artistic merit, we, as a society, are treating the past as if it were part of the present, which it is not. By so doing, we are replicating the cognitive problems that may come with hyperthymesia, a condition in which a person remembers all of life's experiences instantly.

Hyperthymestic abilities may exact a high price. Unable to stop the past from invading the present leads to the lack of discernment of what is truly the past. Trying to separate past from present may become irresoluble, with the affected person lost in a house of mirrors whose surfaces reflect some past point that is now mixed with the sensory experiences of the present. Life becomes arduous or impossible. The present and the future can no longer be met with grace, for they can no longer be distinguished from what has already occurred.

By destroying our nation's monuments, we are in essence destroying the arrow of time. Today is thus a jumble of what is present and past, which is being rewritten or edited to conform to an unyielding ideal. We have created a new and unprincipled mode in which to experience our lives, the screaming "now."

This is a recipe for societal dysfunction on a grand scale, which is what we are witnessing. As with the case of a person with hyperthymestic syndrome, our present life is exhausting our capacities to cope, for we are making no distinctions between the past and its societal rules, and our present time and the norms we observe.

The rioters and malcontents of today want to crash their present into our past, to create something that will be homogeneous. Such a construct cannot advance; indeed, there is an unintended price: If the evolving nature of life and history is obliterated, then future advancement is impossible because our past, present, and future must all be uniform. This is the tragic illogic that pervades the minds of these radicals.

We must, as a society, deploy solutions that honor history, while enshrining respect for those who have been deeply wounded by it. One answer could be a cellphone app that gives many different perspectives when an observer is near any of our country's monuments to individuals whose lives were complex and whose actions are now deemed incongruent with present moral standards.

We should, as a nation, present the totality of history to the public. This will serve to increase knowledge of the ravages of slavery, the Civil War that was fought to end it, and the people and their motivations that caused the war to be waged.

Mantle

The pillars of freedom can only stand if they are embedded in foundations that rest upon the glowing core of our world. These foundations are our faith, our Founding, our families, and our people, which are strengthened by our nation's commitments to education and to science.

These foundations are further imbued with the virtues of vision, hope, gratitude, and forgiveness. These qualities instill clarity, fortitude, discernment, and charity, which are necessary to face our nation's problems in order that we do not dwell in the past but live for the future.

Our government is pocked by an administration and a bureaucratic state that rely on diversion, untrue narratives, and misdirection to cover their own incompetence and their raft of errors. Perhaps paradoxically, it is the lawlessness and permissiveness—which erode the civil society—that precipitate public desires for governmental action, thus increasing the administration's size and reach. This may in time lead to totalistic governance, in which restrictions are imposed on activities, limiting severely the latitude of private or individual actions that were previously permitted.

Political or other groups may be targeted at this point because the regime in power, lacking success or initiative, will seek internal and external enemies to divert the public's attention. This is the cycle we must break.

To illuminate, the faceted side of a crystal must be held closest to the light. It is the many merits of our citizens that permit a path forward to be charted. It is our nation's virtues—which are always vested in the individual and not the state—that constitute the wellspring of all necessary reform.

Upon these foundations stand the pillars of strategic defense, economic security, energy dominance, and military strength. These powers, in turn, support the executive in the conduct of diplomacy, intelligence operations, and homeland security. These are the structures that we must fortify without delay.

Chapter 1, Truth, Precepts:

• In our nation's Declaration of Independence, Thomas Jefferson set unalienable rights as the basis for our Republic, for these rights come from our Creator and not from man; they therefore cannot be abridged.

• Republicans hold that liberty, as promised in our Declaration of Independence, is our birthright.

• It is the recognition of these unalienable rights that separates America's Founding from that of every other nation.

• Republicans believe that the free expression of faith and the sanctity of the American family are prerequisites to contentment and to the enrichment of our nation.

• Government spending and its regulatory power have grown out of control; the federal deficit threatens our nation.

Issues and Problems:

• At the heart of many of our nation's most profound problems is the creation of false realities to inhibit our discernment, thereby blocking our ability to resolve crises.

• Terrorism exists both beyond and inside our borders: Transnational criminal organizations kill more than 100,000 Americans each year through the provision of illegal drugs.

• The release of the Wuhan virus was covered up by the Chinese Communist Party; the lethal spread of SARS-CoV-2 throughout the world was actuated by the People's Republic of China and its president.

• Russia's assaultive war against Ukraine has devastated the European peace and a cradle of world civilization.

Duties and Actions:

• Republicans comprehend that prejudice can never be fought with more prejudice.

• Treating all persons as individuals is the means to vanquish the injustice that can be perpetrated against people based upon racial, ethnic, religious, or social attributes.

• The traits of duty, honor, wholesomeness, and faith constitute our nation's strength and our salvation.

• Neither the pandemic wrought by China nor the infamy perpetrated by Vladimir Putin has destroyed our prayers or our hopes for the future but has focused them.

• American military and energy dominance coupled with restraint in the use of force that commits our nation to battle will provide the stage for America's rebirth.

• Decisions to reduce federal expenditures, including the size and the scope of the federal workforce, must be made through the application of proven business and analytic tools. We cannot keep spending money we do not have.

• We must institute rigorous and auditable practices to ensure professionalism in government.

• Our purpose must be the creation of an extremely lean government workforce that is apolitical. A primary objective should be to remove political activism from the bureaucracy.

CHAPTER 2

FAITH

Religious faith must be celebrated in America if our country is to survive. Our faith in God permits us to meet the challenges of life and to address the problems of our nation and the world.

Imagine set before us is a door, and beyond it is incalculable wisdom: All we need do is open it, and everything behind it can be ours. That door is the Holy Bible. From its incomparable truth, we must seek and attain the tools of leadership and the belief in a better world to come.

President Abraham Lincoln's peerless insight guided a country at war with itself, for, in this giant's estimation, we must never wonder whether God is on our side; our greatest concern must always be that we are "on God's side, for God is always right." Truly, this imperative must drive our nation.

Faith

The first foundation is faith. Religious faith must be celebrated in America if our country is to survive.

It is through darkness that the brightest light shines and makes the totality of existence visible. It is only through God's limitless love that we gain the stature and the resilience to face the wrongs we have committed, individually and as a nation, in order that we may repent, change, and embark on a better course.

This has been America's journey. It must be what we demand of the world.

As Christians and Jews, we proclaim Judeo-Christian values, for they are American values. No one of another faith or of no faith ever need fear these values, for they represent tolerance, forgiveness, and love for all humankind, for to profess otherwise would be to blaspheme the name of God.

Through the majesty of his example, the Lord demonstrated the nature of goodness. What is agreeable is not necessarily synonymous with what is good, for pleasantries and banalities may hide deceit or compromise. Too often, we are kind but not good, for we are benevolent but not wise.

Jesus was not agreeable nor was he courteous when he "overturned the tables of the money changers," but he was good. This is our standard.

We bear witness that goodness demands a selfless heart as we journey through pain, for such intent summons us to oppose evil. It is through this trek that growth occurs—within us and in those we touch—so that we may face a world that is forever renewed.

Though immensely difficult, we must confront the world as it is, not what narratives claim it to be. Our world is racked by sin. We dare not shy away, for to do so would permit the ascendance of elements contrary to God's plan.

Through the power of God, we must unite our families and the world's nations. This is our duty as servants of righteousness; this is our obligation to all those who thirst for truth and for deliverance.

I write not of globalism, for this, if ardently pursued, can cause great harm. Neither should we seek global governance, for it would surely reduce the worth of men and women as individuals. No, when we posit a unity of purpose for the countries of the world, we seek to pose a simple question: Are we living in accordance with God's word or are we violating it?

Fellowship and Ideals

The scholar and author C. S. Lewis stated, "I believe in Christianity as I believe that the sun has risen: not only because I see it, but because by it I see everything else." This is a truth that many Americans recognize, for it is through our belief in God that we gain the strength to face what must be faced without resort to falsehoods.

Our might granted to us by God is our armor, which permits us to meet the challenges of life and to address the problems of our nation and the world. In his farewell address to the country, Ronald Reagan said, "don't be afraid to see what you see."[10] This brief statement summarizes the quintessence of vision, which is to see the world in its totality, without presuppositions, which erode perception.

By assessing our faults, we acquire the tools to grow. America's journey documents this truth, for it is in submission to a forgiving God that we observe the course of our Republic.

Virtues

Imagine that set before us is a door, and beyond it is incalculable wisdom. All we need do is walk up and open it, and everything behind it can be ours. That door is the Holy Bible.

As mortal beings, we can never approach the majesty of God. However, we can advance in knowing him and our obligations through committed reading of God's word.

---

[10]https://www.reaganlibrary.gov/archives/speech/farewell-address-nation

The best preparations require patience and sensitivity. The great deeds of the leaders I have known necessitated that they be measured in their spoken words, for this trait is essential to the exercise of prudence.

God gives each of us important work to do, for I have learned that wisdom comes from humility. Great men and women realize that the accomplishment of seemingly small, inconsequential tasks prepares them to undertake that which is gargantuan, for to do what is small and bereft of rewards requires humbleness, which is the bedrock of all august achievements.

The acquisition of knowledge and its application require discernment. The choices we make have consequences for ourselves, our families, and our nation. Through God and our supplication to his word, we gain insight, by which the world's problems may be addressed.

Secretary of State Pompeo told me that in Egypt, in 2019, he visited the newly inaugurated Cathedral of the Nativity of Christ, which is the largest church in the Middle East. It was built in a land where the persecution of Christians occurs though ten percent of Egypt's populace is of Coptic Christian faith. As secretary of state, he proclaimed that every individual must be permitted to worship freely, within their own faith, as they choose.

In that magnificent cathedral, Secretary Pompeo witnessed God's hand at work: President Abdel Fattah al-Sisi said all Egyptians were one and will remain one. What a marvelous message. Truly, we can persevere in the knowledge that God ultimately heals the deepest of wounds, for we all live in a world of his creation.

We must extend charity to those who have hurt us, while seeking forgiveness for our own misdeeds in the realization that absolution is rendered only by a loving God. This is the truth that binds our world, for where others may see differences, those who are inspired by the Lord's beneficence see similarities and opportunities for fellowship.

We, as Americans, must all learn that the first step in solving the world's problems is clarity of sight, for without it, insight is impossible. Vision is a cardinal virtue.

Our Lord, in Jeremiah, warned us, "foolish and senseless people, who have eyes but do not see, who have ears but do not hear: Should you not fear me? . . . Among my people are the wicked who lie in wait like men who snare birds and like those who set traps to catch people. . . . their houses are full of deceit; they have become rich and powerful. . . . Their evil deeds have no limit; they do not seek justice."

These are the terrors of our time that push persons and nations apart. In politics and in international affairs, as in our own lives, our minds and the narratives that we have imbibed or assembled taint our vision. Unfortunately, the internet and social media frequently compound these errors.

Most national problems, which are said to be irresolvable, can be solved if only both sides perceived the world without suppositions. Stridency and willfulness are fortified, however, by a media that seeks to entrench division and discord among the many in order to convey wealth and power to the few.

Narratives and the appearance of false virtue, rule. Technology has introduced great advancements, but when it is used as a vehicle for propaganda and control, it becomes a bludgeon to move people from what they, themselves, know, to what others want them to believe.

Our political adversaries must never be met in cities aflame, but within a landscape where competing ideas are cultivated and permitted to flourish, rather than being culled by gigantic corporations that have no precedent in human history. Bipartisanship can only be achieved if clarity and reality are manifested in our nation's political discourse.

Our vision must also extend into the future and involve pathfinding. Proverbs tell us that "Where there is no vision, the people perish."

After his presidency, Ronald Reagan wrote, "To grasp and hold a vision that is the very essence of successful leadership." Our nation must again be led by men and women of vision that they may grasp the future and not be stunned by it. Vision, in the sense of clarity of perception and in the ability to conceive what could be, is a gift that is a virtue offered to us all by a loving and merciful God. We must use it but not be blinded by it.

The second virtue is hope. Elements in our country seek to divide our nation by generating political power through racial discord and exploitation. Through these instruments, radicals bereft of God and often inspired by Marx, Lenin, or Mao, seek to take from us the joy and the pride we have in our country. This, we must never let them accomplish.

As believers in God's infinite mercy, we know that where there is no joy or pride, hope is forfeit. And where there is no hope, the value and the sanctity of life, including that of the unborn, is diminished and may vanish.

We must restore the joy and pride that must imbue our Republic and touch every citizen or future citizen of our land. America is not faultless, but no nation has pondered or has tried to correct its faults more than the United States. We are proud, for we are free, but in this realization, we are obliged to be humble, for we know our strength comes from our obedience to God and the unalienable rights he has bestowed upon each of us.

Where there is hope, there is liberty, even if there is constraint. For hope dwells in our hearts, and this gift permits us to be free no matter the physical bounds we may face.

It is hope that permits a prisoner of war, in his or her own mind, to dwell in freedom. It is hope that allows the sick and the immobile to roam their memories and to think of a new and better day. It is in hope that we dream of our bountiful and benevolent country, which we know—through our prayers—will soon reclaim its glory as it casts aside its menaces.

The third virtue is gratitude. It is gratitude that substantiates our thankfulness and our responsibility to the nation that has been bequeathed to us.

Prayers begin with our expression of gratitude to a loving God. Prayers for our nation similarly rest on our recognition of what has come before, for this is the foundation upon which we must build.

In this world, how do we honor those who have sacrificed their bodies and their lives to build America, the greatest nation in history? We express gratitude to those who have shed their blood so that we may be free; we express gratitude to those who marched across bridges—in the face of great oppression—through our recognition of what they accomplished.

Gratitude is passed through generations. We thank those who came before us, for to do so is to begin to understand the trials and the difficulties they bore as well as the limitations they accepted, for it is our present consideration of these tests that grants us self-effacement in our conduct of affairs.

By looking to the future, we also express gratitude for what our nation might become. By this act, we connect the past, the present, and the future in our efforts, as individuals and as a people.

The fourth virtue is forgiveness. It is formative, for it creates who we become. Without a relationship with a loving God who forgives our sins, who among us would have the moral courage to peer into his or her own heart to discover and to begin to correct the wrongs we have committed?

As in each of our lives, our sorrows, our joys, our failings, and our accomplishments form what we will become. It is through forgiveness that we advance both as individuals and as one united people. We are all destined to sin, but through our devotion to God, those who are faithful may be blessed with the courage to acknowledge sin, to fight to overcome what is wrong, and to reflect on a journey to righteousness, which is forever incomplete but must be constant.

We must not parse or strain our nation's history to remove that which is objectionable, to strike down monuments that remind us of a different time that was less just. We must learn from our history and its markers, so that we may never repeat the transgressions of the past as we build our nation's future.

May we marshal these virtues so that with intrepidity we may confront the extraordinary challenges before us. It is these virtues that our Founding Fathers used to form the Declaration of Independence, the United States Constitution, and the Bill of Rights.

The Public Square

America must always be a land of hope and never one of fear. I believe with all my heart that the steps of our nation are established by our Lord, for God knows everyone, though everyone does not know God.

In our lifetimes, many in our country have taken the concept of the separation of church and state to mean that we must separate church from state. The two statements are not synonymous. Nor would any of our Founding Fathers believe them to be so.

The profession of faith in God is not inimical to the Establishment Clause, which became part of the Bill of Rights because faith was expected within America's public square. The clause was intended to bar the creation of a state religion, not remove religion from public life, for our Founders understood that faith and the ethical values that religion instills are essential to curb the powers of government.

Today, our world is scarred by selfish and villainous acts. What is our answer? It is to bring faith back into public life.

Thomas Jefferson authored A Bill for Establishing Religious Freedom, which he introduced to the Virginia Assembly in 1779 while governor. Jefferson wrote, "that Almighty God hath created the mind free, and manifested his supreme will that free it shall remain by making it altogether insusceptible of restraint."

Roger Williams, who founded Rhode Island, is said to be the first official to publicly call for the separation of church and state. Later, Thomas Jefferson would write that the Establishment Clause of the First Amendment to the Constitution, which forbade the inauguration of a state religion, built a "wall of separation between the church and state."

What is misunderstood and is mischaracterized today is that this wall was not to remove religion from our consideration of governance but was to protect the sanctity of the church and other faiths from the encroachments of temporal authorities who may ensconce themselves in government. We, in our arrogance, have banished religion from our schools and from our public squares. In doing so, we have forgotten our Founders' intent.

In his inaugural address on March 4, 1797, John Adams said America should "patronize every rational effort to encourage schools, colleges, universities, academies, and every institution for propagating knowledge, virtue, and religion among all classes of the people . . . as the only means of preserving our Constitution from its natural enemies." In the same address, Adams stated that he considered a "respect for Christianity among the best recommendations for the public service." Do these remarks sound as if our second president sought to banish religion from our houses of learning or from our government?

This was never the intent, nor could it have been at the time of our nation's creation, for in that age, humanity and its progress were viewed as inseparable from a belief in God. It is godliness that must be our touchstone as a society. Our government and certain private forces that hold power must never be permitted to shield God's word from our view or our grasp, yet a powerful assemblage of elites holds that what is right is wrong and what is good is suspect.

This ship must be righted. How then are we to consider the separation of church and state? Part of the answer can actually be found within the architecture and the sculpture of our nation's Temple of Justice.

Consider the stately beauty of the United States Supreme Court building. Built ninety years ago, this marble structure was designed in the neoclassical style. Its Eastern Pediment is not observed by most visitors, for they enter through the West.

It is, however, the Eastern Pediment that is most important, for its triangular frieze depicts history's great lawgivers. In its absolute center is Moses, holding the tablets of the Ten Commandments.

Approaching this massive sculptural relief, we observe that the tablets are blank, though their sheer size would have easily accommodated all the words handed down to us that constitute the Ten Commandments. These enormous tablets are unmarked because the Ten Commandments differ in their wording and order between the Roman Catholic, Protestant, Orthodox, and Jewish faiths. Therefore, if the words of the Commandments had been chiseled into the frieze's stone, the east entrance to America's highest court of justice would show preference to one faith over others.

Desiring that the religious wars of Europe, which spanned centuries, would not find refuge in America, our Founders forbade the establishment of a state religion. This is the wisdom that the Eastern Pediment purveys. There is, however, an even more important meaning. The essence of the separation of church and state to our Founding Fathers was to prevent the deification of government or its representatives.

This truth, in its articulation of the proper conception of the separation of church and state, was first enunciated by Christ, as recorded in the synoptic Gospels of Matthew, Mark, and Luke. No human mind, in the time of Imperial Rome, could summon this statement's depth or pith; it may thus be deduced that this pronouncement is divine.

Matthew 22:21 records: "They say unto him, Caesar's. Then saith he unto them, Render therefore unto Caesar the things which are Caesar's; and unto God the things that are God's." Mark 12:17 relates: "And Jesus answered and said to them, 'Render to Caesar the things that are Caesar's, and to God the things that are God's.' And they marveled at Him." In Luke 20:25, we find the same discernment.

Jesus did not say that certain human activities were outside God's authority. Instead, he proclaimed the godly and the physical spheres of humankind and in so doing provided the world with a means to live both within its earthly constraints and still obey the Father.

Idolatry and Communism

The United States and the People's Republic of China are fundamentally different because we respect the individual, while they venerate the collective. Technology has enabled Communist China to transmute the collective into an incipient, all-encompassing mind. Theirs is an anthill in which the Chinese Communist Party is queen. Their nation is constituted by a hive mind in which individualism is an illusion and the state is god. This must never be America's future, for if this occurs, we will have lost much more than our country, we will have lost our souls.

Our Founders believed that the state must never be sanctified. They comprehended the horrific excesses that issued from the deification of the emperors of ancient Rome.

Our Founders, being wise statesmen, understood the wrath that the kings and queens of Europe discharged when they believed themselves to be divine. A nation's laws are forever incomplete, but they may be completed by our adoration of God's laws, for God is omniscient.

We must never idolize the state, which the left attempts to do, for this is the essence of Marxism, and through it, the rejection of our Lord and his creation. Our government is not God; we must not allow it to pose itself as an object of worship, which provides manna to the people. For the state's harvest is not created by any miracle, but seized—only to be given out, often to the same constituents who incur its debt.

If state and church are conjoined, so are their dominions. There would be no separate religious and secular authorities, but one entity: This is not America; it is Iran. The full realization of faith cannot come if our government dominates our lives, for that is antithetical to the Logos, which is the word of God.

The promises of an all-powerful state, which are the gilded lures of communist regimes, are often attractive, but false. Statists offer heaven on earth. Such a prize, in return for total submission to governing authorities, constitutes both too much and too little.

The state has never and can never establish a utopia on earth, for heaven is not of this world. This promise by totalitarian governments is too much, but neither can such despotic regimes match a scintilla of the magnificence offered to each of us by God, for our bodies are trappings for our souls and our souls are unaffected by empty promises that would be false even if we were feted with all the treasures of this planet.

Communism posits that men and women are purely material in nature; indeed, the name of Marxism's theoretical base is dialectical materialism. Where has the quest for heaven on earth led the world? It has created over one-hundred-million corpses in the last century alone.

This is not God's rule, but Lucifer's. Satanism, which proposes no constraint on any behavior, no matter how abhorrent, may seem different from communism. In fact, both these abominations act as pincers that emanate from a central point to crush all those they control.

What China is today, America could become tomorrow, if we do not bring faith and its power back into the public square. A technocratic, all-powerful state that is dominated by a single party, which is backed by internet, corporate, and social media interests, would possess the power to eclipse our Republic as it decimates individual liberties.

Only through the acceptance of faith and through the embrace of our founding principles may we guard our country against such a catastrophe. To do so, we must be true to the dual natures that God has granted us, for we were created to be both spiritual and physical—that we may know peace within ourselves, so that we may dwell in one nation, undivided.

Chapter 2, Faith, Precepts:

- Judeo-Christian values are deeply American values. No one of another faith or of no faith ever need fear these values, for they represent tolerance, forgiveness, and love for all humankind.

- Though immensely difficult, we must confront the world as it is, not what narratives claim it to be.

- By assessing our faults, we acquire the tools to grow, for wisdom comes from humility. Strength granted to us by God is our armor, which permits us to meet challenges and to address the problems of our nation and the world.

- God is love: Therefore, we must extend charity to all. This is the truth that binds the world, for where others may see differences, those who are inspired by the Lord see similarities and opportunities for fellowship.

Issues and Problems:

- The separation of church and state was not meant by our Founders to remove religion from our consideration of governance. The separation was to protect the sanctity of all faiths from the encroachments of government and those in authority who would seek to deify themselves, to amass even more power.

- Most national problems, which are said to be irresolvable, can be solved if everyone perceived the world without suppositions. This is often difficult, for radical forces, which can include technocratic, media, or business interests, distort reality for their own gain.

- Ronald Reagan stated, "To grasp and hold a vision that is the very essence of successful leadership." Our vision for the future must be clear, involve pathfinding, and not unnecessary acrimony.

Duties and Actions:

• Our Founders believed that the state must never be sanctified. We must not allow our government to trample our religious rights nor make itself an object of worship.

• The United States and the People's Republic of China are fundamentally different because we respect the individual, while they venerate the collective.

• Technology has enabled Communist China to become what America must never be: a hive mind in which individualism is an illusion and the state is god.

• We must guard against the merger of intrusive surveillance technologies and government.

• Our Republic is in danger of being eclipsed by an all-seeing, all-powerful state that is dominated by a single party that is backed by internet, corporate, and social media interests.

• Freedom and not domination by an unquenchable government must be our guiding principle.

• What China is today, America could become tomorrow, if we do not bring faith and its power back to the public square.

• Only through the acceptance of faith and through the embrace of our founding principles may we guard our country against catastrophe.

CHAPTER 3

FOUNDING

The American Experiment is unique in history in its conception of liberty, which is freedom from oppressive government and its yoke.

We are a nation that rests on the rule of law and not the imperfections present in all humankind. Our Founders created what would become the most powerful nation ever to exist. In doing so, they forged a living example of how freedom must expand through the generations for all humanity.

As men, our Founders were flawed. As authors of human advancement, there is no greater congregation of political geniuses in history. This is America's heritage.

Founding

There is no America without the Founding. The American Experiment is unique in history and is essential to all humankind. The Founding of our country was made possible by the assembly of men of extraordinary vision.

A nation is not forged in perfection but evolves according to its people and its principles. Our forebears' dedication to expand liberty led to the ensuant establishment of freedom as the birthright of all, though this necessitated the Civil War and battles, both before and within my lifetime, against segregation.

We have the capacity to extend America's quest to embody reverence, equality, prosperity, and security if we embrace as a single people what has been bequeathed to us. To do so, we must approach our Founding in humbleness and in gratitude.

The word parrhesia first appeared in the work of the playwright Euripides, who was a contemporary of Socrates. Parrhesia means to speak truthfully and boldly. Democracy before its collapse in ancient Greece reflected the evocation of this term. The fracturing of America—by those who would destroy our country—demands that we speak with complete candor concerning the fault lines of our Republic.

Our Founding Fathers drew on two superlative traditions to create our nation and our principles as a people. Judeo-Christian precepts of compassion, forgiveness, and tolerance were combined with the most incisive and illuminative thoughts of philosophers and statesmen from Ancient Greece and Rome. Political concepts, developed during the Enlightenment, were carefully considered: These ideas included the works of John Locke and Montesquieu.

Our Founders placed their trust in God, believing that he had inspired the principles that they extracted and assembled to create our Republic: a nation unequaled in its dedication to liberty, for our country rests on the rule of law and not the imperfections present in all humankind. As men, our Founding Fathers were flawed. As authors of human advancement there is no greater congregation of political geniuses in all history.

America's cherished principles of liberty and personal agency have allowed successive generations of citizens to enjoy ever-expanding freedoms, unknown before our nation's Founding. These principles must be maintained so that they may be passed down to generations yet unborn.

We must distinguish between fundamental rights and rights that are accrued by actions. Our Founders understood that the bases for the abolition of slavery and for the universal freedom of humankind were present in the conceptualization of unalienable rights as expressed by Thomas Jefferson in the Declaration of Independence.

Gravity

The politics of the time, the harsh social norms, and the cultural structures inherited from Great Britain blocked our Founders' predominant intent to institute universal freedom at the time of the creation of our Republic. In their generation, the Founders could impede the expansion of slavery, as was done in the Constitution, but they could not abolish it, no matter their determination. Slavery in the eighteenth century was too powerful a force, for it was deeply entrenched, having existed throughout history.

It is impossible to envision all the unrealized hopes for freedom held by Americans who came to our country in bondage. We cannot summon the agony that was experienced; we can only imagine what these brave men and women might say if they could stand outside time and gaze at the course of our country:

> Across an ocean of pain, I was taken to America, not to be freed but to be consigned to dehumanizing purchase, arduous servitude, beatings, torments, and abuse in the field or at a station I never sought. My family separated, its members bought and sold, my anguish so visible to all, ignited a spark, for earnest people, who were themselves free, knew freedom was a condition they did not earn but was, in fact, the birthright of humanity as ordained by the Creator of the universe.
>
> A great war secured the promise of my freedom but not its exercise, for humanity is imperfect and too frequently those with power

oppress the powerless. The night, however, is always followed by a new day. America is now living up to the promises of its Founding.

Equality, fellowship, and forgiveness have washed upon my country's shores. What is ordained by God must never be taken away, nor do we dare allow those with power to strip or to curtail individual initiative or the strength that resides in our families. This is most often accomplished in the twenty-first century through the tender of insincere promises, which, in fact, are traps to rob us of our agency as citizens— who are not controlled by the government but are, always, its superior.

We must hold this history of extreme abuse in our hearts as we consider the nature of our Founding. The statues of our Founders are not preserved in contrived ignorance of the fact that the majority of these men were slaveholders. These statues are cherished despite this evil, for these men surpassed their own injurious faults to reach forward so that freedom would increase through time, thereby instigating the maturation of our Republic as a vessel for liberty.

Documents

Both Thomas Jefferson and James Madison derived their concepts of property and happiness from the ideas of the English political philosopher and physician, John Locke, as expressed in his *Second Treatise on Government*. Locke wrote, "Every man has a property in his own person. This nobody has any right to, but himself. The labour of his body, and the work of his hands, we may say, are properly his."

Thus, property rights, correctly understood, guarantee the individual dominion over his or her own body and what may be created through its exercise. This is the basis for freedom, which derives from the Ten Commandments. The commandment, "Thou shalt not steal" expresses an absolute prohibition against slavery, for slavery, by definition, is the theft of that which is most central to any person, their own being.

Appropriate property rights, therefore, cannot be rescinded, for they are oppositional to theft and, thus, consistent with God's law. Emancipation would not have been possible without a comprehension of the concept of property as expressed by Locke, Jefferson, and Madison.

It is not coincidence that the Fifth and Fourteenth Amendments both speak to the subject of rightful property as expressed by Locke. Indeed, the Fourteenth Amendment was to mark a turning point in the expansion of freedom for all Americans; thereafter, an "equal protection of the laws" was to be applied to every citizen. Our country has fallen short of a prompt and universal application of this right, but this was not due to the structure of the Constitution and its amendments, but the flawed nature of humanity, which is all too frequently corrupted by prejudice.

Freedom, Liberty, and Slavery

From Montesquieu, our Founding Fathers adopted the principle of the separation of powers. Our Founders understood from their study of tyrants through the ages that despotic rule has one cognate: It is the concentration of power without any checks or balances. Reflecting on the capriciousness and the cruelty of King George III, our Founders incorporated Montesquieu's conceptualization into the fabric of our nation.

If through the desire of some utopian end, our country destroys or renders effete the separation of powers, we will have succeeded not in creating a paradise but in destroying all we have. In 1887, Britain's Lord Acton would phrase memorably the threat that set in motion the American Revolution.

According to Acton, "Power tends to corrupt; absolute power corrupts absolutely."[11] In humility and in consideration of our cherished principles, we are obligated to ponder this timeless observation, for the meaning of this apothegm is now betrayed by those who would accrue unlimited authorities at the people's expense.

The amalgamation of powers leads to abuse. The separation of powers leads to decency, honesty, cooperation, and moderation.

The separation of powers must also be considered in the context of our nation's being a Constitutional Republic and not a pure

[11]https://www.dictionary.com/browse/power-tends-to-corrupt-absolute-power-corrupts-absolutely

democracy. Our Founders believed that democracy, unchecked, could disintegrate into mob rule, which would threaten rights that are unalienable.

The Constitution was established as the supreme law of our country to safeguard our nation from devolving into anarchy, particularly in a time of crisis. The intent of the will of the people was designed to be realized through representative democracy. This was established to moderate political passions, which may be transitory and injurious, thereby permitting reasoned discourse and prudent decision-making.

What is transcendent is that which moves through time, for its substance illuminates without reference to its age and is thus, by definition, of universal significance. We venerate the images of Washington, Jefferson, Madison, and our other Founding Fathers, for they etched within our country's soul transcendental truths that, in time, permitted freedom to be attained by every American.

Liberty

Our Founders understood that freedom is destroyed if virtue is not prized. Virtue is the prerequisite for freedom, for it provides the boundary that enables the exercise of freedom by an individual without unduly limiting or infringing upon the rights of others, thus safeguarding the exercise of freedom in its totality. Slavery, oppression, and segregation are inimical to virtue; the fact that these three obscenities subsisted in our Republic testifies to their prior entrenchment despite the luminosity of our Founder's conception.

In his letter of June 21, 1776, John Adams wrote, "it is Religion and Morality alone, which can establish the Principles upon which Freedom can securely stand." It is this conviction that motivated the abolitionist movement, which built the Underground Railroad to be a corridor for escape for slaves, so that they might reach free states.

Liberty is freedom from molestation by an obdurate government or authority. Liberty, as promised in our Declaration of Independence, is thus only possible if limited government is practiced and not enlarged, for expansive government, through its sundry actions, subverts individual agency and choice, ultimately destroying liberty.

There can be no greater certainty than that God's covenant is with the individual and not the collective. It is this relationship that is the basis for unalienable rights, for these rights cannot be annulled by humankind for they are not of our creation. This is the essence of the immortal legacy that Thomas Jefferson, James Madison, and the other authors of America's creation left to the world.

It is incontestable that three great leaders, Abraham Lincoln, Frederick Douglass, and Martin Luther King, all understood this inheritance, for within the palisade of liberty, designed by our Founders, each of these three visionaries labored to construct a more perfect union that would entrench principles of freedom and equality for all. In Abraham Lincoln's Lewiston, Illinois, speech of August 17, 1858, he spoke words that should be treasured throughout time, for Lincoln, who was our nation's first Republican president, understood completely the magnificence of the Founders' creation:

> They erected a beacon to guide their children and their children's children, and the countless myriads who should inhabit the earth in other ages. Wise statesmen as they were, they knew the tendency of prosperity to breed tyrants, and so they established these great self-evident truths, that when in the distant future some man, some faction, some interest, should set up the doctrine that none but rich men, or none but white men, were entitled to life, liberty and the pursuit of happiness, their posterity might look up again to the Declaration of Independence and take courage to renew the battle which their fathers began—so that truth, and justice, and mercy, and all the humane and Christian virtues might not be extinguished from the land; so that no man would hereafter dare to limit and circumscribe the great principles on which the temple of liberty was being built.[12]

This is the reason why all Americans should respect our Founders and our country's birth. As men who served to build a mighty nation, the Founders exceeded their own personal limitations, in order to establish the means wherein future generations of Americans could

---

[12]https://quod.lib.umich.edu/l/lincoln/lincoln2/1:567?rgn=div1;view=fulltext

reach past the limits that our Founding Fathers, as men of their times, could not overcome. This is their gift, which established our nation.

There is great hubris in those who would castigate our Founders. What makes these modern critics believe that they would have acted more humanely than did our Founders, if they had lived in that time, a time at which women in England were still burned at the stake for treason, after first being garroted?

The eighteenth century was marked by intense brutality: Slavery and cruel and unusual punishments existed throughout the earth, as both had been worldwide scourges throughout history. Do these critics not know this?

Such detractors have not shown themselves capable of building, in our time, one iota of the works for which our Founders fought—so the world would one day be marked by freedom and not by bondage. That our Founders could not achieve all they dreamed—in their own time—was a product of their age, which constrained their aspirations.

Modern critics of America would probably wish not to know that in 1860, *The New York Times* reported horrendous actions decreed by the king of Dahomey, a land situated within what is now the West African nation of Benin, which was a major conduit for the intercontinental slave trade.[13] According to the record:

> A great pit has been dug, which is to contain human blood enough to float a canoe. Two thousand persons will be sacrificed on this occasion. The expedition to Abeakouta is postponed, but the King has sent his army to make some excursions at the expense of some weaker tribes, and has succeeded in capturing many unfortunate creatures. The young people among these prisoners will be sold into slavery, and: the old persons will be killed at the Grand Custom.

In fact, these rites were long-established in the Kingdom of Dahomey. Do the moral hypocrites of our day not realize that a number of African nations and chiefdoms have apologized for their role in the slave trade? For example, in 1999, President Mathieu Kerekou of Benin expressed contrition for his region's role in the slave

---

[13]https://www.nytimes.com/1880/12/05/archives/public-massacres-in-dahomey.html

trade, which sacrificed or executed tens of thousands of people while selling millions into appalling bondage throughout the world.[14] Slavery did not begin in America, but it was fought in our country and contested by our Navy and by our Marines globally.[15]

Instead of reaching back more than two-hundred years to denigrate our Founders, the present claimants of virtue should work to free the planet from slavery—as it is practiced today. Why do they turn a blind eye to the enslavement and the genocide of Muslims in China and the human trafficking of women and children across the globe, for in absolute numbers, more people are enslaved today than in any time in history. Indeed, a recent United Nations report states, "The 2021 Global Estimates indicate there are 50 million people in situations of modern slavery on any given day, either forced to work against their will or in a marriage that they were forced into. This number translates to nearly one of every 150 people in the world."[16]

Slavery is a stain on our nation's history. It is deplorable that such an institution existed anywhere. Our nation's treatment of Indigenous Americans also represents an unconscionable chapter in the formation of our Republic and its westward expansion. To pretend, however, that slavery just existed in America is to reduce radically the magnitude of the crime, for as with conquest, it existed everywhere.

More than twelve million persons were sent to the New World aboard slave ships in what is known as the Middle Passage. The trans-Saharan slave trade to North Africa, to the Middle East, and to other parts of the world, displaced and imprisoned at least ten million other Africans.[17] In addition to this horrendous toll, millions

[14]https://www.blackhistorymonth.org.uk/article/section/pre-colonial-history/the-history-of-the-kingdom-of-dahomey/

[15]https://www.history.navy.mil/research/library/exhibits/anti-slavery-operations-of-the-us-navy.html

[16]https://www.ilo.org/wcmsp5/groups/public/---ed_norm/---ipec/docu ments/publication/wcms_854733.pdf

[17]https://books.google.com/books?hl=en&lr=&id=iWUXNEM-62QC&oi=fn d&pg=PR11&ots=zhCkxlB8pE&sig=Roag435iRJV3eGfgcNUkk7LDG9s#v=on epage&q&f=false

more were enslaved within sub-Saharan Africa, itself. Of this totality, fewer than two percent of the enslaved of African descent were
taken to what is now America.[18]

The institution of slavery is often taught as a peculiarly American practice. This assertion is untrue and does grave injustice to the
millions of people today who are trafficked in many lands or who
are enslaved, due to their religious beliefs, by the People's Republic
of China.

Wars

Beginning in ancient times, the taking of captives, and turning them
into slaves, replaced warfare that was marked by rampant extermination. The term Carthaginian peace derives from the viciousness, the
devastation, the murder, and the enslavement that followed Rome's
victory over Carthage after the Third Punic War.

This type of warfare has been part of the world's history since
language was first transcribed, for before the cruelty of Rome, the King
of Assyria, Ashurnasirpal II, during his reign in the ninth century BC,
soaked Asia Minor in blood. Shockingly, such assaultive wars and
rampages reached their zenith in the past century, for Hitler, Tojo,
Stalin, and Mao all sought to enslave those they did not murder.

Slavery has always existed and has been present on every inhabited continent. The word slave, in part, derives from Slav, the most
numerous European ethnolinguistic group in the sense of shared root
languages and overarching cultural identities.

Slavs were seized in great numbers in raids carried out by the
Crimean Tatar state from its founding in 1441 until its conquest in
1783 by Catherine the Great. The Crimean Khanate, which constituted this state, was, in fact, the direct descendent of the Golden
Horde, which was begun by the Mongols in the thirteenth century.
Indeed, it is estimated that the enslavement of Europeans, beginning
in the early modern period that commenced with the Muslim

---

[18]https://www.pbs.org/wnet/african-americans-many-rivers-to-cross/
history/how-many-slaves-landed-in-the-us/

conquest of Constantinople in 1453, may be numbered in the millions, with most captives being sent to North Africa and to the heart of the Ottoman Empire, having been taken by assorted slavers, including Barbary corsairs and English or Dutch privateers.

Oceans

The expansion of slavery on an intercontinental scale was made possible by developments in oceanic transportation that occurred in the sixteenth century. This precipitated the extension of trafficking in enslaved persons of African descent to the New World and eastward, to the Indo-Pacific, in addition to its continuous practice within the Ottoman Empire.

With the enlargement of slavery across continents came an emerging abhorrence of this trade in Europe and in the colonies, for this oppression's viciousness was increasingly recognized as a vitiation of God's covenant. In the latter part of the seventeenth century, slavery was racialized in order to maintain its practice during the Age of Enlightenment. This obscene and unpardonable act to legitimize slavery, in minds capable of capitulating to self-deception, has been one of the root causes of discrimination against peoples of African origin. The notions of racial superiority or inferiority are wrong, are without bases, and are completely unacceptable.

In this century, ISIS (the Islamic State of Iraq and al-Sham, or, alternatively, termed ISIL, the Islamic State of Iraq and the Levant), transnational criminal organizations, and the People's Republic of China have systematized murder and slavery. Parts of Libya, areas of the Democratic Republic of the Congo, and all of Mauritania still practice slavery in some form. No inhabited continent is presently free from this abuse and butchery.

There is no higher duty than to extinguish this execrable practice from the earth. All senior officials in our federal government must realize that decisive action in this war must be preeminent among their responsibilities. The destruction of ISIS by the Trump administration was a crucial first step toward the goal of eliminating slavery worldwide and the trade in enslaved people.

As we stamp out the vestiges of prejudice and discrimination within America, it is incorrect to deduce that racial discrimination always underlies slavery. Slavery can and will arise wherever the powerless fall prey to those who rule by brute force; the trafficking of people across our southern border, often for the purpose of sexual exploitation, constitutes a testament to this fact. Slavery can also be the consequence of utopian objectives, for such desires are fraught with risk, for totalistic states view their citizens and others as shards of wood with which to build empires, which are invariably deemed forever incomplete.

By rejecting England's yoke, America's colonists took the first concrete step for every American to be free one day. This was Thomas Jefferson's and the Founders' vision for the new country to come, for liberty must often be defended assertively if it is to be enshrined and enjoyed individually. America must stay this course by believing in our Founding, which was enabled by the guiding hand of God.

Chapter 3, Founding, Precepts:

• The Constitution was established as our supreme law to safeguard our nation from devolving into anarchy.

• America's Founding Fathers surpassed their own personal limitations to reach forward so that freedom would increase through time, thereby instigating the maturation of our Republic as a vessel for liberty.

• This is the Founders gift to every subsequent generation of Americans; it is one of the greatest gifts ever offered. We must accept this legacy and its promise and not castigate it.

• It is impossible to envision all the unrealized hopes for freedom held by Americans who came to our country in bondage or that of Indigenous Americans whose societies were destroyed or gravely damaged.

• We cannot summon the agony these persons felt, but we can rededicate our nation to the principles of our Founding, for they transcend time and offer great hope for a better future for every American.

• The will of the American people was designed to be realized through representative democracy; this can only be obtained through a separation of powers between the legislative, executive, and judicial branches of government, but this separation is threatened.

Issues and Problems:

• In building a new nation, our Founders established the means wherein future generations of Americans could reach past the limits that could not be overcome in the direct aftermath of the Revolutionary War.

• Slavery is a stain on our history. It is deplorable that such an institution was tolerated anywhere, but it has always existed throughout the world. Indeed, slavery and forced servitude exists today even within America's borders.

• In this century, the terrorists that comprised ISIS, transnational criminal organizations, and the People's Republic of China have all systematized murder and slavery. Parts of the Middle East and Africa still practice slavery in some form. No inhabited continent is presently free from this grave sin.

Duties and Actions:

• Slavery can arise wherever the powerless fall prey to those who rule by brute force; the trafficking of people across our southern border, often for the purpose of sexual exploitation, offers testament to this fact. As Americans, we are obligated to fight slavery wherever it exists, beginning at our border with Mexico.

• Slavery is also the consequence of utopian objectives that are unrealizable, for totalitarian countries view their citizens as disposable components with which to build empires that are deemed forever incomplete. This is the primary reason China's, Russia's, and Iran's vision for the world must be fought.

• By rejecting subjugation by Great Britain, American colonists took the first concrete step for every American to be free one day, for liberty must be defended assertively if it is to be enjoyed individually.

• Due to our nation's story, we are obligated to be a voice for freedom. To do so, we must lead by example.

• We must fulfill our history, not abandon or denigrate it. America must stay this course by believing in our Founding, which was enabled by the guiding hand of God.

CHAPTER 4

FAMILY

It is the glory of the American family that illuminates the world. A parent's love is unique and cannot be replicated. To substitute algorithms, technology, and social media for the family is potentially as destructive as any threat now facing our country.

Technology has introduced great advances, but when it is used as a vehicle for propaganda and control, when it is misused to remove our children from the embrace of those who love and shelter them, it becomes an acid, corrosive to our children's natural development.

Married, two-parent families reduce the incidence of abortion, which is often precipitated by insecurity. A law is not rendered good automatically. It is rendered good if it is just, and it is just if it derives from God's word. Our nation's laws must support the vibrancy of the American family, which is nourished by the gift of children.

Family

The family will always be the irreplaceable unit of humankind. It must never be deprecated. Children prosper in the presence of loving parents. The insertion of the state's ambitions between parents and their children is impermissible. This encroachment must be fought by our declaration that the family is to be honored. No governmental power can ever replace the value of a loving parent to a child.

The essence of communist and totalitarian regimes is to replace the family with the state. The result is always the same: moral degradation and dissolution. In contrast, it is the magnificent nature of the American family that illuminates the world.

The expression of faith anchors families through prayer and through love. Fused with moral courage and hard work, the American family has built a mighty nation. Unless we act now to assert the primacy of family, of devotion, and of morality, our nation cannot be strong. And if America is not strong, the world will be at the mercy of tyrants.

The American family is at risk, and if it is toppled, America will fall. Our institutions and our media continuously denigrate the importance of nuclear families, though children are most likely to succeed when surrounded by loving adults who care for and balance each other.

It is said that there are no perfect families, but there is perfection in trying. This is what is demanded; this is the debt owed by one generation to the next. Only loving families, be they biologically related or not, can flourish in our modern, mechanistic age.

I know friends who never knew a parent's love. I know adults who experienced abuse when they were children. There are gaps in their hearts that take a lifetime to fill, which cause enormous pain.

How can we as a society reduce abuse and increase the potential for love in accordance with God's laws? We must prize what we wish to create and not disparage it. Wholesomeness is not a dated term: It is the basis for healthy moral development. Children must be taught by example that being a good parent is central to life.

Our children must always be protected from age-inappropriate material. Unfortunately, groups, which are part of the left, seek the indoctrination of youth through lures, which may be abhorrent. This occurred in both the Soviet Union and in Cuba. It is now occurring throughout America.[19] State and local governments have no more important duty than to stop these detestable activities without delay.

It is of the utmost importance that children be taught that the equality of men and women is a guiding principle of our nation. Of equal significance is the rejection of racial prejudice or discrimination in all its forms. The teaching of these precepts fortifies the family; their abrogation destroys cohesiveness and growth.

These were the lessons I learned. My grandfather, Philip, was a leather worker employed by small manufacturers in New York. His standard was flawlessness in all that he did, no matter how small. He was a learned and pious man: I remember vividly that not one important moment in my life transpired without my grandfather's being there.

Principled and caring, my grandfather was born in the nineteenth century in Russia; he loved America in ways in which few today can comprehend, for he witnessed the savagery of the pogroms. My grandfather, despite many difficult obligations, always placed his love of God and his care of our family above any desire for personal comfort. I owe him a tremendous debt for he demonstrated the centrality of love.

My grandfather taught me to respect the importance of hard work. Everything that I have accomplished is the result of these simple lessons. It is with deep sorrow that I contemplate children left alone, without loving parents or caregivers to guide them and to instill the lessons that many of our citizens take for granted.

A parent's or a grandparent's love is unique and cannot be replicated. This is why our society must value families, for nothing else may substitute for a mother's loving care for a sick child or a father's teaching his son or his daughter how to throw a ball. Elites may disparage these ordinary and familiar acts, but it is these everyday steps that author who we become.

---

[19]https://spectator.org/public-schools-gender-radical-reshaping/

There are, of course, many different types of families; any one of which can be a sublime vehicle for childhood growth and societal cohesion. In our nation, we must embrace all American families as we place our children's needs first. Sound child-rearing patterns must be based on love and never on fashion.

For the American family to thrive, we must return to our time-honored principles of mutual respect, care, compassion, and rectitude, for dangers and incipient threats to our nation's families must be met with actions. Pernicious isolation, abortion, attempts to nullify biological reality, and systemic educational failures must be challenged if our families are to be vibrant.

Invention, Technology, and Loss

Philo Farnsworth began development of his image dissector, critical to the electronic transmission of moving pictures, while still a teenager, after watching the motion of a plow in a field. In 1927, when he was twenty-one, Farnsworth built and later demonstrated the world's first completely electronic television. After the Second World War, his invention was copied and integrated into the national consciousness. This was American innovation at its finest, but it has had unintended consequences.

Farnsworth's invention and the personal computers and smart phones that came after it have allowed humanity to inhabit a synthetic world for much of each day. These cyber-immersive technologies have divorced many children and adults from living in a reality constrained by physical limits. This is extremely addictive.

Worship and reality have become secondary for so many who dwell in an unreal universe dominated by the internet, social media, and online gaming. The psychological and societal ramifications of the creation of these false realities, as well as the resultant developmental challenges placed on children, are not fully understood.

The technological revolution of this century is altering human nature, for the essence of being human is to dwell on a plane that is both physical and spiritual. The first is tangible; the second involves our souls.

The internet was supposed to serve the cause of freedom and offer enlightenment and educational opportunities for children and families. Billions of people who use the internet expect freedom in communication. Technology providers, however, have made themselves sieves that select which viewpoints are acceptable. This is in part due to a function of what they are, for in order to preserve their corporate positions of monopolistic dominance, they must offer the pretense of continuous improvement, even if the improvement conveyed is errant or destructive of the bonds that have enriched and enabled our society.

Fictions that disparage our nation and its Founding are propagated to support a new ruling class that attempts to substantiate a false religion that is rooted in Marxism. This cover is convenient for it masks corporate rapaciousness with a cloak of seeming beneficence, which is paid for through the toil of the disadvantaged in America and in many countries throughout the globe.

Isolation

Cyber-immersive technologies have divorced many young people from living in the real world. The past years of social and scholastic isolation, due to the pandemic, have increased substantially the costs of immersion within a cyberworld, absent the guiding hands of caring adults.

The threats of loneliness, online bullying, and the narrowing of perspectives must be reduced through concerted attention. Strong families are fundamental, for it is the family that must guide our youth in traversing a digital landscape that is both enthralling and compulsive.

True loss cannot be measured until all that is lost is realized. Media is now pervasive in its reach due to the internet and social networks. This envelopment creates alternative realities within social bubbles. Most damaged are our children, who, too often, would rather live in a simulated world, in preference to the actual one with its demands and challenges.

Unbound by a moral compass, media companies operate as global businesses and thus seek to maximize profits and returns for investors worldwide. Truth is often not marketable for it may be difficult or distasteful to accept; therefore, it is not prized.

If a child's online involvement is not monitored, there is potential for the manifestation of depression, abuse, exploitation, kidnapping, or suicide. This must not be—as a nation we have to realize that strong schools and teachers are but a partial cure, for they cannot replace the importance of intact families.

To substitute algorithms, search engines, smart phones, and social media for the family is as potentially destructive as any threat now facing our nation. Technology has introduced great advances, but when it is used as a vehicle for propaganda and control, when it is misused to remove our children from the embrace of friends, teachers, and families, it becomes an acid, corrosive to our children's natural development. A future is upon us in which we must not let artificial intelligence (AI)[20] pose as an oracle to our youth; we must establish human bonds wherever possible, as we guard against those that are empty.

We must bring our nation back to family, for within it lies the answers to how we must balance the enticements and the promises of materialism and technology, so that they do not trample eternal truths. The federal government must always act to promote the family as the essential basis for our nation and not defer to corporate or special interests, which may be contaminated by foreign influences.

Any action that promotes the separation of families, except in cases of illegalities and abuse, is inherently wrong. It must be understood that while government does not possess the capacity to make families strong, government does possess the means to make families weak. It has done so by denigrating the role of fathers and by placing itself between parents and children.

The insertion of the state between children and parents is appropriate in cases of abuse. This is a judicial matter and must not become a bureaucratic exercise that seeks control or disruption, in order to convey power to the state. Laws, executive orders, and regulations oppositional to families and their creation must be rescinded.

---

[20]https://hai.stanford.edu/sites/default/files/2020-09/AI-Definitions-HAI.pdf

Expectations, Challenges, and Excellence

The social ramifications of COVID-19 are vast. The lasting damages to the psychological health of the youth of our nation cannot be overstated.[21] These affronts are compounded by factors present in the United States before the advent of the pandemic. The maintenance of America demands that our nation extols excellence. If expectations and challenges are not promulgated, our society may soon wither, and our children will fail to meet their potential.

Dr. John Calhoun studied animal behavior and its implications for human overpopulation. In 1954, Calhoun joined the National Institutes of Health; fourteen years later, Calhoun conducted experiments that produced results with implications for human conduct. The National Institute of Mental Health supported Calhoun's study, known as Universe 25, which commenced in 1968.[22]

Confined to a well, the fecundity of the study's animals was to gauge the effects of overpopulation within a set area. To stimulate reproduction, every need and want were provided. Only the size of the enclosure was fixed, though as it was designed, it could hold more animals than would ever, in fact, be present.

The experiment produced prodigious growth in the subject population until the 315th day. Deprived of the struggle intrinsic to nature, for water, food, sex, domain, and position, the character of the animals changed irredeemably. They degenerated.

Reproduction slowed to a standstill; many animals became abnormally violent, absent any provocation; they also exhibited aberrant behaviors, including cannibalism. Other groups within the subject population spent the totality of their existence alternately gorging or grooming themselves, exhibiting no interest in group welfare or interaction.

Before the experiment reached its second year, all reproduction ceased. What was to be a test of overpopulation became an exercise

---

[21]https://www.unicef.org/press-releases/impact-covid-19-poor-mental-health-children-and-young-people-tip-iceberg

[22]https://www.iflscience.com/universe-25-the-mouse-utopia-experiment-that-turned-into-an-apocalypse-60407

in extinction. Certain results of this experiment may be seen as a window with which to view the societal fissures of our times.

Any contemplation of the human condition must promote challenge and competition as necessary predicates for prosperity, individual happiness, and advancement. Such societal challenges have included Martin Luther King's mission to end racial discrimination, President Eisenhower's response to the placement by the USSR of a satellite in orbit,[23] President Kennedy's quest to land Americans on the moon before 1970, and President Reagan's call to vanquish the Soviet Union, to forestall the evil it perpetrated.

America and its present leadership have not committed our nation and its youth to important new tests; instead, political, business, and academic elites venerate ostentation and mediocrity. Our nation's standard must be excellence. In an intensely competitive world, any other metric will strip the United States of its strength and its purpose.

The isolation wrought by the pandemic induced traumas and voids within America's youth that are consonant with aspects of malaise, stupor, and deterioration. In earnest contemplation of the human condition, we must again realize what President Kennedy understood: For young people to prosper, they must be challenged. We, who have eyes to see, are obligated to observe that abundance without effort precipitates indolence and disillusionment, which may only be alleviated by the guiding hands of intact families, not uncaring and rapacious bureaucrats who seek only to increase their own dominion.

President Kennedy's vision spread throughout the globe. For example, many nations in the Middle East have built impressive space agencies. Of note are the United Arab Emirates' recent accomplishments. The genesis and the programs of its space agency not only form a substrate to advance science in the Middle East, this basis creates the capacity to explore the unknown. This is the legacy of President Kennedy's dream, which has suffused the planet, to become the inspiration for the creation of enterprises, in numerous

---

[23]Sputnik 1 was launched by the space program of the Union of Soviet Socialist Republics (USSR) on October 4, 1957.

countries, to conquer the mysteries of space.[24] Truly, for America's children to be strong and to lead productive lives, they must always be challenged and not be coddled.

Loss of core values at home, including faith, family, and patriotism, will precipitate the degradation of our country without any analyses of costs. We want our children and the children of the world to travel throughout our solar system in this century, not cry about past wrongs or imagined slights.

To explore and to grow requires that we meet great tests. We must face the future bravely as one united people. We must race toward it.

Children

Children are the basis for society and must never be sacrificed for convenience or for material wealth. As a nation, we must offer alternatives to abortion. Though my wife and I are not blessed with children due to the protracted illness I endured, I earnestly believe, as it is written in Psalms, "Children are a heritage from the Lord, offspring a reward from him."

Margaret Sanger was the founder of Planned Parenthood, the nation's leading abortion provider. Sanger was an arch racist, whose stated and promulgated intent was the eradication of the Black race.[25] Abortion has deprived tens of millions of Black children the ability to draw their first breath, for they were destroyed in the womb.[26] This is an abomination worthy of the Third Reich, not America.

The decision by the Supreme Court to overturn Roe v. Wade returns the power to regulate abortion to the states. The ruling reflects America's system of federalism. Our Founding Documents do not reference abortion; this matter, therefore, lies within the purview of our states according to the Tenth Amendment to the Constitution.[27]

---

[24]https://www.unoosa.org/oosa/en/ourwork/space-agencies.html
[25]https://www.physiciansforlife.org/seven-quotes-by-planned-parenthood-founder-margaret-sanger/
[26]https://rtl.org/multicultural-outreach/black-abortion-statistics/
[27]https://constitution.congress.gov/constitution/amendment-10/

Justice Samuel Alito, writing for the majority, stated, "The Constitution does not confer a right to abortion; Roe and Casey are overruled; and the authority to regulate abortion is returned to the people and their elected representatives."[28] Many commentators and abortion advocates have decried this new opinion as upturning the precedent established by Roe. Yet, precedent cannot rest on sand. This is as true today as it was when Plessy v. Ferguson was overturned by Brown v. Board of Education.

Life begins at conception and is sacred because every soul bears the image of our Creator. I have come to believe that abortion is not the answer, for abortion is the nullification of life.

Abortion severely harms minority communities. Millions of Black, Latino, Indigenous, and other minority children have never been born because of it. This monumental loss has, without question, deprived our nation of millions of citizens who could have made profound contributions to America while enjoying life.

Unfortunately, the horrendous condition of extremely high abortion rates within minority populations is often the result of governmental programs that hinder the formation of two-parent families in these communities. Married, two-parent families reduce the incidence of abortion, which is often precipitated by uncertainties and insecurities, which may, for single mothers, be tantamount to abandonment. What is clear is that desertion during pregnancy can be a cause of severe depression or, in some cases, suicide.

Stable, two-parent families strengthen the support a child receives, endowing parents with greatly enhanced abilities to care for children. Abortion statistics reflect these facts, for abortions occur with far greater prevalence among single women.[29]

Government cannot substitute for intact, two-parent families. Government is not the answer to God's promise, which can only be realized through the promotion of the family as the principal foundation for our society. I, therefore, pray that our nation will find

---

[28]https://constitutioncenter.org/blog/divided-supreme-court-overturns-roe-abortion-precedents
[29]https://www.cdc.gov/mmwr/volumes/70/ss/ss7009a1.htm

solutions that support life as well as the individual agency of each mother in need.

A law is not rendered good automatically. It is rendered good if it is just, and it is just if it derives from God's word. This is the basis for our unalienable rights, which I believe should be granted to all human life, including life within the womb.

What can people acting in faith and in deep concern do to reduce the incidence of abortion? In addition to the recission of laws that hamper the creation of new families, we must offer a true choice: the choice for the unborn to be raised by loving, biological parents or to be adopted by parents who will provide adoration and care.

If abortion were outlawed in every state in America, which will not happen, its practice, though curtailed, would still exist and be augmented by chemical abortifacients, which are now responsible for sixty percent of abortions. We must be watchful, too, for tainted abortifacients may proliferate in underground markets, for such drugs are available on the internet.

The distribution of non-prescription fentanyl is facilitated directly by actions by the Chinese Communist Party at our southern border and across our nation. We, therefore, must be concerned that cartels, facilitated by the Chinese Communist Party, could supply contaminated drugs to our citizens that will kill pregnant women while inducing abortions, which would devastate our society.

Adding to our concerns is the fact that the Chinese Communist Party also stands guilty of enforcing its decades-long pogrom that has subjected its own citizens to brutal, forced abortions. This terror has reached its apex in China's repulsive actions against its Muslim citizens in the so-called Xinjiang Uyghur Autonomous Region in Northwest China.

Call

Within America, we must demand that a more humane and comprehensive solution to the issue of abortion be created. We must devise an alternative that supports the dignity of the birth mother in all circumstances.

The first step is to realize that providing an alternative to abortion is a national emergency. A countrywide, anti-abortion hotline, employing an N11 code, should be established. This code is a three-digit telephone number that can be designed to ensure strict privacy and confidentiality.

Our churches should partner with synagogues, mosques, and temples, to join with foundations, states, and federal authorities, to create a new three-digit telephone number, similar to 9-1-1. Recently, a national suicide hotline, 9-8-8, has been instituted as a new N11 code. These numbers are administered by the Federal Communications Commission.

To counter abortion, the new N11 number could be called by any young woman or couple who are in need and who otherwise might contemplate the termination of a pregnancy. This new facility will save young lives.

This new national phone number would immediately put the caller in contact with a counselor who would provide comprehensive information on the range of government, church, and charitable services that are available to help individuals through pregnancy, birth, and a child's infancy. Alternatively, this new number would put young women or their principal relatives in touch with a national network of fully vetted and caring families who are ready to adopt any baby who is yet unborn.

Certainly, there have been efforts to establish parts of this proposal. What is needed now is an integrated endeavor to assemble and to launch a more comprehensive undertaking. Crucially, such an effort must be coupled with programs to educate young people on the lifelong economic and personal consequences of having a child before marriage, so that unwed pregnancies, a primary cause of abortions, may be reduced.

Composed of several reinforcing components, this endeavor to end abortion must be available to all women without regard to social or economic status, or any other trait. Our humanity requires that our nation be composed of one neighbor helping another, one family opening its doors, and one young woman offering abundant life to the child she carries.

With the resources we regularly expend in building a bridge, our nation and its houses of worship can build a never-ending pathway to life, in accord with each of our beliefs and creeds. The overturning of Roe must not induce national strife but the rebuilding of our nation's soul, which rests on faith, family, fellowship, and, most blessingly, children.

Chapter 4, Family, Precepts:

- Only loving families can flourish in our modern, technological age.

- Children must be taught by example that being good ensures a lifetime of happiness and contentment.

- No governmental power can ever replace the value of a loving parent to a child.

- Wholesomeness is not dated: It is the basis for healthy moral development and a thriving society.

- We must return to our time-honored principles of mutual respect, compassion, and uprightness.

Issues and Problems:

- Isolation, abortion, attempts to nullify biological reality, and systemic educational failures must be challenged if American families are to be vibrant.

- Our society must honor families, for nothing else can substitute for a parent's loving care. Elites may disparage a mother's and father's simple acts, but it is growth within the structure of our family that authors who we become.

- The distribution of non-prescription fentanyl and other drugs is facilitated directly by actions by the Chinese

Communist Party at our southern border and across our nation. This stream of suffering and death must end immediately.

• Unbound by a moral compass, media companies operate as global businesses and thus seek to maximize profits and returns for investors worldwide. Truth is often not marketable; it is therefore not prized.

• Worship and reality have become secondary for many children who inhabit an unreal universe dominated by the internet, social media, and online gaming. The technological revolution is altering human nature, for the essence of being human is to be both physical and spiritual.

• The internet was supposed to serve the cause of freedom and offer enlightenment and educational opportunities for children, but for many families it has become an inferno of separation that breeds discontent and loss.

Duties and Actions:

• Children are the basis for society and must never be sacrificed for convenience or for material wealth.

• We must bring our nation back to family, for within it lies the answers to how we must balance the enticements of materialism and technology, so that they do not trample eternal truths that define true happiness and fulfillment.

• Our nation's standard must be excellence. America's present leadership has not challenged our nation and our youth; instead, political, business, and academic elites venerate mediocrity and conformity. This must change.

• A countrywide, anti-abortion hotline, employing an N11 code, should be established. This code is a three-digit telephone number, similar to 9-1-1, that can be designed to ensure strict privacy and confidentiality.

• To create a viable alternative to abortion, which is being facilitated by the nationwide proliferation of drugs that terminate pregnancies, the N11 number would offer a full range of counseling and services to any young woman or couple who are in need and who otherwise might contemplate the termination of a pregnancy.

CHAPTER 5

IMMIGRATION AND BORDER SECURITY

The first obligation of any nation is to ensure that its borders are secure. The Biden administration has failed this test and subverted this requirement. Billions of people desire to become Americans, but our nation cannot accommodate the whole world. This realization should be self-evident, but it is not.

America accepts far more legal immigrants than any other country. This fact does not satisfy leftists within our government, our media, and many of our corporations. They believe that our country has no character, is borderless and formless, and may be bent into any desired shape.

Societal cohesion is one of the most important attributes of national strength. Unity is fractured by the present emphasis on the race, the ethnicity, or the country of origin of America's citizens; this errant emphasis is, however, propounded by disingenuous elites.

Immigration and Border Security

Our Judeo-Christian heritage and our unalienable rights, fortified by our belief that only an educated people may truly enjoy both liberty and prosperity, have created the America we cherish. We dare not lose it. Our country was once called a melting pot, for people from every nation on earth have freely chosen to become Americans. This is because of the nature of our country and our citizens.

The left and many Democratic politicians would have us believe that our country is not endowed with character, is borderless and formless, and is malleable to the extent that it may be bent into any shape that is desired. I dare these activists to convey such thoughts to the Gold Star Parents who have lost children in defense of our country. I dare these deceitful politicians to tell our nation's brave warriors—who have lost their sight, their hearing, or their limbs— that America has no meaning. This, these pretenders have not the courage to do, but they will hector us, for they believe that there is no such thing as a country that may express its own dominion.

All countries ultimately rest on the strength of their people. Our nation and the abundance and the safety we enjoy require that we manifest a growing population that is young, for this is the prerequisite to maintaining a resilient and productive workforce.

America accepts far more legal immigrants than any other country.[30] It is in our national interest to continue to welcome large numbers of legal immigrants and to assimilate all those who lawfully seek to

---

[30]https://www.pewresearch.org/fact-tank/2016/05/18/5-facts-about-the-u-s-rank-in-worldwide-migration/

become Americans. What must be required of new citizens or aspirants for citizenship is respect for our borders and for the rule of law, respect for our Founding and its legacy, respect for the creeds and faiths of others, respect for the family and for education, and respect for hard work. These commitments are the cornerstones of our Republic.

Solidarity and Cohesion

Societal cohesion is one of the most important attributes of national strength. Unity is fractured by the present emphasis on the race, the ethnicity, or the country of origin of America's citizens; this errant emphasis is propounded by disingenuous elites. We must not be concerned with appearances or with statistics that place people into segmented groups, for such hollowness tells us nothing about how individuals order their lives or how they yearn to contribute to our nation.

Physical differences between people must never be used as the means to divide our nation, though foreign and domestic forces seek to ply dissension and civic unrest on this basis. Subordination to such a callow and evil course must never be tolerated for it would destroy the progress we have made as a nation. To render people as stereotypes, bound within discrete cohorts, is beneath the dignity of our country, though such conceptions are advanced by the Biden administration's actions.

Demography concerns factors resident in human populations that serve to describe groups statistically. America faces demographic challenges, which are shared by other nations. Now is the time to begin considering these concerns. Such questions, however, should never involve the racial or the ethnic composition of America, nor the country of origin of immigrants, nor the percentage of foreign-born Americans as contrasted to naturally born citizens.

The inquiries to be addressed must concern the size of the population sought for America and its composition by age group. We must also consider the skills and the educational levels that new, legal immigrants should possess, so that they will add substantially to our nation's economic might and to the creation of new jobs and businesses.

Issues precipitated by the intended assimilation of large numbers of new citizens require careful planning and integration into our nation's overarching immigration strategy. National requirements, immigration policies, and potentially corrosive forces must be considered.

Borders and Security

The first obligation of any state is to ensure that its borders are secure. The Biden administration has not only failed this test, it has subverted this requirement. President Biden's actions in allowing a flood of illegal immigrants to pass through our southern border are unpardonable: They constitute a grievous offense, for the president has demonstrated that he does not comprehend that the difference between legal and illegal immigration is as great as the distinction between purchase and theft.

Legal immigration must serve the interests of American citizens; it must never place incumbrances on the men, women, and children who constitute our nation. Billions of people desire to become Americans, but our nation cannot accommodate the whole world. This realization should be axiomatic, but it is not.

The federal government is responsible for the maintenance of our nation's borders and our immigration, asylum, and refugee policies. Sanctuary cities or states crush the rule of law, by disregarding the Supremacy Clause of the Constitution (Article VI, Clause 2) that renders state law subordinate to federal statutes and to treaties made in accordance with the Constitution.

By blocking or by hindering law enforcement actions by the United States Immigration and Customs Enforcement (ICE) agency, sanctuary cities or states are acting in an inherently unlawful manner that is deeply injurious to our Constitutional Republic. Sanctuary cities and states must be eliminated for America's immigration system to function.

Our nation can benefit substantially from a reconstituted immigration system that prioritizes immigrants, who, by their talents, will add materially to our nation. This does not mean that every immigrant must be a PhD. It does mean that the vast preponderance of adult immigrants must be skilled and be able to add immediately to our nation's economy and to the communities in which they settle.

Our exploding national debt compels us to focus government assistance on our own citizens' needs and not those of aliens. America's schools are failing. This situation is compounded if our schools continue to be flooded with undocumented and unaccompanied children who must receive K-12 education, in accord with the Supreme Court's 1982 decision in Plyler v. Doe.[31] With our students' test scores plummeting, America must first secure our children's future before additional burdens may be borne; this focus may only be accomplished by taking decisive actions to stem the flow of illegal aliens into America, for our nation's tax base is depleted by the entry of so many unskilled or unaccompanied persons.

Morality requires that we establish priorities, for if we champion every cause with the same fervor, we will accomplish nothing and will lose our way. Our federal government's first commitment must be to our citizens, including—most especially—those who have served in our armed forces. Help to immigrants must come after our citizens' requirements are met.

The care of Americans in need, including homeless veterans, must be our absolute priority, as opposed to aiding those who would abrogate our borders and laws. Being an illegal immigrant does not mean that someone is a bad person or is undeserving of compassion. Most illegal immigrants have suffered and have sacrificed to reach our nation.

The proper ordering of competing needs is stated in 1 Timothy 5:8, in which care for one's own, and, especially for those within one's house, is prioritized.[32] We can, as a country, show compassion. This, however, must be tempered by our allegiance to a moral order that reflects societal objectives as well as the clear privations of our citizens, which include personal safety in the presence of transnational

---

[31]https://www.uscourts.gov/educational-resources/educational-activities/access-education-rule-law
[32]https://biblehub.com/1_timothy/5-8.htm

gangs that have been enabled and enriched by the Biden administration's border policies.

Assimilation

Assimilation may be defined as "the process of becoming . . . a part of a country or community rather than remaining a separate group."[33] Demagogues contend that the purpose of assimilation is the destruction of cultural and religious identities in order to placate a dominant group of Americans.

The forced assimilation of Indigenous people and nations within America did occur. This was attempted by means of family separation and by indoctrination through childhood education. Immigrant groups, in the past, battled similar actions that were designed to achieve homogeneity.

Such policies have never and will never represent conservatism nor the veneration of the individual but are, instead, emblematic of compelled servility as ordered by the state. Forced assimilation must be rejected unequivocally for it subverts personal agency.

Assimilation properly understood and practiced is the means wherein immigrants weave their identities into the fabric of our country. This embodiment rests upon our laws, our history, and our traditions, thereby permitting new or aspiring citizens the opportunity to participate fully in everything America has to offer.

Assimilation is the integration of immigrants into the weft of our country; it must never be construed or ordained to be the robbery of preexisting and valued traditions. Assimilation should never demand the renunciation of cultural or religious practices, for to do so would be to rob our nation of the richness and uniqueness of customs and precepts found throughout the world.

Every aspect of our nation's life reflects the diversity expressed through cross-cultural enrichment and its many gifts. America is America because this plentitude has been brought to our shores.

---

[33] https://www.oxfordlearnersdictionaries.com/definition/english/assimilation

The use of English, our country's common language, facilitates education, work, commerce, political affiliation, and upward mobility. We must never allow our society to degenerate into combative factions. Absorption of our nation's founding principles is thus crucial, for our society must never become Balkanized.

Requirements, National Wealth, and the Future

In the United States, as in many other lands, national wealth and power are, in part, a function of the size of our population. This issue merits attention and action.

Present estimates project that America's population will exceed 400 million persons by 2060.[34] Our national goals should be to exceed this figure substantially and to add an additional 100 million people to this number by the turn of the century.

We must substitute legal immigration for that which is illegal. America can remain the most powerful nation on earth for the foreseeable future if we grow our population from 338 million in 2022 to 500 million or more by the year 2100. Such growth must be designed to support our nation's principles, not replace them.

China's population is almost certainly in severe decline, due principally to that nation's one-child rule, which led to the selective abortion of females on an appalling scale. After being in place for thirty-five years, the rule was rescinded in 2015. The damage wrought, however, is enduring and multiplicative, for China must now deal with a disastrous disparity between the number of young men and the number of women of childbearing years.[35]

China's population is aging at a rate that is unprecedented for a large country. A phenomenon known as the "4-2-1 problem" is widespread, wherein four elders and two parents must be cared for by one working-age descendent. This is fundamentally due to the one-child policy. This inverted pyramid also places differential pressures on

---

[34]https://www.numbersusa.com/news/us-census-bureau-immigration-will-drive-us-population-over-400-million-2060

[35]https://www.statista.com/statistics/251129/population-in-china-by-gender/

women who wish to join the work force, for, in China, women traditionally care for their parents and grandparents.[36] Thus, young women bear additional disincentives to begin families.

It is possible that China's population may be reduced by almost half by the year 2100, with its citizenry declining below 750 million people.[37] This reduction will also derive from intense urbanization, which tends to induce small families, and the exodus of China's citizens to nations of greater freedom and opportunity.

Reports indicate that perhaps half of China's wealthiest citizens seek to move to another country or place permanently.[38] This number is massive. Hong Kong was a prime destination for this cohort, but Beijing's larcenous repression of Hong Kong's promised independence and the forced incorporation of the former colony into the communist party's totalistic system, in abrogation of the 1984 Joint Sino-British Declaration, eroded the benefits previously conferred by emigration from China to Hong Kong. Thus, Beijing's treachery may result in its elites moving to more distant locations from the mainland, further hampering China's economy.

India, too, will see a gradual decline in its population but is expected to be the only country with a citizenry that numbers more than one billion people through the turn of the century. India will thus increase its relative strength in comparison to China.

Population collapse feeds on itself. If births and immigration do not exceed deaths, a nation's population will enter a spiral that portends future dissipation. For example, Japan, Italy, and other advanced nations also exhibit dangerously low birthrates.[39]

Population growth is a function of the number of children born per couple and the age at which women give birth, for starting families earlier permits more generations to be born in a given space of

---

[36]https://www.prb.org/resources/chinas-concern-over-population-aging-and-health/

[37]https://www.bbc.com/news/health-53409521

[38]https://www.wsj.com/articles/BL-CJB-24030

[39]https://data.worldbank.org/indicator/SP.DYN.CBRT.IN?year_high_desc=false

time. Population growth also derives from the net influx of people to a country.

In developed nations, the population replacement rate, to maintain constancy in population size, without immigration, is 2.1 births per female. In developing countries, with poor health systems, the birth requirements to maintain a given population are higher, for fewer females reach child-bearing age.

Given America's present birthrate, constructive immigration is imperative for stability, growth, and prosperity. The average number of children born is now 1.7 per woman in the United States, which is insufficient, by itself, to maintain the present size of our nation's population.[40] Immigration, therefore, represents a vital mechanism for population stability and growth, for demographic strength results from the achievement and maintenance of a youthful workforce able to support our nation's unfunded liabilities, which currently exceed 100 trillion dollars.[41]

Without legal immigration, America would weaken in all domains of national power, for our population would decline precipitously. The question, therefore, is not whether we should have immigration but what steps must be taken to ensure a strong system that is consistent with our values of fairness, compassion, and excellence.

America benefits enormously from the dynamism generated by the aspirations of new entrants to our country. What is broken today is not legal immigration but the uncontrolled influx of undocumented immigrants who claim asylum status.

Substantial levels of legal immigration, coupled with reductions in abortion, and a national understanding that large families are a necessary component of America's future, will promote adaptability and resilience, which will support our nation's economy as well as our security. Immigration, however, must never mean lawlessness.

---

[40]https://www.cdc.gov/nchs/data/nvsr/nvsr68/nvsr68_13-508.pdf
[41]https://www.forbes.com/sites/realspin/2014/01/17/you-think-the-deficit-is-bad-federal-unfunded-liabilities-exceed-127-trillion/?sh=74bcb1cd9bf8

We are obligated to consider the present crisis on our border with Mexico.

Human Dignity, Trafficking, and Solutions

America's southern border has become a locus for human trafficking and thus human misery. A pillar of humanity is nationhood, which upholds liberty and dignity. Without national borders, we will have neither: The people trafficked by transnational criminal organizations will be subject to every crime and degradation perpetrated by the cartels that profit from this illicit trade. We must complete the wall and apply technology to other areas of our border in which the construction of a wall is impractical or is insufficient.

The Biden administration refused to complete the wall the Trump administration began, thereby signaling to millions of disadvantaged persons as well as those who would harm our citizens that they may cross into our country without documentation. President Biden has sowed mayhem and fostered needless death along our southern border by maintaining an insufficient force of Border Patrol Agents. Predictably, cartels took advantage of the Biden administration's infatuation with globalism, which encompasses the incineration of America's boundaries.

The unwillingness of the Biden administration to defend the southern border empowers transnational criminal organizations that ply lethal narcotics, prostitution, and human trafficking on a scale never before seen in our nation's history.[42] The present number of Border Patrol Agents is a fraction of the Internal Revenue Service (IRS) personnel proposed to be added to the federal work force pursuant to President Biden's deeply irresponsible budgetary actions.[43]

President Biden has avoided meeting Angel Families, who have lost loved ones to violence committed by illegal immigrants. The Biden administration has refused to acknowledge the National Day

[42]https://usafacts.org/data/topics/security-safety/crime-and-justice/homeland-security/border-patrol-agents/
[43]https://www.forbes.com/sites/robertwood/2022/08/11/irs-to-add-87000-new-agents-more-crypto-tax-enforcement/?sh=7f7fa72b3213

of Remembrance for Americans Killed by Illegal Aliens, which was declared by the Trump administration.

President Biden's lack of compassion for American families who have been devastated as a consequence of his open-border policies is beneath contempt. The acceptance of carnage that is denominated in the murder of our fellow citizens, so that leftist precepts may adhere, is not beneficence. It is not concern for the dispossessed who have few options: It is the gutting of the rule of law.

The undocumented immigrant population in America is not known but could exceed twenty million persons. Hardships do not end when the downtrodden enter into America illegally, for many, new tribulations begin, for transnational criminal organizations control the preponderance of illicit and clandestine passages across our border with Mexico. A significant percentage of those who pass illegally are subsequently obligated to work for these cartels—whose crimes cross all fifty states.

Of even greater magnitude in its ability to inflict suffering and death is the transportation of proscribed drugs, including fentanyl, which is illegal unless it is prescribed. Fentanyl, which is made illicitly from compounds produced in China, is now killing Americans at a rate that surpasses the battle-related deaths our nation suffered, on average, per year, in every war fought with the exception of the Civil War.[44]

In its destruction of America's means to uphold national sovereignty, the Biden administration is aiding and abetting this slew of crimes. You do not improve something by destroying its foundations—you obliterate it. This is what President Biden is orchestrating, either due to calculation or due to indifference compounded by incompetence.

America must have complete control over its borders. This is no longer the case, and the results are repulsive in terms of human misery.

---

[44]https://www.dea.gov/stories/2022/2022-02/2022-02-16/fentanyl-deaths-climbing-dea-washington-continues-fight

Outrage

Organ harvesting has been performed on Chinese political prisoners and Uyghur Muslims. Practitioners of Falun Gong, which is a manifestation of traditional Chinese spiritual themes and exercises, are targeted for organ harvesting, for elements within the Chinese Communist Party succeeded in labeling Falun Gong as heretical; its observance was thus banned in 1999.

These outrages involving nonconsensual organ harvesting occur daily in China and occur elsewhere: According to written congressional testimony given in 2019, the threat of this crime has appeared on America's southern border.[45] Can there be any doubt that criminal cartels that are known to burn their rivals alive, would harvest organs from children, and in so doing kill them, when such body parts can bring hundreds of thousands of dollars per victim to a cartel and its brokers?[46]

The organs harvested from one person can be sold on global black markets or on the dark web for enormous sums, since there is a worldwide shortage of organs harvested legally; this is, in part, caused by cultural practices that eschew organ donation, as is the case in China. It is thus virtually certain that Latin American children are being sold and murdered near our southern border by criminal cartels for this execrable trade. Our media has not endeavored to investigate this matter; the American public has thus been kept unaware or ill-informed of the probable extent of these crimes, which are facilitated by America's porous boundary.

The United Nations' Protocol to Prevent, Suppress, and Punish Trafficking in Persons, Especially Women and Children, requires parties to the protocol, including America, Mexico, China, Russia, and the majority of the world's nations, to criminalize human trafficking. Particular emphasis is placed on interdicting such crimes as perpetrated by transnational criminal organizations. Further, Article

---

[45]https://www.congress.gov/116/meeting/house/109140/witnesses/HHRG-116-HM11-Wstate-BallardT-20190326.pdf ·

[46]https://www.acamstoday.org/organ-trafficking-the-unseen-form-of-human-trafficking/

3 of the protocol states, "Exploitation shall include, at a minimum, the exploitation of the prostitution of others or other forms of sexual exploitation, forced labor or services, slavery or practices similar to slavery, servitude or the removal of organs."

In 2020, the Department of State's *Trafficking in Persons Report* was sent to congress pursuant to The Victims of Trafficking and Violence Protection Act of 2000. This law sets standards for preventive and punitive antitrafficking measures; it further seeks to aid victims. The report is our government's tool to engage other nations in order that these stated objectives be realized, but our nation cannot lead if we do not follow our own laws or international agreements to which we are party.

The Department of State's report remains a crucial resource to assess antitrafficking efforts worldwide in support of the twenty-five million people trafficked and denied their basic human rights. The policies of the Biden Administration have undercut the efforts that were broadened by the Department of State during Secretary Pompeo's watch.

By permitting trafficked persons to be crossed into our nation, without a staunch interdiction and suppression of the transnational criminal organizations that engineer this trade, the present administration is, in effect, facilitating the commission of crimes that we, as a nation, are obligated to combat by law, as stipulated by the Thirteenth Amendment to the Constitution and by our international commitments. I believe this dereliction of presidential duties to be an impeachable offense: I contend this judgement is consistent with Alexander Hamilton's argument in Federalist No. 65, in which he wrote that impeachment could remedy an "abuse or violation of some public trust."[47]

The present administration's policies are deeply flawed and succeed only in establishing our southern border as open, though lackies within the administration call it closed. This anarchy and its concomitant subterfuge must end.

---

[47]https://avalon.law.yale.edu/18th_century/fed65.asp

The administration focuses its concern on slavery as it existed more than 150 years ago. It pays scant attention, however, to the slavery that exists today—across our borders and throughout our nation. This misdirection is nauseating. President Biden should be fighting the slavery his mindless policies have entrenched, but this is evidently beyond his ken.

Solutions

The Trump administration understood that an open border constitutes a magnet. Good people, many in dire need, are drawn to it, but so are criminals, gangs, and terror suspects. We must be absolutely clear: Our nation must maintain control over our borders.

Cognizant of the Biden administration's abandonment of the policies and the physical barriers established by the Trump administration, waves of illegal immigrants are now crossing into our country. Border patrol is overwhelmed: This perilous situation, which puts both the lives of our agents and those who seek to enter our country at severe risk, is eviscerating our country's unity.

Our deeply broken border immigration system can only be fixed by integrating a number of partial solutions. Physical boundaries do work; if they did not, people would not have locks on their homes and their businesses.

Walls must be supplemented by increased numbers of Border Patrol Agents; their ranks should increase by approximately fifty percent to at least 30,000, given the challenges and dangers faced.[48] Also critical are vastly expedited means of administering immigration cases.

In terms of technology, new types of drones will be crucial to an expanded security effort. These airborne vehicles could be guided by predictive algorithms that will enable increased border apprehensions while minimizing the degree of human resources employed.

---

[48] https://usafacts.org/data/topics/security-safety/crime-and-justice/homeland-security/border-patrol-agents/

The Department of State was deeply involved in structuring and negotiating the remain in Mexico policy, which required asylum seekers to stay in Mexico until their hearing dates. Although this policy was effective, it does not constitute the comprehensive solution our nation must attain.

A true, regional response is needed at our southern border. On September 20, 2022, President Biden responded to a question as to why the southern border is now overwhelmed; he said, "This is a totally different circumstance. What's on my watch now is Venezuela, Cuba, and Nicaragua. And the ability to send them back to those states is not rational. You could send them back and have them — we're working with Mexico and other countries to see if we can stop the flow."[49]

President Biden's first point is salient, for emigration from three despotic, socialist regimes in our hemisphere has, indeed, overstressed our border because the Biden Administration has consciously decided not to fill the gaps in the southern border wall built by the Trump administration, nor provide adequate numbers of Border Patrol Agents. Perhaps, President Biden intends to dissuade emigrants from Venezuela, Cuba, and Nicaragua from entering the United States by turning our country into a replica of such radical, autocratic states, whose governments are detested by their own people.

The latter point made by President Biden about his working with Mexico to eliminate the border crisis is, of course, not true in any operational sense. The Biden Administration has made no comprehensive and meaningful effort to stem the flow of illegal aliens into America; the system on our border has devolved into a twisted chasm run by transnational criminal organizations that should be viewed as the equivalent of terrorist groups and be treated as such.

To address the present perilous influx of people, contraband, and crime, which has no precedent, our nation must address asylum law.

---

[49] https://www.whitehouse.gov/briefing-room/speeches-remarks/2022/09/20/remarks-by-president-biden-on-the-disclose-act/

We must suspend an illegal immigrant's "right" to seek asylum on self-professed grounds.

Putative asylum seekers should be obligated to request refuge in the first country to which they travel. This is the essence of a regional response, which must be adopted immediately to answer the present crisis. Obviously, nondocumented immigrants from every nation, not contiguous to America, enter first, if traveling by land, countries other than our own. It is to such nations that asylum claims should be tendered. The Biden administration has belatedly embraced this imperative but in an adulterated form, which will accomplish almost nothing. President Biden's plan contains an egregious loophole, which is the acceptance of online applications for asylum, even from those traveling from faraway lands.[50] This is unacceptable; a new administration must prioritize the core principle of meaningful asylum reform.

The misapplication of our statutes has allowed individuals to self-proclaim that they are entitled to asylum. United States Code specifies, "To establish that the applicant is a refugee within the meaning of such section, the applicant must establish that race, religion, nationality, membership in a particular social group, or political opinion was or will be at least one central reason for persecuting the applicant."[51]

None of this applies to the vast majority of illegal aliens entering our nation surreptitiously, most often to feed on our nation's social welfare programs and to improve their economic situation. Their transit, however, is facilitated by President Biden, who seems intent on not fulfilling his oath of office.

Rather than addressing this ongoing disaster, the Biden Administration continues to provide incentives for illegal immigration. On September 30, 2021, Secretary of Homeland Security Alejandro Mayorkas released updated guidance that stated that his department will no longer detain or deport individuals based on their illegal status

---

[50] https://abc13.com/biden-administration-mexico-border-title-42/13230234/
[51] https://uscode.house.gov/view.xhtml?req=granuleid:USC-prelim-title8-section1158&num=0&edition=prelim

alone, noting, "The fact an individual is a removable noncitizen therefore should not alone be the basis of an enforcement action against them."[52] This is the active abrogation of law.

Our government should not evaluate whether individuals deserve asylum or refugee status by first allowing them to live in our country. The determination of status must be made before an individual crosses our borders. The situation on our southern border is so ruptured that new laws should be written without delay.

We must replace current statutes with those that make sense. General principles should require that asylum claims be made outside our country and that such claims should comport with a formal presidential declaration that persons from a particular country or region have, indeed, been subject to persecution on the basis of race, religion, nationality, membership in a particular social group, or political opinion.

Such formal proclamations would be measurably different from today's standard in which a "reasonable possibility" of persecution, held in the aspirant's mind, is enough to enable the applicant to settle in our nation—to await a hearing before an immigration judge. The present system allows leftist lawyers to coach asylum seekers on what to say, perpetuating this farce. Required court appearances, however, usually never occur, for these immigrants disappear, often without a trace, within our country.

Sagacity should require that the United States Code in these matters reflect the United Nation's definition concerning victims of genocide as set out in General Assembly Resolution 260 of December 9, 1948, which entered into force January 12, 1951.[53] This description noted that victims were "in whole or in part, a national, ethnical, racial or religious group," which was subject to "(a) Killing members of the

---

[52]https://www.usnews.com/news/national-news/articles/2021-09-30/dhs-issues-new-priorities-for-arrests-and-deportation

[53]https://www.un.org/en/genocideprevention/documents/atrocity-crimes/Doc.1_Convention%20on%20the%20Prevention%20and%20Punishment%20of%20the%20Crime%20of%20Genocide.pdf#:~:text=Convention%20on%20the%20Prevention%20and%20Punishment%20of%20the,in%20accordance%20with%20article%20XIII%20The%20Contracting%20Parties%2C

group; (b) Causing serious bodily or mental harm to members of the group; (c) Deliberately inflicting on the group conditions of life calculated to bring about its physical destruction in whole or in part; (d) Imposing measures intended to prevent births within the group; (e) Forcibly transferring children of the group to another group."

Although these principles apply to victims of genocide, they can serve as a sound basis upon which to redraw our asylum and refugee laws; further, they could be expanded to include persons who are victimized based upon other factors. Crucially, such a finding of harm—instigated through the employment of new asylum laws—should be made by the president and not by the person seeking asylum.

After such a presidential declaration is made, members of the group at risk should then be able to make their case if they can prove group affiliation. This is the means to resolve the ever-increasing number of asylum cases rapidly and fairly.

Present

The foregoing does not resolve the situation of illegal immigrants who presently live in the United States. New laws and regulations are required. All undocumented immigrants should be obligated to register with federal authorities within a specified period of time, which should not exceed four months. After the registration period, all illegal immigrants who have a criminal record must be expelled as should all concerned persons who fail to register.

Unbelievably, we now allow illegal immigrants with criminal records entry into our country, for the standard is that only perpetrators of "particularly serious" crimes, generally taken to mean aggravated felonies, are automatically barred from making asylum claims. This leniency places our nation's citizens at grave risk and is wholly unacceptable. The prevention of crime and loss must be our priority, not an afterthought.

Law-abiding, undocumented immigrants, who already reside in our country, should be permitted the opportunity to stay in America if multiple criteria are met. We must take into account that many of these aliens acted on the basis of *de facto* law as expressed by the Obama and the Biden administrations.

Undocumented immigrants who can assert their maintenance of ongoing, meaningful employment should be permitted to stay in accord with the achievement of special work visas. Exceptions to this qualification should be made on the basis of special, enumerated circumstances.

With this foundation in place, America should consider extending qualifications to apply for citizenship to undocumented persons after they exhibit ten years of exemplary conduct within our country. Our actions should reflect the fact that the present situation is compounded in its difficulty by the presence of children of undocumented immigrants who were born in America and are thus our fellow citizens. This fact, alone, should mandate our immediate attention to this divisive situation.

As a condition of application for citizenship, affected persons should be required to demonstrate their commitment to assimilate, including the attainment of basic proficiency in English. After the noted ten-year period, applications for citizenship should be folded into the existing process for prospective legal immigrants.

Security, common sense, fairness, and mercy must mark our country. This articulated plan would constitute a fresh start in immigration policy. We must hope that all people of goodwill may see the necessity of embracing these realistic and compassionate precepts as a way forward, which will help mend a molten rift in our nation.

Chapter 5, Immigration and Border Security, Precepts:

• A pillar of humanity is nationhood, which upholds liberty and dignity. Without national borders, we will have neither.

• Security and the application of law, commonsense, and fairness must mark our country's immigration policies. The Biden administration refuses to complete the wall the Trump administration began, thereby signaling to millions of disadvantaged persons that they may cross into our country without documentation.

• In its destruction of America's means to uphold national sovereignty, the Biden administration is abetting heinous crimes that include the importation of illegal drugs, human trafficking, and the exploitation of children. Unbelievably, we now allow illegal immigrants with criminal records to enter and to stay in our country.

• It is in our national interest to continue to welcome large numbers of legal immigrants and to assimilate all those who lawfully seek to become Americans. Assimilation is the integration of immigrants into the heart of our nation; it is not the excision of preexisting or valued traditions.

Issues and Problems:

• Legal immigration must serve the interests of American citizens; it must never place incumbrances on the men, women, and children who constitute our nation's citizenry.

• The federal government is responsible for the maintenance of our nation's borders and our immigration, asylum, and refugee policies. Sanctuary cities or states crush the rule of law, by disregarding the Supremacy Clause of the Constitution that renders state law subordinate to federal statutes made in accordance with the Constitution.

• Physical differences must never be used as the means to divide our nation, though foreign and domestic forces seek to ply dissension and civic unrest on this basis. We must never place people into segmented groups, which tell us nothing about how individuals order their lives or yearn to contribute to our nation.

• America must secure our children's future before accepting additional burdens; this may only be accomplished by taking decisive actions to stem the flow of illegal aliens into America, for our country's tax base is depleted by the entry of so many unskilled or unaccompanied persons.

Duties and Actions:

• America benefits enormously from the dynamism generated by new legal entrants to our country. What is broken today is not legal immigration but the uncontrolled influx of undocumented immigrants who claim asylum status.

• We must address asylum law and suspend an illegal immigrant's "right" to seek asylum on self-professed grounds.

• Walls must be supplemented by greatly increased numbers of Border Patrol Agents, whose ranks should increase by at least fifty percent. Vastly expedited means of administering immigration cases are critical, as is the deployment of advanced technologies to secure the border, including new classes of drones.

• Solutions must be wrought to contend with the large number of undocumented immigrants who already reside in our country, for many have children who are American citizens due to their birth in the United States. In developing solutions to this difficult problem, the safety and the welfare of American citizens must come first.

CHAPTER 6

STRENGTH THROUGH PEOPLE

China, Russia, and other belligerent nations seek to seed racial turmoil and division within the United States, as the Soviet Union did. Though our country has addressed racism earnestly, American exceptionalism is rejected by the left for it destroys their concept of humanity's being a uniform mass.

Material possessions must never be held as being of supreme importance or as being indicative of the true worth of an individual, for our worth as human beings is created by God and not by our industriousness or fortune. The left seeks to disrupt our society; this includes the nature of men and women and the status of motherhood, which should be revered but is now denigrated.

> As society becomes unmoored from its religious foundations, elites assert that we can become the authors of our own creation and alter the essential nature of humanity, for it is not fixed. These assertions are false: We live within our time and bear obligations to society; we are part of history but do not control its entire course. We do not possess the power to void God's will.

Strength Through People

Unconstrained illegal immigration is not the only threat our nation faces. China, Russia, and other belligerent nations seek to seed racial turmoil and division within the United States.

This stratagem is not new, nor has it only been practiced in our country. Numerous directors of the Central Intelligence Agency and secretaries of state have contended with disinformation and propaganda campaigns that targeted our nation.

Misinformation involves the spreading of false information, whether it is known to be false or not. Disinformation is differentiated from misinformation. Disinformation is defined by an absolute intent to spread false information to cause societal discord.

Propaganda may use misinformation, disinformation, distortion, obfuscation of counterevidence, and various manipulative techniques, in a deliberate and systematic manner, to obtain political or other ends that are often contrary to independent choice. These results may be designed to demoralize or stigmatize targeted populations. Propaganda in its Leninist and Maoist applications is often merged with agitation, which coerces or summons selected groups to act on behalf of a state's or an entity's objectives.

Today, the Chinese Communist Party's United Front Work Department seeks to influence groups across the globe, commanding intelligence and information operations, to secure Chinese objectives. Information operations may be defined as the acquisition of information and its use, presented in a propagandistic context that often employs elements of behaviorism, including operant conditioning using positive and negative stimuli, to achieve policy goals.[54] In their pursuits, the PRC's intelligence assets are mirroring the work of three intelligence arms that were active in the United States before and during World War II.

History

The militarist, Japanese Black Dragon Society was begun in 1901 to contest Tsarist Russia in the prelude to the Russo-Japanese War of 1904 and 1905. By the 1930s, the Black Dragon Society had spread to the Middle East and to the United States, seeking to establish ideological beachheads for Imperial Japan.

The Federal Bureau of Investigation (FBI) was aware of this Japanese organization; agents of the FBI tracked its activities. The Black Dragon Society had a different racialist message than that of the German American Bund, which sought to legitimize Nazi Germany. The German American Bund was an insurrectionist organization that began in 1933; it was tethered directly to Nazi leaders and was the result of a plan instituted at the behest of Adolf Hitler's deputy, Rudolf Hess.

While each organization sought to spread hate and division within America, their objectives differed. The Black Dragon Society sought to ignite a race war between Americans; the German American Bund propounded the fictional superiority of people of German ancestry over all others, as it vilified Jews. This despicable Nazi organization held a mass rally in Madison Square Garden in 1939 but was disbanded in 1941 at the onset of the Second World War, after its first leader was imprisoned, and its subsequent head fled to Mexico.[55]

Scholar Ernest Allen, professor emeritus, Department of Afro-American Studies, University of Massachusetts Amherst, has

---

[54]https://www.rand.org/topics/information-operations.html
[55]https://www.britannica.com/topic/German-American-Bund

documented actions of the leader of the Black Dragon Society within the United States. Major Satokata Takahashi, ensconced in the United States before the war and married to an American, attempted to inflame racial discord through propaganda and through the connections he established with Black separatist groups.[56] Though this plan did not achieve its objectives, it provided part of a template for other foreign groups, by using incendiary rhetoric to enlarge existing racial tensions within our country.

During this time, Soviet information operations, designed to impact American public opinion, became deeply entrenched. Since its founding in 1919, the Communist International (Comintern) sought to establish global communism. A number of prominent American and British citizens rallied to this malicious cause. Democratic Congressmen Samuel Dickstein, a staunch anti-fascist, also served, surreptitiously, as a paid agent of the People's Commissariat for Internal Affairs, which is abbreviated from the Cyrillic as NKVD. This was a predecessor organization to the KGB (Committee for State Security), which was formed in 1954.[57]

The Moscow bureau chief of *The New York Times*, Walter Duranty, won a Pulitzer Prize, which has not been rescinded, for his mendacious and highly destructive reporting for his paper concerning Vladimir Lenin, Joseph Stalin, and the USSR, during the formative period for Soviet communism that began after the Bolshevik Army's victory in the Russian Civil War and the formation of the Soviet Union in 1922. Duranty's reporting from Moscow lasted through 1936.

Duranty actively sought to override reports by English journalist Malcolm Muggeridge and Welsh journalist Gareth Jones that concerned the magnitude of the famine that communism induced in Ukraine, which claimed up to ten million lives. This horror was due to direct starvation and to birth defects resulting from inadequate nutrition.

---

[56]https://www.researchgate.net/publication/291327339_Satokata_Takahashi_and_the_Flowering_of_Black_Messianic_Nationalism
[57]https://archive.nytimes.com/cityroom.blogs.nytimes.com/2013/05/22/a-street-named-for-a-soviet-spy-goes-largely-unnoticed/

Walter Duranty was paid by Stalin's regime and, in all likelihood, was blackmailed by the Kremlin. Coercion was easily wrought, for Duranty was an occultist and most probably a Satanist. He shared a close association with the infamous British Satanist Aleister Crowley, with whom he enacted blasphemous rituals, designed to bring forth ancient, malevolent deities, while both were in Paris years earlier.[58]

Jones was subsequently assassinated in Manchukuo, a puppet state of Imperial Japan.[59] His murder was almost certainly at the behest of the NKVD.

Born to a father who was a prominent socialist and a Labour Party Member of Parliament, Muggeridge, himself, was drawn to communism in his early adult life. He, however, was so repulsed by what he saw in the Soviet Union that he became a noted conservative, whose dispatches, essays, and books deeply influenced William F. Buckley and Ronald Reagan, thereby serving to stimulate the birth of the modern conservative movement in the United States.

Governors

From the 1930s onward, as part of a plan conceived by the Comintern, the Soviet Union broadcast to the world grievous episodes of segregation and discrimination, which occurred in the United States. Two Democratic governors, whose racism exemplified aspects of the Jim Crow laws that scarred our nation during this time, were, in effect, used by Soviet information operations.

Orval Faubus, in 1957, employed the National Guard to prevent Black students from attending and thus integrating Central High School in Little Rock, Arkansas. Predictably, the USSR used this racist act to ignite the international community against "American democracy."

Faubus's actions and the resultant narrative were destroyed, however, through decisive actions by President Eisenhower, who

---

[58]https://www.patheos.com/blogs/eidos/2020/10/the-lies-they-tell-us-our-betters-and-the-stories-we-believe-walter-duranty/
[59]https://www.goodreads.com/book/show/8677636-gareth-jones

ordered the deployment to Little Rock of 1,200 soldiers of the 101st Airborne Division. The state's National Guard, which had interfered with the students' admittance to the school, were then placed under federal orders, ending the crisis.

This pattern was repeated in 1963 when Alabama's Democratic governor, George Wallace, standing at the doorway of the state's university in Tuscaloosa, attempted to block the matriculation of two Black students. To break this assaultive act by the governor, President Kennedy federalized the state's National Guard, thereby upholding the students' rights.

In these two cases, determined presidential responses, which thwarted un-American actions by state governors, defended the Supreme Court's landmark desegregation decision of 1954, in Brown v. Board of Education. Despite these restorative federal actions, the Soviet Union amplified these racially based clashes and others, to attempt to sow greater racial discord within America and to thus reduce America's stature abroad.

What is different today from these historical episodes and conflicts is that Chinese, Russian, and Iranian information operations spread disinformation about the status of our society. Each of these nations would have the world believe that America has not addressed racism.

Unfortunately, this propaganda is ingested and spewed by American broadcasters, social media companies and influencers, and progressive politicians. Wounds that should be healed are opened; lesions that should not exist are highlighted and amplified, so that they appear to exemplify the current condition of our Republic, rather than be seen as exceptions to the general comity of our country.

We must assess information operations that are now actualized to spread racial discontent. This is particularly true of falsehoods involving America's southern border. As stated, America welcomes far more legal immigrants than does any other nation.

Our country's immigrant population is more than four times the number of non-native persons in any other land.[60] America's true

---

[60]https://www.pewresearch.org/fact-tank/2016/05/18/5-facts-about-the-u-s-rank-in-worldwide-migration/

status as a beacon for freedom should be broadcast, but this cannot happen if our media, in all its forms, dwells on our country's failures and not our triumphs that far exceed those of any other nation.

American exceptionalism is an anathema to the left for exceptionalism destroys their concept of humanity's being a uniform mass. Such malicious factions therefore seek ways to disrupt that which is laudatory.

Genesis, Good, and Evil

The nature of evil is freedom misused and unbound. Evil is thus corruption; indeed, the expression of evil by autocrats scales in relation to their power. Many conservatives are hobbled in their ability to combat evil for one cannot contest what one cannot conceive.

Three vectors, each with demographic consequences, threaten to destroy America's status and power. The first, abortion, may be fought through education, through adoption, and through the adoration of the family as the basis for civilization.

The second vector is the avowed preference for many young women to defer having children, to have small families, or not to bear any children at all. No society can hope to flourish if motherhood is not central. Motherhood must be revered.

In a commencement address at Wellesley College on June 1, 1990, First Lady Barbara Bush said, "At the end of your life, you will never regret not having passed one more test, not winning one more verdict or not closing one more deal. You will regret time not spent with a husband, a friend, a child, or a parent."

Barbara Bush's statement is a marvelous conception of life. We must exemplify this sentiment by seeking balance in our lives, so that generations now living or unborn may benefit from this matriarch's exceptionally thoughtful reflection. As a society, we must extol that true happiness comes from family, for though we all like nice things, material possessions must never be held as being of supreme importance or as being indicative of the true worth of an individual, for our worth as human beings is created by God and not by our industriousness or fortune.

The third vector concerns a new peril, which did not exist a decade ago: It involves the natures of men and women. If our society becomes unmoored from its religious and its philosophical foundations, we may fail to comprehend that the essential nature of humanity is fixed, for we are not the authors of our own creation. Humanity is not a giant machine or a collection of servers that may be altered in the quest for mechanistic improvement or change.

Adrift

"We are all that exists" may be a common thought, but it is not a correct observation. Each of us lives within our time and bears obligations to the society that surrounds us; we are part of history but never constitute the entirety of its course; we thus never possess the power to vitiate one scintilla of God's will.

America and the West are faced with intensely radical forces that seek to demolish the differences between the sexes, which exist not only between humans but throughout the entirety of mammalian and avian life. Does no one in our media or in corporate America have the courage to say, "Stop, consider what you are doing to our nation's children?"

There is no third sex nor can there ever be one. Indeed, such a creation would violate the Lord's design as well as any secular theory of evolution. The concept of a third sex, or one sex transposed as the other, exists only in a mind that is devoid of serious inquiry.

If we propel each sex to blur into the other, which can only be accomplished by denying all that is real, humankind will destroy God's primary creations: man and woman. We will thus commit deicide, for to obliterate the sexes is to attempt to murder God. The realization of this travesty, though impossible, is Marxism's prime objective, for by slaying God, humankind would establish itself as the arbiter of all things.

We should not confuse, as a society, what is normative with what is permitted, and we should not confuse what is permitted with what is good or advantageous. To forgive is different than to condone.

Acceptance of a fact is not the same thing as acceptance in a personal or in a moral sense. In the first instance, we have no choice: A fact is a fact. The second connotation of acceptance defines our moral self, for our heart is the embodiment of our soul.

We all must live within our society and its laws, even those which we may consider wrong. If a law is unjust, we must work to change it, for history proves this to be the most advantageous and expedient course to correct past injuries.

Our society, state legislatures, the federal government, and our nation's courts must reciprocally accept that we, as individuals and as a people, are endowed with the unalienable right to hold beliefs that are consonant with our understanding of God's word or our creed. This unalienable right, to hold our own beliefs, grants each of us the prerogative to peaceably protest what we hold to be improper or unjust. This right is of such importance that it is established by the First Amendment to our Constitution. To censure what we do not understand is unwise. To censure what we, ourselves, know, through God's grace, cannot be but wrong.

Statement

When Health and Human Services Secretary Xavier Becerra, testifying before the Senate, cannot bring himself to say the word "mother," we are in danger of no longer living in a country, but in a madhouse.[61] Faith venerates mothers as the bringers of life, yet this man could not speak the word from his lips. Such leftist absurdity is offensive, for it degrades motherhood, which is the basis for all civilization.

Children are now made to think that they can change their sex or that there are no differences between the sexes. Neither assertion is true, nor will such sentiments ever be true.

Somehow, our society has reached the point in which a medical doctor, who is a four-star admiral in the United States Public Health Service Commissioned Corps and serves as the assistant secretary

---

[61]https://www.dailywire.com/news/watch-bidens-hhs-sec-grins-as-he-refuses-to-say-the-word-mother-instead-of-birthing-people

for health in the United States Department of Health and Human Services, forcefully asserts that children deserve "gender-affirming care."[62] Young children should therefore be the authors of their own diagnoses, even though childhood, puberty, and adolescence are marked by intense changes in personality, deportment, and preferences, for the brain is not fully formed until a person reaches their mid-twenties.[63]

To employ the left's risible but highly destructive logic is to assert that if a child states that he wants to become a pirate, we should proceed to gouge out his eye and chop off his leg. This is representative of an insanity that can become a contagion, which will, if unanswered, destroy countless children.

No country can withstand the manufactured infertility of a substantial percentage of its youthful population. If a girl receives puberty blockers that are followed by courses of testosterone, the child will, almost certainly, be rendered infertile for life, for she will have never passed through female puberty and will therefore be incapable of conceiving a child.

Planned Parenthood advocates puberty blockers such as leuprolide acetate,[64] a drug that has been used to chemically castrate adults who are sex offenders. Planned Parenthood's website notes to children, "Sometimes during puberty the changes going on in your body might not line up with your gender identity. . . . Your gender identity is real, and there are medical treatments you can use to help your body better reflect who you are."[65]

In fact, the concept of gender identity that is differentiated from a person's sex is recent and is highly controversial. It was articulated first in 1955 by Dr. John Money,[66] a psychologist and author who helped establish the Johns Hopkins Gender Identity Clinic. This

[62]https://nypost.com/2022/05/02/rachel-levine-doctors-agree-on-need-for-gender-affirming-care-for-trans-kids/

[63]https://www.ncbi.nlm.nih.gov/pmc/articles/PMC3621648/

[64]https://www.plannedparenthood.org/learn/teens/puberty/what-are-puberty-blockers

[65]Ibid.

[66]https://pubmed.ncbi.nlm.nih.gov/13260820/

became the first medical institution to perform reassignment surgeries in the United States, until such operations were stopped on clinical grounds.[67] However, years later, a reconstituted Hopkins clinic would again make referrals for surgery, in seeming deference to an emerging, politicized context.[68]

Dr. Money's reputation was eventually shattered by the publication of the extraordinarily contemptable and abusive details of the reassignment case of David Reimer, whom Money treated from infancy through childhood. Sadly, Reimer would take his own life at the age of thirty-eight.[69]

The pivotal role that Dr. Money played in both the creation of the concept of gender as being differentiable from sex and the establishment of the first major clinic in America that performed reassignment surgeries, is reminiscent of the work of two other doctors. The once celebrated, 19th century physician, Moritz Schreber, introduced pedagogical methods in Germany and in other parts of Europe that promoted chastisement and the wearing of torturous devices by children to enforce proper posture and, spuriously, rectitude.

Dr. Schreber's own son, Daniel, ultimately became insane, though he was one of Germany's leading jurists in his time; two of Daniel's siblings also succumbed to profound mental illness, with one committing suicide. The damage wrought by Dr. Schreber's childrearing methods may be inferred, in part, from Sigmund Freud's and Carl Jung's commentaries concerning the case of Dr. Schreber's son.

The larger, societal consequences of Moritz Schreber's advocacy are difficult to measure. The noted Swiss philosopher and psychologist Alice Miller contends that Dr. Schreber's "poisonous pedagogy" had deep and lasting psychological ramifications for those impacted.

---

[67]https://www.wsj.com/articles/paul-mchugh-transgender-surgery-isnt-the-solution-1402615120

[68]https://archive.thinkprogress.org/johns-hopkins-transgender-surgery-5c9c428184c1/

[69]https://embryo.asu.edu/pages/david-reimer-and-john-money-gender-reassignment-controversy-johnjoan-case

It certainly may be argued that incorporation of Dr. Schreber's pedagogical methods instilled a receptivity to brutality within the minds of affected Germans, Austrians, and other Europeans born during the pre-World War I and interwar periods. Thus, the savagery displayed by the European Axis powers in World War II may have been shaped, in part, by the inhumanity of the childrearing methods advocated by one of Germany's leading physicians, beginning in the mid-nineteenth century. Of course, Dr. Schreber's methods are today totally discredited, but the damage they inculcated may have served as a substratum that allowed the most vicious leaders in history to attain power.

More recently, in our own country, our medical establishment permitted what are now deemed atrocities to be committed. Dr. Walter Freeman II was born to a family of physicians in 1895.

Dr. Freeman pioneered psychosurgery and coined the term lobotomy for his favored procedure, which he first performed in 1936. The surgery detached the thalamus from its connections to the frontal lobes of a patient's brain. After a decade in which he performed hundreds of these surgeries, Dr. Freeman focused on a simpler procedure, which he often performed without surgical gloves or a mask: This operation was termed a transorbital lobotomy; an icepick-like instrument was inserted beside the patient's eye and hammered upward, thereby permitting the surgeon to reach the patient's brain to dislodge crucial connections.[70]

Twenty thousand lobotomies of various kinds were performed in the period between 1942 and 1952. Almost immediately, respected neurologists and surgeons raised alarms about the procedures, which often left patients in a vegetative or zombie-like state. The operation, however, was heralded by the media and by public commentators in the postwar period as a breakthrough with scant side effects, though famous patients, including John F. Kennedy's sister, Rosemary, had already been grievously harmed.[71]

---

[70]https://www.britannica.com/science/lobotomy#ref205578
[71]https://www.jfklibrary.org/learn/about-jfk/the-kennedy-family/rosemary-kennedy

Of obvious but neglected concern was the nature of Dr. Freeman's traveling roadshow, for he would motor from town to town, performing his surgeries after superficial examinations of the individuals who would become his victims. Dr. Freeman, an accomplished photographer, would take before-and-after pictures of his subjects. He argued that his photographs and the changes in expressions in his patients' faces were indicative of improvement, though such analyses proved nothing.[72]

Although this horrendous surgical procedure was all but abandoned, due to the realization of the errors committed and because of the introduction of psychotropic medicines in the early 1950s, such as chlorpromazine, the lobotomy did, however, live on through the efforts of Dr. Freeman. In 1960, he performed a transorbital lobotomy on his youngest patient, who was not mentally ill or incapacitated but was a rambunctious, twelve-year-old child.

The horrors inflicted on this boy are recounted in his memoires, *My Lobotomy*.[73] This book, by Howard Dully, should be required reading for those physicians and therapists who seek to operate on children to change them permanently.

In the case of lobotomies, the surgeries were often performed to make individuals conform to societal norms or be more tractable. Adolescents and young adults living in difficult or complex family situations were thus at increased risk of being subject to this heinous operation—due to coercive forces.

Irreparable Harm

Today, different procedures and hormonal therapies are advanced to alter irrevocably our children and fellow citizens. A total of 2.1 billion dollars will be spent on reassignment surgeries in 2022; expenditures for such procedures are expected to grow at a compounded rate in excess of eleven percent per year through 2030, to reach an

---

[72]https://videocast.nih.gov/summary.asp?Live=29010&bhcp=1
[73]https://www.npr.org/2005/11/16/5014080/my-lobotomy-howard-dullys-journey

annual expense of five billion dollars, before inflation. This new industry could potentially entrap more than 1.3 percent of our nation's youth.[74] This is unacceptable, but reassignment procedures on our children have increased at a prodigious rate for the past ten years; this trend, if not arrested, will, in all likelihood, continue.[75]

Categorization of humans by sex is considered biological in nature; a large segment of America's medical establishment now differentiates gender from biological sex and deems gender a psychological, social, or cultural construct.[76] Therefore, if this dichotomy is to be respected, it makes no sense to alter a patient's physical body, profoundly affecting their health and their reproductive capacity. This is because the desire to conform to another sex is presently deemed by elements of the medical establishment to be not necessarily innate but to be essentially a product of social conditioning. In the sense of conformation to societal expectations, reassignment surgeries may be viewed as simulacrums of the discredited psychosurgical procedures of the past.

If there is no distinction between biological sex and gender ascription, then internal discord between these two attributes is an illness, which should first be treated with therapy and the in-depth evaluation of possible causal factors. Instead, proponents of surgical interventions and hormonal treatments view the incongruence of a patient's biological sex with his or her asserted internal and social expressions, to be something that is physically broken. Thus, the manifested incongruence may be repaired through surgeries complemented by the administration of drugs; the intervention is thus viewed as being akin, in its modalities and in its basis, to the fixing of a compound fracture or a cleft palate.

Supposed authorities believe a mismatch in physical and psychological attributes may be efficaciously corrected by surgery and

[74]https://www.grandviewresearch.com/industry-analysis/us-sex-reassignment-surgery-market

[75]https://www.cbsnews.com/news/sex-change-treatment-for-kids-on-the-rise/

[76]https://www.psychologytoday.com/us/blog/old-school-parenting-modern-day-families/201907/time-move-beyond-gender-is-socially-constructed

associated care. Gender dysphoria, particularly in children, should, however, first be given a chance to pass, for it most probably is a stage.[77]

Reports indicate that eighty percent of children diagnosed with gender dysphoria grow out of it, for it "recedes with puberty" in most cases.[78] If the condition is persistent, it should be treated as a psychological malady that requires intervention within the discipline of mental health, without making unalterable changes to the patient through the destruction or the remodeling of healthy tissue.

Victims

Childhood abuse is one of the world's most devastating scourges; tens of millions of Americans, of all ages, are survivors. Reported cases of child abuse in 2020 in our country comprise 618,399 victims, including 1,713 fatalities.[79] The total number of cases, including those that are unreported, is undoubtably much higher, though there are certain positive trends, which concern the vector of reported instances.

The damage wrought by child abuse is a cause for a myriad of evils; abuse inevitably produces profound sorrow within the victim, which may lead to suicide or an intense desire to change oneself physically in order to become another person. Unlike the facts of the Reimer case, many young people who seek reassignment surgeries are, no doubt, survivors of childhood abuse, which they answer through seeking to change their outward self for their internal pain is too difficult to bear.[80] As a nation, we must fight abuse in all its forms. Its obliteration must become our country's priority if we are to safeguard America's children and thus our future.

---

[77]https://www.transgendertrend.com/children-change-minds/
[78]https://www.ncbi.nlm.nih.gov/pmc/articles/PMC5841333/
[79]https://www.statista.com/topics/5910/child-abuse-in-the-united-states/#dossierContents_outerWrapper
[80]https://www.ncbi.nlm.nih.gov/books/NBK532313/

In their actions, America's elites and elements of the medical establishment now support surgeries to alter irreparably physically healthy patients as a first course of action to relieve psychological pain. This is an inversion of the Hippocratic Oath, which is to first do no harm. This error is extraordinarily damaging to our nation and to all those involved.

Historians lament the creation of eunuchs who served the Chinese emperors or who held stations in the Ottoman Empire, but we, as a society, are eerily silent concerning the present approximations of such crimes, which are occurring with increasing frequency. We are now witnessing an appalling breach of human rights and personal agency, for children and adolescents cannot exercise informed consent.

The consequences of these reassignment procedures duplicate the effects of the sterilization programs perpetrated by fascist and communist states, which continue in this century. This is impermissible.

We, as citizens, must demand answers: Why does President Biden, through his administration's actions, vitiate the safety of our nation's most vulnerable children? Why is this pernicious agenda not stopped immediately?

We must understand that not every supposed medical advance is an advancement. Let us reflect on the misery caused by Dr. Schreber and Dr. Freemen; let us take direct steps so that such mistakes are not repeated.

Evil is not necessarily intentional. It may result from a combination of unplanned actions generated by disparate ideas that coalesce to form something that is deeply injurious. Therefore, for evil to be fought, it must be recognized and be decried. If we, as a nation, allow the off-label use of drugs that are routinely prescribed to treat sex offenders, so that a child's puberty and maturation may be blocked, we will continue to circle a moral abyss, whose tide will become ever more difficult to contest.[81]

Our touchstone, as in so many things, must be our Lord's message of love. We cannot stand idly by when our children are

---

[81] https://cnsnews.com/article/national/lucy-collins/what-woman-documentary-puberty-blocker-used-chemically-castrate-sex

threatened by the most radical forces our nation has ever known. We are witnessing a union of indifference, indecision, and wickedness, which is expressed by elites and by members of the medical community. This pretention of care oozes with a false sanctimony that would make Lucifer proud.

Parallels

Female genital mutilation (FGM) has brutalized more than 200 million women and girls worldwide, who are alive today, according to the World Health Organization of the United Nations.[82] FGM is the excision of external female genitalia or the severe injury to female genital organs for religious or tribal reasons. This form of mutilation is universally decried across developed nations as being an absolute denial of the victim's humanity, sexuality, and rights, as declared by numerous international bodies and conventions.

The Centers for Disease Control and Prevention, in 1990, estimated that 168,000 females, living in the United States, had either undergone this procedure or were at risk.[83] Congress acted and in 1996 passed a bill that became law: The statute made FGM illegal when performed on girls under 18 years of age. Implicit in this action is the understanding that any group that tolerates this practice risks placing itself outside our nation's fabric and our commitment to human rights.

The Department of State has been deeply involved in women's issues since the Reagan administration; the department's interagency groups and international actions have sought to eliminate the blight of FGM from the earth. Pursuant to my duties involving global issues, I remember vividly my explaining this practice to Robert McFarlane while we served together in the White House; he was shocked and could hardly believe that FGM existed in the twentieth century. Decades later, in 2018, the Secretary's Office of Global Women's Issues (S/GWI at the Department of State), which supports the rights and the empowerment of women and girls globally, recounted the Trump administration's efforts in this regard.

---

[82]https://www.who.int/health-topics/female-genital-mutilation#tab=tab_1
[83]https://www.ncbi.nlm.nih.gov/pmc/articles/PMC1381943/

The United States Agency for International Development (USAID), which operated under the secretary of state's guidance and that of the National Security Council (NSC) in the White House, launched a three-year initiative in Kenya to use local engagement to eliminate this ghastly practice. This project is known as "Koota Injena: Clan Engagement as a Tool for Abandonment of CEFM [Child, Early, and Forced Marriages] and FGM/C [Female Genital Mutilation/Cutting] and Promoting the Value of the Girl." Numerous in-country accounts contend that this initiative has been a success, with Kenyan assemblies and elders of the Gabra community declaring FGM illegal in 2020.[84] On March 5, 2021, the President of Kenya oversaw the Kisima Declaration in which Samburu elders renounced CEFM and FGM/C.[85]

The empowerment sought for girls throughout the world is what we must seek in order to contest unwarranted surgeries that alter God's plan. As a society, we must celebrate masculinity and femininity in order that children become acclimated to accepting these gifts in their own lives. I am convinced that by blurring the distinctions between the sexes, we have created an atmosphere in which confusion about identities is rife.

There are many differences between the sexes that cannot be altered and will always mark someone as either male or female, no matter what is averred. Reproductive cells differ between the sexes; this is unalterable: A person with spermatozoa is male; a person with ova is female. This distinction is also observed by scientists in every one of the approximately 16,000 mammalian and avian species now living on earth. Humanity is part of this creation.

To be strong, we must be noble, but we cannot be noble if we do not act. With very rare exceptions for treatments to address specific congenital issues, we, as a nation, must hold that so-called gender affirming care involving drugs and reassignment surgeries must be made illegal until a person reaches the age of eighteen.

---

[84]https://newsroom.amref.org/fgm/2020/09/top-most-gabra-leaders-outlaw-fgm-and-early-child-marriage/

[85]https://amrefusa.org/news/samburu-elders-publicly-declare-to-no-longer-practice-fgm/

Chapter 6, Strength Through People, Precepts:

• The nature of evil is freedom misused and unbound. Its expression by autocrats scales in relation to their power.

• Misinformation involves the spreading of false information, whether it is known to be false or not. Disinformation is defined by an absolute intent to spread false information to cause societal discord. Our media is guilty of both.

• Despite the dreams of technocratic elites, humanity is not a machine or a collection of servers that may be altered in the quest for mechanistic improvement.

• America is confronted by intensely radical forces that seek to demolish the differences between the sexes, which exist not only between humans but throughout all species of mammals and birds.

• To deny the different natures of manhood and womanhood can only be accomplished by denying all that is real. To attempt to destroy God's primary creation is impossible, though the realization of this travesty is Marxism's prime objective, for by it, humankind would falsely establish itself as the arbiter of all things.

Issues and Problems:

• We should not confuse, as a society, what is normative with what is permitted; we should not confuse what is permitted with what is good or advantageous.

• When the secretary of the Department of Health and Human Services, testifying before the Senate, cannot bring himself to say the word "mother," we are in danger of no longer living in a country, but in a madhouse.

• Children are now made to think that they can change their sex or that there are no differences between the sexes.

Neither assertion is true, nor will such sentiments ever be true. A total of at least 2.1 billion dollars was spent on reassignment surgeries and associated measures within the United States in 2022; expenditures for such procedures are expected to grow at a rate in excess of eleven percent per year through 2030, to reach five billion dollars.

• If there is no distinction between biological sex and gender ascription, then internal discord between these two attributes is an illness, which should first be treated with therapy and the in-depth evaluation of possible causal factors. Elements of the medical establishment now support surgeries to alter irreparably physically healthy patients as a first course of action to relieve psychological pain. This is an inversion of the Hippocratic Oath, which is to first do no harm.

• Surgical interventions and hormonal treatments are proffered almost casually. Reports indicate that eighty percent of children diagnosed with gender dysphoria outgrow it, for it "recedes with puberty" in most cases.

Duties and Actions:

• We must demand answers to these questions: Why are surgeries on children that result in sterilization not stopped? Why does the Biden administration take no action to safeguard our nation's most vulnerable?

• Female genital mutilation (FGM) has brutalized more than 200 million victims of all ages according to the United Nations. This form of mutilation is universally decried across developed countries as being a denial of humanity, sexuality, and basic rights, yet we allow reassignment surgeries to be performed on children and adolescents in our country. This must be outlawed. Unless specified to treat specific congenital issues, so-called gender affirming care and reassignment surgeries must be made illegal until the age of eighteen.

CHAPTER 7

EDUCATION

To nullify what someone may become, so that even they do not know what God intended them to be, is impermissible. An entire generation will fall short in realizing their dreams if persistent failures in education and training are permitted to continue.

James Madison stated, "The advancement and diffusion of knowledge is the only guardian of true liberty." America is in danger because malignant forces are betraying our children's future by denying them the opportunities conferred through education. America cannot remain the world's leading economic power if we do not act.

Excellence demands that we learn what we do not know. The introduction of leftist propaganda and the protection of failing teachers means that our schools are not instructing our children. Access to quality education is fundamental and is dependent on school safety, opportunity, and parental consent and responsibility. It is no accident that statists oppose vouchers, charter schools, school choice, and home schooling. This is because choice equals freedom, and freedom demands the reduction of government in our lives.

Education

"The advancement and diffusion of knowledge is the only guardian of true liberty." This statement by James Madison must be heeded, for as historian Will Durant observed, "A great civilization is not conquered from without until it has destroyed itself from within."

America is in danger. Forces in our midst are betraying our children's future by denying them the opportunities conferred through education. President Randi Weingarten of the American Federation of Teachers and other leftists have arguably crippled our nation's schools.

An entire generation of Americans will fall short in realizing their dreams if persistent failures in education and training are permitted to continue. This potential fault is more damaging than any external threat. We must be competitive to be respected, for this attribute is necessary to secure our Republic; it will be lost if our educational system is set upon a quagmire.

Timeline

Sarah was born in 1779, just three years after the Declaration of Independence was proclaimed. She was ten when she witnessed George Washington's being sworn into office in New York City.

In the year 1859, James was born; he met Sarah when he was nine, and she told him many stories about the Founding of our Republic before she died that year. James lived to the age of ninety, and, in his last years, befriended Thomas, who was born in 1939.

Thomas is still alive today and his great granddaughter, Amber, was born in 2019. Amber will live well into the twenty-second century and may travel to the Moon or to Mars. Amber is but one person removed from James who knew Sarah, who witnessed George Washington's inauguration as president.

This particular chain of people is imagined but the reality of this possibility is not. Our country is still nascent and emergent, though we brim with unequaled accomplishments.

We have fed multitudes and have forestalled great famines through the creation of new varieties of cereal grains. We developed entirely new classes of products and industries, too numerous to mention. We defeated Nazi Germany, Imperial Japan, and the Soviet Union. We landed Americans on the moon a total of six times, with twelve astronauts' walking upon the lunar surface.

Education permitted these accomplishments, which are each singular in history. American education, however, is now at risk at every level. Though we still lead the world in the sciences, in engineering, and in mathematics, our position of dominance in these domains is threatened by internal and external forces.

Safety

To nullify what someone may become, so that even they, themselves, do not know what God intended them to be, is impermissible and is not consonant with American principles. Access to quality education is fundamental and is dependent on three correlates: safety, opportunity, and parental consent and responsibility.

Safe Schools and Role Models

Student safety must be prioritized. The murder of seventeen people at Marjory Stoneman Douglas High School, in 2018, demanded concrete action as did the atrocity at Sandy Hook Elementary School in 2012, but both attacks were met with unresponsive measures. Clarity and purpose are essential if our nation is to avoid another massacre.

Nineteen precious children and two adults were murdered by a lone shooter at Robb Elementary School in Uvalde, Texas, in 2022. Answers and not political rhetoric are required. This demands pertinent action and the application of established principles adapted from our nation's military.

Hundreds of millions of guns are owned by law-abiding citizens who venerate our Bill of Rights. Millions more, however, are held illicitly by criminals aided by a southern border that is porous, allowing arms trafficking. Therefore, a ban on rifles that resemble military weapons in appearance will not restrict the ability of those with murderous intent from obtaining lethal arms.

While focused programs to foreclose the opportunity of individuals with a history of violence or who are mentally ill and have demonstrated dangerous behaviors, should be a priority, general gun control is an ineffective means to curtail attacks at schools, which may also be carried out using a vehicle or a bomb. Our Navy protects its vessels through the adoption of a layered defense. We must protect our schools and our children this way.

The first layer is the formation of a defensive zone to obtain advantage; the second layer is intelligence gathering; the third, interception; and the fourth, point defense. Many of these layers are in place in our nation's schools but are not integrated. America must erect a cohesive system of defense in all schools, for each layer reinforces and depends upon the others.

To form a defensive zone, the threat must be specified. Students with mental health issues or histories of violence or abuse must be assessed and, if appropriate, reported to cognizant local and national authorities; enhanced data management and notification must be prioritized.

Students at risk often lack adult models of virtuous behavior; this is compounded by a popular culture that erodes once-sacrosanct moral precepts, instilling nihilism and despair. Social media further exacerbates isolation by limiting human interaction. To impart values that will shape students, enriched standards of behavior must be demonstrated.

Our veterans, including those with disabilities, should be employed to serve as school mentors, character coaches, and after-school instructors. These men and women can instill leadership, compassion, courage, and the importance of health and fitness.

Veterans, serving in our schools, could spot troubling behaviors, to alert school officials to potential threats. This would be responsive to the 2002 Secret Service and Department of Education report, *Threat Assessment in Schools: A Guide to Managing Threatening Situations and to Creating Safe School Climates*,[86] for had the report's measures been followed, targeted gun or other violence in schools could have been reduced.

This report considered how the Secret Service operates through anticipating and evaluating potential threats. Veterans could become essential bridges between school officials who, under the report's guidelines, are charged to conduct threat assessment inquiries, and law enforcement, which is obligated to conduct threat assessment investigations.

These two types of assessments, using different institutional skills and vantage points, must form a continuum. Trained veterans would fortify this endeavor, while providing a special perspective concerning the anticipation of violence, which is obtained through military training. Such a national program would be affordable and could employ 200,000 veterans, whose salaries could be covered by a mix of federal, state, and local funds.

Interception concerns the maintenance of a defense perimeter to bar a threat from its objective. Effective physical barriers might have stopped the national tragedies that have occurred in our schools.

In accord with other concerns such as fire safety, if entry or exit from a school can be controlled through a series of physical measures, the security of the institution is enhanced. Such hardening must be the product of a fusion of ideas from architects, students, teachers, school administrators, law enforcement officers, firemen, and veterans, for the physical plant of each school is unique.

---

[86]https://www2.ed.gov/admins/lead/safety/threatassessmentguide.pdf

Point defense is the final boundary against targeted school violence. It is, by definition, a last-ditch effort. In this, we need not reinvent the wheel: Schools may be protected by the same means used to secure airports, courthouses, or government offices.

In these venues, select personnel are armed. Law enforcement officers in schools should carry guns. State and local school systems should consider whether contract security personnel, veterans, or teachers should also be armed.

The introduction of armed veterans, supplemented by a hidden-carry program for teachers or the addition of more armed guards or officers, attached to schools, should be considered as a key component of any time-urgent point defense, for experience shows that school assaults may end before any outside police force can arrive on school premises, much less make entry to apply force. In every case, it is imperative that all those armed in schools be subject to routine psychological screens designed and implemented by professionals.

Too many so-called gun-control measures represent either an uninformed or a political diversion that cannot staunch targeted violence aimed at our schools. No system of protection is perfect, but the erecting of multiple layers of defense provides the surest means to enhance the safety of America's students, teachers, and administrative personnel.

Global Competition

Failing schools must not mean that our children are destined to underperform or wane. If institutions betray student and parental trust, we must build new avenues for true learning to flourish. The fight we must wage for the soul of America can only be sustained if our nation's system of education is reformed.

We must initiate new modes of teaching and not wallow in failure. Educational success does not accrue from compounding mistakes: It results from excising constraints, and what is polluted, so that new growth can occur.

We have poured enormous sums of money into kindergarten through high school (K-12) education with scant results. Money alone is not the answer. Money can be spent wisely, or it can be mis-spent or be squandered.

The Organization for Economic Co-operation and Development (OECD) is a multilateral association, which succeeded a prior entity established to help oversee the Marshall Plan, which rebuilt Europe after World War II. Its convention went into force in 1961, to support worldwide economic development and trade. Thirty-eight member countries, having transparent, market-based economies, compare important societal and economic data.

Education at various levels is compared by the OECD across member countries, which comprise three-fifths of world gross domestic product (GDP); the organization does not, however, include China, India, or Russia.[87] Data from the nations that comprise the OECD are often combined with that of non-member countries to form educational achievement assessments across nations.

American educational results if compared with nations who spend a fraction of our per-pupil costs, demonstrate that we have fallen.[88] Of the thirty-eight countries evaluated by the OECD, America spends far more than the OECD average and exceeds the per pupil expenditures for K-12 and tertiary or post-secondary education (involving colleges, universities, or trade schools) of other countries, save Luxembourg, Iceland, Norway, and Austria.

If only K-12 costs are considered, America spends 3,800 dollars more per pupil than the OECD average.[89] This represents expenditures that are approximately thirty-seven percent more than the OECD mean. Indeed, certain states, such as New York, and cities, such as Baltimore, whose test scores are disastrous, have K-12 per-pupil expenditures that are extraordinarily high in comparison to those of other nations, states, or cosmopolitan areas.

---

[87]https://www.oecd.org/about/document/ratification-oecd-convention.htm
[88]https://data.oecd.org/eduresource/education-spending.htm#indicator-chart
[89]https://www.realclearpolicy.com/articles/2021/12/10/five_facts_on_k-12_education_in_the_us_807264.html#!#:~:text=The%20U.S.%20spends%20about%20%2414%2C100%20per%20K-12%20student,and%20the%20UK%2C%20in%20addition%20to%20other%20nations.

Students in the People's Republic of China outscore American students in all the educational categories considered, though their per-pupil expenditures are modest. Categories measured include reading comprehension, mathematics, and science scores.

American students, by comparison, are particularly deficient in mathematics and in science, which are the two subjects most highly correlated with professional success in our technological age. Of the seventy-nine countries assessed by the Program for International Student Assessment (PISA), a global study conducted by the OECD, American students ranked 36th in mathematics, 17th in science, and 12th in reading, behind China, Estonia, Poland, the Republic of Korea, and other nations.[90] (Macao, which practices its own distinct method of education, reflecting Portuguese influences, is taken as part of China, but Hong Kong is counted separately in this enumeration [Hong Kong's educational system reflects British methods due to its status as a former colony].)

America cannot remain the world's leading economic force if we do not immediately recognize these signs. If the United States should fail because of the deficits induced by those who endeavor to change the nature of our country, the world will enter a phase dominated by tyrants. Our alliances will be jeopardized, for self-interests will propel nations to partner with others not in decline. This is why the leftist educational establishment, as epitomized by the president of the American Federation of Teachers, is so dangerous. The malfeasance exhibited directly empowers the leaders of China, Russia, and Iran, who look to our schools to chart our deterioration.

Public schools must be forced to compete for students with charter, private, and religious schools, in addition to homeschooling. Competition will improve student performance and, if necessary, break apart and reconstitute public schools that are deficient, if individual schools continue to underachieve. We must insist that symbols of mediocrity be overcome and never papered over. A school is

---

[90] https://www.oecd.org/pisa/PISA%202018%20Insights%20and%20Interpretations%20FINAL%20PDF.pdf

not a building but a place of learning. If it fails in its mission, it is no longer a school but a pile of bricks and iron.

If public schools are to exist and to fulfill their original mission, they must educate our youth, so that they can compete with any students on earth. This is simply not the case today for the overwhelming majority of our public-school pupils.

We are in the midst of a national crisis in education, which has been exacerbated by unjustified and inordinate school closings imposed during COVID, which have reduced student test scores. Student performance has declined precipitously, for our children were deprived of crucial in-person support, the company of their classmates, and, in many cases, adequate connectivity to remote lessons.

The National Assessment of Educational Progress (NAEP) released the *Nation's Report Card* for 2022, which the organization, as mandated by Congress, conducts in various disciplines. Under the title, "Largest score declines in NAEP mathematics at grades 4 and 8 since initial assessments in 1990," the summary of the report states:

> In 2022, the average fourth-grade mathematics score decreased by 5 points and was lower than all previous assessment years going back to 2005; the average score was one point higher compared to 2003. The average eighth-grade mathematics score decreased by 8 points compared to 2019 and was lower than all previous assessment years going back to 2003. In 2022, fourth- and eighth-grade mathematics scores declined for most states/jurisdictions as well as for most participating urban districts compared to 2019.[91]

Interminable lockdowns and curricula focused on leftist grievances led to the most significant declines in test marks since records have been kept, wiping away decades of student progress. The devastating response to the pandemic showed the true nature of many putative leaders in America's educational establishment; their actions placed the needs of our children last.

---

[91]https://www.nationsreportcard.gov/highlights/mathematics/2022/

Student Debt and Engagement

On March 30, 2010, President Obama assumed federal responsibility for educational loans; thereafter, the student became not a mind to be taught, but the means of transfer of federally guaranteed monies to universities and colleges. There is no incentive, whatsoever, for schools to contain costs. Predictably, costs pursuant to the attainment of degrees are spiraling out of control.

It has estimated that federal student loan debt has increased from 187 billion dollars, in 1995,[92] to more than 1.6 trillion dollars in a recent survey.[93] Private student loans supplement federal student loans but account for less than 7.6 percent of total student debt. The function of originating student loans must be returned to the private sector.

President Biden on August 24, 2022, announced college loan forgiveness for those who make less than 125,000 dollars per year.[94] This action was both illegal and unethical, for it would pass debts, incurred in the attainment of advanced degrees, to the majority of Americans who have not attended college and do not benefit from the increased earning potential that a college education normally confers.[95]

Our nation's highest court on June 30, 2023, repudiated President Biden's plan to impose debt forgiveness, which would have been paid for by America's farmers, machinists, police officers, and all who must scrub their hands at night because of the jobs they perform during the day. President Biden's plan was theft. Thankfully, the Supreme Court, in its decision, struck down this obvious attempt to buy votes, which most probably altered the results of the 2022 midterm elections.[96]

---

[92] https://www.cbo.gov/publication/56754

[93] https://www.forbes.com/advisor/student-loans/average-student-loan-statistics/

[94] https://abcnews.go.com/Politics/president-biden-announces-student-loan-forgiveness/story?id=88736949

[95] https://www.epi.org/publication/almost-two-thirds-of-people-in-the-labor-force-do-not-have-a-college-degree/

[96] https://www.npr.org/2023/06/30/1182216970/supreme-court-student-loan-forgiveness-decision-biden

The massive industry that is higher education should be forced to cut their ballooning administrative staffs and salaries. As a condition for any future federal aid, these institutions must be required to paydown a percentage of loans for those former students who are in actual need of help.

Such institutions may count their endowments in billions of dollars. These places of learning have overcharged their students: They must use their secreted wealth to undo some of the damage they have caused.

Knowledge

We must recognize that school choice and not socialist proselytization is necessary to reform our schools. To promote this restoration, we must act.

America's public school system is composed of boards within districts. School boards set policies that affect all aspects of education; they govern public education through the establishment of budgets, course structures, class sizes, the training of teachers, collective bargaining, the appraisal or the engagement of district superintendents, and other crucial matters.

In recent years, radicals have sought and attained positions on our nation's school boards. These malicious actors often do not have children of their own enrolled within a given school system during their elected term. The officials' purpose is to implement the transference of Marxist or other radical precepts to children. This is often done under the pretense of care or inclusion; such masquerades are accomplished most readily when parents acquiesce due to group pressures, inattention, or the acceptance of disingenuous platitudes offered by school board members, administrators, or teachers.

Election to school boards and their attendance must become central emphases for conservatives. Only direct parental involvement in a child's education is more important. If these three objectives are accomplished, our schools will quickly improve; if these goals are not attained, the educational fabric of America will continue to erode, perhaps irretrievably.

One immediate step that should be considered to block patently political actors is to require that candidates for school boards have a child or a grandchild enrolled in the school system at the time of their election. School boards should be run by parents and by the guardians of our children; such candidates should be American citizens. We cannot allow radicals, who may be controlled in an orchestrated manner across states, to destroy the education of our children.

Before college, subject mastery must be paramount. The substitution of criticism for knowledge is the essence of the progressive agenda that seeks to alter our nation, which now encompasses the misrepresentation of the feminine and masculine traits that are intrinsic to existence and maturation.

Criticism cannot precede knowledge; criticism must follow the attainment of knowledge and the practice of discernment. This natural order is disrupted and reversed in our schools, so that students are required to criticize what they do not yet understand.

Why has this deeply flawed approach to the attainment of knowledge propagated? Causes that are manifold have led to this fault. Teachers' unions, teachers, and administrators are all party to this pernicious errancy.

When the members of teachers' unions attain tenure that can almost never be taken away, teachers may cease being teachers and become an advantaged class, answerable to no one, including parents. The alternative is simple: We should insist that school districts reward great teachers and fire incompetents, but this, unions and politicians will not allow, for the imposition of mediocrity defends their purview. This is why we must insist on change: Students must come first, not the defense of inept teachers within a broken system.

The introduction of leftist propaganda and the protection of failing teachers means that our schools are not teaching our children. Our colleges and universities have merged with powerful unions and our government to become an Educational Industrial Complex. It is this edifice to waste, to political indoctrination, and to underachievement that we must dismantle in order to rebuild our educational system.

America suffers from having too many educational administra-tors and bureaucrats and too few qualified teachers. This situation has ossified due to the primacy of unions coupled with the suppres-sion of parental rights. Under the Biden administration, well-mean-ing parents have been subject to state surveillance and arrest for merely speaking their minds at school board meetings. This is intolerable.

Vouchers, to empower parents and to grant them true choices as to the education of their children, are the way forward. The massive structure that is the Department of Education must be torn down and replaced with a small federal office that numbers its staff in the hundreds and not in the thousands. Freed from this bureaucratic over-mind, America's parents will be enabled to chart marvelous courses for their children's education and fulfillment.

Mediocrity is never comfortable with what it does not under-stand. Excellence demands that we learn what we do not know: This is the standard that we must entrench for our children; barriers to this goal must be removed with great expedience.

With freedom of choice will come excellence and advancement. This is the lesson of American history.

As we remake the classroom through the widespread use of vouchers, we must also empower home schooling by providing the means for parents to form their own associations and receive allot-ments. We must apply lessons learned due to in-home instruction during the period of COVID-19.

Students learn in different ways. Technology now exists to map each student's optimum mode of learning, creating individualized means to enable each pupil to master required subjects. Ideally, a student's best method for study should be determined and embraced. Libraries of online courses, taught by master teachers, should be employed to supplement in-person teaching.

The Necessity of Choice

It is no accident that statists universally oppose vouchers, charter schools, and school choice. This is because choice equals freedom, and freedom demands the reduction of government in our lives. This is something the left cannot abide.

Action is necessary. We must embrace an expansive definition of school choice. Aside from a core curriculum of English, logic, mathematics, history, civics, and science, parents must be able to choose their child's coursework. This is a parent's God-given right, and the state has no right to oppose it. Students must not be exposed to material that is not age-appropriate, but progressive educators throughout our country are confusing students in order to ply collectivist goals, which require the destruction of societal cohesion.

Rules and customs derive from the experiences of many generations. They must not be vitiated in order that children be taught to embrace new totems that are alien to the American experience.

Parental rejection of current, public-school curricula is one of the reasons why homeschooling is exploding in popularity. This increase is also due to the exodus of many talented teachers from their profession because of disruptive student behavior, which is omnipresent in our public schools. Bringing discipline back into the classroom must be central to educational reform.

Discipline in schools is practiced by our most important economic competitors, including China and India. Focus and discipline are essential to learning; I could not have achieved my life's wishes if these two traits had not been already embedded within me as a consequence of my prior education in public schools. Subject mastery, particularly in the STEM fields of science, technology, engineering, and math, is the doorway to the future, but each of these subjects requires intense concentration, which is impossible in overly permissive environments.

To buttress our efforts in preparing students for the STEM fields, the concept of inclusion must be reimagined. We must make it mean that children can attain entry into a field or occupation of their dreams.

Students will not fulfill their ambitions through diversity training based on the color of their skin or their religion. They will realize their dreams, in our world's interconnected economy, by being able to compete successfully with young people in every other nation.

Students must be held accountable for their behavior in class. Cellular phones have no place in the classroom once teaching begins. The ability to work at grade level, self-control, concentration, and deportment are fundamental to learning, but are too often not prized or demanded.

Learning cannot occur in the absence of discipline within the classroom. Maturity in personal conduct begins with the acknowledgment that disruptive or grade-inappropriate behavior is unacceptable within schools, for it is irreconcilable with the rights of others and the attainment of knowledge. Concentration is a skill that is necessary in order that complex materials may be studied and learned; this facility is impossible if there is not decorum in the classroom. Respect, manners, and teamwork must be demanded if they are to be acquired.

Maturity is demonstrated when students begin a project or a course of study and are compelled to complete it. To pass failing students is to denigrate their attainment of their potential. Such actions, which have become endemic, help no one, for they consign students, who frequently come from disadvantaged backgrounds, to destinies bound by unfulfilled dreams.

The failure to maintain discipline in the classroom is dangerous. It is a major cause for educators to leave the profession, for personal safety has become a concern for many teachers and their families. We must insist on schools that are safe and welcoming for all students and faculty members.

A rectified establishment must not resemble the educational caste system that is in place in China. Unlike China, failure on a test must not mean that a student's academic career is derailed. Students must be given multiple opportunities to make up work and to correct mistakes.

Many students who fail, correct their path, and continue with their education. This is why General Educational Development (GED) courses or High School Equivalency Tests (HiSET) or programs are essential. They provide a pathway for students to attain their goals through study.

Independence

Trades offer young Americans the chance to be independent soon after graduating high school. There is great dignity in self-sufficiency, in being able to buy a home, and in being financially secure enough to support a family.

Our country must secure this avenue of prosperity upon which many of our nation's children will depend. Machinists, mechanical technicians, welders, and automotive specialists are vital as are professionals in many other trades. America's high schools must develop vocational educational tracks, beginning in the ninth grade, which will lead to apprenticeships after graduation.

There must be specialty coursework available to train aspiring students in diverse fields—from chefs to bakers, to artists or computer support technicians. College is not right for everyone, for many the advent of state-of-the-art vocational education will be the answer to dreams of a fulfilling livelihood and future.

Working with industry, we must also create junior-college programs to build a cadre of manufacturing engineers to permit American factory production to expand. To support high-paying jobs for working Americans, our government must link U.S. company participation in federal contracts to corporate support for such initiatives. This educational goal, if attained, will facilitate increasing numbers of competitive factories to be built in our country, permitting us to regain control over our supply lines, thus restricting Chinese economic suasion.

In his biography of Steve Jobs, Walter Isaacson related that President Obama was informed by Jobs, in 2011, that Apple factories could have been built in America rather than in China, potentially employing hundreds of thousands of Americans, if our nation had available engineers.[97] Jobs stated that he needed manufacturing

---

[97] Walter Isaacson, "Steve Jobs," (Simon & Schuster, 2011), 546–547.

supervisors with basic engineering skills. Such production engineers could have been educated rapidly in community colleges and in trade schools if the required initiative had been established. Nothing was done, but this is a capacity that we can build.

We must use our universities as magnets to attract the best minds from around the world to create new industries and businesses in America. This resource, however, is in danger of becoming a liability. Foreign students in the sciences, in mathematics, and in engineering are now choosing to return to their home countries in increasing frequency, instead of creating new lives for their families in America.

It is imperative that the vast majority of foreign students be retained here, where they achieved their mastery of subjects so vital to our nation's growth. If we accept foreign students into our country to study STEM subjects, we must induce the overwhelming majority of these students to stay in the United States, so that their education may be put to work in America.

If large numbers of students return to their home countries, our universities will have succeeded in not strengthening America, but our economic competitors. Vetting by means of artificial intelligence, special visas, expedited citizenship, and enhanced immigration opportunities for the immediate families of foreign students, could be used to channel the best minds in the world to make America their home, enriching our country and creating new jobs for all Americans.

Pathways

Minority students may be at a disadvantage in their attainment of subject mastery due to substandard schools and harsh urban environments. Minority students have the same aptitude as other Americans to be successful in STEM coursework at the collegiate level, but what is frequently absent is adequate preparation.

Many gifted students do not succeed because they lack the necessary foundations that should have been acquired before their ascension to college. This is especially true in mathematics, for knowledge in this essential discipline is cumulative and rests upon a ladder of attained understanding that increases in difficulty in each grade. Therefore, we must recalibrate our junior colleges so that minority and disadvantaged students may fill educational gaps in order that they may become successful baccalaureate candidates in demanding disciplines.

For many students, a remedial preparatory program, taken at a junior college, could be a means to secure a successful transition to a college or a university. As part of this initiative, swift adaptation of educational programs and practices pioneered within the United States military would be of great assistance.

Conceptual Failures, Indoctrination, and Subversion

Perhaps no single individual has placed a greater stamp on America's system of education as it exists today than Dr. John Dewey. A philosopher of significant intellectual scope, Dr. Dewey is most remembered for his books, essays, and speeches that shaped avenues for reform in education, beginning in the first decades of the last century.

Dewey's conception of the classroom departed from previous models. The transference of accumulated knowledge and skills to students was to be replaced as the main objective in primary and secondary education by psychological mechanisms to form the pupil as a person. The teacher was therefore obligated to preference what a student thought over what a student knew; the acquisition of knowledge was thus waylaid.

Although Dewey's writings are complex and subject to interpretation,[98] what is clear is that they released a whirlwind that has severely compromised learning and the transmission of knowledge, for Dewey argued that the traditional goals of education were not as important as schools' shaping students to be moral, so that they may take part in a democratic society.

---

[98] https://www.iwp.edu/articles/2018/02/01/the-tragedy-of-american-education-the-role-of-john-dewey/

At first, such goals seem laudable and not necessarily at odds with learning or the imbibing of knowledge; this, however, is not the case. A chief reason for this deleterious course is the untethering of transmitted morality within the fabric of our public schools from religious precepts, shared by all the world's major religions. Dewey saw no true place for the collected religious wisdom of the ages inside the classroom. Morality was thus cast adrift; this situation has been used by radical forces to transform our schools and thus transform America.

The imposition of Critical Race Theory, The 1619 Project, and fallacious gender studies curricula are posited as moral imperatives, though they are not. Indeed, they represent the antithesis of moral action. In his 1919 work, *Moral Principles in Education*, Dewey stated:

> Moreover, the society of which the child is to be a member is, in the United States, a democratic and progressive society.
>
> . . . .
>
> There cannot be two sets of ethical principles, one for life in the school, and the other for life outside of the school. As conduct is one, so also the principles of conduct are one. The tendency to discuss the morals of the school as if the school were an institution by itself is highly unfortunate. The moral responsibility of the school, and of those who conduct it, is to society. The school is fundamentally an institution erected by society to do a certain specific work,—to exercise a certain specific function in maintaining the life and advancing the welfare of society. The educational system which does not recognize that this fact entails upon it an ethical responsibility is derelict and a defaulter.[99]

These sentences, as seen through the contorted prism of the leftist activists and Marxists among us, as well as the enticed, are a recipe for the imposition of socialism and radical, progressive ideas. The adoption of Dewey's approach has permitted the influx of preposterous precepts, heretofore unknown, that out-Herod even the most committed communists in their assiduous levying of wholly new ideologies centered about deeply distorted views of race and sex.

---

[99]https://www.gutenberg.org/files/25172/25172-h/25172-h.htm

These machinations by leftist are given cover by Dewey's concentration on democracy. Though an objective of our political system, democracy unbound may degenerate into mob rule, which would constitute a direct assault against our Republic.

Democracy, if not counterbalanced by the understanding of unalienable rights and the nature of our representative government, which was designed to limit transient sentiments that may be injurious to society, can thus be repurposed by radical forces to use the levers of our mode of government and our open school system to destroy our country, as does a serpent that eats its own tail. Our schools cannot be strong if Dewey's fallacious and deformative ideas are left to stand. They must be removed from our educational institutions, root and branch. Parents have no option but to take point in this necessary quest.

Today, leftist politicians do not stand for America, while many Republican politicians do not stand for themselves, but cower, for fear of being smeared with invectives that reverberate through social media. Unfounded charges of racism or of racial animus are an acid that is destroying our Republic.

We must not bow to a mob that employs epithets to accrete power at the expense of veracity. We must say what must be said to protect our nation's children.

America is the greatest force for good the world has ever known, but the Democratic Party and its leadership have salted racial discord in our nation's educational establishment. The Democratic Party has a long and deeply troubling history of using racial division and discord to attain and hold power. Conservatives belong to the party of Abraham Lincoln, not to the party of the Confederacy.

Obstacles

Patently adult materials have proliferated within America's public schools under guises of inclusion or the exploration of the concept of gender. Such poisonous outrages are both defended and denied by school officials and leaders of a benighted educational establishment that would rather see well-meaning parents arrested, than curb the abuse that has been allowed to propagate in our schools.

What leftist activists and their sycophants cannot dismiss is the proof parents have read to schoolboards across the country. We must remove grossly inappropriate materials from our schools. This campaign must begin on the first day of a Republican presidency.

In our technological age in which the synthetic cyberworld threatens to overtake that which is real, leadership is required to ensure that America always exalts the individual and never the collective. All group prejudice is destroyed if every person is understood to be a unique and irreplaceable creation of God. This was Martin Luther King's vision.

Rather than understand that prejudice can never be fought with more prejudice, the left has created new totems to instill racialism and hate. The left understands that it must denigrate America before it can subdue our country.

Critical Race Theory (CRT) is Marxist in its presuppositions. It is neither critical nor a theory, but rather a reconceptualization of communism, which stems from the work of the communist theorist Antonio Gramsci, who considered freedom, servitude. When Gramsci wrote his *Prison Notebooks*, from 1929 through 1935, while imprisoned in Fascist Italy, he conceived of a new emphasis for socialism that differed from the economic class struggle central to Marxism.

Gramsci proposed that cultural hegemony was at the core of the oppression that ensnared the working class. Cultural values, according to Gramsci's critique, as established by an oppressive, acquisitive stratum, are designed to suffuse throughout the populace, ensuring compliance to norms that derive from organized religion and its precepts that venerate the family and individual responsibility.

Therefore, to unseat traditional conservatives or liberals from power, religion must bear the brunt of a broadly based ideological attack, to eviscerate preexisting values, which were once viewed as sacrosanct. This assault is structured to pave the way for the new world to come, which is framed to extol equity and sameness.

The success of Gramsci's stratagem is palpable. America's elites are predominantly no longer those who venerate religious or traditional societal values. Beneath our liminal view, a new elite has arisen that eschews religion, its teachings, and the train of moral reasoning that has existed for millennia.

First, this new, manufactured morality is imposed on students of all ages. Second, the substitution of Gramsci's vision for that of America's Founders is propounded within our schools.

This communist framework has devastated every nation that has embraced this totalism. Do the beguiled not see that these vortices, created by the left, are but veiled attempts to cleave the American people, in order to turn racial discord into power for a self-anointed political class?

A theory is an explanation for phenomena that is widely accepted by a reputable scholarly community. Critical Race Theory is not what its name implies, for it was put forward as a political instrument, defined by its propagandistic intent.

Critical thinking requires the unbiased explication of complex issues based on evidence. The 1619 Project, which substantiates Critical Race Theory, is a screed, condemned by scholars for its gross inaccuracies. The 1619 Project is centered on the unsupported premise that the Founding of America had as its primary intention the defense of slavery.[100] In fact, America's Founding sought to dislodge the British substantiation of slavery, which was then a tool of Britain's empire and was entrenched in the South during the period of colonization.

Attention must be drawn to these misrepresentations if they are to be halted and reversed. Unfortunately, Environmental, Social, and Governance (ESG) and Diversity, Equity, and Inclusion (DEI) training regimes and constructs too often constitute façades to instill Marxist thought within the piths of institutions that had been at the forefront of societal advancement and the creation of prosperity for

[100] https://www.nas.org/blogs/article/pulitzer-board-must-revoke-nikole-hannah-jones-prize#_ftn3

all Americans. The destruction of our nation's businesses, government, and institutions must be stopped.

Diversity means nothing if diversity in thought is absent. Inclusion is laudable but must never be achieved at the expense of the exclusion of others. Equity is not synonymous with equality.

Equality in opportunity must be inviolable. This, however, is not equity. Equity is instituted for factions to impose equivalence in outcomes, which may be unearned. Equality is applied to individuals to ensure fairness in the potential for each person to succeed in accord with their own abilities.

True diversity recognizes the myriad of differences between people and celebrates them. Equity does not support diversity but instills a suffocating homogeneity that is incompatible with individual merit and achievement. If American schools seek equity, they will ensure that both China and India will eclipse the United States and become the world's leading economic and technological powers.

Forced equity in outcomes can only be attained through tyranny, for persons are dissimilar in talents and in capacities. Thus, equity, as pursued by the left in order to attain and to ossify institutional power, is incompatible with diversity as a point of logic, for absolute sameness and difference are not reconcilable within a given system.

Critical Race Theory is a political enterprise, intended to reapportion power through expropriation; it is not a window with which to view our world. Being woke today demands adherence to Marxist lies about the nature of humanity, which masquerade as revealed truths, as well as a gnawing myopia that requires that everything be seen through the lens of race.

Wokeness and its handmaidens, Critical Race Theory and The 1619 Project, are presented as idols to which we must bow down. Never. We cannot allow the left to transform America's classrooms into segregated infernos built upon implanted hatreds constructed by unaccountable elites and those they bribe or hector.

We have made too much progress as a nation to return to a time when people were judged by the color of their skin and not "by the content of their character." The 1619 Project, woke ideology, and

Critical Race Theory deface Martin Luther King's monumental contributions to America, by placing racial identity, and not individual character, as the determining factor of existence.

Being not only antithetical to morality, these doctrines, as enforced by social media, render people as living obituaries of themselves, thwarting individual progress and the ability to start over. This is deeply objectionable.

There is no place, in any primary or secondary school, in any college or university, for students to be taught that race, color, religion, or economic status determine who they are and what they will achieve. Any curriculum that categorizes schoolchildren by the color of their skin or on the basis of their ancestry or religion is an atrocity that does not belong in the classroom.

It is because we do not deny our past and our nation's grievous errors that we must be steadfast on this principle: We will never allow our country to segregate again or to deny freedom to any citizen. As God gives us strength, we must move heaven and earth to ensure that no child is ever categorized by any attribute determined at birth or outside their control.

Too many brave men and women have died in service to our country, fighting against tyrannies in other lands, to let these progressive abominations, which go by a raft of misleading names, to find a home in America's classrooms. What we do not accept in foreign nations, we must never abide within our own country.

Using race to divide a nation and blaming people for the crimes of their ancestors, or persons they might resemble, are tools of totalistic or autocratic states. Such provocations have no place in America.

Course

On the collegiate level, our institutions of learning are shattered intellectually as they are splintered by race. These malevolent conditions are inflamed by the Chinese Communist Party (CCP), which focused on exporting its means of scholastic domination and recruitment through the creation of Confucius Institutes on or near American campuses.

Secretary of State Pompeo designated these institutes to be foreign missions, thereby curbing their march, greatly reducing their number, and ensuring their ultimate demise. We must continue to be watchful at home: Our universities cost many tens of thousands of dollars per year, but too often demand severe regimentation and indoctrination.

China, in fact, is reconstituting its mechanisms to obtain access and control within America's colleges and universities, for it sees the Biden administration as weak. Indeed, the present administration has proven itself unwilling or unable to protect freedom of speech on America's campuses or to empower students who are Chinese nationals to break free of the control exercised by their country's intelligence agencies.[101]

This obsequious course is oppositional to the policies that must be instituted.[102] Describing the Chinese Communist Party's threat to America's institutions of higher learning in his December 9, 2020, speech at the Georgia Institute of Technology, Secretary Pompeo expressed the urgency of this crisis.[103]

Addressing the university's president, Ángel Cabrera, its faculty, and its students, Secretary Pompeo stated, "[W]e see too often on American campuses that there is silence and censorship. It's being driven by the Chinese Communist Party."

"[M]any of our colleges are bought by Beijing," the secretary warned, as he implored that our government must "talk with the American people" about this threat. This conversation, however, is not presently taking place.

---

[101]https://www.propublica.org/article/even-on-us-campuses-china-cracks-down-on-students-who-speak-out

[102]https://www.globalatlanta.com/pompeo-warns-of-chinese-influence-on-u-s-campuses-in-georgia-tech-speech/

[103]https://2017-2021.state.gov/the-chinese-communist-party-on-the-american-campus/index.html

According to a recent Center for Security and Emerging Technology (CSET) report, there are more than 46,000 students from China studying the sciences, engineering, or mathematics in America as undergraduates. An additional 76,000 students from China pursue these subjects in our country at the graduate level.[104] The number of American students in China, comparably situated, is an infinitesimal fraction of these numbers.

Many of these students from Communist China are the sons and daughters of party members or of military officers. Our universities are not only educating our most ruthless economic competitor; they are also aiding China in its building of weapon systems that may one day outclass our own.

We must not facilitate our nation's self-immolation. The Biden administration's self-deception and acquiescence must stop, for it is more than myopia; it is more than turning away from a hard problem: It is abject stupidity in the face of a destructive force that is corrupting our country by buying the institutions we hold most dear. Bilateral programs in education with China must support the economic and security objectives of our country, or these programs must cease.

Under no circumstances should our institutions of higher learning enable China's military. Seasoned national security officials and professionals such as Roger W. Robinson, Jr., the former chairman of the Congressional United States-China Economic and Security Review Commission and the chairman of the Prague Security Studies Institute, who served with me on Ronald Reagan's National Security Council staff, worked tirelessly to stop this intrusion. In the wake of COVID-19 and more than one million dead in our country alone, the path Roger and other patriots helped chart must become a national imperative, but this has been thwarted by

---

[104]https://cset.georgetown.edu/wp-content/uploads/CSET-Estimating-Chinese-STEM-Students.pdf#:~:text=Across%20those%20STEM%20fields%2C%20there%20are%20around%2046%2C000,to%20more%20than%20half%20at%20the%20graduate%20level.

progressive objectives, which seek to understate the threat posed by China.

The left has for decades insisted on taking God out of the classroom but festoons the walls of our schools with images of Lenin, Mao, and Che, though each was a mass murderer. Lenin ordered the execution of Czar Nicholas II, his wife, and their young children. Mao's Great Leap Forward killed tens of millions of his own citizens, and Che, with his own hands, murdered opponents as he helped design a system of concentration camps in Cuba, where priests, dissidents, gay people, and other blameless persons met unspeakable fates.

This assemblage of some of history's greatest criminals deserves everlasting condemnation, but, instead, they are heralded by professors, academics, and teachers as well as the hypnotized students they influence. We must eliminate this demonic veneration from our classrooms.

Communist imagery must be banned in public schools, for these pictures are no more acceptable than are portraits of fascist leaders. As for colleges and universities, as a predicate for the transfer of federal funds, school presidents should be required to sign a pledge to promote American values, respecting all faiths, our Founding, the family, the right of free speech, and a commitment to scientific openness.

If universities become breeding grounds for neo-Marxists, they should be excluded from receiving any federal funding. We must proffer nothing to educational institutions that use their freedoms to undermine our nation. Neither can we continue to support colleges and universities whose administrative staffs far outnumber their full-time faculty members. These places of higher learning must cut their administrative staffs to levels below that of their full-time faculties or they must be defunded, in whole or in part, by the federal government. Bloated administrative staffs are not only wasteful but they all too often serve as instigators in the entrenchment of neo-Marxists precepts.[105]

---

[105]https://www.wsj.com/articles/the-stanford-guide-to-acceptable-words-elimination-of-harmful-language-initiative-11671489552?mod=opinion_lead_pos2

Steps

In its June 29, 2023, decision to end racial preferences in college and university admissions, the Supreme Court of the United States upheld our Constitution and its Fourteenth Amendment that requires equal protection under the law, as well as Title VI of the Civil Rights Act of 1964, which prohibits racial discrimination in all activities that receive federal financial assistance.[106] In so doing, the court took an important step toward national unity built upon our country's being a meritocracy.[107] This action must not be allowed to be undercut by educational administrators who may employ proxies that may in practice be strongly indicative of an applicant's race, to permit admissions to be once again based on a factor that is corrosive to fairness and societal progress. Constant vigilance must be maintained if this pivotal legal decision is to have teeth.

Any college or university that grants preferential admission or grades on the basis of sex, religion, creed, race, or ethnicity should be sanctioned immediately and, in due course, stripped financially of all federal grants, loans, and tuition assistance. Institutions of higher learning that confer admission based upon traits not intrinsic to student performance deny excellence, its quest, and its attainment.

Who is most hurt? If a less apt student receives preference over another applicant who has demonstrated greater acuity, society is ultimately wounded, with the truly disadvantaged among us being most harmed.

This result may seem counterintuitive. In fact, if we hamper excellence, we upset the life courses of gifted individuals, who, through their industry, may better the lives for everyone through the creation of that which did not exist, and which might not have even been imagined.

Our best students must have avenues to attain their potential, not be held back due to quotas or social engineering. Imagine the

---

[106]https://www.hud.gov/program_offices/fair_housing_equal_opp/title_vi_civil_rights

[107]https://www.supremecourt.gov/opinions/22pdf/20-1199_hgdj.pdf

course of our nation and of science if the great physicist Richard Feynman had been denied entry to an elite university: It is conceivable that deprived of truly challenging educational opportunities, Dr. Feynman might not have worked on the Manhattan Project or become a Nobel Laureate—whose work laid foundations for new industries and modes of mathematical and scientific inquiry.[108]

Dr. Feynman attended the Massachusetts Institute of Technology as an undergraduate and studied for his doctorate at Princeton University. His academic career and his profound contributions to the world might have been derailed, however, due to prejudice and quotas.

Richard Feynman sought first to be admitted to Colombia University, but that institution, which is a member of the Ivy League, rejected Feynman's undergraduate application because he was Jewish. In 1935, when Feynman completed high school, quotas still existed for many elite colleges and universities. Unbelievably, such quotas still exist today, though institutions attempt their obscuration and camouflage.

Asian students are the frequent targets of this unconscionable discrimination. This practice must be stopped immediately; further, the Supreme Court's ruling on this matter must not be subverted by machinations that may be difficult to dissect. All institutions of higher learning must be placed on notice: Quotas, hidden or not, will never be tolerated.

America must sanction colleges and universities that accept funds from adversarial states, such as China, Russia, or Iran. Under penalty of making false statements to federal officials (18 U.S.C. § 1001),[109] school presidents should be required to provide accurate lists of all foreign donors. A school's leadership must also be obligated to certify that its institutional funding is not being provided by cutouts that are serving adversarial regimes.

---

[108] https://www.eejournal.com/article/richard-feynman-and-quantum-computing/

[109] https://www.justice.gov/archives/jm/criminal-resource-manual-908-elements-18-usc-1001

Although America's universities are being attacked through the insertion of racial politics, social engineering, and division, any list of the world's leading universities is dominated by our nation's schools. Maintaining this edge and retaining recent graduates in the STEM fields are essential to our economic growth and our national defense.

Truth and Privilege

The worst crimes are those we do not remember, for our mind, seeking to preserve our soul, does not allow remembrance. Let us commit, this very moment, to restore wholesomeness in our schools and decency in our country.

Many Democratic politicians seek to rewrite American history, which is quite difficult if you do not understand it. Nowhere is the lack of essential knowledge of this political class more in evidence than in their discussion of privilege.

Privilege is not granted to those who earned its outward manifestations; it is granted to those who did not. Privilege is defined as, "a special right, advantage, or immunity granted or available only to a particular person or group."[110] Privilege does not accrue to the societies that attained the bases for advancement but to the nations and societies that did not.

Privilege is apparent in America and in Europe because, for hundreds of years, the West constituted the world engine for scientific discoveries, technological and engineering progress, and most of the great advances in mathematics. This is the gift that America and Europe have given the world, which should be respected and not denigrated, for such achievements are not a source of shame. Nor must they be a source of selfish pride, for these advances are an

---

[110]https://www.encyclopedia.com/social-sciences-and-law/law/law/pri vilege#:~:text=priv%C2%B7i%C2%B7lege%20%2F%20%CB%88priv%20 %28%C9%99%29lij%20%2F%20%E2%80%A2%20n.%20a,in%20the%20 form%20of%20a%20franchise%20or%20monopoly.

everlasting heritage for all humanity. If we do not learn from each other, we will covet, which is a great sin, for it precipitates conflict.

Three scientists shaped the modern world: Sir Isaac Newton, James Clerk Maxwell, and Albert Einstein. Without these three European men, the world would not exist as we know it. Only in the West could such geniuses reach maturation, for as Newton said of René Descartes, "If I have seen farther than others, it is because I have stood on the shoulders of giants."[III]

Before Newton there was Galileo Galilei. Before Maxwell there was Michael Faraday, and before Einstein, who was the embodiment of genius, there was Maxwell. Within the West, a scientific legacy begun by Galileo, developed a chain of unbroken, superlative thought, unequaled in world history and replicated nowhere else in such spectacular magnitude.

Without these three men and the inventions and innovations that were made possible by their achievements, billions of people could not have been born, for their fathers and mothers would have been bereft of modern technology, rendering our world incapable of supporting its multitudes. Without these three men, there would be no developing world, for the developed world would not exist.

The information conveyed in the preceding paragraphs is today not usually stated for fear of offending, but if we are afraid to offend, we fail, as a society, to educate. This is the true crime, which is being committed by a politically correct elite that enjoys every luxury obtained as a consequence of Western science, while this self-admitted overclass denigrates, in the very same moment, the societies that were the bases for such discoveries and inventions.

A hypocritical elite and a fawning media, who are enraptured by insincere proclamations of compassion, either know themselves to be liars or are devoid of basic historical knowledge, though they profess to understand technology. They act as jealous bullies who come upon a magnificent sandcastle on the beach, only to smash it

---

[III]https://documents.pub/document/5-universal-laws-of-motion-universal-laws-of-motion-newtons-laws-of.html?page=1

due to spite, rendering the beauty of the creation unobservable to others.

Inheritance is practiced and granted in every nation on earth. Thus, what appears to be privilege in the West is actually an inheritance, and if we reject inheritance as an institution, we block the most central motive of humanity, which is the desire to create a better, more prosperous world for our children.

Horizons

President Biden should have demanded a renaissance in America's schools, but he is too indebted to unions, leftist activists, and other special interests to do his job. America has expanded freedoms throughout the world while creating its economic engine, though these accomplishments are belittled by the Biden administration. I am obligated to ask: Do they not know that our children must have pride in our nation if they are to succeed?

Who are the beneficiaries of this circus of malpractice that is robbing our children of their pathways to excellence? They are our adversaries. If the radical left continues to control our schools and universities, we will lose our country, for it will become indefensible. What dictators, who are our foes, could never accomplish on the battlefield, they will reap in the classroom.

Students must be taught that America's Founding was a watershed in world history. They must learn that our nation is exceptional. They must internalize that the United States is not the moral equivalent of China, Russia, or Iran.

My dear wife Terry and I care deeply about learning. This day, we have the capacity to extend America's quest to embody reverence, equality, prosperity, and security to many generations yet unborn if we embrace all that has been bequeathed to us through the sacrifice and the patriotism of our countrymen—in their dedication to enhancing liberty in order that it be the birthright of all. We must consider the extension of this pursuit to be a primary quest in each of our lives.

Chapter 7, Education, Precepts:

• Failing schools must not mean that our children are destined to underperform or wane. If institutions betray student and parental trust, we must build new avenues for learning to flourish.

• If public schools are to exist and to fulfill their original mission, they must educate our youth, so that they can compete with any students on earth. Money alone is not the answer. Money can be spent wisely, or it can be misspent or squandered.

• School choice and not socialist proselytization is necessary to reform our schools. Public schools must be forced to compete for students with charter, private, and religious schools, in addition to homeschooling. Competition will improve student performance and, if necessary, break apart and reconstitute public schools that are deficient.

Issues and Problems:

• President Randi Weingarten of the American Federation of Teachers and other leftists have arguably crippled our nation's schools. To impart values that will shape students, enriched standards of behavior must be demanded.

• Subject mastery is paramount. The substitution of criticism for knowledge is the essence of the progressive agenda that promotes Critical Race Theory (CRT). The 1619 Project, which substantiates CRT, is a screed centered on the unsupported premise that the Founding of America had as its primary intention the defense of slavery.

• Election to school boards must become a central aim for conservatives.

Duties and Actions:

• When teachers' unions require tenure that can almost never be taken away, teachers become an advantaged class not answerable to parents. School districts must reward great teachers and fire incompetents.

• Vouchers that grant choice in education are the way forward; we must also empower home schooling by providing the means for parents to form associations and receive allotments.

• The Department of Education must be torn down and replaced with a small federal office that numbers its staff in the hundreds and not in the thousands. Education is most properly a local issue.

• Students will not fulfill their ambitions through diversity training based on color or religion. To buttress our efforts in preparing students for the STEM fields, the concept of inclusion must be reimagined. We must make it mean that children can attain entry into a field or occupation of their dreams and be competitive with anyone, anywhere.

• Many gifted students do not succeed because they lack the necessary foundations that should have been acquired before college. We must recalibrate our junior colleges so that minority and disadvantaged students may fill educational gaps in order that they may become successful baccalaureate candidates in demanding disciplines.

• Any university that grants preferential admission or grades on the basis of sex, religion, creed, race, or ethnicity should be sanctioned and, in due course, stripped financially of all federal grants, loans, and tuition assistance.

• Trades offer Americans the chance to be independent soon after graduating high school. There is dignity in self-sufficiency and in being financially able to support a family. America's high schools must develop vocational educational tracks, beginning in the ninth grade, which will lead to apprenticeships after graduation.

CHAPTER 8

SCIENTIFIC INTEGRITY

America's scientific and medical institutions are at risk. Integrity is critical. Science cannot be static for absolute knowledge is unattainable.

A broken system, if discovered, can be revised, ignored, or left to fail and be replaced. Untrue narratives replace reality if a broken system is maintained without revisions, in order to preserve existing bases of power and control.

Lockdowns, school closures, and compelled vaccinations in the military and in schools are emblematic of the severe damage induced by the pretention of science and not its practice. If scientific information is adulterated, government, businesses, and institutions are hampered in their ability to use evidence within the context of policy. To claim to know what cannot be known must not resonate in science but be understood as politics, which raged as a storm during COVID-19. Science and the practice of medicine have been confounded by governmental and non-governmental betrayals of the public trust, enabling injurious deceit within our nation, which is impermissible.

Scientific Integrity

The integrity of America's scientific and medical institutions is in doubt. We must understand essential elements of the scientific method to discern where our nation's conventions and establishments have faltered, so that we can oversee revisions and advancements.

Each of us approaches life with the understanding that issues, conjectures, or theses must be continuously addressed. To face these challenges, we collect data or rely on its accumulation by various sensors, which include private and government entities, online sources, and presumed authorities.

Data, including measurements, descriptions, numerical assessments, and statistics must next be arrayed in context to produce information that is useful. Due to actions that constitute the appropriation of policymaking by a medical, bureaucratic elite, this stage was corrupted during the pandemic. The creation of policy during this crucial time was often not informed by science but was misled by what was falsely presented to be set knowledge.

The lockdowns, school closures, and compelled vaccinations in the military are emblematic of the severe damage induced by the pretention of science and not its practice. A testament to this dissimulation is the vaccination of young men and male adolescents throughout the country, which increased the prevalence of myocarditis in these populations.[112]

---

[112]https://pubmed.ncbi.nlm.nih.gov/35076665/

Powerful forces within America's medical establishment, including pharmaceutical companies and the National Institutes of Health (NIH), as well as our intelligence community and the World Health Organization (WHO), altered the background that enveloped SARS-CoV-2 through their repudiation and destruction of competing observations. This cost many precious lives through induced impoverishment, suicide, and the public's reluctance to obtain vital medical testing for other maladies during the lockdowns.

If the scientific information offered is adulterated, government, businesses, and institutions are constrained in their ability to use evidence properly within the context of policy. Thus, obtaining meaning from shared experiences is rendered useless.

Another challenge arises when the background of an issue presented to decision-makers is altered. This may result from viewing an object or a problem from different vantage points.

These perspectives result in the same object, at the same moment in time, being pictured against two dissimilar backgrounds. There is no harm if both perspectives are considered, but if one is culled for political reasons, errors in decision-making are frequently triggered.

Information properly presented leads to pathfinding, which charts a course forward. A process of iteration and refinement should cover the steps of data collection, the presentation of information, and sensemaking.

After necessary repetition of analyses, salutary actions should be instituted. Policymaking is supposed to be practiced this way. This is especially true in preparation for crises that have an expected incidence of occurrence; the process, however, is broken.

The NIH failed the nation in this regard and must be thoroughly reformed. Before we can consider changes to our nation's policies, we must correct this fault. This requires national leadership that understands and promotes appropriate processes to effect change, not politically expedient actions, whose public acceptance is gleaned through the application of an echoic corporate media.

Politics raged as a storm during COVID-19 because our perceptions of the arc of need were confounded by presuppositions and by bureaucratic betrayals of the public trust. These acts damaged clear-sightedness, enabling our nation to be deceived.

To claim to know what cannot be known must not resonate in science but be understood as politics. The fear propagated during the pandemic did not allow discernment to occur. Instead, medical bureaucrats acted as handmaidens to the politicization of science.

Statements only have power if we are able to question their validity. Questioning presumed facts permits evidence to be amassed to support a belief as well as negations that may dislodge convictions. After questions are asked and answered, the validity of a given statement is either enhanced or rejected.

An inability to question statements results in the acceptance of assertions that may be untrue. This happened routinely during COVID-19; the largest companies the world has ever known vied with China in dismantling dissenting opinions. This can never be allowed to occur again.

The ability to question is essential to the scientific method, for orthodoxy is displaced by heterodoxy, which is then established as the new orthodoxy, only to be replaced by a new heterodoxy. Such a process repeats without end. During the pandemic, the corruption and the misappropriation of the scientific method was deleterious to public health, our economy, and our national security; this debasement has increased in scope during the Biden administration, for false narratives are now not rejected by President Biden even when they are discovered.[113]

A Broken System

The author of the destruction of billions of dollars in wealth on what was once one of the world's largest cryptocurrency exchanges, Sam Bankman-Fried, pledged eighteen million dollars through his FTX

---

[113]https://www.military.com/daily-news/2021/07/29/biden-orders-military-move-toward-mandatory-covid-vaccine.html

Foundation[114] to TOGETHER, a study consortium, which before FTX's allocation, conducted research on the common drug ivermectin and its efficacy in treating COVID-19. TOGETHER found ivermectin ineffective in this purpose,[115] but the presence of actors such as Bankman-Fried within the domain of research and its funding must give us pause.

During this same period, Bankman-Fried became one of the Democratic Party's largest donors,[116] second only to financier George Soros. To what extent is our nation's system of medical research corrupted by malicious agents who may be seeking to steer medical studies based on profit motives and not public health?

The reach of malefactors in this sphere can fracture consideration and reasoning. These trespassers must be stopped.

There must be extreme transparency as to funding sources and potential conduits of influence for studies of this moment. We must not allow deceitful entities to attain billions of dollars through stratagems to direct outcomes. We must observe that our enemies can be part of this form of insurgency, for the Chinese Communist Party undercuts American policymaking through its propagandistic arms and intelligence operations, which target American politicians, including a Democratic senator[117] and a Democratic congressman on the House Permanent Select Committee on Intelligence.[118]

A broken system, if discovered, is revised, ignored, or left to fail and be replaced. If a broken system, however, is to be maintained, without revisions, in order to preserve existing bases of power,

---

[114] https://ftx.medium.com/the-ftx-foundation-for-charitable-giving-5ae53178dce
[115] https://www.cato.org/sites/cato.org/files/2022-07/regulation-v45n2-for-the-record.pdf
[116] https://www.latimes.com/politics/story/2022-08-12/sam-bankman-fried-ftx-political-donations
[117] https://www.cbsnews.com/sanfrancisco/news/details-chinese-spy-dianne-feinstein-san-francisco/
[118] https://www.realclearpolitics.com/articles/2020/12/18/intelligence_panel_republicans_swalwell_compromised_by_fang_ties_144884.html

untrue narratives must replace reality. This is our nation's present state, but deeper questions must be raised.

The future is composed of unknowable actions by uncountable agents. False narratives may constitute a manufactured future, which can be exploited by its authors for money and power, for to conceive such a counterfeit future is to command it. Evolving artificial intelligence may instigate or hide these threats.

The embrace of nonrealities is facilitated in our age if belief in God is eschewed. This fact is oppositional to the argument that religion obscures reality. Truly, religion commands us to live in the world God created for us, not a make-believe world that we, ourselves, have conjured into mock existence.

The future is frequently feared; therefore, politicians offer palliative answers that are unreal, understanding that apprehension motivates desires for comprehensive responses to difficult problems. The answers frequently proffered, however, do not respect actuality, but must, nonetheless, be maintained or reality will flood in, erasing the falsehoods that give comfort. This is the reason totalistic dreams are stagnant and unyielding, for their creation is the result of ignoring reality, not embracing it. A dictatorial and overly simplistic conception of the world is incompatible with science, for science is the quest for truth.

Veracity

The scientific method requires the creation of a hypothesis to explain or to predict a given phenomenon; experiments are next conducted. Peer review both before and after publication of experimental results either vests a hypothesis with credibility or serves to discredit it.

Experimental results must always be considered with skepticism until there is a substantial body of confirmational outcomes that accrues over time. Open debate of such results establishes new knowledge. This knowledge is always subject to further review and the generation of new hypotheses that promise more explanatory or predictive power.

These new hypotheses may ultimately cause new theories to be proposed and to be accepted. Present knowledge may therefore be displaced by new insights.

Science starts with experiments that are often numerous, in order to support or disprove a hypothesis. As researchers experiment, they construe similarities and patterns. Scientists eventually create a theory that captures these patterns and has explicatory strength.

The scientific community can then use these patterns and a resultant theory to attempt to explain phenomena that are observed but have not actually been studied through experimentation; scientists can use this same process to forecast future phenomena. This capacity for abstraction is the essence of science but was rendered almost nonexistent during many of the stages of the pandemic. This was done by scientific and medical bureaucracies that may have been intent on masking their own adjunctive culpability for the creation of the virus through gain of function experiments conducted at the Wuhan Institute of Virology or another nearby facility.

Analysis and Pathfinding

Obtaining counterexamples to an established theory often occurs in the context of not challenging the original theory but through conducting a set of experiments for some other purpose. A consequential explanation of observed results, which clashes with an established theory, causes reassessment and the modification of recognized science.

This process of experimentation, observation, and questioning yields new theories and forms a never-ending chain that allows science to progress. Implicit in this process is the understanding that our conception of reality is always an approximation.

Data are observations of variable reliability made by humans or by sensors; data become useful after being placed in context to produce information. The examination of information and its interpretation—to assess its meaning—are necessary to create knowledge. Understanding what information means requires that we make sense of accumulated data within relevant contexts.

The ultimate essence of reality is beyond human grasp. This means that science cannot be static for we are always moving toward something that we cannot obtain, which is absolute knowledge. Totalitarian systems of thought, however, rest on the idea of the availability of truth without God. Reality in its totalistic form is therefore dependent upon our intentions and not our quest for enlightenment. Such a conception of knowledge is antithetical to the scientific method.

Options as to the use of knowledge arise after it is contrasted with existing conceptions of reality, which are affected by observations or resultant actions. The acquisition of knowledge is a dynamical process. Complex problems require analytic tools, not bureaucratic inertia or obstinance.

In life, pathfinding is essential. Too often, particularly in matters involving governance or involving public health, progress is uncertain and may be riddled with self-imposed obstacles that are counterproductive.

Pathfinding to determine a course of action, in its quantitative sense, is the process, aided by computers, of finding the shortest path to a goal. This technique, which is accomplished in the context of policy, may be combined with decision analysis, with weights assigned to different policy objectives that must be solved simultaneously, in order to address complex problems of importance that touch many different domains.

Policymakers must determine the relative importance or weights of different objectives. These factors are established through the consideration of the comparative value of each objective in contrast to other competing goals.

Solution bundles are contrasted and assessed in order to derive the best policy choices given multiple objectives, for each goal may have distinct levels of importance. Different bundles may be proposed by assembled expert teams, each with cross-competencies.

After applying weighting factors, composite scores can be rendered. Several teams should work in opposition to ensure the broadest range of views and plans are presented to decision-makers.

This process aspires to find the best pathway to accomplish various criteria, each vital, so that solutions may be attained in the most direct way, with the least adverse consequences. This needs to be done in a competitive environment in which multiple analytic teams bring different viewpoints to the issues at hand. This is required to produce critical analyses that promote excellence and not acquiescence or manufactured harmony at the expense of competency.

By understanding how multivariate decision analysis should be performed, we ensure that America's sciences will never again be commandeered by a coterie of duplicitous bureaucrats. Unfortunately, Dr. Anthony Fauci, director of the National Institute of Allergy and Infectious Diseases (NIAID), who also served as the chief medical advisor to President Biden, permitted few appropriate or competitive analyses to be performed during the pandemic.

Knowledge

To further understand how science has been corrupted, we must consider perception. We hold that we know things through observation, though observation may be biased or incorrect. What we expect to happen in the future is entrenched by the frequency that a suspected fact is encountered in the past as well as the power of the incidence of its manifestation. What is frequent or what is unique is remembered and is projected forward in time.

Empiricism concerns the enlargement of knowledge through repeated observations. Presuppositions based on past events, however, should not be confused with evidence but rather be tested against it. In addition, we believe that we know things, often wrongly, if they are conveyed to us by an authority. Arguments from authority are often not explicative, though they predominated during the pandemic.

Inductive reasoning offers the prospect of new knowledge; deductive reasoning does not. For a deduction to be valid, the truth of the premises must guarantee the truth of the conclusion. Thus, while insights may be attained through deduction, any insights are necessarily derivative.

Misdirection may be discovered through the application of parsimony, an important tool in science. Isaac Newton described this principle as the admittance of "no more causes of natural things than such as are both true and sufficient to explain their appearances."[119] This elaboration contains a crucial element of this approach to discovery: The hypothesis selected through this means must encompass observed facts, even if such facts add complexity.

Emphasis on logic and the rejection of the unnecessary compounding of entities or observables should be standards that undergird inquiry. This frequently is not the case.

In America today, the use of contested or unsupported charges of medical noncompliance or of scientific heterodoxy, or of insurrection, are propounded to suppress dissent. The result is a stifling of needed scientific, medical, or political discourse, for words that impute guilt to individuals, for conjectured crimes, are carelessly asserted. Such indictments are magnified through social media's instigation of acquiescence to prevailing narratives.

Forced conformity serves elites, the media, and the bureaucratic state, for it is through such submission that people are herded and manipulated. This conformity enhances the ability of statists to shepherd people toward specific objectives, which, in turn, serve the needs of the technocratic overclass that benefits from knowing that their conceptions of the future will be realized in some form due to governmental actions. This posture facilitates rent seeking, which is the manipulation of public policies, which affect economic conditions, in order to obtain wealth in the absence of correlative, productive contributions. It is thus often the case that government waste is sought and not fought by bureaucrats and their beneficiaries because such waste permits this odious practice.

Conspiracies

The confusion concerning the prevalence of conspiracies and conspiracy theories is designed to create a haze that obscures truth. The road to truth may be termed a conspiracy and a true conspiracy may

---

[119]https://www.goodreads.com/quotes/7883642-we-are-to-admit-no-more-causes-of-natural-things

be heralded as veracity. The People's Republic of China's concerted obfuscation of the true origin of the Wuhan virus is a prime example of the declaration of a putative conspiracy that is designed to misdirect.

There need not be a fixed, initial design for a narrative to evolve that has the attributes of a conspiracy. Many individuals, in many lands, may desire the attainment of similar objectives. They may act independently or in concert with each other in small or large groups. The false collusion narrative involving President Donald Trump and Russia exemplifies this threat, for it embroiled an entire administration, doing great harm to our country.

In these cases, the result of disparate or coordinated actions created overarching vectors that propelled emergent narratives or doctrines, the formations of which were, in part, accretive, representing the sum of many small acts. This process accounts for the fact that while some presumed conspiracies appear to be well designed and coordinated, others do not. Thus, objectives may be shared, while individual actions may not be organized, leading to claims that something is a conspiracy when it, in fact, may be a coalescing of interests that overlap to some discernable degree.

Substitutes

"When the facts change, I change my mind. What do you do, sir?" This assertion may have been expressed by the economist John Maynard Keynes; it is also attributed to others. This statement addresses the fact that knowledge is not fixed.

Policies are not substitutes or analogues for science. Policies may rest on science, but they must not be confused with it. Policies may apply science correctly or misapply it; as such they are always distinct from science, though they may reflect it.

During the height of the pandemic, which occurred on the Biden administration's watch, America did not lead. We did not even follow.

Very complex policy issues such as America's response to SARS-CoV-2 require a multidimensional approach in which experts and stakeholders are brought together so that decision analysis techniques may be employed to optimize actions across multiple domains. Unfortunately, the bureaucratic mind detests multivariate methods, for the solutions attained frequently diminish the administrative province of control. This is because appropriate actions may be optimized for results that potentially not only encompass a particular bureaucrat's fiefdom, but areas overseen by others. Any splitting of bureaucratic control is usually unacceptable to officials who are protected from responsibility, though they may wield immense authority, as was the case with Dr. Fauci.

The National Institutes of Health and the Centers for Disease Control and Prevention, and the National Institute of Allergy and Infectious Diseases, which is one of NIH's twenty-seven separate centers for research, dismissed contrarian voices, though such opinions were expressed by world authorities on epidemiology and on public health.[120] Instead, our country was bound by bureaucrats and their acolytes in the media.

Dr. Fauci is an immunologist and a physician, who has served as the director of NIAID since 1984. His background was, without question, too narrow and too permeated by his own interests to consider the pandemic in comprehensive terms. The result was a disaster, with America's having one of the worst pandemic outcomes in the developed world.

Never did Dr. Fauci consider adequately the economic costs and dislocations of his actions; never did he consider the price paid by our nation's children for his dictatorial fever nor the dreams that his actions in effect crushed. Dr. Fauci and his cohort overrode the intuition of a president, who did not wish to shut down America. Such is the strength of the medical industrial complex and the deep state that a career bureaucrat prevailed over a president, and, in so doing, caused grievous harm.

We cannot permit this mode of action to be accepted, but COVID-19 permitted science to be butchered and be misused by a rapacious bureaucracy. This catastrophe must motivate us to change our system exigently, for evil is most easily vested when it is proclaimed to be a mercy. Never again should this chain of actions be tolerated.

---

[120]https://gbdeclaration.org/

Scientific integrity is at grave risk, for statists and politicians seek the trappings of unquestioned knowledge. Such pretenses can convey powerful and enthralling narratives, but this occurs at the price of corrupting science.

A bureaucrat will try to conflate policies with science and science with policies. Special interests will cloak the unearned benefits that they seek, and unethical politicians will disguise an expedient policy as a scientific imperative, to prevent its contestation.

Regrettably, scientists within government and those who are tethered to government grants or institutions, may, themselves, become bureaucratic as a consequence of the fusion of grantmaking and grant seeking, the quest for academic or private-sector positions, or—for university professors—the pressure of publishing imperatives. This constellation of forces is a hindrance to the proper practice of science, for it propels consensus positions, which are contrary to the spirit of inquiry, which involves skepticism.

The value of NIH grants for biomedical research represents by far the single largest funding source in this field.[121] A consequence of this power is control. The NIH notes:

> The NIH invests most of its $45 billion budget in medical research for the American people.
> Over 84 percent of NIH's funding is awarded for extramural research, largely through almost 50,000 competitive grants to more than 300,000 researchers at more than 2,500 universities, medical schools, and other research institutions in every state.[122]

In the wake of COVID-19 and its pernicious consequences that have imperiled our nation and the world, a comprehensive assessment must be initiated of NIH grantmaking, its influence, and its ability to gear science and medicine toward governmental or group

---

[121]https://www.nih.gov/grants-funding
[122]https://www.nih.gov/ABOUT-NIH/WHAT-WE-DO/BUDGET#:
~:text=The%20NIH%20invests%20most%20of%20its%20%2445%20
billion,schools%2C%20and%20other%20research%20institutions%20in%20
every%20state.

objectives at the expense of truth. The means to conduct this assessment must involve independent, multidisciplinary teams.

Team B

We are deluged with information; often, however, we need less information and the application of more wisdom. To claim a mastery of facts that are not facts, must not taint science but be considered to be a part of politics masquerading as incisive knowledge.

Groupthink has been defined as "a pattern of thought characterized by self-deception, forced manufacture of consent, and conformity to group values and ethics." It is antithetical to scientific inquiry and integrity. Scientific inquiry, not groupthink, inclusion, or sops to equity, is the basis for consequential growth across a spectrum of disciplines and objectives.

The explosion of knowledge in every academic field, particularly in science, requires that gifted students pursue increasingly narrow disciplines, to enable the mastery of germane materials. Thus, the individual pursuit of knowledge is often extremely constricted.

Subject competency and investigation have eclipsed random intellectual inquiry, particularly across unassociated fields. This narrowing of the intellectual mind limits the accurate perception of the world, for commonalities, dependencies, and junctures, across different areas of knowledge, may not be discerned or integrated. This is a fundamental issue that our society must address, for it is the fusion of ideas and information that arises across disparate fields that often leads to the acquisition of new knowledge, which supports economic and social development.

Analyses that are competitive and include teams drawn from outside the federal bureaucracy can offer an important avenue to rapidly improve assessments of critical issues. Contention is the means to disrupt the malaise and the groupthink intrinsic in established bureaucracies.

Ill bureaucracies rely on diversion, untrue narratives, and misdirection to cover their own incompetencies and their raft of errors.

Competitive analyses have the potential to unseat entrenched predicates that tarnish subsequent investigations by creating false parameters or premises.

Concerned that Soviet nuclear strategy was predicated on achieving superiority in opposition to the United States that would grant the USSR strategic warfighting capabilities, President Gerald Ford instituted a competitive assessment to the Central Intelligence Agency's National Intelligence Estimate. At stake was the potential of the USSR to reduce America's strategic forces to the point of diminishing our deterrent due to limiting our second-strike capability, or the Soviet Union's use of its burgeoning strategic missile forces as tools for international suasion and coercion at a time in which the United States embraced détente.

In opposition to the CIA's estimate of Soviet strategic force structure and intent, a Team B was formed, under the direction of the noted Harvard historian, Dr. Richard Pipes,[123] who would become Ronald Reagan's most senior White House advisor on the Soviet Union. Dr. Pipes and his team found severe conceptual and methodological errors in the bureaucracy's appraisal of the strategic threat posed by the USSR.

This independent evaluation would prove critical to the Reagan administration in closing America's window of vulnerability in strategic forces, through programs to supplement America's Triad of nuclear systems. Combined with an emphasis on protection through the inauguration of the Strategic Defense Initiative (SDI), Team B's work laid the foundation for the dismantlement of the Soviet Empire through the use of selective pressures applied to stressed segments of the USSR's military and geostrategic establishments.

True competitive analyses could have uncovered the flawed assessments that led to the Iraq War and to America's protracted and arduous engagement in Afghanistan. Properly employed,

[123]https://www.commentary.org/articles/richard-pipes-2/team-b-the-reality-behind-the-myth/

competitive analyses hold the potential to reduce government spending and to refocus the attention of Washington to matters of central concern to the American people, as opposed to costly and peripheral policies and actions, which have, nonetheless, garnered substantial support within the bureaucracy. The employment of competitive analyses during times in which the nation faces medical emergencies must, in future, be considered obligatory.

Discernment

The ability to question an authority is central to our living in a free society as opposed to an autocracy. The impermissibility of raising doubt is the hallmark of totalitarianism. It has no place in science or in America.

The problem of scientific integrity must be placed within the greater context of societal confusion concerning reality. Because of social media and the internet, narratives are attaining a strength, an incidence, and a vibrancy not seen since the preindustrial age. We must recognize that the momentary acquisition of a digital soapbox to shout absurdities or banalities should never be confused with the knowledge or the capacity to convey meaningful ideas.

We must combat societal reliance on untruths in order that we may advance through thoughtful comprehension, astuteness, and the application of the scientific method. This process, however, must not create dictatorial powers within government, within the private sector, or within other institutions. A perceived orthodoxy must never be permitted to silence other voices.

The accumulation of power in any entity or domain, though perhaps originally purposed to rescind misinformation, is too easily repurposed to spread misinformation and to censor discordant voices. The best antidote to incorrect or to misleading information is more information, not censorship.

When people are lost, intellectually or morally, and shown the truth, they may become angry. But it is at this juncture that an inflection point is reached, presaging change. Altering our nation's present trajectory is essential; therefore, we must not be afraid of instigating righteous outrage, for to do so is to do a great service for our country.

The scientific method is not oppositional to the quest by religious adherents to discover God's plan and his majesty. Science and religion are not two antagonistic and different magisteria.

In Proverbs 11, we find great wisdom. The Bible states, "The Lord detests dishonest scales, but accurate weights find favor with him." The acquisition of knowledge and just action are dependent on our use of correct measures. Without such conduct we are cast at sea without the means to reach any shore.

Science rests on faith, faith in the purity of a process in which truth, even if difficult, is exalted. Thus, science can be the discovery of God's plan and is, therefore, not in conflict with the Divine, unless an attempt is made to nullify the Lord's design.

To believers, science involves encountering God's magnificence. Conversely, if we believe ourselves to be as God, we, in fact, prove ourselves to be abject fools. America and the West stand at a decision point: Are we to build upon thousands of years of human thought, moral reasoning, and advancement, or are we to place our trust in a self-selected overclass that wishes to fashion the world to reflect their own projections of inerrant design and absolute conformity?

Chapter 8, Scientific Integrity, Precepts:

• The ability to question is essential to the scientific method, for orthodoxy is displaced by heterodoxy, which is then established as the new orthodoxy, only to be replaced by a new heterodoxy. Such a process repeats without end.

• The scientific community uses patterns and resultant theories to attempt to explain phenomena. The capacity for abstraction is the essence of science but was hindered during many stages of the pandemic.

• The future is composed of unknowable acts. False narratives may constitute a manufactured future, which can be exploited by its authors for money and power, for to conceive such a counterfeit future is to command it.

• During the pandemic, the corruption and the misappropriation of the scientific method was harmful to public health, our economy, and our national security; this debasement has increased in scope during the Biden administration, for false narratives were embraced for political reasons even when they were discovered.

• Policymakers must determine the relative importance of different objectives. These factors are established through the consideration of the comparative value of each objective in contrast to other competing goals.

Issues and Problems:

• Our perception of reality, the scientific method, and discovery must not be dependent upon intentions, political posturing, or ideology. Such conceptions of knowledge are antithetical to the scientific method.

• The Chinese Communist Party undercuts American policymaking and scientific integrity through its propagandistic arms and intelligence operations, which target American politicians, businesses, and academic institutions.

• America has not developed proper structures to combat Chinese information operations. In the United States, the accumulation of power in any entity or domain, though perhaps originally purposed to combat disinformation and foreign intelligence operations, is too easily repurposed to spread misinformation and to censor discordant voices.

Duties and Actions:

• The process to fuse scientific knowledge with policymaking must find the pathway to accomplish various objectives so that solutions may be attained directly, with the least adverse consequences. This needs to be done in a competitive environment in which multiple analytic teams bring different viewpoints to the problems at hand.

• There need not be a fixed, initial design for a narrative to evolve that has the attributes of a conspiracy. Many unrelated individuals may desire the attainment of similar objectives. Confusion concerning the prevalence of conspiracies is designed to obscure truth. This façade, used against us by our adversaries, must be destroyed.

• Truth may be termed a conspiracy, whereas a true conspiracy may be heralded as veracity. The Chinese Communist Party's concerted obfuscation of the origin of the Wuhan virus is a prime example of the declaration, by media, of an alleged conspiracy that is designed to misdirect real inquiry. Such stratagems must be challenged.

• Very complex policy issues such as America's response to SARS-CoV-2 require a multidimensional approach in which experts and stakeholders are brought together so that decision analysis techniques may be employed to optimize actions across multiple domains. Unfortunately, the bureaucratic mind detests these inclusive methods. The results can be disastrous. The rebuilding of America's scientific institutions and their ability to inform policymakers is urgent. Competitive sources of analysis, not suppression of contradictory views, is mandatory.

CHAPTER 9

PILLARS

The actions of our government must, at all times, hold the needs of the American people as our North Star. America must convey resolve through moderation and precision in international affairs. An obligation of governance is to consider the world as it is and to weave together tools that encompass the entire range of national power, including economic, military, and geopolitical capabilities. The employment of these levers must reflect a sober vision of the future and our country's place in it. This has often not been the case.

Our nation has repeatedly employed the force of arms as a geostrategic instrument during the past quarter century, often without clearly defined objectives. Leadership demands precise consideration of what must be attained to benefit and safeguard the American people.

> Too often, what can be achieved overshadows what must be done. The bloat in our government and the errors committed in our nation's security policies are frequently the result of confusing the capacity to overpower, which may be temporary, with the necessity to act. Distinguishing between these two conditions requires wisdom and forbearance.

Pillars

In the preceding chapters, I discussed the foundations for freedom for our nation and the world. I will now direct my attention to the principal pillars of our nation's power in the sphere of security, which rest upon such cardinal standards.

An obligation of governance is to consider the world as it is and to weave together disparate policy tools that encompass the entire range of national power, including economic, military, and geopolitical capabilities. These attributes and levers, to support our nation, must reflect present and future currents and trends.

Blessed with wealth, our country has manifested an inclination to lavish money at problems. This is frequently disadvantageous, for root causes may be hidden by a jamboree of ill-conceived or disingenuous actions.

Our nation has repeatedly employed the force of arms as a geostrategic instrument during the past quarter century. Our wars in the Middle East demonstrate that the application of inconstant power is less effective than the strength of our example. That is, if we convey our resolve through moderation and precision in our deeds.

We may conceptualize the problems inherent in policymaking and the necessary procedural changes that should be made by considering three overlapping categories of actions. These sets are constituted by, first, what must be attained; second, what can be achieved; third, what should be accomplished. Too often, what can be done overshadows what must be done; this is often detrimental, for possessing the capacity to do something does not mean we should automatically commit to doing it.

The bloat in our government and the errors committed in our nation's security policies are often the result of confusing the capacity to decree with the necessity to act. Distinguishing between these two conditions requires wisdom and forbearance. Therefore, we should consider what should be done as being the fusion of what must be accomplished, due to exigencies, with what can be attained, due to our capabilities. This adaptive process, when governed by the application of our core principles, which must always reflect decency, humanity, and the wise and measured use of strength, will lead us to prudent policy goals that our nation can initiate, sustain, and uphold.

The news cycle and the dynamics of politics often summon actions even when no action might be better. Our Founders did not seek to establish an efficient government in the sense of its planned capacity for rapidity in its tasks and endeavors. The separation of powers was, in part, designed to allow contemplation and thus restraint, for our Founding Fathers, in their scrutiny of history, believed that government had a greater capacity to do harm than to do good.

With the dawn of the nuclear age in 1945 and with the Soviet Union's explosion of its first nuclear device in 1949, swiftness was sought in our government's decision processes. This capacity should have been generally restricted to matters involving weapons of mass destruction, which demand speed and certainty in response, or emergencies and isolated matters that require prompt action. It was not.

In the ensuing decades, all of government sought to become proactive, for this was initially viewed as efficiency and keenness. In fact, we have sacrificed wisdom too frequently in exchange for a mirage built upon superficial achievements that are trumpeted to maintain political power; such actions have often turned out to be errors, which have contorted our system of government as bequeathed to us.

The Founders were very concerned that our Republic not devolve into an autocratic organism. Unfortunately, the modern bureaucratic state believes that its purview concerning governance conveys to it the *de facto* ownership of government.

The concept of ownership in Roman law encompassed three seemingly contradictory attributes: the right to use what is owned without destroying it, the right to reap fruits from what is owned, and the right to waste or to destroy what is owned.[124] The bureaucratic state assumes that its ownership of government transfers to its masters the right to reap benefits from their positions as well as the prerogative to destroy that which they distain. These are great dangers that must be answered through meaningful changes in the administration of government—to bar the potential for a totalistic bureaucratic state.

A dictator need not be a lone human being; a dictatorship may be constituted by a technocratic bureaucracy or, in the future, an advanced artificial intelligence. A sebaceous, self-proclaimed, technocratic overclass, which is globalist in nature, seeks the permanent installation of a bureaucratic state that it can control. In doing so, this putative overclass, populated by billionaires and an imitative media, seek the capacity to intensify a single spark until it becomes an inferno, so as to attain and to ossify power at the expense of the public trust. This is the essence of dictatorial rule: to take one voice and to impose it on many.

Representations and Despotism

Totalistic rule may take many forms, but it is always initiated through the exploitation of human flaws. As recounted in the Ten Commandments, coveting is a most costly sin. To desire to possess what belongs to someone else is to covet. The nature of this fault is to set a person against his neighbors and a countryman against his fellows.

Covetousness is often shrouded by an assertion of blame or privilege. This is the essence of the social justice movement that seeks to mask envy and pillage, attendant to the redistribution of

---

[124] In Latin, *jus utendi, jus fruendi, jus abutendi*

wealth, with the espousal of the supposedly noble purpose of equity. Nothing could be further from the truth than this ruse, for perfect equity requires perfect tyranny, for each person's gifts are different and, therefore, not equivalent.

To take what is not earned or what is not freely given is to steal. Theft is the basis for every autocratic regime. In each case, totalistic governance suborns theft by terming it beneficence. This would only be true if charity were typified by the slaughter of millions of persons, which is the harvest that has been reaped by the train of fascist and communist regimes that proliferated in the last century, permitting their remnants to still maintain today.

Coveting reduces all human conduct to the physical realm denominated by possessions and wealth. This is perhaps the greatest crime of this failing, for we are each far more than our physical selves: What we possess that we can touch is the least of our God-given gifts.

Convergence

If America does not reflect a balance between the material and the immaterial—in what we touch and what we feel—we will fall. Sixty years ago, the Dutch economist Jan Tinbergen, recipient of the Nobel Prize in 1969, conjectured that the Western economic and the Soviet economic systems were destined to converge. Other prominent economists, including fellow Nobel Laureate, Paul Samuelson, of the Massachusetts Institute of Technology, and Robert Dorfman, of Harvard, undertook computational analyses that demonstrated theoretical support for Tinbergen's hypothesis.

The fall of the Soviet Union in 1991 and the rejection of communism by the former members of the Warsaw Pact proved Tinbergen's conjecture to be false, for it lacked any empirical support. Of the 193 sovereign states that comprise the membership of the United Nations, only the Democratic People's Republic of Korea (DPRK), the People's Republic of China, Vietnam, Cuba, and Laos are self-declared communist nations. All have markedly different systems; all but the DPRK embrace some level of capitalism—albeit with rigid governmental controls.

Since the advent of the communist dictatorship in Laos in 1975, which has subsequently eschewed certain Marxist dictates, no country on earth has formally embraced communism as its form of government, though people in many nations have girded under the yoke of leftist leaders, including some who were professed communists.[125] The dictatorships we see in so many countries today may feign socialist or utopian motives, but this is only to misdirect people who are exploited.

Though the convergence of Soviet and American economic systems never occurred, there is today the prospect of a convergence of American and Chinese political, academic, and business institutions or interests. America has veered dangerously to the left at the instigation of elected officials who are neo-Marxists, members of the deep state who seek unbridled power, and academic and corporate elites who demand control over the levers of government.

Russia, under Vladimir Putin, and China, under Xi Jinping, must be understood as kleptocratic autocracies, though both countries have professed markedly different forms of authority. Each government has ruled and has been enriched by theft on the greatest possible scale. This must never be America's path.

Though still incipient, there is a danger of our nation becoming a repressive kleptocracy, for the juncture of an unprincipled executive with a compliant Federal Reserve, which enables the party in power to print money to purchase constituencies, represents a profound threat to our Republic. It is this threat that the Biden administration epitomizes through its sundry actions. Therefore, President Biden and his cohort must be stopped: This can only be done through the election of a Republican president.

Dissemination

Today, conglomerates that dominate Hollywood also control America's media, publishing, and news platforms. Foreign influences,

---

[125]https://www.britannica.com/biography/Vladimir-Voronin

most particularly from China, are insinuated within our media through the cooption of multinational companies founded and ensconced in our country. China offers American companies access to its markets and to its capital if the Chinese Communist Party deems such inclusions to be in its strategic interest. Thus, access to Chinese markets creates substantial pressures for companies to obey Beijing's dictates.

American media, when it is beholden to China, influences our public and our institutions so that they will submit to China's intentions. Our news sources reverberate with patent falsehoods that are the product of China's intelligence services, as exemplified by the narrative that the PRC's many actions to obliterate access to crucial virus research and related data, known to be once held by the Wuhan Institute of Virology, constituted either expected or benign practices.

The results of this toxicity induced by foreign actors are propagated through social media and are amplified by technology companies, by Hollywood, and by Wall Street. The American public deserves news and analyses devoid of veneers and narratives conceived by an adversarial state. Often, they do not get it.

We are now confronted with a socioeconomic malaise within our country that may constitute the inauguration of the prophesized convergence of communism with our system of governance and our market-based economy. Certain trends that support convergence have been gradual; others have been rapid or explosive.

Creative destruction, although derived from Marxist thought, has been applied to capitalism. The Austrian American economist Joseph Schumpeter was Paul Samuelson's thesis advisor when Samuelson was at Harvard.[126] Schumpeter's "gale of creative destruction" has been emplaced within free market mechanisms; it attempts, in Schumpeter's words, to explain the "process of industrial mutation

[126] https://www.informs.org/Explore/History-of-O.R.-Excellence/ Biographical-Profiles/Samuelson-Paul-A

that continuously revolutionizes the economic structure from within, incessantly destroying the old one, incessantly creating a new one."[127]

Though creative destruction may serve useful purposes in market economies that operate with limited governmental controls, it can also be misused to promote radical change with unknowable consequences. The left seeks to wipe away what was, in order to institute what they believe must be. We need, therefore, to be attentive to the use of forms of creative destruction that instigate undue profit-taking by elites, the accretion of political power by vested interests, and rent seeking, which is constituted by the accumulation of unearned revenues that result from affiliations with politicians or bureaucrats, who implant plans that misappropriate resources within the fabric of government.

Social isolation and despair, which were supercharged by the unnecessary and deeply harmful lockdowns instituted during the pandemic, create public malleability that, if left unabated, can result in pathways to despotic rule. Central to the imposition of tyranny is an assault on religion, for faith is the source of fortitude and of resistance.

The Reign of Terror in France, which lasted from 1793 to 1794, the Russian Revolution, which lasted from 1917 to 1923, and the Cristero War in Mexico, which lasted from 1926 to 1929, are examples of revolutionary fervors that led to mass campaigns against organized religion, which presaged numerous massacres. Each of these revolts was deeply injurious to the countries in which they occurred.

When the organs of the state, including its judicial and enforcement arms, effect the primacy of the state above a citizen's obligations to God, a nation stands in severe jeopardy. No Founding Father and few presidents would find this reordering of allegiances acceptable.

An oppressive, dictatorial state can never abide the faithful, for the faithful subordinate themselves to a higher law that is not the product of man. Unalienable rights are not temporal in nature but

---

[127] https://journals.sagepub.com/doi/abs/10.1177/0539018413497542#:~:text=J oseph%20Schumpeter%2C%20who%20is%20credited,Schumpeter%2C%20 1942%3A%2083).

are vested in our nation's laws to preserve the order of creation. Without freedom of conscience, no freedom is possible, for while government governs the crimes of men, citizens must hold such freedom as is necessary to contest the crimes of government.

The Process President

We cannot know the future, either individually, as a government, or as a nation. Our ability to reason can, however, confer astuteness and with it our nation's ability to picture a future within projected confidence brackets, concerning expectations, which must also address alternative visions. In this manner, a presidency that venerates process can employ analytic tools, history, philosophy, psychology, and deep stores of knowledge, which are held within our country, to project depictions of probable futures along with suitable policy responses. This is not foreknowledge but the appropriate anticipation of events. Sadly, administrations, both Democratic and Republican, have not used the decision tools that are available.

One example of these methods and their application is Bayesian search theory, which enabled the United States Navy to find the USS Scorpion (SSN-589), a nuclear submarine that was lost with all hands in the Atlantic in 1968.[128] This application is rooted in Bayes theorem, which is a statistical means to improve a hypothesis by vesting it with bases of experiential knowledge.[129]

Bayesian search theory permits the addition of new knowledge gleaned from the accrual of information and facts to refine and limit a hypothesis until it pictures the actual situation that exists. Thus, in its essence, this theory is a means of pathfinding. This is the type of tool decisionmakers within our government should employ: There are many others.

The disjunction and pity is that the United States and the United Kingdom developed the field of decision analysis, with the great polymath John von Neumann defining many early advances after

---

[128]https://mitsloan.mit.edu/alumni/math-magic-and-a-lost-city-gold
[129]https://plato.stanford.edu/entries/bayes-theorem/

having been a part of the Manhattan Project. This is our nation's heritage, but it is forgotten and unused by presidencies and administrations that are devoid of process. This deficit has hurt our country in the conduct of foreign affairs and national security policy.

Perhaps worse, history and philosophy are often not considered in America's policymaking practice. Although psychological profiles of Axis leaders in World War II helped inform our nation's military strategy, the intelligence community's transmittal of such analyses, judged by the results exhibited, appears to be forgotten or neglected as a means to attain needed insights concerning our adversaries.

In philosophy, lawlike statements, proposed to picture the future, may garner their legitimacy through their numerical inerrancy as successfully projected hypotheses, which have been proposed and validated in the past. Alternatively, a different means of entrenchment may result from the magnitude and not the frequency of an impelled postulate. Such projections should be fused with analyses of history and bases of institutional knowledge to inform a process presidency. Unfortunately, such an administration does not now exist, for analytic tools are of no use in presidential decision-making if human judgement is not ceaselessly applied throughout the sensemaking process.

A searing example of the harm induced by a lack of scrupulousness is presented by the Biden administration's stumbling attitudes toward Russia and the war in Ukraine. The universe of possible outcomes concerning ongoing and future developments in Russia and the challenges posed to the United States, our NATO partners, Ukraine, and the people of this region may be reduced by reflection on the significance of present developments in this sphere.

Philosopher John Rawls termed the space in which we restate, reconsider, and adjust our beliefs, such that they may be projected reasonably to describe parts of the future—the reflective equilibrium. By employing this approach, the president and the National Security Council, aided by analytic tools that hone decision-making, should be able to discern what steps will confer the most substantial benefits to our policies concerning Russia, including the potentialities of a post-Putin state. There is no indication, however, that this rigor in process has or is taking place, no matter the momentous stakes involved.

It is a savage inconsistency that certain policymakers appear more apt to receive guidance from a shrouded oracle, in the form of an artificial intelligence agent, than to equip themselves with analytic tools that can actually be understood, which have been used and evaluated over the course of decades. The simple explanation for this is laziness, which has no place in the Oval Office.

Though we cannot know how Russia will evolve in the aftermath of President Putin's removal or death, four concerns must dominate our pathfinding in order to yield outcomes supportive of our national interests. Of primary importance is the security of the thousands of nuclear weapons in Moscow's arsenal: Should Russia collapse, these weapons must not be conveyed to unstable parties, including terrorist groups. Second, oligarchs must not command a future Russian state, for their interests are inimical to that of the Russian people as well as NATO's security concerns, for these billionaires accrue wealth by manufacturing instability. Third, while resumption of sales of Russian fossil fuels on world energy markets will help curtail inflation, this can only occur after that nation accepts the conditions demanded by the present litany of sanctions. Fourth, China must be thwarted in any plan to conjoin itself with the state or states that succeed Russia as we now know it, for this would permit China to dominate much of Eurasia. These four matters will be considered in the chapters that follow.

Foundations and Pillars

Those who would be leaders of our nation must take care so that the instruments of policy are not confused with the foundations that support our Republic. Instruments, such as tax policies, regulations, defense expenditures, alliances, and international agreements, can change over time.

The ever-present question for the conservative concerns what must be conserved versus what must be changed due to the march of time and the increasing acceleration of technological change. This demand requires that policy implements be always subject to reexamination or sharpening. Our nation's moorings, however, should be grounded in principles that do not change. These principles, as related, are our faith, our Founding, our families, our borders, our strength through people, our modes of education, and our scientific integrity. Together, these principles constitute our North Star.

The instruments of governance, their application, and their degree of employment are not fixed; President Eisenhower's use of the levers of government differed from President Reagan's approach, yet both administrations were highly successful, for they attained the crucial goals of comity, prosperity, and peace for the American people. The selections of the sets of instruments by both presidents were correct and necessary for their respective times. These two giants shared the same principles but understood that true conservatism is not dogmatic but dynamic, for its time-tested principles—held and espoused—convey great strength to the bearer even when policy options are difficult or fleeting.

America must be on guard, for external and internal forces seek to fracture our Republic; these forces have studied models for revolution, which they intend to execute. To protect against such threats, we must fortify the pillars that constitute our means to uphold the security of our nation. In so doing, we must contemplate and realize the nexus of local, regional, and domestic goals with national objectives and international security policies.

Lower energy costs lead to economic vibrancy and to freedom from foreign coercion. These benefits were conveyed by the Trump administration's creation of American energy dominance, which has since been destroyed by the Biden administration's obstinance in effecting its stultifying convictions.

The cry of climate change has become a cudgel to subdue dissent. This myopia, as expressed by President Biden, vivifies the fear of what cannot be known, thereby destroying commonsense and needed action.

In opposition to the Biden administration's collectivist priorities, job stability and growth underwrite self-esteem and advancement. These merits were cast to the wind by unprecedented government spending, which ignited levels of inflation not experienced in over forty years.

Security at home and abroad is purchased by military strength and the judicious employment of force where necessary. The Biden administration's disastrous withdrawal from Afghanistan, in contravention of military advice proffered by combatant commanders, emboldened President Putin to conduct an illegal war that has placed world peace and economic solvency at risk.

To chart a deliberate course from this slew of misjudgments and misdeeds, four pillars of national strength must be considered in detail, for these pillars confer capabilities. These are embodied by, first, our strategic and tactical nuclear assets; second, economic security; third, energy dominance; fourth, conventional military forces and alliances.

These pillars confer means to achieve objectives, which are constituted by the organization of the National Security Council in the White House, whose statutory members are the president, the vice president, and the secretaries of state, treasury, defense, and energy. Derivative instruments include diplomacy, intelligence and counterintelligence, and the maintenance of homeland security, which includes elements of law enforcement, as well as cybersecurity.

To preserve our nation and to reinforce its strength, we must act with great discernment and seek bipartisan solutions where possible. We cannot, however, place politics above the needs of our country: The challenges we face are too momentous.

The following chapters are based on a lifetime of study and ceaseless discussions with experts and leaders in the fields of business, economics, technology, energy, intelligence, education, law enforcement, statecraft, and military strategy and procurement. Though I have been extraordinarily fortunate to know decisionmakers and leaders throughout the world, the most important conversations of my life have been with Americans whom I meet every day.

The conception of threats, positions, and recommended actions related in the following chapters reflect my discussions with Americans of every background and occupation. I can state on the basis of my experience that the combined wisdom of our nation's citizens far outstrips that of any statesman, academic, politician, or group of such people. It is the American citizenry who must be served, and it is their insights that must be harnessed to break the present cycle of despair and the poverty of purpose that grips our country.

Chapter 9, Pillars, Precepts:

• A dictator need not be a lone human being; a dictatorship may be constituted by a technocratic bureaucracy or, in the future, an advanced artificial intelligence. The modern bureaucratic state believes that its purview concerning governance conveys to it the *de facto* ownership of government. This is unacceptable.

• When the state, including its judicial and enforcement arms, effects its primacy above a citizen's obligations to God, a nation stands in severe jeopardy. No Founding Father would find this reordering of allegiances acceptable.

• Totalistic rule may take many forms, but it is always initiated through the exploitation of human flaws. As recounted in the Ten Commandments, coveting is a most harmful sin. To desire to possess what belongs to someone else is to covet. The nature of this fault is to set a person against his neighbors and countrymen.

• Covetousness is often shrouded by an assertion of blame, which is the essence of the social justice movement that seeks to mask envy, pillage, and redistribution of wealth, by the espousal of the supposedly noble cause of equity.

Issues and Problems:

• America has veered dangerously to the left at the instigation of elected officials who are neo-Marxists, members of the deep state who seek unbridled power, and elites who demand control over the levers of government.

• Foreign influences are insinuated within media through the cooption of multinational companies resident in our country. Conglomerates that dominate Hollywood also control America's media, publishing, and news sources. We are now confronted with a socioeconomic malaise within our country that may constitute the inauguration of the convergence of communism with our system of governance and our market-based economy. This toxicity is propagated through social media and amplified by technology companies and by Wall Street.

• America must remain America; we must demand news and analyses devoid of veneers and narratives conceived by adversarial states.

Duties and Actions:

• We must discern what must be conserved versus what must be changed due to the increasing acceleration of technology. Policy tools must be subject to constant reexamination. Our nation's moorings, however, should be grounded in unchanging principles, which are our faith, our Founding, our families, our borders, our people's strength, our modes of education, and our scientific integrity. Together, these principles define America.

• The United States must be on guard, for external and internal forces seek to fracture our Republic; these forces have studied models for revolution, which they intend to implement. To protect against such threats, we must fortify the pillars that constitute our means to uphold the security of our nation. In so doing, we must integrate local, regional, and domestic goals with national objectives and international security policies.

• A process presidency is essential, for the full panoply of analytic tools must be used given the problems faced.

• To preserve our nation, we must act with great discernment and seek bipartisan solutions where possible. We cannot, however, place politics above the needs of our country: The challenges we face are too momentous.

• It is the American people who must be served, and it is their insights that must be harnessed to break the present cycle of despair and the poverty of purpose that grips our nation.

CHAPTER 10

PEACE THROUGH STRENGTH

America's preparedness across the spectrum of conflict dissuades belligerent powers from attacking our nation. Nuclear war is unconscionable. It is important to grasp that it is our broad range of capabilities that support deterrence, thereby averting global devastation.

Deterrence is the prevention of aggression due to the fear of unacceptable counteraction. It is to avert conflict by ensuring that any first strike by a belligerent will be unsuccessful and ruinous to their nation. Our actions must enforce this certainty.

The Islamic Republic of Iran is apocalyptic in its composition and in its actions. This is why Iran must never be allowed to possess nuclear weapons, for any rational strategic calculus may be jettisoned at any time by that radical state.

The tactical nuclear armaments that America now possesses are few in number, which is dangerous given Russia's capabilities. China is expanding its nuclear forces markedly while engaging in unprecedented militancy. Therefore, America must ensure the future capabilities of our strategic forces as we guard against new threats, including biological warfare.

Peace Through Strength

Tens of thousands of nuclear weapons have been created since the dawn of the atomic age in 1945; thousands still exist in the inventories of the countries that possess these armaments. America's preparedness across the entire spectrum of conflict dissuades belligerent powers from attacking our country and our allies. Though nuclear war is unconscionable, we must grasp that it is our broad range of capabilities that substantiates deterrence, thereby averting a war that would devastate the world.

Attentive strategists have advanced our nation's understanding of conflict in the nuclear age. Dr. Henry Kissinger examined the complexity of nuclear deterrence. Indeed, he rose to national prominence upon writing *Nuclear Weapons and Foreign Policy*, in 1957, published for the Council on Foreign Relations.[130] In his *Foreign Affairs* article of the same year, titled, "Strategy and Organization," Dr. Kissinger declared, "Whatever the problem—whether it concerns our military strategy, our system of alliances or our relations

[130]https://books.google.com/books?id=ZbuZDwAAQBAJ&pg=PT13&source=gbs_selected_pages&cad=2#v=onepage&q&f=false

with the Soviet bloc—the nuclear age demands above all a clarification of doctrine."[131]

This challenge was accepted by Herman Kahn, who was a physicist, strategist, and futurist who founded the Hudson Institute in 1961.[132] As one of our nation's leading multidisciplinary policy institutions, Hudson has continuously innovated in the development of national security policy, fusing data and views from numerous domains and disciplines in order that new insights be obtained.

No book is more aptly titled than Herman Kahn's *Thinking about the Unthinkable*, published in 1962, for it concerns nuclear war and deterrence.[133] Though six decades have passed since the publication of these cited works, the search for strategic clarity in America's postwar conduct of military and foreign affairs is still challenging.

Dr. Kissinger's and Mr. Kahn's books are among a substantial library of works on nuclear strategy by theorists, for the issue has dominated national security policies in the aftermath of World War II and the use of nuclear weapons to end that global catastrophe. Since beginning my service as a member of the defense group of the National Security Council staff during the Reagan administration, I devoted large measures of time to the study of the nuclear doctrines of the nations that have acquired or have sought to obtain nuclear weapons. The realities of the nuclear age—and the severe threats posed—leave our nation's policymakers no choice: We must confront America's strategic threats and options.

To begin, we must examine our first nuclear adversary's principles, for Soviet and American doctrines were different. America has held that no intact victor can emerge from a nuclear exchange that can be unbounded in its potential for escalation. The issue of strategy, therefore, concerns the force structure and doctrine that should be adopted to best support deterrence, thereby preventing the advent of war. The corollary to this policy is to limit escalation at every stage of nuclear conflict, should it occur.

---

[131] https://www.foreignaffairs.com/articles/united-states/1957-04-01/strategy-and-organization

[132] https://www.hudson.org/

[133] Herman Kahn, "Thinking about the Unthinkable," (Avon, 1962).

Soviet nuclear doctrine stressed warfighting and war-winning capabilities. The former Soviet Minister of Defense from 1967 to 1976, Marshal Andrei Grechko, made clear that Soviet strategic doctrine and its fundamental tenets should not be obscured but heralded to serve the interests of the state. He thus articulated doctrines that stressed warfighting capabilities as being necessary at every level of conflict.

Soviet Marshal Vasily Sokolovsky's influential volume, *Military Strategy: Soviet Doctrine and Concepts*,[134] was premised on the belief that war could be won on any level of conflict if appropriate preparations, strategies, and weapons were in place. This included nuclear war, despite its obvious costs to all belligerents. Based on its authors' original translations of documents, *The Role of Nuclear Forces in Current Soviet Strategy*, by Leon Gouré, Foy Kohler, and Mose Harvey, explicated the war-winning themes that coursed through the USSR's nuclear doctrines.[135]

Soviet strategic thought encompassed many stratagems that sought to forge the communist regime's possession of thousands of nuclear weapons into not only tools for combat at various levels or stages of warfare but as bludgeons for psychological manipulation and control, within the USSR, itself, and in nuclear and non-nuclear states allied against communism. Strategic concepts formed by Soviet planners still reverberate in Putin's Russia and in Xi's China. The ideas formed by Soviet theoreticians are studied in Iran and in the Democratic People's Republic of Korea. This is why the study of doctrines formed fifty and sixty years ago, in an empire that no longer exists, is important. We must understand the implications of Soviet nuclear doctrine, including its applications as an implement of non-kinetic belligerence and intimidation, if we are to comprehend

---

[134]Vasily Sokolovsky, "Military Strategy: Soviet Doctrine and Concepts," (Pall Mall Press, 1963).
[135]Leon Gouré, Foy Kohler, and Mose Harvey, "The Role of Nuclear Forces in Current Soviet Strategy," (Center for Advanced International Studies, University of Miami, 1974).

principles now held within totalistic regimes; this is necessary to chart a path to peace and security for America.

Deterrence and its Correlates

Bernard Brodie, who preceded Henry Kissinger and Herman Kahn as one of America's foremost nuclear strategists, framed part of our conception of nuclear weapons in terms of deterrence. The concept of deterrence may be defined as the prevention of aggression due to the fear of unacceptable counteraction. It is to avert armed conflict by the establishment of the certitude that any first strike by a belligerent force will be unsuccessful in its aims and be disastrous for the aggressor. Our actions in peacetime and in wartime must enforce the certainty that an adversary's post-strike position will be inferior to their pre-strike situation in relation to the balance of forces.

Deterrence arises from strength and never from weakness because weakness invites belligerency. Unilateral restraint in the maintenance and disposition of forces does not support deterrence, for deterrence cannot arise from unilateral restraint if such restraint circumscribes power in the face of burgeoning threats. Unilateral restraint can signal weakness, which may begin a dangerous cascade of responses by nations that believe they are unbound.

Meaningful, stabilizing strategy must pose a convincing deterrent composed of strategic systems, which are complementary and thus, as a force, survivable, for deterrence is a function of the credibility of a nation's armed strength as seen by an opposing state. To deter effectively, we must be capable of posing accurate and certain counteraction that is unacceptable to an adversary, given its beliefs, values, and intentions. This includes, by definition, states that hold that a nuclear war can be fought and won. This is the essence of the rationale for America's Triad of land, air, and submarine-based strategic nuclear forces.

American nuclear policy is a product of presidential directions to the Departments of Defense and Energy. It is also a product of our strategic forces in being as well as their technology, accuracy, yield, and readiness.

The budgetary atmosphere, Congress, and prevailing strategic philosophies, held by our country and by potentially belligerent states, combine with geopolitical events and intelligence assessments to define threats, costs, opportunities, and programs. A strategic doctrine, to be relevant, must codify the strategic forces, doctrines, and threats at hand as well as those that may evolve.

While the term balance of forces concerns the number, disposition, and readiness of military assets, revolutionaries have embraced a different and broader measure. The term correlation of forces originated with Vladimir Lenin's conception of revolutionary commitment, as demonstrated in the Bolshevik Revolution. According to communist theorists, such dedication is one of the most important metrics that conveys a state's power and its willingness to fight. The relevance of the term, however, is applicable in other circumstances, and its germaneness may be separated from its origin.

Correlation of forces, which is manifested in the willingness of a combatant force to sacrifice itself in order to attain its objective, is important in the consideration of a military that is defending a homeland. The term is also relevant to our consideration of deterrence in the face of fanatical states such as Iran, whose theocratic rulers constitute a millenarianism, which is a religious sect or aberrant ideology that holds that the end of history is upon us, in which the nature of the world will profoundly change. Tyrants who have embraced this precept view any sacrifice to be permissible: The glories that await the faithful must be attained even if millions die. Therefore, the term, correlation of forces, as used in this sense, may permeate the minds of America's enemies in their expressions of agonistic radicalism. Though this concept, centered upon fanatical resolve, is not vested in Western strategic thought, this is not the case elsewhere.

The Islamic Republic of Iran is apocalyptic in its composition and in its actions, as was Nazi Germany, though the fundamental beliefs of each of these fascistic states differ in almost every respect. Such regimes do not recognize any limits: The capacity for unrestrained actions is inherent to their very structure and existence. This is why Iran must never be allowed to possess nuclear weapons, much less those that could be mated with ballistic missiles.

Any rational strategic calculus may be jettisoned at any time by such a radical state. We must not, as a nation, project our ethical values or our perceptions of reality onto a theocratic state that has proven it does not share our basic precepts concerning liberty and the value of life. It is supremely dangerous to believe that some glib arms control agreement can restrain the Iranian regime from obtaining weapons of mass destruction.

As we pierce the underlying dogmas of such a repressive state, we must, by manifesting overwhelming military power, make it absolutely clear that Iran will never be permitted to exist as a state armed with nuclear weapons. This commitment must be an imperative for our country and our allies.

Tactical Nuclear Weapons and Boundaries

There are thresholds in geopolitics and in warfare that are immediately recognized. Other thresholds, though ultimately realized, are not acknowledged in real time. In such cases, only by the examination of changes that in hindsight appear supercritical, and thus representative of overwhelming transformation, may we comprehend that a significant threshold was crossed.

The progression from clandestine assaults or limited incursions to war may or may not be recognized when such acts occur. The first use of a weapon of mass destruction may immediately change the battlespace or be unseen or be denied and concealed to stem escalation.

The use of a tactical nuclear weapon may be seen as a limited employment of a drastic battlefield weapon, or it may signal an escalation toward an apocalyptic nuclear conflagration. Nuclear war must be deterred, but we cannot do so unless America and our allies possess the full range of weapons that can deter an adversary's use of a nuclear weapon at any potential stage of conflict.

Should we lack capability or will at a specific level of escalation, this will be exploited by an adversary either in an actual war or in the preliminary preparation of the battlespace. Putin's avowed willingness to use nuclear weapons in the context of the war in Ukraine constituted his ploy to bolster the perceived military capacity of Russia, which has proven insufficient in a conventional war. The equation of war was thus posed by Putin to be viewed through the prism of Russia's superiority in the number of tactical nuclear weapons it deploys; this stratagem was articulated to endeavor to deter the West's actions in support of Ukraine.

Tactical nuclear weapons may be considered battlefield armaments. In general, they possess lower yield and reduced range in comparison to strategic nuclear weapons. There is, however, no hard line that separates tactical nuclear weapons from strategic arms, in that their labels pertain to their use and characteristics, though arms control treaties have attempted to delineate acute differences in the two classes of weapons.[136]

A tactical nuclear weapon employed by a belligerent against a civilian population center would immediately be classified as a strategic attack, for the protection of a nation's citizenry is paramount in any democracy. A tactical nuclear weapon used to attack a key communication or energy node may present a grey area. Depending on the nature and the circumstances of the attack, it may be construed by the affected nation as either strategic or tactical in nature.

War games have documented that the use of any nuclear weapon could escalate quickly into a general nuclear war. A leader's statements, a nation's force structure, the choice of delivery system, the yield of the weapon, the target, and the context or stage of battle in which the strike occurs, all weigh upon the determination of the nature of the assault and the appropriate response. Given these complicating factors in assessing the quality of a nuclear attack, the range of tactical and strategic nuclear weapons our adversaries hold must be met with reciprocal and countervailing capabilities. This is necessary to support deterrence and to provide the means to respond in a limited way, without

---

[136]https://www.cnn.com/2022/09/26/europe/russia-ukraine-tactical-nuclear-weapons-explainer-intl-hnk-ml/index.html

increasing the scale of conflict. Every rung on the ladder of nuclear escalation increases the likelihood of a general nuclear exchange.

Of special concern are next-generation weapons, being developed by our adversaries, which could diminish the threshold for the tactical employment of nuclear weapons of reduced yield. A tactical nuclear exchange, at whatever level, would dramatically increase the potential for global nuclear war by escalation or miscalculation.

America must retain tactical nuclear weapons to deter this type of aggression. Advanced weapons must be pursued if they are necessary to overmatch potential belligerents, for an unrestrained war cannot be won.

Assault

Vladimir Putin sought global relevance and the reestablishment of a Russian empire through his war against Ukraine and his caustic energy policies, for Russia is by many measures a failed state in severe demographic decline. Putin abrogated the 1994 Budapest Memorandum in which Russia guaranteed Ukraine's territorial integrity in exchange for Kyiv's elimination of its nuclear arsenal. This deceit provided a steppingstone for Russia's strategy, which, in Ukraine, has sought victory at any cost.

Putin has endeavored to compensate for his nation's military failures, as demonstrated in the cities and steppes of Ukraine, with nuclear threats. The Kremlin realizes that an attack with conventional weapons against any North Atlantic Treaty Organization (NATO) state will result in the overwhelming defeat of Russia's forces. Moscow, however, believes, with some justification, that the West is hobbled by indecision. This is why Putin asserted Russia's nuclear might through deliberate threats. We must not succumb to Putin's or a successor's disingenuous ploys.

The Biden administration's fear of escalation is, in fact, inherently destabilizing for it demonstrates weakness, which the Kremlin uses to its advantage. Fear has set the stage for increased carnage in Ukraine, in a war that could have been won quickly by Kyiv, if President Biden provided weapons of decisive lethality in an expeditious manner.

The employment of a low-yield, tactical nuclear weapon by Moscow is possible. On June 2, 2020, Executive Order 355 was promulgated by Russia's president; it is titled: Basic Principles of State Policy of the Russian Federation on Nuclear Deterrence. This document is the Russian Federation's public description of its nuclear policies.[137]

The purpose of the Russian doctrine is the "protection of national sovereignty and territorial integrity of the State, and deterrence of a potential adversary from aggression against the Russian Federation and/or its allies."[138] The document further stipulates that, "The decision to use nuclear weapons is taken by the President of the Russian Federation."[139]

Most of Putin's executive order concerns the employment of nuclear weapons by the Russian state in response to a nuclear strike. There are, however, exceptions. The document states, "The Russian Federation reserves the right to use nuclear weapons in response to . . . aggression against the Russian Federation with the use of conventional weapons when the very existence of the state is in jeopardy."[140]

In the case of Ukraine and in the case of any independent nation that Russia's military threatens, the United States must warn the Kremlin that actions to liberate parts of Ukraine, held by Russia under the charade of false referendums, or areas in other nations, such as Transnistria in Moldova, do not constitute an attack on Russia, for Putin's claims of dominion are false. To provide teeth to this doctrine of nonrecognition, we must hold the People's Republic of China accountable economically and financially if Putin or a successor were to detonate a nuclear weapon, for China has facilitated the Kremlin's military onslaught against Ukraine. China has not condemned this assaultive war nor made it difficult by imposing sanctions upon Russia. Instead, it continues to purchase Russia's energy and minerals.

---

[137] https://www.globalsecurity.org/wmd/library/news/russia/2020/russia-200608-russia-mfa01.htm
[138] Ibid.
[139] Ibid.
[140] Ibid.

The United States' trade in goods with China amounted to more than 656 billion dollars in 2021.[141] The entirety of this trade and the Chinese and American equity and bond holdings that prop up the Chinese Communist Party should be openly placed at risk to persuade President Xi Jinping to constrain the Kremlin from ever acting on its nuclear threats.

If the Kremlin should employ a nuclear weapon, Taiwan would almost certainly be attacked by China, for the Chinese Communist Party would believe that America's attention would be focused on Europe, conveying enhanced freedom of action to China's military. Iran would be further animated to attack Israel with nuclear-armed missiles; if fission or thermonuclear weapons were not available, radiologic warheads could be used.

After Putin first threatened to use nuclear weapons in Ukraine, China should have been put on notice by the Biden administration. Our nation should have crafted and made the following policy absolutely clear to President Xi: If Moscow should detonate a nuclear weapon, America will devastate the Chinese economy through our cessation of trade and capital investments.

There is no public indication that the Biden administration adopted this obvious and prudent course. It is thus imperative that China understand that a Republican administration will hold it accountable for Russia's use of any nuclear weapon. Xi has pledged his allegiance to Russia; he must be made to answer for his actions should Russia cross the nuclear threshold. We must take every step necessary to avert escalation to the use of nuclear weapons in any regional conflict.

The tactical nuclear armaments that America now possesses are few in number, which is dangerous, for Russia, alone, holds ten times as many battlefield weapons.[142] With the withdrawal from our inventory of the Tomahawk Land Attack Missile—Nuclear (TLAM-N) between 2010 and 2013, our nation's tactical nuclear inventory consists

---

[141]https://www.newsweek.com/us-china-economies-stall-tensions-rise-over-pelosi-taiwan-visit-1730137

[142]https://www.reuters.com/world/what-is-russias-policy-tactical-nuclear-weapons-2022-10-17/

of bombs that are to be carried by fifth-generation F-35 strike fighters, which are replacing fourth-generation fighters in this role. These bombs would also be shared with certain NATO allies, in time of war, whose air fleets include specifically designated tactical aircraft, as prearranged by nuclear sharing agreements.[143]

The Biden administration released an unclassified version of its Nuclear Posture Review (NPR)[144] in October of 2022.[145] The new review is the fifth since this process was established in 1994. Since then, reviews were undertaken every eight years, to promote continuity. The Biden administration broke this established precedent by rejecting this time interval, for the Trump administration conducted a comprehensive NPR in 2018. That review charted a prudent course for updating America's Triad and improving America's tactical nuclear posture, to support deterrence, but stabilizing initiatives were cancelled or undermined by President Biden in order that disingenuous narratives be promulgated.

Several actions specified in the 2022 NPR are of enormous concern. In the field of tactical nuclear weapons, President Biden's cancellation of the Sea-Launched Cruise Missile (SLCM-N) not only threatens America's tactical nuclear deterrent, the termination of this vital program increases the chances that misinterpretation will occur during hostilities. The Biden administration, by terminating the SLCM-N, makes our nation overly dependent on low-yield W76-2 nuclear warheads, which will be carried by Trident D5 missiles aboard ballistic missile submarines.[146]

The launch of a Trident missile equipped with low-yield warheads of tactical value may not be differentiated by an adversary from our launch of an otherwise identical missile that carries multiple, high-yield, strategic reentry vehicles. This increases the chances

---

[143]https://www.nato.int/nato_static_fl2014/assets/pdf/2022/2/pdf/220204-factsheet-nuclear-sharing-arrange.pdf
[144]https://media.defense.gov/2022/Oct/27/2003103845/-1/-1/1/2022-NATIONAL-DEFENSE-STRATEGY-NPR-MDR.PDF#page=33
[145]https://fas.org/2022-npr/
[146]https://www.defensedaily.com/first-w76-2-finished-pantex-january-nnsa-says/nuclear-modernization/

of unintended nuclear escalation, for a single D-5 carrying a loadout of twelve W88 warheads, each with a 475-kiloton yield, would represent 400 times the explosive power of the same missile, if armed with two W76-2 warheads.

The firing of a single Trident missile that carries one or two low-yield reentry vehicles may expose the position of one of a small number of American ballistic missile submarines, thereby engendering another avenue for escalation by a belligerent force. Trident missiles carrying lower-yield warheads were intended to supplement the SLCM-N, which would be carried by attack submarines or surface ships; the W76-2, carried by the Trident, was not designed to replace the SLCM-N. The Trident, W76-2 system is most valuable in dissuading a country with few nuclear warheads and constrained anti-submarine warfare capabilities from escalating to the employment of nuclear weapons. The SLCM-N has broader applications over a range of scenarios involving all adversarial, nuclear states.

The SLCM-N upon launch would be recognizable as a tactical system, for the weapon's non-ballistic course, similar to that of an aircraft, would not be subject to misinterpretation during a crisis; the flight profile and speed of this cancelled cruise missile is completely unlike that of a sea-launched ballistic missile.[147] The SLCM-N program's termination therefore increases the chances of an initial nuclear exchange, involving several weapons, to become a global nuclear war that could claim hundreds of millions of lives.

By cancelling the SLCM-N, the Biden administration unilaterally renounced a system with global reach and flexibility in its staging, applications, and capabilities that was to have been obtained at a relatively low cost. By focusing on appearances and disingenuous narratives rather than facts, the Biden administration, through this action, has made nuclear escalation a more prominent threat.

The Biden White House and Pentagon must not eclipse a future administration's prerogatives in the domain of strategic offensive or defensive systems. America's Triad became operational in 1959,

---

[147] https://media.defense.gov/2018/Feb/02/2001872886/-1/-1/1/2018-NUCLEAR-POSTURE-REVIEW-FINAL-REPORT.PDF

though the Soviet Union demonstrated this multidimensional capability first.

Today, the nuclear forces of Russia, China, India, and the United States are all based upon the concept of a strategic Triad. By deploying forces on an array of platforms, by land, sea, and air, deterrence is supported because a disabling first strike is all but impossible if each arm of the Triad is structured to correspond to the threat.

Strategic deterrence reduced the chances of conventional wars becoming global conflagrations in the aftermath of World War II. The perilous stakes present in any nuclear exchange led to caution and forbearance in confliction zones or in regional wars in Europe, Asia, and the Middle East. The nuclear forces of the United States and the Soviet Union provided a backdrop of stability through the absolute certainty of retaliation in response to a first strike.

Nikita Khrushchev's removal of the USSR's nuclear-armed intermediate-range ballistic missiles (IRBM) from Cuba, during the 1962 crisis, occurred primarily because of the assurance by President Kennedy of overwhelming American escalation, should the missiles not be withdrawn. Post de-escalation, the United States removed its Jupiter IRBMs from their base near İzmir, Turkey, and from sites within Italy. The Cuban Missile Crisis was governed by America's strategic capabilities and our nation's resultant ability to deter, thereby providing space in which quiet negotiations yielded the peaceful resolution of this perilous episode. America's deterrent capacity, as exemplified by the structure of our nuclear forces, is central to our understanding of the totality of how President Kennedy and his advisors avoided global war—without compromising our nation's principles or forces.

In the case of the Cuban Missile Crisis, multifaceted deterrent forces on both sides, coupled with sound intelligence and warnings by the CIA's Directorate of Intelligence, which determined that the USSR was placing nuclear warheads in Cuba, allowed President Kennedy to act prudently and not precipitously. This combination of a spectrum of strategic forces and intelligence capabilities is the foundation for deterrence. This bedrock has been greatly enhanced by America's emphasis on defensive systems, employing advanced radars, anti-ballistic missiles (ABM), and Aegis cruisers and destroyers, which possess inherent anti-ballistic-missile capabilities.

Critical Actions and the People's Republic of China

The People's Republic of China is expanding its nuclear forces while engaging in unprecedented bellicosity. Over time, China may pose a greater threat in the nuclear domain than Russia, Iran, or the DPRK.

Chinese President Xi Jinping seeks global dominance in a world he plots to control through the Chinese Communist Party. The Chinese economy eclipses the Russian economy by one order of magnitude. China's gross domestic product is now second to our own.

With callous and unbridled ambition, Xi seeks to mold the existing world order into a system of global governance controlled by Communist China through its prophesied future supremacy in all forms of international power. China, therefore, represents the greatest threat that America has faced in the modern era, for no other nation that has contested the United States has possessed China's relative economic power or population.

China is tempting global catastrophe in its ill-administered gain-of-function experiments that could release another deadly pathogen, in its subjugation of freedoms in Hong Kong, in its threats against Taiwan, in its construction of militarized, artificial islands in the South China Sea, and in its tests of new classes of nuclear-capable weapons, including orbital hypersonic glide vehicles (HGV). Secretary of State Pompeo, in London, on January 30, 2020, termed the Chinese Communist Party, "the central threat of our times."

China's orbital hypersonic missiles, which can carry nuclear warheads, are a grave threat to world peace in that they have the potential to limit strategic warning. The diminution of strategic warning could escalate the risks of global nuclear war due to miscalculation. The enhancement of America's nuclear deterrent is thus essential, for our forces must continue to be resilient and be capable of coping with reductions in warning times that could arise from technological or doctrinal innovations.

China today represents an unmatched danger to the free world, for it is acting in a manner contrary to the most basic human objectives and expectations. In consideration of the pandemic that China induced and in recognition of Beijing's other bellicose actions, America's allies and many other states finally concede the threat that is posed; I believe they now embrace the assessment Vice Admiral John Poindexter, Robert McFarlane, and I made in our book, *America's #1 Adversary*, published in 2020 by Fidelis Publishing.

Harnessing the might of emergent technologies, new media, and coercive forms of manipulation and censorship, defined as sharp power, China manifests a belligerent form of historical and geopolitical revisionism, which it directs against America and other countries it seeks to dominate or usurp, including many of its neighbors in the Indo-Pacific region. To be stopped, China must be contested.

Post 9/11

In the aftermath of 9/11, a new articulation of American strategy might have checked our enemies more purposefully and perhaps more comprehensively than any single military action, if we had clearly stated that what such extremists hold most dear, their domains, redoubts, and means of support, would be devastated by us, in response to any future terrorist use of a weapon of mass destruction. A coherent strategy for the post-9/11 world was not developed. Our country and our brave servicemen and women have paid dearly for this abrogation of the core responsibility of national leadership.

This is an arena that must be navigated with precision and strength. President Reagan in his March 23, 1983, defense address, proclaimed a profound shift in American nuclear strategy with these words, "Wouldn't it be better to save lives than to avenge them?"

Defense is different than deterrence, though it should enhance it. Defense is to pose effective interdiction once confrontation is apparent; it is to oppose an attack.

Simplicity can be its own reward. A modern strategy for addressing the threats we now confront must be conceptually similar to Ronald Reagan's Strategic Defense Initiative and draw from the lessons it conveyed. It must also maintain the sufficiency of our Triad and apply technologically advanced answers to the array of new threats we face.

The Strategic Defense Initiative was named and championed by John Poindexter, then deputy assistant to the president for national security affairs. Admiral Poindexter received his PhD in nuclear physics after review of his thesis by two Nobel Laureates and the famed physicist Richard Feynman, who would be awarded his Nobel Prize the following year.

John Poindexter thus understood the technological requirements necessitated by the Strategic Defense Initiative to a degree that was all but unmatched by any senior government official or scientist. Crucially, he understood that the enunciation of the program by President Reagan would stress the Soviet military and scientific establishment to a point beyond their ability to cope.

The announcement of the Strategic Defense Initiative by President Reagan rendered the USSR's land-based and sea-based missile forces meritless to a substantial degree as internationally accepted and enduring measures of national power, for the vaunted military utility of these weapons would be diminished, and thus uncertain, as the United States deployed defensive systems. This drove the Soviet Union into a technological race that helped ensure its demise.

Are there strategic policies and choices that can be enunciated that would help neutralize the nuclear threats posed by Russia, China, or other potentially belligerent states? Certainly, a precisely articulated strategic doctrine is needed. Thus, proper doctrinal choices are compulsory and will be of immense benefit to world stability and peace, whereas choices made through the opaque lens of puerile narratives will invite disaster.

We must be concerned that if the weakness manifested in the Biden administration's catastrophic withdrawal from Afghanistan be repeated, our homeland's safety will be placed in grievous jeopardy. The often-proposed substitution of imagined arms control accords for nuclear capabilities is neither acceptable nor wise. Such pablum will be viewed by our adversaries as American fragility and thus as an inducement for their caustic adventurism.

Whereas the United States initially faced only one other adversarial nuclear state after the USSR's explosion of a nuclear device in 1949, made possible by its theft of American and British nuclear secrets,[148] the ensuing decades added great complexity to our strategic calculus. America and our allies now face two adversaries that control nuclear arsenals. Other belligerent states either possess limited numbers of nuclear weapons or are on the cusp of attaining such arms.

Though Russia's and America's present nuclear capacities are far greater than China's, Beijing is arming itself at an unparalleled pace, building hundreds of intercontinental ballistic missile (ICBM) emplacements. These are in addition to China's ballistic missile submarine (SSBN) force, which is being modernized, and China's development of a stealth bomber that is expected to be capable of carrying nuclear missiles. As with the Soviet Union before it, China's assertive march toward a multidimensional strategic and tactical force composed of nuclear weapons and precise delivery systems has been facilitated through espionage,[149] illicit transfers of technology, and the purchase of dual-use materials and systems, including those designed for use in space.[150]

Faced with an adversary that, for the first time, possesses wealth that in certain ways is almost equal to our own, America must innovate constructively if we are to preserve an implacable deterrent posture against China, Russia, Iran, and the DPRK. A Strategic Defense Initiative for our time, the SDI II, which should exemplify President Reagan's vision of defense in depth, is mandatory.

---

[148]https://www.britannica.com/biography/Klaus-Fuchs
[149]https://www.cbsnews.com/news/report-china-stole-nuke-secrets/
[150]https://www.washingtontimes.com/news/2023/jan/3/chinas-nuclear-forces-built-part-us-technology/

Strategic Clarity and Tactical Uncertainty

Our nation's senior officials should deem it crucial to articulate policies in the context of providing certainty in a world permeated with disinformation. There is no more important realm for the assertion of clear policy objectives than that involving the greatest power held on earth.

False narratives or unreal histories are often propelled by a malignant constellation comprised of foreign actors, demagogues, and an elitist media divorced from reality. Crucial information as well as subtleties may be lost, which is counterproductive in a world imbued with technologies that instigate actions before needed information is often assimilated. We must remember that war is frequently traced to a predicate of miscommunication or disguised malice.

Clarity of voice is the *sine qua non* of effective statecraft and principled leadership. It is essential to consequential arms control. Such strategic clarity should not be confused with realpolitik, which lacks a moral core.

We cannot, in our information age, speak imprecisely. A new paradigm is required: Dr. Miles Yu, former principal advisor on China policy to Secretary of State Michael Pompeo, has been at the forefront of this conceptualization that balances the employment of clarity with the need for tactical uncertainty.

Strategic clarity is the means to impart critical advantages through the clear articulation of national objectives with regard to potential adversaries or enemies. Strategic clarity helps to preclude conflicts and aids in deconfliction by clearly delineating stakes. Such a policy rests on the certitude of actions that uphold declarations.

Clear-sightedness permits insight that allows us to frame plausible goals and perspectives for the future. Moral clarity and strength are critical to operationalize these imperatives. The world is dynamic: Leaders must comprehend that communication derives from what is understood and often not what is said. Thus, diplomacy's objective is to ensure that what is grasped is what is conveyed, which is difficult.

Tactical uncertainty is the means to confound adversaries or enemies as to the tools and methods we will employ to enforce a national policy governed by strategic clarity. This conceptualization must be undergirded by our appreciation of the world as it exists, not by narratives driven by geopolitical convictions that are often static or blinding.

In the domain of nuclear weapons, our enunciation of policies must be clear. The corollary to this statement is that the projected outcome of a nuclear exchange must never grant potential adversaries the foreknowledge that their use of nuclear weapons will convey any subsequent advantage vis-à-vis America's arsenal.

Unilateral Disarmament

First-generation nuclear weapons employed fission, the splitting of atoms, to create explosive force. Second-generation weapons employ fission to trigger fusion, which is the power of the sun. New, third- and fourth-generation nuclear weapons could be more focused in their conveyance of energy and in their possible uses.

The Department of Energy (DOE) and the National Nuclear Security Administration (NNSA) are tasked with the design and the establishment of protection, safety, and effectiveness procedures for America's stockpile of nuclear explosives. Each year, a Stockpile Stewardship and Management Plan is issued.

Beginning with the first detonation, codenamed Trinity, in New Mexico, in the summer of 1945, America conducted over 1,000 actual tests of nuclear weapons. The last series of tests ended in 1992, in anticipation of the Comprehensive Nuclear-Test-Ban Treaty (CTBT), which has not been ratified by the Senate.

America's nuclear stockpile is thus assessed through the employment of highly complex mathematical models and simulations. America's safety hinges on the suitability of these activities that simulate the myriad of elements necessary for a nuclear bomb to detonate. America's national laboratories must be adequately resourced in this domain; the potential for controlled fusion experiments to document simulations may be of benefit in the future.[151] It will, however, take a substantial period of time to perfect such types of enhanced simulations. We must thus revisit our testing protocols.

It is time to undertake a comprehensive review of the adequacy of the present, simulated testing regime in light of new developments in fusion research, but I fear that the Biden administration or its successor may declare America's continued commitment to the un-ratified Comprehensive Test Ban Treaty, with no preconditions, despite indications of Russia's and China's noncompliance. This would potentially inhibit our ability to deploy next-generation nuclear weapons, which promise enhanced dependability without the requirement for recurring, underground testing.

Our nation cannot be defeated from without, but we can defeat ourselves from within, through the substitution of facile dreams for hard realities. In addition to its cancellation of the sea-launched SLCM-N program, which was designed to restore a capability America once possessed,[152] the Biden Administration's NPR strikes crucial nuclear capabilities and long-established postures.

The 2022 NPR specifies that America's only megaton-class weapon, the B83-1 gravity bomb, is to be removed from service, though for many scenarios, this modern weapon, which was first deployed in 1983, is vital to defeat deeply buried and hardened targets. The 2022 NPR further specifies that the "formal role of nuclear weapons" will no longer include service as a "hedge against an uncertain future."[153] This is code for the destruction of many or all of America's nuclear weapons that are not deployed but are kept as part of our nuclear stockpile, given that the Trump administration's NPR of 2018 stated, "Our hedging strategies must also help mitigate and

---

[151]https://www.energy.gov/articles/doe-national-laboratory-makes-history-achieving-fusion-ignition

[152]https://www.heritage.org/defense/commentary/the-nuclear-sea-launched-cruise-missile-worth-the-investment-deterrence

[153]https://media.defense.gov/2022/Oct/27/2003103845/-1/-1/1/2022-NATIONAL-DEFENSE-STRATEGY-NPR-MDR.PDF#page=33

overcome unexpected technical risks throughout the life cycle of U.S. nuclear capabilities, and must mitigate risk in the development, deployment, and operation of U.S. nuclear forces."[154]

At a time when Russia is rapacious and China appears intent on more than tripling the size of its nuclear arsenal by 2035,[155] the planned reduction of America's stockpile would constitute a supremely reckless act that will only embolden our adversaries and enemies.[156] Given these indicators, what additional steps might the leftists who now hold power in our government take to disarm America's strategic deterrent should President Biden be elected to a second term or be replaced by a like-minded successor? We must unfortunately contemplate craven acts that would be crushing and may have only been stayed in their adoption by the Biden administration due to Russia's war against Ukraine and the consequential evisceration of peace and order in Europe.

We should be concerned that comprehensive nuclear talks with China and Russia would be broached, in order that "unprecedented" reductions in nuclear systems be achieved. If negotiations were to commence, China's and Russia's gamesmanship may be expected to be placated by a Democratic administration and therefore inure to our adversaries' benefit. Thus, acquiescence by an irresolute administration could be used to inscribe a narrative that will falsely posit American strategic strength while inducing disarmament, for this is a leftist imperative.

Although seemingly wedded to the maintenance of our Triad, composed of ICBMs, ballistic missile submarines, and bombers, a Democratic president may delay the procurement of the Ground Based Strategic Deterrent (GBSD), which has recently been named the LGM-35 Sentinel. This system is to replace the Minuteman ICBM.

---

[154] https://media.defense.gov/2018/Feb/02/2001872886/-1/-1/1/2018-NUCLEAR-POSTURE-REVIEW-FINAL-REPORT.PDF
[155] https://news.yahoo.com/china-nuclear-arsenal-set-more-073246653.html?guccounter=1
[156] https://www.state.gov/wp-content/uploads/2021/10/Fact-Sheet_Unclass_2021_final-v2-002.pdf

The Sentinel should attain an initial operating capability (IOC) in 2029. Since our existing ICBM force is now fifty-years old, any delay in deployment would be catastrophic to the maintenance of our land-based deterrent. A Democratic administration could thus sidestep into a two-legged Dyad, which would consist of SSBNs and bombers, while Russia and China would each retain strategic Triads, now enhanced with HGVs.

A Democratic administration could announce a unilateral moratorium on the development of strategic, as opposed to tactical, antiballistic missile systems, and invite Russia and China to do the same, which they will never in practice do, for the boundary between strategic and tactical ABM systems is no longer clearly demarcated, due to technology and operational doctrines. To this point, a Democratic administration could hobble our bomber fleet by announcing that the new B-21 Raider bomber will be rendered incapable of carrying nuclear weapons and that the B-52 re-engining program will be cancelled. (In 2011, the Mach 1.2 B-1B bomber was modified to make it incapable of carrying nuclear weapons.)

Any of the foregoing actions is unacceptable. Any combination would be ruinous to deterrence.

No First Use

In contravention of all precedents since World War II, a future Democratic administration could declare a no-first-use policy with regard to nuclear weapons, which will undermine and degrade America's ability to respond to a range of fateful threats. A no-first-use doctrine would place America at a grave disadvantage in responding to a large chemical or biological attack, thus eviscerating our deterrent posture.

We need the ability to answer a strike that employs weapons of mass destruction (WMD) with the armaments we have, not ones that we do not possess and will never develop. This capacity is intrinsic to deterrence across a wide spectrum of potential threats.

America's strategy concerning weapons of mass destruction, nuclear forces, and arms control demands clarity of voice. Disorganization in the proclamation of policies, which affect ongoing force structure decisions, undermines deterrence, prolongs strife, and inhibits resolution by involved parties. There has, however, been a concerted attempt to obfuscate President Obama's and President Biden's policy objectives.

In his remarks on nuclear security made on January 12, 2017, Vice President Biden declared that retaliation in the wake of a "nuclear attack should be the sole purpose of the U.S. nuclear arsenal." In the same statement, Vice President Biden averred that once unstated future conditions were established, "the sole purpose of nuclear weapons would be to deter others from launching a nuclear attack." Thus, the term "sole purpose" is operationally equivalent to "no first use."

Vice President Biden also stated, "Given our non-nuclear capabilities and the nature of today's threats—it's hard to envision a plausible scenario in which the first use of nuclear weapons by the United States would be necessary. Or make sense."

Today, we must realize that such a hypothesis is not true. The present pandemic has killed more than two-and-a-half times as many Americans as World War II. If, in the future, such a level of carnage issues from a planned, non-nuclear attack, it is difficult to envisage how a conventional response would be sufficient to reestablish deterrence. The absurdity of Joseph Biden's dictum is so patent that his 2022 NPR rejected his idea: The review, which was commissioned by him, states:

> Consistent with prior reviews, our nuclear strategy accounts for existing and emerging non-nuclear threats with potential strategic effect for which nuclear weapons are necessary to deter. We concluded that nuclear weapons are required to deter not only nuclear attack, but also a narrow range of other high consequence, strategic-level attacks. This is a prudent approach given the current security environment and how it could further evolve.[57]

---

[57] https://media.defense.gov/2022/Oct/27/2003103845/-1/-1/1/2022-NATIONAL-DEFENSE-STRATEGY-NPR-MDR.PDF#page=33

Electromagnetic Pulse, Weapons Development, and Strategic Defense

It is the effectiveness and surety of America's nuclear response that secures deterrence against the array of WMDs that we face. These include nuclear, chemical, biological, or electromagnetic pulse (EMP) weapons of devastating or annihilative capabilities.

New nuclear weapons could employ intense EMP fields to surmount our military's current EMP hardening. Such a weapon would wreck electronic devices, civilian power transmission, and interrupt the provision of electricity to military bases within the United States that are served by commercial powerplants.

Factions within adversarial nuclear states may adhere to strategies that hold that a nuclear EMP attack is not necessarily the equivalent of nuclear war. Such conceptions are destabilizing but can only be operationalized if the United States does not pursue EMP offensive and defensive measures.

The 1.2 trillion-dollar infrastructure bill, signed into law in November of 2021 by President Biden, allocated millions of dollars for studies on how to protect critical infrastructure from the effects of an electromagnetic pulse, which could be induced by the explosion of a nuclear weapon or by other means. What the spending bill did not do, however, is initiate a multi-billion-dollar program to build national EMP preparedness, to harden our electric grid, which would protect our military assets, infrastructure, businesses, and citizens. This was not funded, though the requisite studies had, indeed, been completed by the EMP Commission, which was empowered by the National Defense Authorization Act for Fiscal Year 2006.[158] This commission released its report to Congress and to the White House in 2008.[159]

What are the potential consequences of such inaction in the face of this present danger? An EMP attack against the United

---

[158]https://irp.fas.org/congress/2008_hr/emp.pdf
[159]https://empactusa.org/app/uploads/2014/06/A2473-EMP_Commission-7MB.pdf

States could, in a period of months, result in more deaths than a limited nuclear strike against the homeland. These deaths would be due to the collapse of infrastructure, which would block food and medicine production and delivery and deny the necessity of electricity to millions.

The severe supply-chain problems of today would be amplified a thousandfold. The Biden administration's recalcitrance to address this threat, despite its spending trillions on matters of far less importance, is not the prioritization of preparedness measures but an abdication of the grave responsibility vested in our president to protect the American people.

It must also be noted that a massive solar flare, if on the scale of the Carrington Event of 1859, would devastate our electric grid if it is not hardened.[160] Such phenomena, on smaller scales, occurred in 1921 and in 1989, due to coronal mass ejections. A massive solar storm, of similar magnitude to the Carrington Event, missed our planet by just nine days in 2012.[161] Preparedness for the range of possible EMP events is no longer optional; it is mandatory.

Force Structure and Stability

The preservation of the strategic Triad through concerted programmatic actions to build a force of a minimum of 150 B-21 Raider bombers, at least twelve Columbia-class SSBNs, and 400 or more deployed Sentinel missiles, is imperative. Indeed, a force of 175 B-21 bombers may be necessary to replace the B-1s, B-2s, and B-52s that are planned to be retired from service. The Biden administration, however, has not committed to the number of B-21 bombers to be built.

Numerous governmental and industry assessments place the Biden Administration's procurement plan at 100 aircraft. This total is two-thirds of the minimum number of new bombers America must possess. If history be any guide, a second Democratic

---

[160] https://wisconsintechnologycouncil.com/history-a-perfect-solar-superstorm-the-1859-carrington-event/
[161] https://news.berkeley.edu/2014/03/18/fierce-solar-magnetic-storm-barely-missed-earth-in-2012/

administration would not increase this number but decrease it to less than 100. Such a course would put our nation at risk, though it will placate the Code Pink left.

The Sentinel force will replace 400 Minuteman III missiles and is scheduled to achieve its initial operational capability by the end of this decade. Full operational capability, however, is not expected until 2036, meaning that some Minuteman missiles will be more than sixty-years old before their replacement.

America's development and deployment of the Long-Range Standoff Cruise Missile (LRSO) is critical. Our B-52 force is scheduled to be operational through its ninth decade of continuous service. It is not a platform that can penetrate defended sites; therefore, a modern standoff weapon is required if the B-52 is to continue as a component in our Triad. The LRSO is also a hedge against a defensive breakthrough that could impair our stealth bombers from reaching their targets undetected.

Crucially, our maintenance of a capable bomber fleet exacts huge defensive expenditures from adversarial states. If not for our strategic bomber force, these defense expenditures would, in all likelihood, be redirected to offensive weapons. The fact that bombers are slow in comparison to missiles is an unmatched factor in crisis de-escalation, permitting precious time in which strategic forces may be recalled.

Our undersea strategic forces are at risk; immediate measures must be taken to secure the components for both America's Columbia-class and the United Kingdom's new Dreadnaught-class SSBNs. Each submarine will house Trident D-5 missiles, but each nation's warheads will be different and be designed in parallel by each country.

The American warhead is to be a new design, the W93; Britain is defining its blueprint, which may draw on the American design and share certain components. The new warheads of each nation will, however, share the American Mark 7 reentry-vehicle aero-shell casing.[162]

---

[162]https://www.heritage.org/defense/report/the-w93mk7-program-ensuring-the-future-us-nuclear-deterrence

Failure to secure these key programs will result in serious force structure gaps for both nations and presage a crisis similar to that wrought by America's unilateral cancellation of the Skybolt missile in 1962, which did substantial damage to our alliance. This is because Britain terminated both its Blue Steel II air-launched standoff missile and its TSR-2 nuclear-capable strike aircraft in expectation of American programs, which were subsequently cancelled without adequate explanation, in the case of Skybolt, or abandoned in the case of the F-111K strike fighter, due to programmatic issues.

America's alliance with the United Kingdom must be held as inviolable. It must not be subject to the caprice of an irresolute administration. Neither should our constellation of alliances be shortchanged.

Shared purpose with our NATO partners as well as our alliances with Japan, Australia, the Republic of Korea, and what should be an expanding relationship with India are essential in countering China's march. We must also make every effort to work with France, a founding member of NATO, as it modernizes its nuclear deterrent, for our military relationship with our oldest ally was harmed by the Biden administration's callous handling of the announcement of the Australia, United Kingdom, United States trilateral security pact (AUKUS). This announcement, which centered on nuclear submarine development for Australia, was made without appropriate diplomatic communications with France, a nation that maintains a significant territorial presence and citizenry in the Indo-Pacific.

Hypersonic Advances

China and Russia, separately or possibly in coordination, seek permanent geostrategic advantages by overmatching our military forces. Hypersonic weapons, which fly faster than five times the speed of sound, are extremely difficult to counter. America must stress the development of advanced defensive and offensive systems.

Hypersonic weapons may be conventional or nuclear; they include missiles, fractional orbital bombardment systems (FOBS), which traverse part of an orbit, and new weapons called hypersonic glide vehicles, which may have persistent orbital capacities. If armed with nuclear weapons, these vehicles could violate the Outer Space Treaty of 1967, to which China and Russia are signatories. Hypersonic weapons may also be armed with electromagnetic pulse devices to disable America's electric grid, causing massive casualties over time.

Key to the capabilities of hypersonic weapons is their ability to reach immense speeds and to maneuver within the earth's atmosphere. These attributes require an enhanced strategic defense if these weapons are to be countered. HGVs are destabilizing, for they can maneuver at speeds that make interception by current anti-ballistic missile systems highly uncertain; thus, to be deterred, they must be overmatched. We must, therefore, fast-track the design of new defensive and offensive technologies.

Chinese hypersonic glide vehicles can orbit the earth, posing for months or years as satellites, before being summoned to attack without warning. Russian HGVs, such as the Avangard, which can carry both nuclear and non-nuclear payloads, can be launched by the massive RS-28 ICBM as well as other missiles.[163]

The Avangard glide vehicle, which can reach speeds above Mach 20, was deployed in 2019, years before our analysts expected.[164] The United States has no known, comparable system within our force structure.

HGVs may contain kinetic or conventional warheads (this capability is in addition to their capacity to carry nuclear payloads). By dint of their unprecedented speed and their ability to evade and to maneuver, kinetic or conventionally armed HGVs could be able to attack American strategic assets in the future. The targets could include missile silos, bomber bases, or submarines in port.

Aircraft carriers or airbases are vulnerable today due to the deployment of intermediate-range HGVs, which are being produced by Russia and by China in significant numbers. China, which

---

[163]https://nationalinterest.org/blog/reboot/russia%E2%80%99s-silo-based-rs-28-sarmat-icbm-looks-killer-182293

[164]https://missiledefenseadvocacy.org/missile-threat-and-proliferation/todays-missile-threat/russia/avangard-hypersonic-glide-vehicle/

pretends to be a reliable trading partner, has recently built a life-sized depiction of a Ford-class carrier on rails, for use as a moving target in the desert it employs for weapons tests.

Development, therefore, of defensive systems, incorporating new technologies, is imperative. The time-urgent design and procurement of anti-HGV sensors and weapons is a necessity.

We should recall that a system of defense priorities was employed by Project Silverplate, in World War II, which enabled B-29 bombers to be rapidly redesigned in order to carry America's first atomic bombs. This system of defense priorities cut through a vast array of bureaucratic red tape, enabling war-winning weapons to be deployed.

It is critical that anti-HGV weapons be recipient of the same type of emphasis, so that bureaucratic indifference be quelled. It should also be recalled that Project Silverplate made use of bomb-carriage attachments from a version of Britain's Lancaster bomber.

To defeat HGVs, America should work closely with our most-trusted allies to glean if any of their technologies may be applicable in defeating this threat. Military leadership is required, but many of our nation's civilian officials, and some of our generals and admirals, appear more concerned with progressive politics and sociological constructs, which should have no presence in our armed forces.

A primary mission of our military should be the fielding of crucial weapons in a timely and cost-effective manner. Too often, however, managerial or programmatic incompetence is masked by feigned concern for social issues. This is not our military's mission.

Dual-use technology transfers from the United States, which have both civilian and military applications, permitted a determined China to leap forward in the design of this new class of hypersonic weapons. Stolen American software, machinery, and data are at the core of China's advance.

America's investors have—without their consent—funded HGV development and other Chinese military programs. Through a complex web of Chinese front companies, subsidiaries, and exchange-traded funds (ETF), American investment capital is financing the research, development, and procurement activities of banned Chinese companies, which are linked directly to China's military. This must end.

America must not degrade our means of defense. In this regard, we should recall that President Carter ordered that the Patriot surface-to-air missile (SAM) system have its anti-missile capability rescinded. This action was in addition to his cancellation of the B-1A bomber on the cusp of its planned production.

In removing the anti-missile capability from a system about to be deployed and in cancelling a new bomber, which had been in development since 1963, President Carter demonstrated weakness, which was not respected. The Soviet Union took no reciprocal actions, for President Carter sought deterrence through unilateral restraint.

Ronald Reagan restored the Patriot's capability against IRBMs. He also ordered that 100 B-1Bs be built, in addition to the B-2 stealth bomber. Ronald Reagan's earnestness and his ability to act on the basis of our adversary's capabilities and not our expectations, which are too frequently governed by errant presuppositions, must frame America's strategic choices in this century.

Convictions may subvert truth if they are immutable. Nevertheless, unsupported convictions and naïve expectations seem to frame everything the Biden administration plans or implements. This must not be so in the realm of nuclear weapons. The stakes are far too important.

It must be remembered that the Soviet Union pursued an antagonistic strategic posture through the 1970s and through the first half of the 1980s. This constituted a crucial substrate for that communist state's use of intimidation in other international domains.

The USSR's military focus was to preempt American strategic forces in order to degrade our retaliatory power. Complementary air, submarine, ICBM, and civil defense measures were pursued by the Kremlin to limit the destructiveness of America's residual strategic capability in the wake of a preemptive Soviet first strike. This destabilizing posture, however, contradicted the expectations of many U.S. planners and decision-makers, for throughout the late 1960s and 1970s their prevailing belief held that once the Soviet Union achieved strategic equivalence, it would limit its nuclear force programs. In fact, the USSR did the opposite and, in so doing, placed strategic stability in doubt.

In 1983, the President's Commission on Strategic Forces, formed by Ronald Reagan and chaired by General Brent Scowcroft, concluded, "If there were ever a case to be made that the Soviets would unilaterally stop their strategic deployments at a level short of the ability to seriously threaten our forces, that argument vanished with the deployment of their SS-18 and SS-19 ICBMs."[165]

Had it not been for Ronald Reagan's grit, clear-sightedness, and determination, the outcome of the Cold War would have been vastly different. Our watchwords must be capabilities and discernment, not rhetoric and disingenuous expectations, grounded in politics.

Indeed, of concern today is the potential deployment by Russia of unmanned, undersea weapons that could house nuclear warheads; these platforms may be able to traverse vast distances and are reported to be nuclear-powered.[166] Such a development is unacceptable and must result in a panoply of appropriate programmatic, diplomatic, and non-military responses.

The Strategic Defense Imperative

For strategic deterrence to maintain, the calculus concerning the outcome of any first strike must be uncertain for the aggressor. Strategic defense complicates this calculus enormously, for the actual capabilities of defensive systems are extremely difficult to ascertain or model with accuracy. This deficit in knowledge promotes stability, which secures peace.

Present and future programmatic elements designed to defeat strategic weapons must be fused and prioritized within a new Strategic Defense Initiative: the SDI II. Disjointed and disparate efforts

---

[165]https://www.nytimes.com/1983/04/12/us/excerpts-report-commission-strategic-forces-excerpts-recommendations-for-mx.html
[166]https://www.news.com.au/technology/pentagon-confirms-existence-of-russian-doomsday-weapon/news-story/16ef0f8642b1699f805f324489942345

must be replaced with unyielding timelines so that America will be defended.

SDI II must investigate the role that space could play in an enhanced defensive frontier. In addition to sensors, the United States has no choice but to explore the deployment of anti-missile systems in space. Advances in HGV technology pose a particular threat that may not be overcome by terrestrially based ABM systems.

A commitment to SDI II would benefit our posture in contesting Russia, China, Iran, and the DPRK. It is the contemplated range of defensive capabilities against a broad spectrum of threats that is most meritorious. Indeed, America's first national ABM system, the Safeguard Program, which became fully operational for a very short period in 1975 and 1976, was deployed principally to defend against a limited Chinese ICBM attack, for technology at that time did not permit the massive Soviet ICBM force to be challenged defensively.

Unfortunately, the Office of the Secretary of Defense (OSD), whose immense size is matched by the latency of its actual productive output, appears incapable of meeting this challenge. Therefore, true bureaucratic reform is a necessity. This will require empowering our nation's warfighters, thus upsetting the department's status quo, which, alarmingly, is now bound by politics.

Although the Chinese or Russian orbital HGVs do not presently threaten the survivability of America's Triad, their speed and their inherent ability to loiter in space are destabilizing, for their stealth, while in orbit, and their swiftness, once committed, could in the future delay, perhaps catastrophically, America's ability to determine the nature and the magnitude of an attack. No specialized defensive systems to counter HGVs have been publicly deployed by our nation. It is not certain that we will be able to defeat these hypersonic vehicles, at least in the near term.

Once an HGV is committed to attack, its heat signature, due to its immense speed, will be observable to a constellation of infrared satellites. One important program known as the Hypersonic and Ballistic Tracking Space Sensor (HBTSS) was initiated by the

Trump administration.[167] It is to be part of the Next-Generation Overhead Persistent Infrared Polar (NG-OPIR) program.[168]

Contracts for this multi-billion-dollar investment were awarded by the United States Space Force, after this service's creation during the Trump administration. The first satellites could be operational by 2025.

Of special concern are Chinese and Russian antisatellite (ASAT) weapon systems, which have not been matched or challenged for decades. On January 11, 2007, the People's Liberation Army of China (PLA) successfully tested an ASAT weapon by destroying a Chinese satellite with a kinetic kill vehicle (KKV) placed into orbit by a solid-fuel, multistage rocket.

On November 15, 2021, Russia tested an antisatellite weapon, which destroyed its target, creating over 1,500 shards in space. Both nations have conducted many other tests of ASAT systems or components. Advances in Chinese and Russian ASAT capabilities thus threaten to blind our assemblage of space-based sensors.

The creation of the United States Space Force by the Trump administration was a pivotal step in securing a reciprocal American ASAT ability. American ASAT programs were quiescent since our ASM-135 ASAT, which was to be carried by a fleet of modified F-15 fighters, was cancelled in 1988, due, in part, to congressionally man-dated restrictions that led to cost overruns and pauses in testing. The errors in the management of that ASAT program must not be repeated, for we must now contend with both Chinese and Russian threats to our space-based systems.

Crystallized by the Trump administration's concerns regarding the magnitude of the Chinese and the Russian ASAT threats, the United States has no option but to deploy ASAT systems expedi-tiously. Such systems, as part of our space force, are also necessary

---

[167]https://missiledefenseadvocacy.org/defense-systems/hypersonic-and-ballistic-tracking-space-sensor-hbtss/

[168]https://news.northropgrumman.com/news/releases/northrop-grumman-to-provide-next-generation-missile-warning-satellites-for-us-space-force

to guard against a breakout of Chinese or Russian space-based weapons that could, in future, be employed to attack terrestrial targets.

Thwarting a Chinese-Russian Bloc

The Sino-Soviet Alliance began on February 14, 1950; months later, the Korean War broke out. The Sino-Soviet alliance began to cleave in the mid-1950s over doctrinal differences. By 1959, relations were in a state of freefall, with the USSR's withdrawing its technical support for China's atomic bomb program, which, nonetheless, did succeed in exploding a nuclear device in 1964.

Although its understandings with China predated the propagation of the Russian-collusion hoax, Russia was propelled further into China's orbit by this fabrication. In November of 2021, Russia announced that a roadmap for future military ties with China had been approved by both nations. Xi and Putin subsequently trumpeted their pact before the Beijing Olympics of 2022. We, therefore, have no choice but to be concerned that a Sino-Russian alliance may mature if Putin or a like-minded successor retains power.

Russia's military technology, which is advanced in certain discrete areas, buttressed by China's ongoing theft of American intellectual property, threatens to equip the People's Liberation Army of China so that, within the next decade, it may credibly approach the military power of the United States. China's economy dwarfs that of its neighbor, but Russia offers energy and mineral resources that China does not possess; thus, Russia's association with China must be stopped.

The fact that the war in Ukraine has dramatically weakened Russia's conventional military power only makes its association with China more important to the Kremlin. China, for its part, covets Russia's resources and views its neighbor as a vassal state whose only future lies as part of a pan-Eurasian entity dominated by Beijing.

Though China has equipped itself with Russian weapons for many years, China and Russia do not yet constitute an actualized combine with shared hegemonic goals, though both nations have articulated a pathway toward this end. Beijing's incendiary ambitions must be restrained from metastasizing into a dynamism that would employ an overt force of arms against Taiwan or nations aligned with America, for such a course could escalate into war with the United States.

The formation of a Chinese-Russian military bloc in this decade would constitute a grave threat to the safety and security of the United States and our allies. China's wealth, population, and irredentism, if coupled with Russia's mineral and energy resources, defense laboratories and plants, intelligence assets, and knowledge, could form a colossus. This union must not transpire, for it could presage regional or, in time, global intimidation or domination by a Chinese-led axis, intent on enforcing its avaricious and assaultive form of communist authority and control.

After Putin

As Putin's era ends, we must broadcast that Beijing's and Moscow's interests are not convergent. Russia's people oppose communism and do not seek to live under any other nation's shadow. China, in contradistinction, has enshrined a neo-imperialist form of Marxism-Leninism to suit the prerogatives of its new emperor, Xi Jinping.

With these facts in mind, America and its allies must use the full spectrum of soft power to delimit and, in time, rupture Russia's relations with China. The world is at risk; we cannot continue the debilitating policy mistakes that began with President Obama's inadequate response to Russia's illegal occupation and annexation of Crimea in 2014.

We cannot permit a Democratic administration to greenlight the next assaultive war, perpetrated by America's adversaries, by demonstrating weakness of purpose and stupidity in planning as was manifested in the Biden administration's calamitous and deadly withdrawal from Afghanistan. We must contest aggression, not signal our incapacity to forestall it.

Of central concern is the status of Russia's nuclear weapons, whose total number almost certainly exceeds 5,000, though less than one-third of this tally is actually deployed. If any of these weapons fall into non-state or terrorist hands or are sold to demonstrably irrational countries such as Iran or Syria, it is Russia, itself, that may be the prime target.

Apocalyptic states, factions, or terrorist movements or cells would wish to limit the proliferation of weapons of mass destruction after they attain such arms. It is thus reasonable that Russia would be held at risk.

The maintenance of Russia's Triad is a massive burden to that country's economy that conveys no advantages. A path to normalcy, solvency, and deterrent capacity is available to Putin's successor. France once possessed a Triad and the United Kingdom held, at varying times, the elements of a Triad. (Though the United Kingdom did not deploy its indigenously developed Blue Streak land-based ballistic missile, America's Thor IRBM was based in the United Kingdom from 1958 until 1963. Missile launch required both British and American concurrence.)

The United Kingdom possessed its "V" bomber force that included the Vulcan bomber, but these planes were abandoned as a nuclear deterrent—in favor of ballistic missile submarines. The present Vanguard-class, which carries Trident missiles, is composed of four boats, with one always on station. It is due to be replaced by the Dreadnaught class, whose lead vessel is expected to be commissioned after 2030.

France's nuclear strike force included S2 medium-range ballistic missiles; later, short-range, mobile ballistic missiles were introduced. France's last ground-based ballistic missile, the Hadès, was dismantled in 1997. France presently relies on a fleet of four ballistic missile submarines, the Triomphant class, which will be replaced by the SNLE-3G submarine beginning in 2035 according to current plans.[169] In addition, France, unlike the United Kingdom, maintains a small inventory of air-launched nuclear missiles, which are of the ASMP type.[170]

---

[169] https://www.navalnews.com/naval-news/2021/11/new-submarines-compared-columbia-class-dreadnought-class-and-snle-3g/
[170] https://missilethreat.csis.org/missile/asmp/

The limited British or French nuclear forces are appropriate models for Russia's nuclear deterrent after Putin's demise. Instead of a sea-based force, it would make sense for Russia's arsenal to be centered around its ICBMs, since such missiles are the most modern and tested part of its present Triad.

Russia under Putin is a pariah. Decommissioning and destroying under international auspices the preponderance of its nuclear weapons should be mandated as a predicate to the cessation of economic sanctions, which must predate Russia's reincorporation into the community of nations after it removes its forces from Ukraine. By adopting the British or French model of nuclear deterrence, Russia can maintain a potent deterrent posture, reduce markedly the opportunities for the proliferation of its nuclear arms, and improve its dire economic position, in part through the reallocation of resources that are presently wasted on a force structure its economy cannot sustain.

Present-day Russia may ultimately splinter into a number of smaller states in the aftermath of Putin's reign. Therefore, the proposed reduction in nuclear arms will yield a more secure and manageable Russian nuclear force that will limit the opportunities for breakaway states, which were once part of Russia, to each be armed with nuclear weapons, thus reducing Moscow's future security and stability. Achievement of this proposed path is of exceptional importance and must be pursued assiduously by a new Russia that is aided by a community of watchful nations.

Bioweapons and Control Mechanisms

In the aftermath of the millions of deaths not caused by nuclear war but by SARS-CoV-2, the risks of a largescale chemical or biological attack are patent, for viruses, in the future, might be weaponized. A no-first-use nuclear doctrine, if embraced by the United States, would make massive chemical or biological attacks more likely, not less. America must eschew such callow posturing, while securing deterrence and meaningful arms control that covers new classes of weapons of mass destruction.

Diseases, in future, may be brought about by natural agents that are propelled by unsanitary and overcrowded conditions. Diseases may also be created and turned into weapons, perhaps unknowingly, for evil may issue from an attempt to do what is initially perceived to be valuable.

A person or group that believes they are incapable of doing harm, will do harm. Arrogance constitutes a severe danger.

The 2020 Nobel Prize for Chemistry was awarded to two scientists, Emmanuelle Charpentier and Jennifer Doudna, "for the development of a method for genome editing."[171] Scientists around the world are developing gene-editing tools that have the potential to benefit humanity significantly. The ability to edit DNA with molecular scissors holds the promise of yielding stunning medical therapies. Such tools, however, may also be made into instruments of cataclysmic harm.

Appropriate concern for the misapplication of such technologies is of the highest importance, for what can be used can be misused. Not only might deadly pathogens be created in the service of evil, but gene-editing tools have the potential to alter the nature of humankind, with unknown ramifications and costs.

In China, a biophysics researcher, in 2018, edited the genomes of two babies before they were born.[172] The researcher was imprisoned for his actions, whose stated purpose was to make the children resistant to HIV through the deletion of a gene.

What is portentous is that the deletion of this gene seems to confer enhanced memory and the potential for enhanced intelligence. Could this have been the hidden reason for this reputedly unsanctioned act?

If the Chinese Communist Party did, indeed, sponsor this research, despite its denials, their actions would harken back to those of Nazi Germany. We must not allow science and medicine to alter the fundamental nature of humankind, to create a world in which

---

[171]https://www.nobelprize.org/prizes/chemistry/2020/summary/
[172]https://sitn.hms.harvard.edu/flash/2018/chinas-genetically-edited-babies-really-happened/

some children are genetically engineered for dominance, while others struggle to exist.

Other uses of gene editing could entail or facilitate the design of weaponized viruses or, conceivably, prions,[173] which are aberrant forms of proteins that can cause neurodegenerative diseases that are fatal.[174] Once the province of science fiction, the reality of such threats is upon us.[175]

There are numerous scenarios that demand our resolve and the certitude of our application. For example, the acceptance and the internalization of extreme climate change propaganda could motivate a radicalized environmental group, which believes the earth to be in imminent danger, to seek a bioweapon to reduce world population, slaughtering potentially billions of persons. Alternatively, a religious millenarianism or a supremacist group could seek targeted but still annihilative objectives. We must confront these types of dangers using all our means of detection—in association with other countries.

The threats posed in this domain cannot be belittled; indeed, the potential now exists to create a new class of pathogens, which must never be tolerated. So-called ethnic bioweapons could be used to target the gene sequences of selected groups; it is imperative at this time to create ironclad barriers to the conception of such horrific weapons through the creation of new modalities in arms control and intelligence gathering and analysis.

Imbued with determination, the world must come together to ban any work that could yield such pathogens. As COVID proves, oversight is needed before the fact, not after. Comprehensive and intrusive laboratory inspection regimes, increased intelligence protocols, and

---

[173] https://pubmed.ncbi.nlm.nih.gov/35581386/#:~:text=In%20particular%2 C%20the%20use%20of%20CRISPR-Cas9-mediated%20gene%20editing, PrP%20leads%20to%20species-matched%20susceptibility%20to%20prion%20 infection.
[174] https://www.britannica.com/science/prion-infectious-agent
[175] https://www.theatlantic.com/magazine/archive/2023/01/anthropocene-anti-humanism-transhumanism-apocalypse-predictions/672230/

meaningful international coordination and agreements are obligatory to prevent such weapons from ever being produced.

We must not allow the militarization of a new stage in science to be used for eugenic or hegemonic objectives. We must not permit science to alter or to rescind the diversity of humankind, to create a world in which global dominance could be achieved with a ferocious, weaponized plague, whose totality could be held in a single laboratory dish.

We must grasp this threat to prevent its emergence. Although it is abhorrent to contemplate, we must imagine what a psychopath might do with an ethnic bioweapon that could devastate opposing armies and innocent populations, through its mechanism of attack on specified polygenic sequences that are unique to the targeted population. This unprecedented nightmare is what we must confront and eliminate.

The foregoing objectives are crucial, though not easily realized, for their articulation will face immediate foreign resistance that will be duplicitous in form and in motivation. It is incumbent upon us to be cautious in our expectations: Adversarial states may not meaningfully cooperate in our quest.

Being cognizant that both China and Russia have exploited media outlets throughout the world in order to wage massive disinformation campaigns, suggesting falsely, among other things, that COVID-19 was developed by the United States as a bioweapon, we must force cooperation through stern inducements, to include, if necessary, severe economic and scientific sanctions. As a nation, we cannot abide the creation of restrictions on our defensive abilities or research; indeed, such constraints must not result from our adversaries' self-serving platitudes that may mask unverifiable activities that are inherently dangerous.

The Chinese Communist Party's allowance of international travel from COVID's point of origin, while restricting internal mobility, caused prior global standards concerning the primacy of the individual, as well as elements of the scientific method, to be tarnished. Foreknowledge of the nature of the virus, which emanated from the city of Wuhan, permitted Communist China to expand as

Western economies receded during the initial, transformative stages of the pandemic.[176] The plague thereby enabled China to breach a solemn treaty obligation, in order to absorb Hong Kong, thwarting promised freedoms.

Rather than seek the truth, governments and institutions have, in large measure, refused to investigate meaningfully the origin of a pathogen that has racked the world. This servility is the result of economic pressure exercised by a totalitarian state that has, in the past, under Mao Zedong, killed tens of millions of its own citizens by collectivization and its arrogant disruption of the natural order.

It is beyond contention that the full effects from COVID on world health will not be known for years, for the prompt diagnoses of many different diseases were impossible during periods of lockdowns. Without time-sensitive diagnoses, other maladies festered, leading to needless illness and death; the cumulative cost of such delays could, indeed, become the greatest price exacted by this terrible virus.

Arms Control and Preparedness

To deter nuclear war, arms control agreements must be married to prudent force structure policies and initiatives. To serve the cause of peace, arms control agreements must be both equitable and verifiable. To be meaningful, they must lead to binding force structure reductions. Further, the reductions of specific systems must enhance and not perturb strategic stability, which is a function of deterrence.

The 1922 Washington Naval Treaty and the London Naval Treaties of 1930 and 1936 were not farsighted, verifiable, or comprehensive in their membership, for Japan and Italy were not parties to the final treaty. The Anglo-German Naval Agreement of 1935, which limited Germany's naval tonnage, was construed differently by both parties, for Nazi Germany errantly viewed the treaty as the beginning of an Anglo-German alliance.

---

[176]https://www.worldbank.org/en/country/china/overview

This misconstruction emboldened Hitler's aims: The treaty did not quash them. Together, these documents failed to prevent global war. Multiple parties to the treaties violated provisions and disguised their substantial preparations for conflict.

Imperial Japan, during this time, camouflaged the construction of the largest battleships ever built as well as an aircraft carrier built on an associated hull.[177] It did so by ordering that massive quantities of netting be directed to its shipyards and factories, to hide the building of these three gigantic vessels. Japan's militarists did not care that the country's fishermen went without new nets. Preparation for war was all that mattered. We must study this lesson.

America's treaties with the Soviet Union to limit nuclear weapons produced disappointing results. SALT I, which was ratified by the Senate and entered into force, and SALT II, which was signed but never ratified, were proven to be both difficult to verify and ineffective in limiting the Soviet Union from dramatically increasing its nuclear forces.[178]

Subsequent treaties with the USSR and Russia never included China. Substantial uncertainties persist as to Russia's degree of compliance with the treaties that came into force.[179]

In its assaultive war against Ukraine, Russia is openly committing war crimes in its air attacks against civilian infrastructure. Such an affront to international norms cannot be ignored, for it demonstrates Russian mendacity, which is incompatible with any reasonable arms control initiative involving nuclear weapons.

Russia's economic woes almost certainly eroded their arsenal of deliverable nuclear weapons far more than any treaty. If China pursues its present course in terms of its acquisition of nuclear weapons, America should take steps to ensure that we induce encumbrances in China's economy to undermine its plans.

---

[177]https://www.thoughtco.com/world-war-ii-battleship-yamato-2361234
[178]https://www.history.com/this-day-in-history/carter-and-brezhnev-sign-the-salt-ii-treaty
[179]https://www.armscontrol.org/factsheets/USRussiaNuclearAgreements

The New START Treaty with Russia had been extended by the Biden administration until 2026. According to President Biden's Department of State:

> President Biden pledged to keep the American people safe from nuclear threats by restoring U.S. leadership on arms control and non-proliferation. . . . The New START Treaty's verification regime enables us to monitor Russian compliance with the treaty and provides us with greater insight into Russia's nuclear posture, including through data exchanges and onsite inspections that allow U.S. inspectors to have eyes on Russian nuclear forces and facilities.[180]

In the aftermath of Russia's war against Ukraine, this extension must be seen as a tremendous misjudgment, for any treaty signed by Putin or his followers is worthless; further, the treaty imposed no limits on China, though the Pentagon believes China could more than triple its number of deliverable nuclear warheads to 1,500 by 2035.[181]

In addition, the New START treaty did not meaningfully address the destabilizing nature of HGVs. On February 21, 2023, Putin announced Russia's suspension of its putative adherence to the New START treaty, providing incontestable proof of President Biden's mistakes in judgement and perception.[182]

While Russian strategic nuclear forces have been constrained, to an unverifiable degree, by past arms control regimes, the nature of Putin's nuclear parlays has reversed any prior expectations of compliance. The difficulties in attaining meaningful and enduring arms control treaties were illustrated in 2019, for the United States was compelled to formally withdraw from the Intermediate-Range Nuclear Forces Treaty (INF), due to Russian non-compliance.

---

[180] https://www.state.gov/on-the-extension-of-the-new-start-treaty-with-the-russian-federation/

[181] https://media.defense.gov/2022/Nov/29/2003122279/-1/-1/1/2022-MILITARY-AND-SECURITY-DEVELOPMENTS-INVOLVING-THE-PEOPLES-REPUBLIC-OF-CHINA.PDF

[182] https://www.voanews.com/a/putin-says-russia-to-suspend-participation-in-start-nuclear-treaty-/6972142.html

Secretary of State Pompeo was central in making this determination, for he directed the government toward this decision.[183] He also sought that steps be taken to include China in three-party talks, while recognizing that multiparty negotiations are extraordinarily challenging, for if handled improperly they can instigate the formation of deleterious unions. China rejected this invitation, for Beijing is committed to building and enhancing its formidable nuclear capabilities.

During the past decade, China's expansion of both its strategic and intermediate-range nuclear forces placed the limits expressed in the bilateral treaties between the United States and Russia in sharp relief. Chinese nuclear forces represent a palpable threat in that their rapid expansion in capabilities is woven into conventional and regional strategies that seek to displace the United States as the pre-eminent power in the Indo-Pacific. America's position, once considered unalterable, is the foundation for peace in the Indo-Pacific and must be preserved.

China's nuclear forces provide a final component in its spectrum of power, which it wields to intimidate and to control. It was not wrong to have sought meaningful arms control agreements with Russia and China. It would be a mistake, however, not to realize that Russia's war against Ukraine and China's actions across a variety of fronts, including its total seizure of Hong Kong and its military provocations and threats against Taiwan, have changed, perhaps irretrievably, the merit of America's pursuing nuclear arms control agreements with either of these countries as presently constituted.

Our conception and paradigm for global arms control must reflect today's realities. Any acceptable arms control regime involving nuclear weapons must include China, for it to be meaningful, but such a comprehensive approach has been rendered impossible by China's conduct, as exemplified by Beijing's refusal to share essential data relating to the genesis and the first occurrences of COVID-19.

---

[183]https://www.nationalreview.com/corner/mike-pompeo-us-withdrawal-inf-treaty/

In the theater of arms control involving adversarial nuclear powers, we can no longer afford to "trust, but verify," a motif that derives from a Russian proverb that President Reagan employed to characterize his approach to arms control. Given Russia's and China's actions, we have no choice but to distrust first before verifying all facts indefatigably. Further, we must never again condone negotiations that devolve into a quest to reduce weapons if such limits might lead to instabilities due to reductions in either the diversity or the survivability of approved platforms.

Arms control must not be used as a tool to thwart our development of offensive or defensive weapons needed to match our adversaries' potentialities. We cannot permit conceivable belligerents to use a myriad of intelligence operations, centered on the manipulation of media across traditional and social platforms, to subvert America's intrinsic right to protect itself through deterrence coupled with defense.

A sagacious approach to stability should also consider India's position. World peace may hinge on India's not being overmatched by a rapacious China. Specific, regional deconfliction and confidence-building measures should be pursued with our encouragement.

We must always keep in mind that arms control can be dangerous if its objectives are not consonant with American and allied interests. As a nation, we must be thankful to the Trump administration for its courageous decision to terminate the Joint Comprehensive Plan of Action (JCPOA), which would have aided Iran in amassing the resources to build nuclear weapons as well as the means to deliver them.

The Biden administration removed sanctions, which the Trump administration imposed on Tehran, pursuant to President Biden's impulsive hope of restarting negotiations to limit what Iran will never willingly limit: its nuclear weapons program. The Biden administration must not resume or actualize this disastrous farrago of deception that would only vitalize a terrorist state through America's submission to Iran's false promises and outright lies.

Our nuclear force structure, defensive systems, intelligence, testing protocols, and arms control aims must serve the objectives of deterrence and stability. The world has not known global war since the first atomic bombs were used; this must give us hope, but this hope must rest on discernment followed by action and not the avoidance of difficult choices.

As we consider the steps we must take as a nation to secure peace and promote world stability, we must enshrine America's illustrious history. We must draw on our record of averting conflict through our substantiation of military preparedness across the spectrum of power. We must recognize that George Washington's admonition, "To be prepared for war is one of the most effective means of preserving peace," has never been surpassed in its profundity or in its application.

Chapter 10, Peace Through Strength, Precepts:

• Nuclear force structure, defensive systems, intelligence, and arms control must serve the objectives of deterrence and stability. The world has not known global war since the first atomic bombs were used. This reality offers hope, but we cannot be complacent, for our adversaries control enormous stores of weapons of mass destruction.

• The nuclear forces of Russia, China, India, and the United States are all based upon the concept of a strategic Triad. Though Russia's and America's present nuclear capacities are far greater than China's, Beijing is arming itself at an unparalleled pace, building hundreds of intercontinental ballistic missile (ICBM) emplacements.

• The progression from clandestine assaults to war may not be recognized when such acts occur. A tactical nuclear weapon used to attack key communication or energy nodes may present a grey area, for such attacks may be denied or be difficult to attribute, though war games document that the use of any nuclear weapon could escalate quickly into a general nuclear war. The inception and the escalation of nuclear weapon use must be prevented.

Issues and Problems:

• By cancelling the SLCM-N tactical nuclear weapon, the Biden administration unilaterally renounced a system with global reach and flexibility in its staging and capabilities that was to have been obtained at a relatively low cost.

• The weakness of the Biden administration has placed deterrence at risk. Putin abrogated the Budapest Memorandum in which Russia guaranteed Ukraine's territorial integrity in exchange for Kyiv's elimination of its nuclear arsenal. This deceit provided a steppingstone for Russia's strategy, which, in Ukraine, has sought victory at any cost.

• At a time when Russia is hostile and China appears intent on more than tripling the size of its nuclear arsenal by 2035, the planned reduction of America's stockpile of nuclear weapons constitutes an unacceptable act.

• Electromagnetic Pulse (EMP) weapons could destroy electronic devices, civilian power transmission, and interrupt the provision of electricity to military bases within the United States that are served by commercial powerplants. The 1.2 trillion-dollar infrastructure bill, signed into law in 2021, did not initiate a comprehensive program to build national EMP preparedness, even though an EMP attack against the United States would wreak devastation.

Duties and Actions:

• In Europe, our nation should be absolutely clear: If Moscow should detonate a nuclear weapon, America will devastate the Chinese economy through our cessation of trade and capital investments, for Xi has empowered Putin.

• America must rebuild its Triad by producing a force of at least 150 B-21 strategic bombers, twelve Columbia-class submarines (SSBN), and 400 or more deployed Sentinel ICBMs. New tactical nuclear systems must also be built.

• Chinese and Russian hypersonic glide vehicles (HGV) can orbit the earth, posing for months as satellites, before being ordered to attack without warning. Tactical HGVs already threaten our conventional forces. A new Strategic Defense Initiative (SDI II) for this century, which will investigate the role that space could play in an enhanced defensive frontier, must be deemed mandatory to secure our nation.

• We must understand new threats to prevent their emergence. In the aftermath of SARS-CoV-2, the risks of a large-escale biological attack are patent, for viruses may be weaponized. The world must come together to ban any work that could yield such pathogens. As COVID proves, oversight is needed before the fact, not after.

CHAPTER 11

ECONOMIC
SECURITY

The subject of economics touches everything. Economic security is essential to national security, for without economic strength, our sources of power will disappear. America's market economy is the means to enshrine the productive contributions of individuals through the uncompelled exchange of the goods produced. Markets are by their nature creative and alive.

America's cherished principles of liberty have allowed successive generations of citizens to enjoy economic mobility and prosperity that is unequaled. China's organized system of pillage and economic imperialism across the world threatens the American worker and thus our way of life. We cannot allow China to control critical materials, global infrastructure, and trade.

We must establish new sets of rules that will prize the American worker and farmer by opening markets globally, while opposing China's deceits. Change cannot come too soon. Indeed, it is critical in the field of international economic affairs.

Economic Security

Economic security is essential for national security, for without economic strength, our nation, in time, would wither and our sources of power would disappear. We must heed warnings of emergent disease, for these indications unfortunately exist concerning the primary basis for civilization, which involves economic relations between nations.

Economic life is a central concern of every state, for the subject of economics touches everything. Abundance and deprivation, resources and inputs, exchanges between parties, and processes wherein decisions are made, all constitute parts of this vast topic.

In his address at the Nixon Library, in Yorba Linda, California, delivered on July 23, 2020, Secretary Pompeo discussed the massive imbalances, built up over decades, in America's relations with China. During his tenure as secretary of state, Secretary Pompeo assembled new policies that precipitated innovative actions to support the Trump administration's doctrine of forthrightness, reciprocity, and justice focused on the citizenries of America and China. Secretary Pompeo, therefore, insisted that we must "engage and empower the Chinese people—a dynamic, freedom-loving people who are completely distinct from the Chinese Communist Party."[184]

---

[184]https://2017-2021.state.gov/communist-china-and-the-free-worlds-future-2/index.html

In transcribing these words, my mind harkens back to Ronald Reagan's great triumphs, which led to the downfall of the Soviet Union. I remember those days vividly, for I served the president as the youngest professional member of the National Security Council staff in our nation's history.

We live in the present, but we must study the past to create a better future. We must think of the world that greeted our fortieth president. Not only were interest rates, energy prices, and inflation metrics explosively high, our principal adversary was living off the largesse of Western democracies. Concurrently, the left speculated that Marxist socialism would prove to be superior to America's market economy. This litany should sound familiar, for these attributes describe the present day.

President Reagan led the free world with unshakable faith in human liberty, which propelled his unambiguous animus to a regime that was the enemy of freedom. President Reagan detested communism and its veneration of the collective at the expense of the individual. He understood its internal contradictions, its corruption, and its dearth of innovation. He comprehended that the command economy of a totalitarian police state could not stand unaided. Ronald Reagan's vision inspired action.

As a direct result of the work of Dr. Norman Bailey, Roger W. Robinson, Jr., and William Martin, my colleagues in the National Security Council's International Economic Affairs Directorate, the Reagan administration successfully derailed the colossal, twin-stranded, Trans-Siberian gas pipeline project. The Soviet Union intended to use this massive pipeline system to dominate the supply of natural gas to Europe. Had this project not been stopped by the Reagan White House, this insidious Soviet initiative would have radically increased Moscow's hard currency income at a crucial time.

If that gigantic project had been completed as conceived, total Soviet domination of West European gas supplies and the near doubling of the Kremlin's annual hard currency income would have been assured. Indeed, Russia's weaponization of natural gas today is emblematic of the use of energy as a tool for coercion.

Then, as now, many businesses cared more about profits than America's security. The Soviet Union's hard-currency financing gap had been funded by Western governments and commercial banks. A consortium of German banks helped finance this Soviet project; later, French banks and the Export-Import Bank of Japan would supply needed capital. These funds facilitated the systematic theft by Moscow of dual-use technologies that permitted its fielding of new weapon systems at a breakneck pace.

Our president, however, was prepared to withstand unprecedented rancor, in order to put in place an economic construct that emphasized American and allied security. Ronald Reagan faced vigorous dissent within his own cabinet as well as from his close friend, Prime Minister Margaret Thatcher. Western Europe would not comply willingly. American export, import, and technology transfer controls would have to be employed.

Beginning in late 1981, the Reagan administration imposed sanctions that prohibited American companies from exporting technologies and material to the Soviet Union that were needed to construct the pipeline. Sanctions were next expanded to enforce these restrictions upon American corporate subsidiaries located in Europe. Ultimately, it took the imposition of U.S. import controls to effect dramatic change; America would close its market to European companies that continued to supply the USSR with equipment based on American designs.

Faced with this ironclad resolve, Western Europe concluded agreements limiting its gas purchases from the USSR. Ronald Reagan's actions curtailed Soviet gas deliveries to Western Europe to no more than thirty percent of its total requirements and ended taxpayer-subsidized loans to the Soviet Union, precipitating an unprecedented realignment in bilateral and multilateral economic and financial relations with that communist state.

The core requirement to effect this shift was to establish a Western alternative to Soviet natural gas. The answer was the development of Troll, the enormous natural gas and oil field in the Norwegian sector of the North Sea. While technically difficult to exploit, this project achieved the objective of diversification in Europe's gas supplies.

At the Williamsburg Economic Summit of May 1983, this blueprint was embodied in one of the most consequential G7 communiqués in history.[185] A new security-driven trade and financial relationship with the USSR was codified. This became the mechanism for global economic recovery, which yielded twenty years of uninterrupted growth and the interruption of the terror posed by the Soviet Union.

President Reagan understood—as we must today—that unrestrained greed begets crime and subverts America's central security interests. Can we, in this century, duplicate what was done in the case of the Soviet gas pipeline?

The cessation of the Trans-Siberian pipeline was part of the most successful implementation of a strategy to achieve geopolitical objectives in modern history. This strategy constituted an operational plan that helped cause the Soviet Union to collapse. It remains unequaled in its scope, depth, success, and consequences for the world.

It was accomplished by the application of pressure on critical nodes that the USSR depended upon for its survival as an empire. The disruption of the gas pipeline to the West; the disruption of Soviet military operations in Afghanistan, which enflamed the public's discord within the USSR; the proclamation of the centrality of faith through America's work with the Holy See; the encouragement of liberative forces in the USSR's constellation of captive nations, including those in Eastern Europe; and the creation of the Strategic Defense Initiative, combined with Soviet economic ossification, foreshadowed a chain of events that ensured the USSR's demise. Pressures induced fault lines in the Soviet state, which could not be ameliorated by actions undertaken by the Kremlin.

Measures by the Soviet regime to free its society from insularity, destitution, and rampant corruption, precipitated a cascade of incriminating responses that hobbled its ruling class, marking the USSR

---

[185]https://www.reaganlibrary.gov/public/2020-09/wmsbrgst.pdf

as a pariah among nations. Internal forces were thus unleashed within the Soviet Union that could not be repressed or mitigated—due to their immensity.

Such a strategy must evolve from a comprehensive understanding of purposes, objectives, and means. In the case of the Soviet Union, an operational plan was enacted by America and its allies that achieved strategic objectives without the resort to war.

What was done to the Soviet economy by the resolute actions of the Reagan administration defines the essence of strategy, for strategy is the formulation of plans to influence the outcome of events. The genius was to achieve these aims through non-military actions, though both powers possessed massive nuclear arsenals.

The Cold War was waged by nine presidential administrations, but it was won by Ronald Reagan.[186] President Reagan understood that the individual must remain superior to the will of the collective. In our enforcement of economic security today and in our future relations with China, we must not forget the timeless lessons this giant taught the world.

Present Dangers

In his paper, "Economic Theory and Mathematics—An Appraisal," Paul A. Samuelson wrote, "Logic is no protection against false hypotheses; or against misinterpretation of reality; or against the formulation of irrelevant hypotheses." We must, therefore, consider the principles that form the spine of our nation's conduct internationally in economics and their impact on the national security of the United States.

International economics cannot be considered in isolation from other geostrategic forces. Therefore, foundational precepts will be discussed, rather than a recitation of numbers that may capture transient or impermanent vectors in our gross domestic product, inflation, oil prices, or stock market valuations. To be of service, it

---

[186]https://thehill.com/opinion/national-security/474669-how-ronald-reagan-won-the-cold-war/

is my intent to describe, in the context of our present moment, America's requirement to define a path forward for economic security, which is the integration of a nation's economy into the global fabric of risks, challenges, and opportunities.

What is remarkable today is that the essence of the market is not comprehended by the world's progressive elites. A market is the means to enshrine the economic contributions of all individuals through the free exchange of the goods they produce. It is by its nature volitional. It is vibrant, creative, and alive.

Governments, however, too often contort markets, eclipsing the freedoms of individuals to trade and to prosper. Markets have endured and brought wealth and dignity to the world since before language was transcribed, but to be free, they must be free of compulsion.

Adam Smith's foundational exposition, *An Inquiry into the Nature and Causes of the Wealth of Nations*, was published the same year as was America's Declaration of Independence.[187] Smith understood that enlightened self-interest, as distinct from selfishness, drove individual actions and promoted the general prosperity as conveyed across nations.

In *The Theory of Moral Sentiments*, published in 1759, Smith argued for an ethical heart and for sympathy for the predicaments of others.[188] These great forces do not contradict each other but serve to reinforce each dynamic.

Beginning in the early part of the last century, economics, as a discipline, became highly quantified. Though differential equations and statistics have been extensively applied to international economics, economists as varied as John Maynard Keynes, Ludwig von Mises, Friedrich von Hayek, and Paul A. Samuelson all cautioned against the rote application of mathematics to economics without a prior comprehension of human motivations. International

---

[187]https://books.google.com/books/about/An_Inquiry_Into_the_Nature_and_Causes_of.html?id=C5dNAAAAcAAJ
[188]https://openlibrary.org/books/OL13561668M/The_theory_of_moral_sentiments

economics must rest on an understanding of human conduct, for human conduct undergirds international affairs in every domain.

Nowhere is conduct in this regard more deleterious than that demonstrated by politicians who have turned their high offices into money-making enterprises for their families. Though beyond the compass of this chapter, this is a disgrace that must be rectified if effective policies are to be implemented.

The Trump administration, before the global pandemic induced by China, created the greatest economy America has ever known. Today, America's economy lies in the hazard.

The natural consequence of inflation is that the nation's citizenry lives for today rather than plans for tomorrow, for the future seems too menacing to contemplate, for unpayable debts are certain to come due. Stripped of our energy dominance, subdued by the Biden administration's disastrous withdrawal from Afghanistan and its imposition of woke dogmas into our military services, subjected to waves of undocumented immigrants coerced by transnational criminal organizations, shattered by inflation due to ludicrous and deeply irresponsible federal spending, and pummeled by lockdowns, looting, and lawlessness, America has been taken to the brink.

What is impermissible for the individual must not be acceptable when attempted by the state, for the Biden administration has coined misery into power. Our task is to convert what is now wasted into useful work; this will lower the federal budget deficit while improving output by stressing efficiencies. Change cannot come too soon. Indeed, it is critical in the field of international economic affairs.

Encounter

Economic security begins with our understanding of freedom. Once a state's power is absolute, it is absolute. Perhaps the most consequential crime of communism is that it cannot even live up to its philosophy of dialectical materialism, for communism allows no meaningful conversation.

The freedom fighter, the iconoclast, the dissident, and the heretic are excluded or, indeed, imprisoned or executed. But it is through divergent views, through their competition or their fusion that humanity progresses. Chinese communism is a falsehood; it has only progressed through theft: theft of a nation and the appropriation of technology and intellectual property from America and our allies.

No major, industrialized country, no international economic or financial institution, asserts that China possesses a market economy with limited governmental controls, for it does not. China's stupendous economic growth is not the result of communism; it is the result of a socialist model similar in form to that implemented by Germany in the 1930s.

This fusion of state control and private enterprise derives its assets from theft on an international scale and from the wholesale appropriation of wealth from China's industrious citizens—who yearn for freedom. Any lasting wealth that is created within China is the product of nonstate enterprises that are exploited by the parasitic rule of the Chinese Communist Party and its favored state-owned combines.

No one in China is free from the clutches of this vindictive state. Those who have achieved economic success are subject to the caprice and the malevolence of the Chinese Communist Party, whose corruption is manifest. In communist China, personal merit and ability mean nothing in comparison to party affiliation or family ties to senior party officials.

Indeed, Chinese billionaires have been forced to relinquish their holdings, lest they disappear into an oblivion not even dreamt of by George Orwell. One manifestation of this domination is the Chinese Communist Party's maintenance of extraordinarily strict currency controls, which all but prohibit the ability of Chinese citizens to transfer their hard-earned money to free countries. The state uses this and other stratagems to effect exploitation and extortion.

Markets operate as self-correcting systems. There is no self-correcting system when a government rules by diktat. If violence and theft become a nation's currency, free trade becomes impossible. In history, the usual progression from such a point has been degeneration followed by war. This price for indifference is a price we dare not pay. Without this understanding there can be no insight.

Looming as hammers to enforce submission are state-controlled digital currencies that will be able to track every individual transaction while collecting taxes without representation. This may be China's future but cannot be America's path. Our nation was conceived, in part, to thwart a king from plying theft; what our Founders could not accept, we must not permit.

Disasters propagate when leaders believe themselves to be infallible. The dreams of autocrats inevitably become nightmares. When hallucinations are promulgated by one authority, ruin, poverty, and death are assured.

It is from reflection on the past that we create the tools to map our future. No party, no government, no person is always correct. Omniscience and omnipotence are not of this world but are of another. When a government or party takes on the mantle of omniscience, one thing is certain, there will be needless death. Communist China has done this and has killed tens of millions of its own people as well as those of other nations, including American citizens and those of our allies.[189]

Mao Zedong witnessed a tiny sparrow that consumed seed in a field, thereby, he reasoned, decreasing the state's harvest. With all the might and the stupidity of a man who deemed himself to be a type of god, Mao then decreed that school children must bring dead sparrows to class and that millions of citizens would be mobilized to defeat an imagined threat, which, before Mao, was valued.

Over one billion birds were exterminated. In so doing, the balance of nature was destroyed, for without sparrows to consume insects and larvae, a cataclysm of starvation was created and unleashed on the Chinese people. Mao's Great Leap Forward killed perhaps forty-five million souls, due to forced collectivization, confiscation, misdirection of labor to iron and steel production, disastrous agricultural practices, inefficient food distribution by centralized authorities, and ecological havoc.[190] This, indeed, was a

---

[189]https://mises.org/library/death-camp-communist-china
[190]https://www.independent.co.uk/arts-entertainment/books/news/maos-great-leap-forward-killed-45-million-in-four-years-2081630.html

great leap, but into the abyss, into a hell in which substantial numbers of villagers turned to cannibalism, for there was no food.

Mao's crime against nature, in the form of the slaughter of sparrows, was only arrested when the great ornithologist Tso-hsin Cheng demonstrated that such forced annihilation created plagues of locusts and other insects.[191] His prize for saving his country came later during Mao's Cultural Revolution.

Stripped of what possessions he had, imprisoned in an animal shed, and forced to perform the most menial labor, this great scientist was taught that in a communist society to be right is to be wrong, for the party is the arbiter of all things and can thus amend history in a moment, eviscerating all human progress, in order to stay its own day of extinction. Today, another reaper has spanned not just China, but the entire globe. The Wuhan virus is demonstrative of Communist China's lack of care and its profligate war against basic human rights.

Chinese civilization existed for four millennia before it was shattered when revolutionary forces introduced an alien philosophy, unsupported by any existent or traditional mode of thought. The formation of the Chinese communist state in 1949 did not mark the culmination of China's progress but signified an epochal fall.

Knowing what is right and doing what is wrong destroys the soul and renders the purveyors of falsehoods incapable of moral action. Where do we see this? This rot is, in fact, everywhere. Today, we confront a rancid goliath, the People's Republic of China.

The citizens of China deserve better than rule by a communist junta that constitutes this century's evil empire. We must challenge President Xi that he yield to China's cries for freedom. We must challenge that he yield to the people's pleas for religious liberty.

The pandemic that began in China and Russia's invasion of its neighbor have shattered the prism through which the United States must see the world; this change is irradiant as it concerns our global economic relations. We have no option but to face new geostrategic realities that cannot be shirked, lest we face intractable conditions

---

[191]https://generalist.academy/2020/11/21/sparrow-smashing/

in the years to come. Therefore, we must comprehend that American weakness in the face of aggression will only beget further assaults against our country, our allies, and our friends.

The entire world is blistered by the war in Ukraine. Substantial portions of that country lie in ruin, the world economy is fractured, and supplies of cereals, fertilizers, and key industrial inputs such as neon have been markedly reduced. Russia has attempted to destroy Ukraine as an independent country and as a people to mask the Kremlin's criminal regime, which has betrayed a nation, so that a selfish elite might steal from everyone else.

This is a global disaster that could have been averted if America and our allies had acted in 2008, when Vladimir Putin invaded Georgia, or in 2014, when he invaded Ukraine. We dare not repeat the same mistakes with China, for it, unlike Russia, is a near-peer competitor to the United States. We, therefore, must rigorously challenge China where we must, while seeking opportunities to work with it where we can.

Failures within Russia have motivated the Kremlin's unrealized geopolitical objectives, which include seizing control of the immense energy resources in the Donbas, confronting NATO by creating a border that stretches from the Baltic Sea to the Carpathian Mountains, and disordering Western economies. Russia, however, is not the People's Republic of China. The challenge China poses is far greater, for it contests our nation in geostrategic reach, in economic power, and in technological advancement.

Moscow's objectives in Ukraine are mirrored by Beijing in the Indo-Pacific. They hinge on the perception that America and its allies are dominated by political discord. Our past inaction in the face of Russia's assaultive acts, combined with Western energy dependencies, created a tinderbox that exploded on February 24, 2022, when Russia began its hideous war against its neighbor.

This series of mistakes, which failed to repulse a revanchist state, must never be replicated. China strives to make the West reliant on resources, on products, and on supply chains that it controls. Through this strategy, and its economic and military might,

China seeks to seize territories to create an empire of unmatched power. This augurs for America's decline if China's plans are not aggressively countered.[192]

China has sickened the world through its treachery in hiding the origin of SARS-CoV-2, thereby permitting its worldwide transference. Its actions in Central Asia, in Xinjiang, in the South China Sea, and on its contested borders with India were prologue to what it has done to Hong Kong and what it seeks to do to Taiwan. China must not be permitted to supplant the United States as the world's preeminent power, for if it does, freedom will be in jeopardy everywhere.

Course

The Trump administration began the arduous task of reforming our intelligence community to focus on the time-urgent acquisition of information relating to Beijing's use of hard, soft, and sharp power; this enormous task was incomplete at the time of President Biden's assumption of office. Today, much of our intelligence community is focused inward, surveilling Americans. Our intelligence and counterintelligence abilities are a shambles and must be reconstituted with great urgency. In the wake of China's recent actions, we must increase our surveillance and proliferate the results of our inquiries throughout our government, our businesses, and our institutions.

Hard power essentially uses force and coercive tools, which may be economic, to obtain policy objectives. Soft power, in contradistinction, involves cooption in the pursuit of shared ends. This had been a sphere of uncontested American supremacy, but such supremacy has now evaporated. China has penetrated Wall Street, our universities, our businesses, and our media, to devastating effect.

As can be seen in the NBA's obsequiousness, Hollywood's obedience, and hedge funds' deference, the Communist Party of China has not only thwarted American soft power, it now exercises a degree

[192]https://www.uscc.gov/sites/default/files/2021-04/Miles_Yu_Testimony.pdf

of control over our institutions through sharp power, which is the imposition of "or else" tactics and stratagems. This form of intimidation lies between hard and soft power, and China is its master.

It is astounding that President Biden still doubts Beijing's earnestness concerning its stated aim to displace the United States as the world's dominant power. Such indolent myopia is contradicted by China's rampage against the international economic order. It is as if President Biden's opinions and actions are formed in deference to some other force that compels his submission to elements of that communist state.

At the height of the global pandemic it created, the Chinese Communist Party did not moderate its detestable objectives; it accelerated them. With utter disregard of its commitments to the United Kingdom and to the people of Hong Kong, China broke the Sino-British Joint Declaration.[193]

This declaration constituted a treaty, granting Hong Kong a high degree of autonomy; China was obligated to maintain Hong Kong's market economy and its freedoms until 2047. It did not. Given China's actions in matters concerning world health, biosafety, and Hong Kong, we must ask: On what important document is China's signature meaningful?

As a nation, and on a bipartisan basis that persists over multiple administrations, we must compile the policy tools, laws, regulations, and customs that can be employed to block China's usurpation of our institutions. Our intelligence community must be continuously tasked to investigate the illicit practices that China utilizes. American companies or institutions that submit to Beijing's direction must be sanctioned and be excluded from participation in any governmental contract, grant, or activity.

Our government and our institutions must work together to ensure that America's economy is not subject to China's control of key sectors or bodies. This requires that all important elements of our nation's relationship with this belligerent state be under constant examination.

---

[193]https://www.state.gov/joint-statement-on-hong-kong/

The total banning of TikTok across the United States is essential, for it is an insidious video hosting service designed by the Chinese Communist Party to indoctrinate and stagger America's children as it serves as a vehicle for intelligence collection. All similar services or apps controlled by adversarial states must be barred. This overarching threat must be vitiated within the United States. Initial examples of forceful action to meet this threat were set by a host of Republican governors, who banned TikTok for all state governmental agencies, employees, and contractors. Other states and the federal government are following this lead.

America should, however, not decouple itself entirely from China's economy, for this would be extremely costly given its size and the myriad of relationships between Chinese and American businesses. Active and resolute reciprocity in our relations with China should be our standard. This principle may be defined as awareness, comprehension, and action.

Countervailing acts are only possible if all Americans are vested with awareness, which is the result of scrutiny. Relations with China, of whatever nature, must not be allowed to place us in a dependent status. Neither should we purpose to divorce ourselves utterly from China, for to do so would limit what suasion and leverage we have in facilitating needed change.

Resource War

China is intent on dominating global infrastructure through its Belt and Road Initiative.[194] Although presented as a means of interconnecting nations across borders, thereby facilitating commerce, the Belt and Road Initiative is something else. China's Belt and Road Initiative is a new form of imperialism.

It is a corrupt attempt to entrap developing countries with loans, which may use national assets as collateral. Countries such as Sri Lanka are paying a terrible price, for these loans are designed to

---

[194]https://hir.harvard.edu/what-does-the-belt-and-road-initiative-mean-for-the-future-of-the-international-integration-system/

ensure noncompliance,[195] leading to the forfeiture of national assets such as ports or mineral wealth.

Beijing also intends to dominate the supplies of strategically critical materials needed for the production of renewable energy and other emergent technologies.[196] According to the United States Geological Survey, we are dependent on imports of such materials as cobalt, manganese, and indium.[197] All are vital in the production of products that will define this century.

Also critical is the production of rare-earth metals, including erbium, neodymium, samarium, and many others. China dominates in the supply of these metals. Further, the secure mining of other critical elements, such as lithium, in the United States or in allied countries, is hampered by environmental restrictions, which are alien to China. Thus, all these elements are subject to Beijing's plan to wage a resource war against American interests.

Beneath the South China Sea is a great store of energy and minerals: Therefore, China's creation of militarized islands in the South China Sea must be contested. President Xi must not be allowed to steal these resources, which properly belong to the nations that brace this sea.

Energy use is directly correlated with income and wealth. Fossil fuels are essential to human development and to the production of a vast array of goods.

China's intent to claim the South China Sea will permit Beijing's exploitation of the immense energy and mineral wealth of this area. We must work with affected nations to lacerate China's hegemonic objectives. The resource war, which Xi seeks, cannot be won by the United States and our allies if we do not recognize Beijing's goals.

---

[195]https://www.msn.com/en-in/news/world/chinas-bri-trapped-sri-lanka-in-debt-chaos/ar-AAW55A6

[196]https://www.voanews.com/a/east-asia-pacific_voa-news-china_studies-reveal-chinas-dominant-position-high-tech-minerals/6206341.html

[197]https://cei.org/blog/u-s-geological-survey-study-underscores-extent-of-import-dependence-for-critical-minerals/

Breakout

Beijing's ambition is to destroy what it views as its geostrategic obstructions. As Ukraine is to Moscow, Taiwan is to Beijing, whose trajectory of conquest centers on the subjugation of that state. The conquest of Taiwan would remove the key strategic chokepoint to a Chinese military breakout, which would threaten the entirety of the Indo-Pacific, including Guam, Hawaii, Japan, and Australia.

Taiwan is the principal supplier of advanced semiconductors to the U.S. economy. If these supplies be interrupted by war or by conquest, America's economy will falter, which will make the United States more dependent on China. Expanded production of semiconductors in America is crucial in providing a safety net for our economy and the world, should China attack Taiwan. The manufacture of semiconductors in the United States also forms a deterrent that will abrade Xi's broader aims of economic dominance.[198]

China's international economic enterprise, which seeks to control resources and supply chains globally, is thus part of a larger strategy that centers on the invasion of Taiwan. Change must come: In his March 2022 trip to Taipei, in the presence of Taiwan's president, former Secretary of State Pompeo declared that America should immediately recognize Taiwan as a "free and sovereign country."[199] This action will support global stability if it coincides with the provision of arms that can overmatch any invading force. Failure, however, to match deeds to words will undercut deterrence and may precipitate armed conflict.

The West must not replicate its errors in failing to arm Ukraine resolutely before Russia's invasion. If through indifference or ineptitude our government allows the People's Republic of China to invade Taiwan, such malfeasance could constitute nearly as great a strategic miscalculation as the appeasement that precipitated World War II.

---

[198]https://www.wsj.com/articles/investing-silicon-semiconductors-chips-taiwan-invasion-tsmc-china-intel-blackrock-asset-manager-11665408814
[199]https://thehill.com/homenews/administration/596851-pompeo-calls-for-us-to-recognize-taiwan-as-free-and-sovereign-country/

During the Clinton administration, China threatened Taiwan, launching ballistic missiles that impacted near that state's two largest ports. This action, in 1996, advertised an overt threat of invasion before Taiwan's first free and direct election of its president. Comprehending the magnitude of the menace, wrought by China, which contested Taiwan's epochal transition to being a vibrant democracy, President Clinton, to his great credit, dispatched not one, but two carrier battle groups to express America's resolve.[200] American naval power deescalated this crisis, for strength secures peace.

Why should America defend Taiwan? Part of the answer is that every president since Truman believed that Taiwan's existence is crucial to America's defense. The 1979 Taiwan Relations Act requires that we maintain Taiwan's defensive abilities to thwart an attack from the mainland.[201]

Presidents from both parties have acted forcefully in demonstrating American resolve. All understood what was at risk.

Today, the capture of Taiwan would severely reduce American prestige and influence in the Indo-Pacific region. America's status as a superpower and as a dependable partner would be placed in the gravest jeopardy, which would invite armed conflict that would impact our nation. Chinese occupation of Taiwan would also eliminate a primary technological and economic partner of the United States. Such compounding losses would devastate America's economy and destroy the livelihoods of millions across our nation.

Markets

Restraint is often admirable; indecision buttressed by incompetence is not. To effect economic security, we are obligated to act decisively: China's ruptures to the international economic order must be curtailed; China's subversion of capital markets and businesses must be stopped; cybercrime and intellectual property theft must be stemmed;

---

[200]https://www.washingtonpost.com/archive/politics/1996/03/11/second-group-of-us-ships-sent-to-taiwan/34280337-be79-4d6e-b859-8046682a37b3/
[201]https://china.usc.edu/taiwan-relations-act-1979

genocide, slavery, and human trafficking must be eliminated; trade alliances and imbalances must be addressed; and crucial history must be remembered.

We must not allow the communist model for development to proliferate, for it is a kleptocracy. It is rule by thieves as is demonstrated by the magnitude of China's theft of intellectual property. It is a system that ensures that there can be no true freedom of thought.

The Chinese Communist Party operates a titanic system of state-owned and state-supported conglomerates; these, in turn, control crucial economic, material resource, and telecommunications sectors all over the world. Well-funded state conglomerates, such as Huawei and ZTE, can thus underbid global competitors to gain significant control over key arteries of the global economy, including infrastructure and trade. This must end.

Chinese state companies, which are governed and directed by the party, do not work for shareholders; they do not benefit the Chinese people. They serve but one master, a communist dictatorship whose vision for world domination derives its purpose from its own particular conception of Marxism-Leninism.

America should not be required to pay for its own extermination. Capital from American investors fund Chinese companies traded on U.S. exchanges. In its 2021 Report to Congress, the U.S.-China Economic and Security Review Commission cited the massive exposure of American investors to Chinese equity and debt securities.[202] American holdings of Chinese equities have, for periods of time, exceeded one trillion dollars; debt holdings amount to many billions more. Precise calculations and verifiable valuations have been made difficult to ascertain, for China uses complicated legal structures and tax havens to mask its activities involving U.S. exchanges.

Today, there are thousands of Chinese companies in the investment portfolios of scores of millions of Americans.[203] The true level of American financial exposure to Chinese state-controlled companies is not fully known, due, in part, to failures in oversight by the Securities and Exchange Commission (SEC) and the Treasury Department.

American investors are not only at risk, they are almost universally uninformed that their pensions and stock portfolios are riddled with holdings in Chinese companies that may be sanctioned or may directly serve China's war machine. That the Chinese Communist Party does not care about American retail investors is obvious; that Wall Street feels the same way is at times all too clear.

This infusion of wealth into China has allowed its regime to eviscerate human rights with impunity, for it believes itself invulnerable due to its intertwining with Wall Street, American industries, and Hollywood. In response, financial, energy, technology, currency, cyber, and data security must become our watchwords, if our investors and institutions are to be free of Beijing's yoke.

According to the U.S.-China Economic and Security Review Commission (USCC):

> As of September 30, 2022, there were 262 Chinese companies listed on these U.S. exchanges with a total market capitalization of $775 billion. This marks a more than half-trillion-dollar drop in the market capitalization of U.S.-listed Chinese firms from June 30, 2022, owing primarily to several major national-level state-owned enterprises (SOEs) delisting in August 2022. Two SOEs remain listed on major U.S. exchanges.[204]

These firms, before the delisting of certain state-owned enterprises, were capitalized at more than 1.3 trillion dollars just months earlier,[205] but this figure was reduced, in part due to President Xi's mishandling of China's economy and the Chinese Communist Party's need for the concealment of its true tools and objectives. According to the USCC: "Five Chinese SOEs announced they would voluntarily delist from the NYSE on August 12, 2022." The commission further noted that,

---

[204]https://www.uscc.gov/research/chinese-companies-listed-major-us-stock-exchanges

[205]https://www.forbes.com/sites/earlcarr/2022/09/01/the-future-of-chinese-companies-listing-in-the-us/?sh=4f539712fd69

"China's Ministry of Finance likely compelled these SOEs to delist to shield information deemed sensitive by the CCP from U.S. regulators ahead of the framework agreement on audit inspections."[206]

Investing in China and in Chinese companies does not serve American investors, for any transitory transparency is manufactured. With the resolute support of the Trump administration, the U.S. Senate, on May 20, 2020, without objection, approved the bipartisan Holding Foreign Companies Accountable Act (HFCAA); the House of Representatives concurred. On December 18, 2020, President Trump signed into law the HFCAA, which amended the Sarbanes-Oxley Act of 2002.[207]

According to the summary of the legislation, written by the Congressional Research Service:

> This bill requires certain issuers of securities to establish that they are not owned or controlled by a foreign government. Specifically, an issuer must make this certification if the Public Company Accounting Oversight Board [PCAOB] is unable to audit specified reports because the issuer has retained a foreign public accounting firm not subject to inspection by the board. Furthermore, if the board is unable to inspect the issuer's public accounting firm for three consecutive years, the issuer's securities are banned from trade on a national exchange or through other methods.

Chinese corporations, which are covered by this law, will be required to use public accounting firms subject to inspection by the PCAOB. This is a noteworthy achievement in protecting both American investors and the nation's security.

As a subsequent measure, the United States, through our Department of State, working in conjunction with other U.S. agencies, must urge America's allies to adopt similar laws or rules. Nations with important capital markets should, of course, be our first priority.

As we close one door, Communist China, abetted by avaricious globalists, breaks through another. The HFCAA does not penetrate

---

[206]https://www.uscc.gov/sites/default/files/2022-09/Chinese_Companies_Listed_on_US_Stock_Exchanges.pdf
[207]https://www.sec.gov/hfcaa

or capture index funds that may include great numbers of Chinese firms. The world's largest asset managers are pouring hundreds of billions of dollars of investment capital into Chinese corporations controlled by that nation's communist party.

China's hope is that global finance will prove too complicated for retail investors to understand, and that its country's true intentions will remain hidden. These assumptions must be proven wrong.

Beijing's fundraising through opaque financial instruments and passive investment funds has passed the trillion-dollar threshold. Senior members of the Trump administration, working with Congress, designed a financial architecture to defend scores of millions of Americans who, without their knowledge, have had their savings, in the form of investments, directed to sanctioned companies or those facilitating egregious human rights abuses or the underwriting of China's military-industrial complex.

It is up to us to address this hidden onslaught, which we did not seek, but must counter. The financial security architecture that the Trump administration was building strengthened investor protections, human rights, and our nation's security; its design owed a great debt to the groundbreaking work of my former colleague, Roger W. Robinson, Jr., who has continuously mapped China's predations over the course of decades. On November 12, 2020, the president signed Executive Order 13959: Addressing the Threat from Securities Investments that Finance Communist Chinese Military Companies.[208]

In signing this executive order, the president determined that the People's Republic of China was "increasingly exploiting United States capital to resource and to enable the development and modernization of its military, intelligence, and other security apparatuses."

The executive order blocked American capital from being used directly to fund the Chinese military-industrial complex. Specifically recognized was China's strategy of military-civil fusion that camouflages the purposes of putatively non-military Chinese

---

[208]https://trumpwhitehouse.archives.gov/presidential-actions/executive-order-amending-executive-order-13959-addressing-threat-securities-invest ments-finance-communist-chinese-military-companies/

companies, which, in fact, are obligated to support China's belligerent actions.

Thus, the ability to peer inside China's maze of companies and their interconnections is imperative but is veiled by the inclusion of unregulated Chinese companies in global equity indexes. The economic-security structure that the Trump administration designed must be completed by creating market transparency for American investors, by banning Chinese companies that support the regime's illegitimate ambitions, and by restricting China's insertions into our media and the companies that control it.

We must not allow millions of American retail investors to be placed in the position of unknowingly funding Chinese companies that abet genocide and slave labor. We must not enable Chinese corporations that are complicit in these outrages as well as the communist party's conduct of intelligence operations and those of its armed forces, including the construction of militarized islands in the South China Sea.

Simultaneously, we must confront the Biden administration, and we must challenge Wall Street and our nation's corporations, for we cannot allow any misguided force to cripple America. The Bureau of Industry and Security (BIS)[209] of the Department of Commerce plays a vital role in stemming China's or Russia's acquisitions of American technology and products that can be reverse engineered, thus imperiling our nation's security and financial wellbeing. Chinese or other entities restricted by the Department of Commerce or by the Department of Defense should be excluded from inclusion in the managed investment portfolios of Americans, but this is often not the case.

There are no universally comprehensive exclusion lists for corporations or businesses that represent belligerent powers in intellectual property theft and illicit technology transfer or for the front companies that service such foreign states. This is because such lists do not govern complex indexed funds or derivative financial instruments. Thus, a company may be banned on one of our government's

---

[209]https://www.bis.doc.gov/

lists, only to be present elsewhere in our economy or to receive no attention in the world of financial oversight. We must harmonize exclusionary lists across government, with special emphasis on instilling such controls in the financial sector.

Opaque and vested financial interests cannot be allowed to govern the long-term security and economic health of the American people. China's business lobby and Wall Street cannot be permitted to continue to influence our corporations or to dictate the fortunes of American retail investors.

American corporations and institutions have been forces for democratic development and market creation throughout the world. Wall Street, Hollywood, and America's companies were critical elements of our nation's soft power, which involves global engagement and the sharing of goals to obtain national objectives.

Today, Hollywood has been infiltrated by China. This creates subversive pressures that impact our nation's media, publishing, and news sources, because the conglomerates that dominate Hollywood also control these industries.

Other strategic threats loom. According to a February 2023 report issued by the Center for Security and Emerging Technology (CSET),[210] titled, *U.S. Outbound Investment into Chinese AI Companies*:

> Based on available data in Crunchbase, between 2015 and 2021, 167 U.S. investors participated in 401 investment transactions—or 17 percent of 2,299 global investment transactions—into Chinese AI companies.
>
> Collectively, observed transactions involving U.S. investors totaled $40.2 billion invested into 251 Chinese AI companies, which accounts for 37 percent of the $110 billion raised by all Chinese AI companies. However, we do not know the exact portion of the $40.2 billion that came from U.S. investors.[211]

Given the emergent criticality of artificial intelligence to America's economy and defense, such investments are deeply troubling and

---

[210]CSET is a think tank instituted within Georgetown University's School of Foreign Service.
[211]https://cset.georgetown.edu/publication/u-s-outbound-investment-into-chinese-ai-companies/

demand scrutiny. In dealing with the Chinese Communist Party and its dominion over all Chinese companies, the issues considered must encompass more than strict reciprocity in relations and investments. We must be concerned that advancements in artificial intelligence, made possible by American investments in Chinese technology companies, will directly benefit the People's Liberation Army and also propel enhanced methods of surveillance and suppression of political dissent or religion within this totalistic nation.

Sadly, we have learned that money can kill, that human rights abuses can be intensified, that our national security can be compromised, and that investor protections are too often given short shrift. Nazi Germany and the USSR were empowered through their attraction of capital and resources from Western democracies. We cannot let history repeat itself through our somnambulant funding of a totalitarian police state, for President Xi counts on greed and short-term thinking to facilitate his nation's emergence as a juggernaut, intent on global hegemony.

Greed is corrosive and is the formula for the loss of our fundamental freedoms. Our strengths must not be allowed to be turned against us, for in this battle, we retain great reservoirs of power. Indeed, we must inform our compatriots that our adversary has miscalculated in choosing financial and business domains as its new theater of warfare, for we dominate these endeavors. American capital markets comprise more than fifty percent of total world equity market value.

America leads the world in net financial assets per capita. The gross financial wealth per adult in the United States is almost thirteen times that in China, and the amount of capital that we can invest far exceeds that of any other nation.

The United States and our allies dominate this arena. The Bretton Woods Agreement of 1944 established the mechanisms that have governed international economic relations, which must not be adulterated.[212] Our dollar is the world's reserve currency—not the

---

[212]https://2001-2009.state.gov/r/pa/ho/time/wwii/98681.htm

nonconvertible yuan. These are the battlements that our nation must hold and fortify.

We are in the position as a nation to stress China's economy and thus thwart its international objectives. If we marshal the core of our nation, which is America's marvelous people, we have the power to make China, Russia, and other belligerent states conform to international norms or suffer increasingly catastrophic economic consequences. What is needed is the will to say no to these adversarial states and the intention to put the American worker and farmer first.

Intellectual Property Theft

There is a worldwide threat of piracy in different forms. We know we must vanquish the pirate off the coast of Africa, but we retract from confronting piracy in the form of intellectual property theft.

Ancient Romans would blind the ortalon, a small songbird, so that it would do nothing but engorge itself before it was subsequently consumed. This is what China is attempting to do to America as it steals our technology and thus our nation's future.

Intellectual property theft by China has caused cumulative, total losses to the U.S. economy that far exceed two trillion dollars in the last ten years alone.[213] This sum, if divided, could have made one in every forty American families, instant millionaires.

Intellectual property theft is a hydra that damages many aspects of our economy. It thwarts incentives for business development, for the specter of theft increases risk. It has been estimated that three-quarters of China's business software market is filled with pirated code. The result: Their software expenditures are a small fraction of comparable spending by American companies, conveying enormous, unearned competitive advantages to Chinese firms.

What is not commonly known is that America's trade deficit does not include calculated losses from intellectual property theft or cyberattacks by China or other nations. Intellectual property theft

---

[213] https://www.nbr.org/wp-content/uploads/pdfs/publications/IP_Commission_Report.pdf

is beneath the greatness of the Chinese people. Yet, when deceit rules a nation, thievery is both expected and demanded.

The U.S. International Trade Commission, in 2011, stated that 2.1 million American jobs were in jeopardy if intellectual property theft continued; many of these jobs were subsequently lost until the Trump administration endeavored to undo this carnage. In 2013, John Huntsman, who served as President Obama's ambassador to China, and Admiral Dennis Blair, who served as President Obama's first director of national intelligence, authored a comprehensive report on intellectual property theft that has since been updated.

They wrote, "it is safe to say that dollar losses from IP theft are hundreds of billions per year," thus underlining that trillions have been lost to the American economy over time.[214] These losses also carry forward as damages to American competitiveness, which is an immense number that is hard to capture, for the initial theft is followed by the ensuing loss of product category dominance and market position.

Part of the answer to these scourges lies in greatly enhanced cybersecurity. Yet America is buffeted by nonattributable cyberattacks, which in certain contexts are instruments of war. China and Russia seek to damage our economy and security while remaining free from culpability.

Cyberwarfare separates us from reality, for it may create a false simulacrum or delete, repurpose, or misuse vital information. Volitional or intended actions may be rendered impossible.

We must be ready to pierce this insidious threat and force accountability in our present age of hybrid warfare that blends attacks of different natures upon vital economic and financial assets, including our energy grid. Deterrence requires that America possess both defensive and offensive cyber capabilities.

Without cybersecurity, our elections, financial and personal data, and infrastructure are vulnerable to attack and compromise. Both managerial creativity and technical competencies are necessary for cybersecurity. The present administration lacks both. This must

---

[214] Ibid.

change; new structures for cybersecurity must be built that significantly enhance our capabilities.

In the Trump administration's National Security Strategy, issued in December 2017, the administration specified concrete actions to improve America's cybersecurity; these measures included identifying and prioritizing risks, building defensible government networks, disrupting malicious actors, improving information sharing, and deploying layered defenses that are persistent. This work is ongoing and gargantuan in scope. Many additional steps, however, must be taken to realize fully the benefits of such initiatives.

A new national laboratory must link together America's cybersecurity assets, which are distributed throughout agencies, businesses, and research facilities. The new laboratory would be partially virtual in that it would integrate these cybersecurity assets. Functional threat groups composed of red or foreign insertion or exfiltration teams must be enhanced or, in many instances, created to challenge our existing systems and defenses before they are attacked. Cybersecurity and the curtailment of online censorship and manipulation are essential and interrelated.

Cybersecurity must become a cardinal component of America's economic security architecture. A permanent presidential cybersecurity committee must be empaneled and have purview over the cyber assets of the federal government. New organizations that evince technical subject masteries rather than bureaucratic gamesmanship must be formed without delay.

President Trump, in 2018, signed into law the Cybersecurity and Infrastructure Security Agency Act. This was an important step in addressing the faults existent in America's cybersecurity, as practiced by our government, but it was insufficient given emergent threats. Additional actions are mandatory. Present federal powers do not possess the technical capabilities, personnel, authorities, or access to the president to implement a comprehensive strategy in this domain.

One of the greatest architects of the computer revolution, John von Neumann, stated that to build dependable computational abilities, reliable systems must be built from unreliable parts. This is our task today, to build deeply layered cyber-defenses that encompass our military, our government, our private industry, our financial systems, and every person resident in our country. To do this, massive funding must be moved from ineffectual governmental tasks and operations to the creation of matchless cybersecurity systems composed of defensive and offensive capabilities.

During Michael Pompeo's tenure as secretary of state, he made cybersecurity for his department, both within the United States and internationally, a core priority. As secretary, he supported the first joint cyberwarfare exercise conducted by the United States and Taiwan. The Cyber Offensive and Defensive Exercises (CODE) were held in 2019 and included participants from American private industry, Japan, Australia, and Indonesia.

In 2020, America conducted forward, joint defensive cyber operations with Estonia's defense forces. These exercises are a part of America's deployment of cyber assets and the United States Cyber Command's involvement in support of the digital security of numerous nations in Europe and throughout the world. This exercise and others proved crucial in our fortifying NATO's ability to interdict the spectrum of cyberthreats created or induced by Russia.

Our exercises have established the vital premise that cybersecurity must involve groups of allies. No nation can succeed alone. Further, American assets that can contest malicious cyberthreats must be forward deployed, adjacent to our friends and our allies that face malevolent actors including governmental and private cadres in China, Russia, the Democratic People's Republic of Korea, and Iran.

Illicit technology transfer is associated with both cyberattacks and intellectual property theft. Front organizations, espionage, extortion, and payoffs are all employed by China to steal our technology. The United Front Work Department, which answers to the Central Committee of the Chinese Communist Party, seeks to obtain intelligence, influence, and control over useful individuals in China and in other countries. To do this, family members of targets are often held at risk, and a system of rewards is proffered for compliance to party objectives.

Military systems, including those considered dual use, in that they serve both the defense and the civilian sectors of our economy, are prime targets. Even the most cursory review of China's newest weapons, including its aircraft, its missiles, and its guns, reveals substantial similarities to U.S. systems.

Our Terminal High Altitude Area Defense (THAAD) antiballistic missile system and Poseidon antisubmarine aircraft have contained counterfeit parts that could compromise mission readiness, performance, or security.[215] In 2011, Democratic Senator Carl Levin, who died in 2021, said, "There is a flood of counterfeits, and it is putting our military men at risk and costing us a fortune."[216] Through the employment of new marking technologies, which could include digital ledgers such as blockchain, we must bring this hidden threat to heel.

Exfiltration of knowledge by capturing or compromising individuals is a constant concern that is concealed by our media. Born in Shanghai, Qian Xuesen studied engineering at the Massachusetts Institute of Technology (MIT); afterward, he became a member of the Jet Propulsion Laboratory, which is affiliated with the California Institute of Technology (Caltech). Qian Xuesen was subsequently stripped of his security clearances due to concerns he was a communist and a spy. In 1955, he was released to China as part of a prisoner trade.

After his arrival, Qian Xuesen became the architect of China's atomic bomb program. Later, he was proclaimed the "Father of Chinese Rocketry," for his work in the development of the Dongfeng ballistic missile.

Presently, foreign students from China studying at the undergraduate and graduate levels in our colleges and universities receive limited scrutiny. A significant cohort of these students in the United

---

[215]https://www.nextgov.com/cxo-briefing/2011/11/levin-chinese-counterfeit-chips-pose-major-threat-to-pentagon-weapons/50089/
[216]https://www.cnn.com/2011/11/07/us/u-s-military-bogus-parts/index.html

States is enmeshed in the fields of science, technology, engineering, or mathematics at the most advanced levels.

It is a sobering thought that any number of these students may be spies for China's military or intelligence services. Reciprocity between Chinese and American foreign student programs must be enforced, in addition to enhanced vetting and the monitoring of each student's educational track.

To redress these threats, America's intelligence community must compile a comprehensive assessment of the laws, tools, illicit practices, and operations that China has employed to effect mastery in the aforementioned domains. Our response must be framed around novel, asymmetric, or covert actions, to involve both our government and our private sector.

Genocide, Misery, and Human Trafficking

The scourges of genocide, slave labor, and human trafficking are not only part of history, but present in our world today. Each is an affront to our Creator and to any moral order.

These atrocities must not be tolerated. Unconscionable abuses are pervasive in what is termed the Xinjiang Uyghur Autonomous Region. In January 2021, Secretary of State Pompeo declared China's treatment of Uyghurs to be a genocide. He did so based on the accepted international definitions of the term. The bipartisan U.S. Commission on International Religious Freedom affirmed his determination.

Secretary Pompeo's successor, Antony Blinken, upheld his designation. Indeed, the Department of State in its *2020 Country Reports on Human Rights Practices: China*, issued on March 30, 2021, reiterated Secretary Pompeo's findings in its statement, writing:

> Genocide and crimes against humanity occurred during the year against the predominantly Muslim Uyghurs and other ethnic and religious minority groups in Xinjiang. These crimes were continuing and include: the arbitrary imprisonment or other severe deprivation of physical liberty of more than one million civilians; forced sterilization,

coerced abortions, and more restrictive application of China's birth
control policies; rape; torture of a large number of those arbitrarily
detained; forced labor; and the imposition of draconian restrictions on
freedom of religion or belief, freedom of expression, and freedom of
movement.[217]

The report lists a litany of outrages, including, "unlawful killings by
the government; forced disappearances by the government; torture
by the government; harsh and life-threatening prison and detention
conditions; arbitrary detention by the government, including the
mass detention of more than one million Uyghurs and other members of predominantly Muslim minority groups in extrajudicial
internment camps and an additional two million subjected to day-
time-only 're-education' training; political prisoners; politically
motivated reprisal against individuals outside the country; the lack
of an independent judiciary and Communist Party control over the
judicial and legal system," among other offenses by the state and by
the party.[218]

Just months before Secretary Pompeo's determination, in appalling disregard for China's known abuses, a leading American media
company, in the closing credits of a major film, produced at a reported
cost of 200 million dollars, thanked Xinjiang's security bureau and
propaganda departments for aiding the company's production.[219]
Where is this corporation's concern for Xinjiang's Muslims? That
a media icon, whose very name is synonymous with Americana,
would stoop this low is deeply troubling, in part because this and
other American and international corporations have provided cover
for China's acts.

---

[217] https://www.state.gov/reports/2020-country-reports-on-human-rights-
practices/

[218] https://www.forbes.com/sites/ewelinaochab/2021/04/02/us-state-
department-confirms-the-finding-of-the-uyghur-genocide-chinese-foreign-
ministry-spokesperson-denies-yet-again/?sh=704427876ba9

[219] https://www.cnbc.com/2020/09/08/disney-thanked-groups-linked-to
-china-detention-camps-in-mulan-credits.html

As part of the Final Solution, the Nazis established the Theresienstadt concentration camp, in what is now the Czech Republic, as a transshipment point for Jews and persons of Jewish descent before their dispatch to the death camps of the East. Theresienstadt, built in a fortified city, also served another purpose.

It was the camp that the Nazis extolled to the international community, to German citizens, and to the International Red Cross as a humane retirement destination for elderly Jews and those who were grievously wounded while serving Germany in the First World War. Virtually all these people were killed, but the pretense wrought by the Nazis provided a degree of cover for their inhuman acts and their mass industrialization of murder.

The genocide that is occurring today in China is different from the Holocaust. Though we recognize that each genocide is unique, they are absolute to the individual.

No event in human history is comparable to the Holocaust, but we must, where appropriate, draw applicable lessons. We, therefore, are compelled to document with revulsion that the business activities of American and international corporations in Xinjiang serve China's purpose of obscuring the nature of its crimes against the Muslims of that land.

The United States has no more important foreign policy imperative than ensuring that genocide is never permitted, is never accepted, and is always vanquished. Thus, our pressure on China must be constant, but it is not. This must change.

Slavery must be fought resolutely: One of the best ways to do this is to empower women everywhere. This is necessary to prevent human trafficking as well as child abuse and exploitation.

Constructive action in these domains was a tenet of the Trump administration. On January 11, 2020, Secretary Pompeo announced the Freedom First initiative for the Department of State, pursuant to the president's proclaiming January as National Slavery and Human Trafficking Prevention Month.

In his statement, Secretary Pompeo wrote that those who wish to bind people in servitude, "deprive their victims of the ability to exercise their unalienable rights of life, liberty, and the pursuit of happiness—an affront to our nation's founding principles." He further stated that our efforts to combat slavery and the associated crime of human trafficking must recognize that "human dignity, autonomy, and freedom are essential to the exercise of our rights and liberties. Delivering on unfulfilled promises of freedom for the millions of people whom traffickers exploit must remain a first priority for us all."

During the Trump administration, the Department of State instituted efforts to quell this outrage. In this regard, Secretary Pompeo obligated tens of millions of dollars to the department's Program to End Modern Slavery, which is a directed initiative focused on regions and nations in which this curse is still prevalent.

Human trafficking remains the fastest growing crime on earth. Our nation must eliminate human trafficking, with particular emphasis on the eradication of trafficking that supports sex slavery. A Republican administration must order that a comprehensive action plan be produced to mount an intensive multifactorial effort to eradicate human trafficking, with immediate enforcement in America.

This plan must be produced within the first ninety days of a Republican president's assuming office. All elements of government will need to coordinate their work with our allies and other nations, elements of the United Nation, advocacy groups, and the private sector.

In future, anti-slavery measures could potentially be aided through the incorporation of blockchain and other technologies to facilitate product tracing, to identify production that stems from forced labor. America's efforts to end slavery must cross administrations and must always be guided by an incomparable vision of human liberty for all people.

Our southern border must be considered broached and thus a dagger to America's proper conduct of international economic affairs, which must respect human dignity. For the twelve-month period that ended in April 2021, total illegal drug-related fatalities passed

100,000 in America for the first time.[220] The illegal distribution of the synthetic opioid fentanyl resulted in about sixty-four percent of these fatalities, equating to approximately 175 deaths each day.

Rather than applaud the Trump administration's deeply moral effort to stem these tides, Democrats, and their representatives in the media, deplored the building of the wall. We are in danger, as a society, of substituting a false morality, centered on appearances and posturing, for true virtue, as contained in the world's sacred texts that have illuminated humanity for millennia. We must turn from this danger as a nation, for if our moral core is forfeit, everything we hold dear, which orbits this central point, will spin outward and soon be beyond our control or grasp.

Trade and the American Worker

In international trade, nothing is more important than fairness for the American worker and farmer. Full stop.

World trade is governed by a number of international agreements, organizations, and treaties. These systems must be overhauled. We can no longer simply rely on good faith, assumed fairness, or trust.

Such articles of expected behavior often function as lip service in a world in which our adversaries look upon trade as another warfighting arena. We have constructed trade agreements that purport to be fair, but these agreements have too often been neither free nor fair.

President Biden's Indo-Pacific Economic Framework (IPEF)[221] acknowledges that the Trans-Pacific Partnership, which the Obama administration negotiated, was "fragile" and unacceptable to Congress.[222] The new framework, however, is not posited as a treaty

---

[220]https://nypost.com/2021/11/17/us-surpasses-100000-drug-overdoses-in-12-month-span/

[221]https://www.commerce.gov/tags/indo-pacific-economic-framework

[222]https://rollcall.com/2022/05/23/biden-outlines-economic-framework-for-us-asian-nations/

subject to the advice and consent of the Senate, nor does it address core trade inadequacies that involve the World Trade Organization (WTO). The new framework is not stout enough to meet our present challenges; it does not incorporate Taiwan; neither does its focus on decarbonization meet the economic realities of today.

President Clinton permitted China to join the WTO based on his administration's acceptance of the Chinese Communist Party's lies. The Clinton administration as well as many Republicans believed that admittance into the WTO would change China; instead, China changed the WTO, for membership provided yet another cloak that Beijing used to cover its massive theft of intellectual property and markets from America and other nations on a scale without precedent.

China, the nation with the second largest GDP in the world, must no longer be able to claim that it is a developing nation, entitled to benefits within the WTO. In addition, the WTO must act with alacrity and stand against any commerce that is based upon enslavement.

Building upon America's multilateral and bilateral alliances, new economic treaties should be negotiated that will become a phalanx, barring China's domination of world trade. Our objective must be the creation of security-driven economic alliances that support reliable and resilient supply chains that link together businesses in many countries, for this approach will constitute a major stimulus to small- and to medium-sized businesses outside China.

Complex international agreements do not necessarily secure America's interests. This realization was the reason America rejected the original iteration of the Trans-Pacific Partnership Agreement. This clear-sightedness also motivated the Trump administration to stress bilateral trade agreements and to stipulate that the decades-old North American Free Trade Agreement (NAFTA) be replaced with a far superior trade pact, the Canada-United States-Mexico Agreement (CUSMA), which is protecting American jobs while improving our trade relations with our friends.

We must establish a new set of rules that will prize the American worker and farmer by opening markets globally, while opposing

China's deceits. The World Trade Organization has been central to international commerce, but it has been coopted by China and must be reformed.

In considering the status of trade issues, we must discern if the core principles of a nation reflect freedom or reflect control. Free trade can only take place between free countries: This is axiomatic. Free trade is impossible if freedom from compulsion is absent. Therefore, we must ask: For whom is free trade free?

Free trade with China is certainly not free for those who labor in internment camps or are threatened with genocide. Those who are disappeared or are made to serve as surreptitious military agents are not free. Indeed, freedom for China's neighbors is impinged by China's territorial ambitions, including those in the South China Sea.

The new Comprehensive and Progressive Agreement for Trans-Pacific Partnership, known as the CPTPP, comprises eleven nations, including Japan, Canada, Australia, Mexico, Malaysia, and Vietnam. The People's Republic of China, the United Kingdom, and Taiwan have all applied to join this pact.

China's interests are inimical to the CPTPP and its members. It should be barred from ascension, lest it pervert this new partnership of nations. The United States should carefully weigh the benefits and costs of joining the CPTPP.

Unnecessary and excessively burdensome environmental controls or the transfer of American jobs to other nations must be assiduously avoided. If these objectives cannot be accomplished within the CPTPP's framework, other concepts must be explored.

Building upon the Quadrilateral Security Dialogue, which involves Japan, Australia, India, and the United States, a new trade alliance could be formed between these nations and the Republic of Korea, Taiwan, Israel, the United Kingdom, and other European states. This revised entity could constitute a security-driven, economic, and financial alliance. It should also secure resilient supply chains that link together businesses in many countries through advanced data systems.

Dependencies on unreliable sources of supply for critical components or materials have costs. In their March 2021 letter that introduced the final report of the National Security Commission on Artificial Intelligence, chairman Eric Schmidt, the former CEO of Google, and vice chairman Robert Work, the former deputy secretary of defense, wrote, "A recent chip shortage for auto manufacturing cost an American car company an estimated 2.5 billion dollars. A strategic blockage would cost far more and put our security at risk."[223]

The creation of new supply chains for medicines and for critical components and strategic materials that do not rely on adversarial states must be prioritized. New legislation should receive attention and consideration as a means to promote supply-chain security. Any action in this regard, however, must not erect new bureaucratic structures; instead, existing elements of the federal government should be reconstituted to deal with our reliance on uncertain or potentially hostile sources of supply for critical items.

We must understand as a nation that communist countries lie until their lies seem more true than truth itself. Since the time of Deng Xiaoping, China asserted that it is and will be a reliable trading party with the West. This is a lie, as can be demonstrated by China's actions during the recent pandemic.

Beginning before SARS-CoV-2 even spread to other nations, China intentionally hid the severity of the novel and deadly coronavirus that it allowed to proliferate. At the same time, the Chinese Communist Party increased its nation's import of personal protective equipment, including surgical gowns, respirators, and face masks, while drastically reducing the export of these items. This is not trade but warfare that is not even concealed, for China believes that Western greed is its best shield.

What must we do? We have the opportunity to use technology to link together vast numbers of businesses throughout the free nations of the world to build supply chains that do not contain companies resident in adversarial states.

---

[223]https://reports.nscai.gov/final-report/chair-and-vice-chair-letter/

Unalterable, digital ledgers, such as blockchain, may provide one means of creating vertical supply chains that do not involve Chinese, Russian, or Iranian companies. Certain products contain thousands of components; only by harnessing the power of technology can we ensure that complex finished goods cannot be subverted by state-controlled entities that withhold or compromise components made in adversarial countries.

Such an approach would constitute a major stimulus to small- and medium-sized businesses outside China. Inducements to erect such new supply chains should be a priority of a global trade compact composed of free nations that appreciate the imperative of economic security in a world that has endured a pandemic that China could have prevented. We must determine which components and materials are strategic so that we may ensure dependable avenues of supply.

We most often think of an alliance in regional terms, but in the case of economic security, it must be global. Can the United States build a new economic alliance that supports democracies and security-conscious trade that is both free and fair and is recognized as such by the American taxpayer? International economic affairs experts Roger W. Robinson, Jr. and William Martin join me in believing we must achieve this goal.

A final component of economic security involves the entire world. We, as a nation, must fight to promote women's rights to become a vital foundation of the foreign policy of the United States. I believed during my time on Ronald Reagan's National Security Council staff and I believe now that if America leads by example and supports boldly women's rights throughout the globe, forces of change and moderation will take root in many countries in the Middle East, in Africa, and in Asia. Sadly, the Biden administration's actions do not match their tendentious rhetoric, for they have betrayed the women of Iran while discounting the progress made in Saudi Arabia, which the Department of State, during the Trump administration helped seed.

Technological development and access to education, media, and family-oriented resources will serve, over time, as counterweights to entrenched, fundamentalist forces. No nation that obstinately continues to suppress women's rights should be considered a true ally of the United States.

Sensitivity to cultural practices if they clearly injure half a nation's population is not sensitivity, but willful blindness on the part of the American Government, which cannot be tolerated. We must listen to other nations; we must respect their paths, should they be at times circuitous due to their creeds, but we, as the United States, are obligated to press for change to improve the rights and the opportunities of women everywhere. In addition, we must also work to improve the rights and the status of children throughout the globe.

Challenge

International economic affairs may be thought of as a Möbius strip, which is a type of twisted loop: Traveling on it flips the orientation realized during each transit. America had hoped that opening global markets, which began in earnest when President Clinton permitted China to join the World Trade Organization, would make China more like us, expanding its people's freedoms. This was a belief widely held by lawmakers, both Democrat and Republican, for many of the ensuing years since China joined the WTO on December 11, 2001. This attitude was wrong, but the threat posed by China was masked by our attention to 9/11 and the subsequent war our country waged on terror.

China has not become more free; it has, under President Xi, become more repressive. Indeed, its tools for the suppression of democratic or contrarian thoughts have been insinuated into our nation and must be removed one by one.

How must we contest China economically in the years to come? The answer is not simple, for it requires mature American leadership and the employment of sound and rigorous processes.

To contest China and belligerent nations, America must be strong across the broadest possible range of indices. To make demands of China, we must first make demands of ourselves. A panopticon is a prison, in the form of a circle, in which one guard in its center can observe every prisoner. China is a panopticon in which the communist party reigns and sees all.

This cannot be the future of the United States. A powerful constellation of technology companies, whose combined wealth far exceeds that of most nations, has colluded with duplicitous politicians and with the deep state to create a virtual prison of online censorship, manipulation, and control that threatens our nation's continued existence as a Constitutional Republic.

This threat has been brought to light by Elon Musk's actions at Twitter, but other technology companies operate on the cusp of perception and beneath the horizon of regulation. The crux of our present dilemma is that traditional American values have been cashiered by the left and by many global corporations, which were founded in America, but whose values are often responsive to global markets and not morality and the American way.

An extremely damaging sleight of hand is proffered by numerous American corporations, private equity firms, and other financial businesses that promote Environmental, Social, and Governance (ESG) and Diversity, Equity, and Inclusion (DEI) business models at home, only to bow and scrape within foreign markets—at the behest of some of the most repressive governments on earth. What these shameless companies demand of America, they ignore a thousand times over in China.

In the past, the federal government has advocated for useful changes in business practices to ensure fairness, equality of opportunity, environmental stewardship, and consumer safety and protection. Today, this proud history of concern for our neighbors and for the environment has been usurped by radicals who use laws, regulations, and business stratagems that rely on pressure to effect neo-Marxist rules to restrain our freedoms, which were expressed by our nation's market-based economy.

Oligarchs and Betrayal

America's population is four percent of that of the world. Thus, globalists within the private sector, academia, and government believe that the American economy must comply with global standards that are pushed through connivence and sharp power by China and other socialist states. This must not be America's path, yet institutions as intrinsic to our economy as the Securities and Exchange Commission are substituting equity-based rules for market-based solutions that enshrine growth coupled with equal opportunity.[224] This betrayal must cease.

Technocratic authoritarians and leftist elites believe that it is necessary to limit sharply or to rescind individual freedoms to bring into being a new age, an epoch after a technological singularity in which machine learning, artificial intelligence, robotics, and bioengineering will supplant humanity as we know it. They, who are advantaged, resemble the leadership and the managerial class that drove the USSR into oblivion. These overlords and the American nomenklatura they control do not represent our nation's greatness. Their outlook violates our history and our nation's promise, yet their presence and their reach are supported by a woke culture, which we must overturn.

That the praying mantis kills and consumes its mate to derive sustenance seems unreal and unnatural when it is first viewed, but it becomes expected after being witnessed time after time. Russian oligarchs are preponderantly gangsters who feed off the flesh of others to destroy nations, for they profit from the instabilities they create. The world cannot allow Russian billionaires to control private armies that pillage entire continents.

Russia must be held continuously responsible for this illicit plague, which has become a global substrate upon which a vast array of criminal enterprises are based. Whether it be the expropriation of mineral riches in Africa, human trafficking across Europe, or espionage and blackmail throughout the world, the crimes committed by oligarchs, who are increasingly based internationally, must be

---

[224]https://www.scu.edu/ethics/all-about-ethics/the-federal-government-and-the-ethical-value-of-esg-policy/#:~:text=The%20Biden%20administration%20%282021-%29%20is%20renewing%20the%20ethical,greater%20ESG%20disclosure%20requirements%20for%20corporations%20%28SEC%2C%20 2021%29.

stopped. Further, they must not be allowed to dominate the Kremlin after Putin.

Intelligence, crimefighting, and judicial tools must bleed into diplomatic and multinational economic negotiations if this threat is to be arrested. The wealth of Russia must not be stollen by the few. It must also not be sold to China by those who seek to launder their actions through affiliations with the Chinese Communist Party.

Economic security for our nation and our allies is one of the most profound challenges of our time. Are we to approach this multifaceted subject in fear or in servility, or are we to summon the greatness of Ronald Reagan, to begin again America's journey to a bountiful future?

America's treasured principles must be maintained so that they may be passed on to generations yet unborn. As a nation we must entrench our belief that the United States is destined to prevail, for we possess the most inspiring force the world has ever known—human freedom. The spirit of free enterprise and the striving for a better life for our families are our nation's heritage. We can live in the past, or live for the future, the choice is up to each one of us.

Chapter 11, Economic Security, Precepts:

• Free enterprise and the quest for a better life for our families are our nation's heritage. Enlightened self-interest, as distinct from selfishness, drives prosperity that enriches the American people.

• In international trade, nothing is more important than fairness for the American worker and farmer. Full stop.

• Our adversaries view trade as another warfighting arena. World trade is governed by international agreements, organizations, and treaties. These systems cannot depend on trust; they must be overhauled without delay.

• We possess tools to stress China's economy and thus thwart its international objectives. America has the power to make China, Russia, and other belligerent states conform to international norms or suffer increasingly dire economic consequences. We must challenge these nations. We must put America's workers and farmers first.

Issues and Problems:

• The gross financial wealth per adult in the United States is almost thirteen times that in China; the amount of capital we can invest far exceeds that of any other nation. Due to a lack of focus, America's economic strength has not been used to fortify our position as the world's leading economic power.

• Genocide, human trafficking, and the provision of illicit drugs are realities today. Unconscionable abuses pervade China and are plied by the cartels that traverse America's southern border.

• The principles of nations with which we trade should be assessed by our government. Free trade can only take place between free countries: This is axiomatic. Free trade is impossible if freedom from compulsion is absent.

• The Chinese Communist Party operates a colossal system of state-owned conglomerates, which control crucial economic, material, and telecommunications sectors all over the world. We must not allow the communist model for development to proliferate, for it is rule by thieves as is demonstrated by the magnitude of China's theft of intellectual property. It is a system that ensures that there can be no true freedom of thought.

• Foreign students from China receive limited scrutiny, though they study science, technology, engineering, and mathematics at the highest levels, while opportunities for American students in China are restricted. This must end: A system of strict reciprocity with China is mandatory.

Duties and Actions:

• China's ruptures to the international economic order must be curtailed; China's subversion of capital markets and businesses must be stopped; cybercrime and intellectual property theft must be stemmed; genocide, slavery, and human trafficking must be eliminated; and trade alliances and imbalances must be addressed.

• A Chinese invasion of Taiwan would eliminate a primary technological and economic partner of the United States. Expanded production of semiconductors in America is crucial in providing a safety net for our economy and the world, should China attack Taiwan. We must challenge China's usurpation of the wealth of the South China Sea.

• Cybersecurity must become a central component of America's economic security architecture. A new national structure must link together America's cybersecurity assets to provide an unprecedented level of defense.

• The promotion of women's and children's rights world-wide is a vital foundation for global economic development.

CHAPTER 12

ENERGY DOMINANCE

Energy is essential to life. It is the foundation for every physical good we make and everything we consume. The Biden administration has destroyed American energy dominance. We must reattain this attribute if we are to possess energy self-sufficiency while also meeting the supplemental demands of our closest allies, thereby influencing energy markets and prices worldwide, in support of our economy, our workers, and our farmers.

The economic growth and prosperity of every nation depend on increased energy consumption. This requirement cannot be met by renewable energy alone, for it is intermittent. Fossil fuels and their production, refinement, and distribution must be supplemented by expansion in the provision of nuclear power. This

> multifaceted approach to energy production is a pre-requisite for adaptation, which creates upward mobility for all the world's citizens. Such needed growth must not be sacrificed to those who seek to instill Marxism globally by cloaking it in the green trappings of radical environmentalism.

Energy Dominance

Never in history has a country retreated from dominance to supplication as quickly as has the United States under the Biden administration in the field of energy. America did not wait for foreign embargoes to be levied; we created our own.

President Biden blocked our receipt of oil from Canada, produced under the world's highest environmental standards, by cancelling the Keystone XL pipeline on the first day of his administration.[225] The Department of Energy (DOE) was later forced by the passage of the Infrastructure Investment and Jobs Act[226] to conduct an assessment of the employment and consumer ramifications that resulted from the revocation of the permit for the pipeline.

According to the department's December 2022 report, the abandoned pipeline was constructed to permit the "delivery of up to 830,000 barrels per day (bpd) of crude oil from the Western Canadian Sedimentary Basin (WCSB) in Canada and the Bakken Shale Formation in the United States to Steele City, Nebraska, for onward delivery to refineries in the Gulf Coast area."[227] As related in the report:

---

[225]https://www.huffpost.com/entry/biden-cancel-keystone-xl-pipeline-permi t_n_60076208c5b6df63a91abf63
[226]https://www.govinfo.gov/app/details/PLAW-117publ58
[227]https://www.daines.senate.gov/wp-content/uploads/2023/01/12.23.22-KXL-Pipeline-Job-Loss-and-Impacts-on-Consumer-Energy-Costs-001245.pdf

President Biden stated that the KXL pipeline "disserves the U.S. national interest," as its construction and operation would not be consistent with U.S. climate goals and it would undermine the global energy and climate leadership role of the United States.[228]

From this vacant and inarticulate argument, President Biden makes clear that he does not understand fossil fuels, for he subsequently begged Russia, Venezuela, and the nations of the Middle East to provide us with oil that our ally and neighbor Canada was anxious to supply.[229] The oil that he sought from Saudi Arabia and from Venezuela is not cleaner than that produced in Canada or in the United States. Neither the care taken in production nor the extensive shipping requirements place either foreign supply as being environmentally equivalent to North American sources.

President Biden's action killed American and Canadian jobs without any adequate reason; indeed, his own experts found that his action could not be derived from an evaluation of the facts.[230] Though a number of analyses are noted in the DOE assessment, the breach in our nation's security and economy is reflected in the following passage, taken by DOE from a Perryman Group (PG) economic evaluation of the pipeline, produced in 2010.[231]

> PG estimated the total impact of construction and development of the pipeline on the U.S. economy. PG estimated that pipeline construction would yield $20.931 billion in total spending and $9.605 billion in output over the lifetime of the project. Additionally, the project would support 118,936 person-years of employment over two years, or 59,468 jobs in each of the two years.[232]

---

[228] Ibid.

[229] https://www.americanenergyalliance.org/2021/08/biden-begs-americas-enemies-for-oil-while-attacking-domestic-producers/

[230] https://www.daines.senate.gov/wp-content/uploads/2023/01/12.23.22-KXL-Pipeline-Job-Loss-and-Impacts-on-Consumer-Energy-Costs-001245.pdf

[231] https://www.perrymangroup.com/

[232] https://www.daines.senate.gov/wp-content/uploads/2023/01/12.23.22-KXL-Pipeline-Job-Loss-and-Impacts-on-Consumer-Energy-Costs-001245.pdf

President Biden has stolen from the American people and has discounted the product and the inherent environmental stewardship of the North American worker. He should be ashamed, for this is idiocy framed as environmental concern. It tricks no one but those who wish to remain uninformed. Security for America and our allies requires ample supplies of energy in all its forms.

Energy is vital to jobs and to economic growth. It is directly correlated with income and wealth, for energy is life.[233] Fossil fuels are essential to human development and will be so into the foreseeable future, for, as we see in Europe, renewable sources of energy are supplementary and not primary in nature. The developing world must have abundant electricity to prosper and to throw off the constraints of poverty.

The Trump administration correctly took pride in achieving the once impossible dream of American energy independence, which it molded so that the nation could become energy dominant for the first time in history. Our country was not only able to satisfy the energy needs of every American, we grew to become a major exporter of liquified natural gas (LNG) to Asia, in direct competition to Russia's and Iran's exploitation of energy markets. This weakened our adversaries.

Acting decisively, the Trump administration promoted the export of American LNG, recognizing that LNG is a fuel that is essential to the realization of our nation's future economic, environmental, and national security goals. Previous actions by a Republican administration and its department of energy have been undermined by President Biden's intent on creating narratives, rather than producing results for the American people.

Natural gas remains the bridge to a future of net-zero-carbon energy that must, for reasons of capacity and technology, be centered on the application of fission power, followed by fusion reactors, should this potential source of unlimited, clean electricity prove commercially practicable. The creation of small modular fission

---

[233]https://link.springer.com/article/10.1007/s40974-017-0072-9

reactors and fusion research, leading to commercially viable plants, must each be prioritized.

One of the principal reasons that we are experiencing alarming fuel prices, supply shortages, and power outages, is the illusion that renewable energy sources are able to fill the gaps created by our staged abandonment of fossil fuels. They cannot.

We must be aware of the environmental costs of renewable energy. We must be cognizant of the fact that renewable energy is intermittent, requiring supplementary energy systems that are thermal or hydroelectric in nature. This constraint substantially increases the cost of renewable energy but is often not considered in the approval process that treats any green energy project with acclamation.

A cause for alarm is the source of the photovoltaic (PV) cells that form the basis for most solar power facilities. China dominates in the production of the constituent parts of photovoltaic cells. According to the *Special Report on Solar PV Global Supply Chains*, composed by the intergovernmental International Energy Agency (IEA), "The world will almost completely rely on China for the supply of key building blocks for solar panel production through 2025. Based on manufacturing capacity under construction, China's share of global polysilicon, ingot and wafer production will soon reach almost 95%."[234]

Critical materials, required in the construction of windmills, are also sourced from China.[235] Due to the Biden Administration, we are now trading the memories of our past dependencies on Middle Eastern oil for actual dependences on China for solar power systems and for the processing and supply of rare earth minerals that are essential to the manufacture of wind turbines.[236] This march toward desolation is compounded by President Biden's failure to maintain America's tariffs against Chinese solar manufacturers, pursuant to Section 201 of the Trade Act of 1974, which permits relief for "domestic industries

[234] https://iea.blob.core.windows.net/assets/d2ee601d-6b1a-4cd2-a0e8-db02dc64332c/SpecialReportonSolarPVGlobalSupplyChains.pdf
[235] https://finance.yahoo.com/news/china-stranglehold-world-supply-critical-073504612.html?fr=sycsrp_catchall
[236] https://www.visualcapitalist.com/visualizing-chinas-dominance-in-the-solar-panel-supply-chain/

seriously injured or threatened with serious injury by increased imports."[237]

In response to petitions from America's solar industry, the Trump administration acted in 2018 to inhibit China's presence in our markets in this rapidly expanding sector. This was done through the application of tariffs as permitted by law.[238] While a December 2021 report by the International Trade Commission (ITC) recommended extending the tariffs by four years, President Biden overruled this federal agency and allowed the tariffs to lapse,[239] no doubt bowing to pressure exerted by China through its phalanx of energy interests, lobbyists, and functionaries.

The Department of Energy in its *Solar Futures Study* of September 8, 2021, detailed the Biden administration's intent that solar energy by 2035 provide 40 percent of America's electricity requirements.[240] President Biden's trade decision is thus catastrophic, for, given this context, the administration's objective to increase America's dependence on solar energy is tantamount to stating that communist China will supply four-tenths of America's electricity requirements by the middle of the next decade.

President Biden has issued a death certificate for the photovoltaic manufacturing industry in America; in doing so, he has betrayed the trust of the American people by placing our nation's future electricity supply, and thus our independence of action, in the hands of an adversarial state. The deceitfulness of the Biden administration in this sphere is patent; we are thus compelled to ask: When will the destruction of our nation's energy industries cease? When will we

---

[237] https://www.energy.gov/articles/doe-releases-solar-futures-study-providing-blueprint-zero-carbon-gridhttps://www.usitc.gov/press_room/us_safeguard.htm#:~:text=Section%20201%2C%20Trade%20Act%20of%201974%20%28Global%20Safeguard,imports%20may%20petition%20the%20USITC%20for%20import%20relief.

[238] https://www.forbes.com/sites/kenrapoza/2022/02/27/how-biden-gave-china-the-solar-industry/?sh=1cbd293372f0

[239] Ibid.

[240] https://www.energy.gov/eere/solar/solar-futures-study

protect our country against the most powerful adversarial state we have faced in this century?

Symbols are important for they proclaim what we hold sacrosanct, but in the name of green energy, bald eagles are being massacred by windmill farms, whose turbine blades act as scythes that gut these majestic birds. This is not the green energy we were promised.

The Obama administration changed the regulations for wind farms to allow these massive installations to kill or to gravely injure thousands of bald eagles each year. In response, we must heed the wisdom of our nation's Indigenous people who decry the multi-decade, federal permits that pardon this slaughter.[241]

The Audubon Society estimated in 2016 that hundreds of thousands of birds of all species could be killed each year by wind turbines.[242] The actual number today could be far higher. Solar farms also kill large numbers of birds, disrupting entire food chains, due to superheated panel surfaces.[243]

According to a study by the United States Geological Survey (USGS), "nearly half of bird species studied were vulnerable to population-level effects from fatalities at renewable energy facilities."[244] This finding merits our concern as does the potential loss of the livelihoods of East Coast fishermen in the wake of the construction of massive numbers of offshore windmills, which may potentially impact shellfish yields severely, according to research that has appeared in the *ICES Journal of Marine Science*.[245]

---

[241] https://indiancountrytoday.com/archive/feds-to-allow-even-more-bald-eagles-killed-or-maimed-for-clean-energy

[242] https://www.audubon.org/news/will-wind-turbines-ever-be-safe-birds

[243] https://www.washingtontimes.com/news/2014/apr/11/death-calif-solar-farms-71-species-bird-found-enti/

[244] https://www.usgs.gov/news/science-snippet/bird-mortality-renewable-energy-facilities-have-population-level-effects

[245] International Council for the Exploration of the Sea: https://academic.oup.com/icesjms/article/79/6/1787/6611678?login=false

Legacy

Fossil fuels are essential not only to the production of goods such as chemicals, asphalt, plastics, and fertilizers, but to human advancement. The demonization of the clean burning of fossil fuels must end. Today, the world faces energy shortfalls that have disrupted critical supply chains, thwarting commerce. Rather than embrace the false totem of climate change, propounded by flawed models, the world must take steps to increase clean fossil-fuel production, with particular emphasis on natural gas.

A question asked by someone who is ill-informed may concern why fuels derived from long dead animals and plants are necessary. The answer is simple: Energy, in the form of fossil fuels, permits us to go places. These places may be reached by any mode of transportation. These places may also be accessed in a classroom, in a home, or in a business, for almost all that we seek to do requires plentiful and affordable power to turn our ideas into actions.

We have many vistas we wish to reach as one united people. What stops us? It is not our lack of boldness. It is not our lack of initiative, steadfastness, or innovation.

What stops us is our government. The Biden administration has done what no other force on earth could have accomplished: It has destroyed American energy dominance. It has demolished what the Trump administration achieved, and, in so doing, stolen the dollars and the dreams of every citizen who yearns to go places, but cannot, for fuel prices, in certain instances, have more than doubled.

Energy is the foundation for every physical good we make and everything we consume. We must fight to take our future back and not place it in the hands of an unaccountable government.

In its role as a shill for the Biden administration, the mainstream press often states that our government "needs adults in the room." Indeed, the Biden administration has proven itself so adult that it could not even find baby formula when our nation's shelves went bare.[246]

---

[246]https://www.msnbc.com/opinion/msnbc-opinion/why-biden-s-response-baby-formula-shortage-disappointing-n1295492

The Biden administration closed down the nation's leading plant that produced baby formula without any backup plan. They did not even ask our allies to increase their production—to ship formula to us. No, they waited until a problem became a crisis because that is what government does. It builds power by flouncing from one self-induced crisis to the next. If our federal government, with the trillions it commands, cannot ensure an adequate supply of baby formula, how are they to be trusted in directing the energy industry in America, which is one of the largest enterprises on earth?

We must challenge the Biden administration as it strips away the last vestiges of American energy dominance, which now lies gutted on the altar of green radicalism. The Biden administration should have learned from the disasters it caused across the entire spectrum of energy production and distribution. It, however, cannot, for it will never learn what it mistakenly believes it already knows.

We must comprehend what we face if we are to contest the actions of the Biden administration. Though rational people believe that others act comparably, this is often not the case. We must plan for chaotic behavior on the part of our political opposition. To match this threat of illogic, we must illuminate what President Biden has obscured.

Supremacy

Energy independence is self-explanatory; energy dominance is not. Energy dominance is the ability through the production of a broad range of fuels and sources of energy, coupled with refining and distribution abilities and alliance agreements, to provide for national self-sufficiency while also meeting the supplemental energy demands of key allies, thus influencing energy markets and prices worldwide. This is what America lost due to President Biden's assumption of office.

Environmental degradation will occur if American energy dominance is not restored and maintained, for it is necessary to ensure clean air, clean water, and the vibrancy of our nation's heartland and cities. This is because abundant power is essential to create the jobs and the prosperity necessary to address environmental concerns within our country and throughout the world.

In contradistinction, the Biden administration's emphasis on initiatives to reduce greenhouse gas emissions, decreases societal and individual wealth. Since the accrual of wealth permits adaptation, President Biden's efforts are inherently counterproductive to enabling people to cope with climate change if it ensues. The loss of energy dominance not only damages American and allied security, it harms developing nations who rely on stable supplies of affordable energy.

Climate change should be studied by our government and by international organizations in the context of the magnitude of consequences as arrayed against the probability of the occurrence of such effects. It is essential to consider the world's capability to influence climate change outcomes at acceptable levels of economic cost. Such a multivariate model will, I believe, demonstrate that the costs inherent in exigent, global reductions in the use of hydrocarbon fuels would overwhelm any benefits that may be attained.

In Africa, population growth in highly congested and impoverished cities, coupled with the pollution that results from the burning of coal or wood in open fires, will result in societal instabilities and the obliteration of national borders. The propagation of diseases is, without question, intensified by overpopulation in cities without adequate infrastructure. By the year 2100, seventeen of the world's most populous cities, comprising 700 million people, will be in sub-Saharan Africa.

Lagos in Nigeria by the turn of this century will, it is estimated, be a city of eighty-eight million; Kinshasa, in the Democratic Republic of the Congo, may be home to eighty-three million people. Dar es Salaam in Tanzania will count seventy-four million souls as its citizens, according to some projections.[247]

---

[247]https://sites.ontariotechu.ca/sustainabilitytoday/urban-and-energy-systems/Worlds-largest-cities/population-projections/city-population-2100.php

It is not possible to know the exact size of these African cities some seven decades from now, but it may be presumed that these metropolises will expand to be far more populous than any city that now exists. The provision of food and water and the elimination of sewage are necessities for urban areas of such scope. Abundant energy is required: These densely populated cities must have oil, gas, and ample electricity for the desalination and the provision of water. Access to education, jobs, transportation, vital supply chains, governmental services, and resources that support human development all depend upon adequate supplies of energy in all its forms.

If plentiful energy is not made available to less developed countries in the coming decades, war, hunger, exodus, radicalism, and pestilence will affect the globe. Adherence to a rigid degrowth agenda, propagated by radical environmentalists, will cause deficiencies and death, perhaps inculcating a more virulent pestilence than the present plague because of the secondary and tertiary effects of energy insufficiencies.

Nations in Asia, Africa, and Central and South America cannot continue to develop and increase their societies' affluence, productivity, health, and wellbeing if abundant electricity and hydrocarbon energy are not available: It is that simple. It is morally wrong to consign the majority of the world's inhabitants to relative poverty and despair in order to inflate the legitimacy of the issue of climate change and apply it as a deceitful tool to redirect wealth and status to elites who benefit from government control and the redirection of money to their enterprises.

I believe our country must embrace a comprehensive path to reattain American energy dominance, for this will enforce global security and the future abundance of energy to all the world's citizens. William Martin, one of the world's leading energy experts and the former deputy secretary of energy during the Reagan administration, refers to the appropriate plan that we envision for the world's energy future as *electricity for humanity*. It centers on American production of natural gas, clean coal, and oil through fracking and other means; it further specifies nuclear power plant production, with an emphasis on building small modular reactors in the near term and commercial fusion reactors before 2050.

Fossil fuels and their production, refinement, and distribution must be supplemented by nuclear power and by renewable energy sources, including solar, wind, hydropower, and geothermal instillations. As technology matures and hydrocarbon resources become limited and more expensive to extract, a natural, market-driven migration to reliance on nuclear power and renewable energy will occur, culminating, we might expect, in the widespread adoption of fusion energy as the preferred, clean source of unlimited power within this century.[248]

No one benefits from runaway inflation and a boom-and-bust approach to energy development, but this is what the Biden administration has instilled by their substitution of mythology for stability. America's economy has been derailed due to the Biden administration's reckless spending and their incomprehension of the centrality of American oil, gas, and coal production to global growth. Instead, they posit an apocalyptic cyclops in the form of climate change, which can only be slain through the immolation of the majority of the world's citizens.

We must understand why this global pretense is being perpetrated. The answer extends to the epoch in which history was first transcribed.

In his superlative examination of ancient worship and ritual across the planet, Sir James George Frazer, in his masterpiece, *The Golden Bough*, discussed kings of archaic times who were also priests.[249] These rulers were believed to wield mysterious powers.

Some dread fear, which emanated from an uninformed contemplation of the world, in the case of a volcano or a storm, or from the mind's eye, in the instance of a dragon or a demon, required that a king not only be a king and thus imbued with all temporal powers, but also a sorcerer, so that he might battle against threats unseen. Such threats were not real but more real than reality for they crowded

---

out astute perception within the collective mind of the polis, which was subjugated to the point of enslavement in order that monstrous forces be slain, though they were, in fact, imaginary.

Climate change has become a false religion, which takes the form of a demon that forces all powers, be they worldly or spiritual, to be transferred in America to a president, and elsewhere, to other national leaders, who would be both kings and conjurers. High priests, in the form of politicized bureaucrats the world over, serve these masters, for the inculcation and the maintenance of spiritual power in these operatives is essential, for climate change is posited as a supernormal force, heretofore unknown.

It would seem on one hand that this stratagem to accrete power is transparent in its avariciousness, and thus almost a prank, yet it is one of the most deceptive governmental actions ever perpetrated. Fear has been transformed into an anvil upon which people are beaten into submission.

Climate and Adaptation

Humanity's journey since the beginning of time has been marked by adaptability. Life is a constant struggle, for new challenges arise every day.

These trials may only be met if we manifest ingenuity and create wealth that can be applied to the problems at hand. Energy is essential to prosperity and must not be constrained if we are to adapt to a world that is ever-changing. Why, therefore, has the Biden administration obliterated, in the face of our enemies, America's energy dominance? Why, in the face of foreign threats and tribulations, has the Biden administration in mere months reversed what has taken decades to accomplish?

The answer to both questions is titanic hubris: The Biden administration believes it, alone, knows the way forward, that it, alone, knows the future. Perhaps President Biden and his cabinet have forgotten that knowledge of the future is the province of God and not of man.

Through its boundless arrogance, the Biden administration has shown that it is not interested in permitting Americans to realize their dreams. It is interested in clamping down on such aspirations through its worship of a false faith. In doing so, President Biden and his followers will not protect the planet's environment, but impoverish people around the world, for abundant energy creates prosperity, which, in turn, permits adaptation. This ability has been essential throughout history to meet challenges. This is what is being stolen. This is what we must restore with great expedience.

Never before has a country abandoned a dominant position so errantly as has America under President Biden in the context of the production of hydrocarbons within our nation's borders.[250] President Biden constrained the exploration, development, and production of American oil by at least two million barrels per day[251] through his imposition of onerous regulations and limits on fracking.[252] He has erected massive roadblocks to our production, use, and export of clean coal[253] and has not provided a template for the future infrastructure needed for our energy companies to supply Asia and the globe with increasing quantities of LNG. These derelictions have empowered dictators, the world over, by increasing allied dependencies on their resources.[254]

It has taken a war in the heart of Europe for the Biden administration to realize the inherent wisdom of the Trump administration's prescient actions to promote the export of American LNG, for the Republican administration recognized that LNG is a fuel that is essential to America's economic, environmental, and national security goals. The Trump administration's accomplishments in the field

---

[250] https://www.americanenergyalliance.org/2022/05/100-ways-biden-and-the-democrats-have-made-it-harder-to-produce-oil-gas/
[251] https://oilprice.com/Latest-Energy-News/World-News/US-Oil-Production-Still-2-Million-Bpd-Under-Pre-Pandemic-Levels.html
[252] https://moneyandmarkets.com/biden-fracking-ban/
[253] https://news.yahoo.com/biden-vows-shut-down-coal-141249268.html?fr=sycsrp_catchall
[254] https://www.csis.org/analysis/biden-makes-sweeping-changes-oil-and-gas-policy

of hydrocarbon energy were undermined by President Biden's intent on serving myths, rather than producing results for the American people.

Levels

Carbon dioxide (CO_2) is essential to life because it plays a central role in photosynthesis; it is not a pollutant. Though it is a trace gas in our planet's atmosphere, it is the most important greenhouse gas after water vapor, for its reaction to infrared light traps heat near the earth's surface. Levels of this gas have risen in the earth's atmosphere since the dawn of the industrial age, for its creation is a consequence of the burning of fossil fuels as well as deforestation, the production of cement, and other causes both natural and manmade.

Global warming is a challenge; it is not a crisis. It is important to understand what is known, what is conjectured, and what is pronounced for political purposes, if we are to understand the dynamics of this issue.

Climate change has been present since the world began. Human-induced global warming is not the greatest threat humanity faces; it must not be construed to be an existential concern, for extreme predictions are falsehoods promoted by those who make money from fear.

Global warming is an issue of manageable dimensions if we take commonsense actions. In 2022, the United States maintained our position in leading the world in reductions in CO_2 emissions, despite our nation's consistent growth in population.[255] In 1973, per capita CO_2 emissions in the United States peaked at 23.08 tons; in 2021, this measure was reduced to 14.86 tons, which constitutes a thirty-six percent reduction.[256] These cuts were predominantly due to market forces in OECD nations, which, for decades, promoted the clean burning of fossil fuels and energy conservation, inducing reductions

---

[255]https://www.instituteforenergyresearch.org/international-issues/since-2005-u-s-has-had-largest-decline-in-carbon-dioxide-emissions-globally/
[256]https://ourworldindata.org/co2/country/united-states

in the creation of anthropologic CO_2 in the United States and allied countries. Japan is second to the United States in its reductions in CO_2 output between 2005 and 2020.[257]

In 1945, in the aftermath of World War II, the United States accounted for 55.5 percent of global CO_2 fossil fuel and industrial emissions.[258] In 2021, though America's economy constituted 24.2 percent of world GDP,[259] our share of global CO_2 creation stood at 13.5 percent,[260] which is fifty-six percent of the CO_2 contribution expected if this number were to reflect our share of the world economy.

We must inquire, therefore, as to which major country is increasing its CO_2 output disproportionately. By far, the biggest offender is China. For example, in 2020, the United States, Japan, and Germany all decreased their respective CO_2 emissions over the prior decade; in contrast, China, Russia, and Iran all increased their CO_2 discharges, with China now constituting 30.7 percent of world emissions,[261] as opposed to America's contribution of less than half that figure, though our economy is much larger.

The suggestion, as magnified by a pandering media, that America and our allies stand as the primary drivers of climate change is incorrect. This falsehood, however, is promulgated by special interests. As with COVID-19, climate science is bureaucratized by federal dictates and grantmaking, making such research and its predictions part of an all-enveloping bureaucracy that frequently cancels alternative views to preserve administrative powers and inertia. Governments will not take the lead in mitigating the rise in global temperatures, people will, and this is why totalistic states will never comply with emission goals.

---

[257] https://www.instituteforenergyresearch.org/international-issues/since-2005-u-s-has-had-largest-decline-in-carbon-dioxide-emissions-globally/
[258] https://ourworldindata.org/co2/country/united-states
[259] https://statisticstimes.com/economy/projected-world-gdp-ranking.php
[260] https://ourworldindata.org/co2/country/united-states
[261] https://www.forbes.com/sites/rrapier/2021/07/23/a-record-decline-in-carbon-emissions/?sh=6ad4d5516280

If free nations enact stringent controls on fossil fuel use, there will be a twofold impetus for adversarial or developing countries to take advantage of this situation. First, nations that have not yet acted will feel less compulsion to enact consequential measures. Second, there is a tremendous incentive for a country, which has not meaningfully curbed its emissions, to not only not act, but to use other nations' restrictive actions for its own economic benefit. This is because energy is a key input to everything that is produced—from apples to rockets.

Efforts to eliminate emissions drive up the costs of any product made under stringent protocols. China, Russia, Iran, and many less-developed countries will never institute such controls; they will only pay them lip service. These nations seek to displace the American worker. Embracing and broadcasting global warming as the key objective for the planet but doing little or nothing to reduce greenhouse gas emissions is a certain route to economic growth for such countries, for competitive advantages will be reaped at the expense of America and our allies. This means lost American jobs and ceaseless economic pain at home. We dare not as a nation let this pillage continue.

The People's Republic of China is substantially increasing its use of coal as a fuel. According to an April 25, 2022, report in the *Los Angeles Times*, "Official plans [in China] call for boosting coal production capacity by 300 million tons this year, according to news reports. That is equal to 7% of last year's output of 4.1 billion tons, which was an increase of 5.7% over 2020."[262]

The Institute for Energy Research notes the following in a 2022 report:

> China's carbon dioxide emissions in 2020 were more than that of the United States, the European Union, and India combined. In 2020, China's carbon dioxide emissions were 10.7 billion metric tons compared to 9.7 billion metric tons for the next 3 largest emitters combined. Since

---

[262]https://www.latimes.com/world-nation/story/2022-04-25/china-promotes-coal-setback-emissions-climate-change

2000, China's carbon dioxide emissions grew by a factor of 3. They increased 1.4 percent in 2020, while most other countries saw a decrease in emissions in 2020 due to lockdowns caused by the coronavirus. In 2020, carbon dioxide emissions were down 10.6 percent in the United States, 10.9 percent in the European Union and 7.3 percent in India.[263]

These numbers should not be surprising, though China's population is in decline, a 2021 report by the Yale School of the Environment notes, "China continues to build coal-fired power plants at a rate that outpaces the rest of the world combined. In 2020, China brought 38.4 gigawatts of new coal-fired power into operation, more than three times what was brought on line everywhere else."[264]

The journal, *NewScientist*, in an essay published on April 26, 2022, corroborates Yale's assessment, writing, "Construction of new coal-fired stations is occurring overwhelmingly in Asia, with China accounting for 52 per cent of the 176 gigawatts of coal capacity under construction in 20 countries last year. The global figure is barely changed from the 181 GW that was under construction in 2020."[265]

Today, China operates more coal plants than the rest of the world combined. By the end of this decade, China's coal footprint may be more than one dozen times that of our nation.[266] China also finances coal plants in other countries and views its construction of such foreign infrastructure as an integral part of its Belt and Road Initiative.

In the United Nations report, *Climate Change 2022: Mitigation of Climate Change*,[267] which is part of the *Sixth Assessment Report of the*

---

[263]https://www.instituteforenergyresearch.org/international-issues/chinas-carbon-dioxide-emissions-more-than-twice-those-of-the-u-s/

[264]https://e360.yale.edu/features/despite-pledges-to-cut-emissions-china-goes-on-a-coal-spree#:~:text=And%20China%20continues%20to%20build%20coal-fired%20power%20plants,times%20what%20was%20brought%20on%20line%20everywhere%20else.

[265]https://www.newscientist.com/article/2317274-china-is-building-more-than-half-of-the-worlds-new-coal-power-plants/

[266]https://americaspower.org/chinas-coal-fleet/

[267]https://www.ipcc.ch/report/ar6/wg3/downloads/report/IPCC_AR6_WGIII_FullReport.pdf

Intergovernmental Panel on Climate Change, the following paragraph pierces prevailing narratives concerning the nature of this issue:

> Globally, gross domestic product (GDP) per capita and population growth remained the strongest drivers of CO_2 emissions from fossil fuel combustion in the last decade (high confidence). Trends since 1990 continued in the years 2010 to 2019 with GDP per capita and population growth increasing emissions by 2.3% yr–1 and 1.2% yr–1, respectively. This growth outpaced the reduction in the use of energy per unit of GDP (–2% yr –1, globally) as well as improvements in the carbon intensity of energy (–0.3% yr –1).[268]

The report also expresses the uncertainties inherent in the models used:

> Modelled pathways with a peak in global emissions between now and 2025 at the latest, compared to modelled pathways with a later peak in global emissions, entail more rapid near-term transitions and higher up-front investments, but bring long-term gains for the economy, as well as earlier benefits of avoided climate change impacts (high confidence). The precise magnitude of these gains and benefits is difficult to quantify.[269]

We must assess these words as undercutting everything that global warming fabulists have told us. In response, we must be realistic. We must wake up and apprehend what is apparent to our nation's adversaries: Fossil fuels are essential to meeting world energy needs and their use can only be meaningfully curtailed as alternative technologies mature and market forces drive their increased adoption. Indeed, natural gas is a key component in the production of ammonia-based fertilizers—without which the world would starve.

Due to the Biden administration's callous policies, natural gas prices have surged; such price increases push fertilizer costs higher, leading to inflation in the prices of the vast majority of foods. On November 10, 2021, the intergovernmental International Energy

---

[268] Ibid.
[269] Ibid.

Forum (IEF), which is composed of seventy-one member nations, noted, "In North America, where natural gas prices have not increased to the same degree as in Europe and Asia, fertilizer price indexes are at their highest level ever – surpassing $1000/short ton, 180% increase compared with the same time last year."[270]

Other countries such as China employ a different process based on coal regassification to produce the basis for fertilizers. The IEF notes, "In China, where most ammonia production is from coal regasification, rising domestic coal prices have also pushed the price of urea (a common ammonia-based fertilizer) higher, up 84% from the same time last year."[271]

The lack of concern for substitution effects caused by narrow policies, which do not adequately consider factors other than the potential for climate change, is startling and often produces effects that contradict the very policies that were intended to be realized. Indeed, Joseph McMonigle, secretary general of the IEF, stated, "The current high prices and scarcity of LNG, particularly in Asia, has led to industries switching from gas to coal and oil and in some cases close down altogether. Major consumers have sounded the alarm, highlighting that the current gas market situation is a threat to the long-term reliability of gas and therefore it is in the interests of both producers and consumers to enhance the availability of gas."[272]

We, as Americans, created the technologies to use fossil fuels cleanly. We must not be constricted by disingenuous rhetoric proffered by an effete administration.

We can no longer permit scientists, economists, and other professionals to be labeled as climate deniers, should they demonstrate the courage to contest the orthodoxy promulgated by leftist elites. Coal use is a brute fact. Clean coal is the means to make this use tolerable in a world in which the burning of wood or dung is used by the poor as sources of energy.

---

[270]https://www.ief.org/news/high-natural-gas-prices-contribute-to-rising-fertilizer-and-food-prices
[271]Ibid.
[272]Ibid.

I do not believe elites generally understand poverty and what it entails. They do not hear the cries of those who seek advancement within impoverished countries.

When I led the first Food for Progress mission while serving on President Reagan's White House staff, I spoke with people in Africa who were in dire need. Having begun these conversations decades ago, I have learned that these wonderful but deprived people understand that absurd posturing and empty promises in the face of imposed hardships are the hallmarks of governmental incompetence. We, for our part, must comprehend that these dangerous traits are iridescent in President Biden's approach to crucial decisions that concern energy and the environment.

Scenarios

We create the witches and the warlocks of our age. Today's ostracization of those who do not comply with the predominant narrative of severe anthropologic climate change is in fact similar in form to the baseless assertions of witchcraft in Europe's early modern period, which began in 1453. Witch-hunts were not inquests at all, for verdicts were predetermined: The act of accusing a person of witchcraft proved the crime. There was no presumption of innocence, for upon arrest the possessions and lands of the accused were immediately confiscated by authorities, leading to massive transfers of unearned wealth to those who would assert certain knowledge where there was none. In essence, this is the case today.

President Biden's energy and environmental policies have constrained oil and natural gas leasing, exploration, distribution, and fracking; in doing so, the Biden administration not only stoked inflation at home, it indirectly funded Vladimir Putin's war machine. Russia's war against Ukraine has exposed the sinews of global economic and energy security. Russia's war has shown that without American leadership and energy dominance, the world may be held hostage by a dictator bent on conquest. Increased prices of oil and gas enriched Russia, incentivizing its invasion of Ukraine: Tens of thousands of Ukrainians are dead because of it.

The loss of American energy dominance means great personal costs due to stratospheric oil and natural gas prices. The inflation and the instability this creates threatens the world's food supplies, through disruptions in the stocks of ammonia-based fertilizers.

As Americans, we know mismanagement when it is paraded before us. The Biden administration is not, however, incompetent in all things; they have proven themselves to be proficient in enacting a radical green agenda, which derives from Marxist principles. President Biden in the domain of energy has proven that he is competent in doing all that is wrong and detrimental to America's interests.

Radical activism supports the degrowth movement, which will impoverish the world; this poverty, in turn, will empower autocrats, who advance their designs when people go hungry. Wind and solar power are not universally applicable, nor are they a total answer to the world's ever increasing energy needs. Renewable energy sources cannot supply base electricity requirements; they are in essence supplementary to hydrocarbon, nuclear, or hydroelectric power where it is available.

Global warming is not an apocalypse, though it is portrayed as one by the media and by scientists and politicians who inveigh against the use of carbon-based fuels for reasons that stem from their desire to increase their dominion. The United States National Oceanic and Atmospheric Administration (NOAA) documents that climate models are inherently "probabilistic." NOAA states the following:

> Unlike weather forecasts, which describe a detailed picture of the expected daily sequence of conditions starting from the present, climate models are probabilistic, indicating areas with higher chances to be warmer or cooler and wetter or drier than usual. Climate models are based on global patterns in the ocean and atmosphere, and records of the types of weather that occurred under similar patterns in the past.[273]

---

[273]https://www.climate.gov/maps-data/climate-data-primer/predicting-climate/climate-models

It is impossible for any climate model to capture the myriad of variables and their interactions years into the future. The magnitude of this inability grows as a function of time, for weather taken over the course of many years constitutes climate.

Climate change forecasts vary from extreme predictions to that of moderate climate change of under two degrees centigrade by the year 2100.[274] We cannot accurately model the amalgamation of countless inputs, which, over time, coalesce to form our climate. If we are to assume that we can predict the future through the turn of this century, we must first ask if such superlative predictive powers have ever been displayed in the past.

We should consider the enormous range of predictions for our present time made by the world's greatest minds a few decades ago. If any of their predictions match our present situation, it is only because all other conceivable predictions were also made. Now selecting those that are right, given the benefit of hindsight, tells us nothing. Neither is the so-called consensus of scientists on climate change determinative.

Science is not consensus; if it were, science as we know it today would be a shell, for science is advanced through the assessment and the incorporation of heterodox views, not through the imposition of manufactured orthodoxy that ossifies existent political power at the expense of progress. Models are inherently speculative and do not adequately consider measures to moderate CO_2 production induced by market forces that are governed by personal choice as manifested throughout the globe.

The factor of prospective efficiencies in energy production is not known and may induce behaviors that are contrary to expectations. With consistent increases of wealth across the globe, the consumption of energy, including the energy embedded in all goods, will likely increase on a worldwide per capita basis.

Economists and analysts have noted that improvements in energy efficiencies can serve as a predicate for increases in the

---

[274]https://www.iea.org/data-and-statistics/charts/temperature-rise-in-2100-by-scenario

consumption of energy per person. This is due to the Jevons paradox, named after the English economist William Stanley Jevons, who observed that efficiencies introduced in steam engine performance, during the Victorian period, actually increased the demand for coal, for its use became less expensive and, therefore, more accessible. Falling costs due to efficiencies therefore stimulated increased consumption at scale.[275] This dynamic has not been adequately addressed in models of future energy consumption, though it is, in fact, well known among scholars in the field of environmental economics.

Dr. Steven Koonin, who served as the undersecretary for science in the Department of Energy under President Obama, is a former professor of theoretical physics at Caltech and the author of *Computational Physics: Fortran Version*,[276] a textbook on modeling physical systems with the aid of computers. Dr. Koonin has raised many pertinent questions as to the adequacy and the sufficiency of models used to forecast climate change decades into the future.

In his book, *Unsettled*, Dr. Koonin has juxtaposed the costs of ill-thought-out climate policies, which destroy global wealth and thus the ability to adapt, with the potential benefits of taking drastic actions to restrict CO_2 and other greenhouse gases, such as methene.[277] Professor Koonin notes that CO_2 that is already present in the earth's atmosphere does not spontaneously vanish even if the world were to achieve net-zero carbon emissions; it can persist for hundreds of years as noted by the United Nations Intergovernmental Panel on Climate Change.

Prudent policies, as enacted by a process president, must weigh costs and risks. This has not been done; instead, scientific data is fed into models that cannot adequately depict what must be projected. As with the scientific community's response to COVID-19, the costs to mitigate the presumed threat are not adequately or meaningfully considered.

---

[275]https://climatalk.org/2021/06/18/jevons-paradox/

[276]Steven E. Koonin, "Computational Physics: Fortran Version," (CRC Press, 1998).

[277]Steven E. Koonin, "Unsettled," (BenBella Books, 2021), 55-59.

The assessment by Dr. Koonin is, in part, shared by Dr. William Nordhaus, the winner of the Nobel Prize in Economics in 2018, "for integrating climate change into long-run macroeconomic analysis."[278] Professor Nordhaus states, "Even if we make the fastest possible turn towards zero emissions, CO_2 will continue to accumulate in the atmosphere, because we cannot simply shut down our economy."[279] Dr. Nordhaus's assessment should seem obvious, but its crystalline nature is shattered by the imposition of misleading narratives by leftists and by global elites who profit from the mass unreason they induce.

Commonsense has been placed in a crucible by leftist academics and scientists, who hold suasion over the statists whose grants enrich the institutions and corporations that constitute the first cause of the present, errant alarm over climate change. This confluence of malign influences is made red hot by communist China and Russia in their promulgation of falsehoods involving the environment and the nature of their own actions.

The foregoing facts will shock those who have imbibed China's and Russia's carefully crafted propaganda that concerns climate change. Communism is totalistic rule that must morph for it rests on a body of catastrophes that has devastated every country in which a form of it was tried. The class struggle was supplanted by communism's supposed war against cultural hegemony and racism. In the last three decades such emphases have been supplemented by cries that the West is destroying the planet and therefore must be squelched if life on earth is to be protected. Reality marks such assertions as abject lies.

As the Soviet Union and its empire imploded, China had its Tiananmen Square. The fabrications and the mendacities that solidified and protected these totalistic states became unsustainable. A new fiction was required if neo-Marxists, communists, and their globalist enablers were to sustain the palisade that they held. Radical

---

[278]https://www.nobelprize.org/uploads/2018/10/press-economicsciences2018.pdf

[279]https://www.swissinfo.ch/eng/sci-tech/environmental-protection_global-warming-goals-impossible--nobel-laureate-tells-swiss-paper/45518376

green ideology was this tool, for it turned the great accomplishments of Western thought and industry into daggers that were supposedly destroying the planet. The answer posed was collective action. It is all a sham.

As conservatives, we must comprehend the reason for the centrality of climate change within the leftist paradigm. As important as is the word, climate, is the word, change. Communists and leftists detest change, which is not of their own making, after they come into power. They do not believe in growing or enlarging the body of the world's wealth but in forever redistributing what presently exists, in order that the totem of equity may be served.

Thus, any change, even change for the better, is to be avoided assiduously. The left views the world as a static system that if upset, will fail. We, who cherish freedom and God's promise, view the world as dynamic, with innumerable opportunities that are ceaselessly created through individual initiative. This difference in perspective is fundamental.

If global warming of a few degrees is such a catastrophe, should it occur, why is observed biodiversity far greater at the equator than it is as one moves away from it, toward the poles? The Roman Climate Optimum, which began during the middle period of the Roman Republic and extended through the initial part of the Western Roman Empire (200 BC to 150 AD), coincided with Rome's greatest achievements and the maximum expanse of its possessions and its influence.[280]

During this period, temperatures in the Mediterranean were unusually warm. Scientists, in their study of climate in this prior geological age, assert that temperatures during this period were hotter than they are today by two degrees centigrade for the same region.[281]

---

[280] https://ancientclimate.philhist.unibas.ch/en/event/the-end-of-the-roman-climate-optimum-and-the-disintegration-of-the-roman-empire/
[281] http://diposit.ub.edu/dspace/bitstream/2445/175978/1/703525.pdf#:~:text=emerges%20of%20this%20trans-Mediterranean%20comparison%20is%20the%20persistent,centuries%20for%20the%20Sicily%20and%20Western%20Mediterranean%20regions.

Crucially, the paleoclimatologists and other scholars, who study this Roman epoch, are interpreting the past, which has left its marks; this is far different than the construction of models to foretell the future. There is compelling reinforcement for the appraisal of the Roman Climate Optimum, based on evidence across many fields, including the recorded ability to plant fruit trees and vines in northern climes in Europe during different centuries throughout the noted era.[282] The Western Roman Empire did not fall when temperatures became warmer but did so when temperatures became colder.

There is a profound contradiction in the argument that momentous actions to restrict the world's use of carbon-based fuels must be taken now, for such actions would constrain economies and limit human adaptation. In fact, there is no means to gradually restrict CO_2 that would thwart the dire consequences inherent in scenarios that represent the worst cases forecasted by climate extremists.

The reality is that radical action to cut greenhouse gases would require the termination of hydrocarbon use worldwide, which is impossible, for it would destroy the global economy, induce mass starvation, and foreclose humanity's ability to adjust. We must assert that human development is the answer to climate change, should it become manifest.

Adaptation for humanity requires prosperity, for it necessitates that we acquire the means to afford costly measures that differ in scope. This level of accommodation will be impossible if we restrict the world's hydrocarbon production and the capabilities it generates. Humanity's future requires that we use fossil fuels cleanly, not abandon them prematurely.

Transference

By the late 1990s, a constellation of elitist forces across the globe coalesced in support of Vice President Al Gore's conceit that global warming was an existential threat. By shaping the future, through narrative creation and entrenchment, this global cabal was able to

---

[282]https://www.sciencedirect.com/science/article/abs/pii/S2352409X21003114

possess knowledge of what was to come and thereby amass extraordinary wealth.

As with the Obama administration before it, the Biden administration seeks to derail America's oil, natural gas, and coal industries. Progressives who have created policy after policy failure, know their ideas do not work. This American nomenklatura, however, understood that ideas have a greater velocity than facts, because ideas may be molded to touch people's emotions.

We, who have eyes to see, must therefore emphasize that American energy production, when free from excessive government regulation or burdensome taxation, is essential to our nation's very existence. In 2021, the energy sector employed 7.8 million hardworking Americans in high-paying jobs.

The paychecks of these fine Americans support businesses in thousands of cities and towns across our country. The American energy industry, in all its forms, represents a central enterprise around which other businesses gather and without which our nation's economy would collapse. This is a most powerful story, which elites in New York, in Washington, and in Hollywood do not want to acknowledge or hear. It is our job to make them listen.

The bountiful supply of energy, in all its forms, produced within our nation's borders and through our offshore drilling platforms, is the means to arrest Russia's, China's, and Iran's ambitions, for each of these belligerent states knows that an America that is not energy self-sufficient, an America that is not energy dominant, is a weakened America. We must show these tyrannical regimes our mettle; we must demonstrate our fortitude, not our adherence to disingenuous political forces.

Collaborating with our allies across the globe, our energy businesses must develop the resources and the infrastructure for global energy and environmental security. This can only be accomplished through our supply of oil and our export of liquified natural gas, clean coal, and nuclear power plants, whose components must be built here and in allied states, lest they be manufactured in Russia or in China.

If we do not commit now to accomplishing these things, international stability will be destroyed as the world will become bound to predatory supply and construction agreements. It is certain that if America and our allies don't build the world's energy and electricity infrastructure, China and Russia will replace us. America's hydrocarbon, nuclear, and renewable industries constitute central piers of American national security, which must be strengthened, not eclipsed. Such support, however, would pierce the left's narratives, so it is proscribed.

Elites contend America's oil, gas, and coal industries are mired in the past and are unable to be part of the world's future. These soothsayers, who view the fueling of their own cars as somebody else's work, could not be more wrong. Oil, gas, and clean coal are the bridges to the world's tomorrows.

These industries provide the basis for the generation of global prosperity that has lifted most of the world out of dire poverty, which has, in turn, enabled individual and societal adjustments, no matter the challenges faced. The Christian humanitarian organization, World Vision, notes, "The world has made huge strides in overcoming global poverty. Since 1990, more than 1.2 billion people have risen out of extreme poverty. Now, 9.2% of the world survives on less than $1.90 a day, compared to nearly 36% in 1990."[283]

Such advancements, which must be burnished, could not have been possible without the use of fossil fuels. Unfortunately, almost 100 million persons have been thrown back into abject poverty due to COVID-19[284] and China's reprehensible actions. Our remedy for those so stricken must be the application of tools that work, not fantasies concocted by elites who have never known want.

Actions

What must be done in the realm of hydrocarbon production and supply? The answers are not difficult but are difficult to enact within a government and media establishment that is bound to mythologies.

---

[283] https://www.worldvision.org/sponsorship-news-stories/global-poverty-facts

[284] https://blogs.worldbank.org/opendata/updated-estimates-impact-covid-19-global-poverty-turning-corner-pandemic-2021

Oil, natural gas, and coal exploration and production must be freed of all unnecessary governmental constraints. The list of these impediments is long but must be revised by regulatory reform and the expansion of oil and gas leases on federal lands, for new leases were all but eliminated by the Biden administration—despite their rhetoric to the contrary.[285]

Clean coal must again be prized, for if the world suffers without adequate supplies of energy, forests will surely be burned for fuel, which will produce massive quantities of black carbon.[286] This is a dangerous pollutant that is known to cause morbidities.

In Alaska, portions of ANWR must be opened to oil exploration and drilling. The Trump administration succeeded where other administrations failed and granted hydrocarbon leases for ANWR. This commonsense action, made in accordance with extremely strict environmental standards and controls, was upturned by President Biden on his first day in office by his issuance of an executive order that instated a ban on drilling; later, his secretary of interior suspended all oil and gas leases for this immense area.[287]

In accord with increasing oil, gas, and coal production, the Department of Energy must continuously assess the adequacy of energy facilities in America. We must not face a future in which arduous regulatory and legal hurdles hamstring our nation's hydrocarbon infrastructure. Of great importance is the adequacy and the condition of our terminals that permit our export of petroleum and LNG to our allies and friends, for this capacity is intrinsic to American energy dominance and, therefore, necessary for global security.

Energy alliances can reduce America's need for military entrenchment overseas, enhancing stability in many regions of the

---

[285]https://www.cnn.com/2022/02/21/us/biden-climate-social-cost-of-carbon-court/index.html

[286]https://www.sciencedirect.com/topics/earth-and-planetary-sciences/black-carbon

[287]https://www.huffpost.com/entry/biden-suspend-oil-leases-arctic-refuge_n_60b677b6e4b0c5658f995387

world. This requires American leadership and our promotion of energy cooperation between neighboring states throughout the globe. Regional thermal-power initiatives can function as repositories of influence and stability, reducing the necessity of certain military deployments; as such, American leadership in this neglected sphere is imperative if our adversaries are to be contested in Africa, in Asia, in South and Central America, and in those nations contiguous to Russia and China.

Geostrategic benefits for America and our allies can be obtained by our championing mutually binding offtake and electricity distribution agreements between adjacent countries. This must be part of our riposte to Russia's and Iran's strategy of making countries in Europe and around the world energy dependent. Of equal importance is that we best China in the construction of international projects, for such facilities are used as vanguards in Beijing's quest for global dominance.

In response to international energy projects built by our adversaries, America and our allies must take the lead by facilitating the formation of multinational, private-sector consortia. New, American-designed coal power plants should employ clean, environmentally sensitive designs that, for example, adopt fluidized bed combustion technologies, as proven in the United States under the sponsorship of the Department of Energy.

The Future of Nuclear Power

Nuclear power is the essential component to meet world energy needs in this century. Measures to reduce CO_2 emissions will not be meaningfully adopted by countries that presently create massive quantities of pollution, including China, Russia, and many countries in Africa and in Asia. Therefore, the quest for very low carbon emissions cannot be successful in the absence of sustained growth in the production of nuclear power across the globe.

The International Energy Agency's (IEA) September 2022 report, *Nuclear Power and Secure Energy Transitions*, bears a descriptive subtitle.[288] It reads, "From today's challenges to tomorrow's clean energy systems."[289] This is one of the most important merits of nuclear power: It is a clean energy solution.

The IEA report notes, "Nuclear energy can help make the energy sector's journey away from unabated fossil fuels faster and more secure."[290] The report further states that,

> Nuclear energy, with its 413 gigawatts (GW) of capacity operating in 32 countries, contributes to both goals by avoiding 1.5 gigatonnes (Gt) of global emissions and 180 billion cubic metres (bcm) of global gas demand a year. While wind and solar PV are expected to lead the push to replace fossil fuels, they need to be complemented by dispatchable resources.[291]

Of equal importance to this statement is this assessment's recitation of the number of Chinese and Russian nuclear plants that are being constructed, for such projects constitute eighty-seven percent of all new nuclear power plants, for the report observes, "Of the 31 reactors that began construction since the beginning of 2017, all but 4 are of Russian or Chinese design."[292]

Unlike our adversaries, safety has been the cornerstone of American reactors in both civilian and naval instillations. Our operation of reactors in difficult sea states in hundreds of nuclear-powered vessels and in the largest array of commercial power plants in the world, places America supreme among nations in nuclear design and environmental protection.

Ever since Eugene P. Wilkinson in 1955, as commanding officer of the world's first nuclear submarine, the USS Nautilus, radioed the words, "Underway on nuclear power," the United States Navy has experienced not one radiological incident in over 6,200 reactor

---

[288] https://iea.blob.core.windows.net/assets/016228e1-42bd-4ca7-bad9-a227c4a40b04/NuclearPowerandSecureEnergyTransitions.pdf
[289] Ibid.
[290] Ibid.
[291] Ibid.
[292] Ibid.

years of operations, involving 526 reactor cores.[293] This is the legacy that we, in concert with our allies, bring to the world.

I believe that America and our allies must offer an alternative to Russian- or Chinese-built nuclear plants that are being erected across the globe, for such protected and hardened plants could, in the future, form a chain of citadels in developing countries, to which Russian or Chinese forces may be ensconced in times of heightened global or regional tensions. The blueprint for such actions has already been documented in Russia's war against Ukraine and in its occupation of the Chernobyl plant.[294] To this point, a November 30, 2022, report by the Royal United Services Institute for Defence and Security Studies states:

> Ukraine's nuclear power plants served three purposes therefore in the invasion plan: to function as reliable shelters for Russia's troops and military personnel, equipment, command posts and ammunition depots; to gain control over Ukraine's energy system, because nuclear power plants are responsible for generating more than 60% of Ukraine's electricity; and to provide the option to obtain leverage for blackmailing European countries with the risk of radiation pollution as a result of possible accidents at nuclear power plants if they attempted to intervene."[295]

We cannot allow a constellation of nuclear plants built and controlled by Russia or China in Africa and in other continents to serve these purposes. In response, a means to effect allied dominance in this field would be the establishment of an international entity that former Deputy Secretary of Energy William Martin and I propose be called the Allied, Nuclear, Secure, World, Electricity Response (ANSWER).

---

[293] Numbers as of November 2021: https://www.world-nuclear.org/information-library/non-power-nuclear-applications/transport/nuclear-powered-ships.aspx#:~:text=Lloyd%27s%20Register%20shows%20about%20200%20nuclear%20reactors%20at,of%20these%2C%20and%20the%20US%20Navy%20over%205400

[294] https://www.bbc.com/news/av/world-europe-61049656

[295] https://static.rusi.org/359-SR-Ukraine-Preliminary-Lessons-Feb-July-2022-web-final.pdf

The agreement of April 16, 2023, regarding the joint provision of nuclear fuel internationally, reached between the United States, Japan, France, the United Kingdom, and Canada, is a positive step.[296] This agreement was made in the Nuclear Energy Forum held in Sapporo, Japan. We must control, as allies, the supply of nuclear fuel for commercial reactors that are in place or being built across the world. Much more, however, needs to be done.

The United States, Japan, the Republic of Korea, France, the United Kingdom, Canada, and private companies within these nations, have in the past competed in providing nuclear plants and related services within their own borders and in foreign, purchasing nations. Competition between the enumerated states must be transmuted into cooperation if these countries, which constitute the heart of the Free World, are to contest China and Russia in the provision of nuclear power plants globally.

The successful construction and operation of new nuclear power plants in purchasing nations is, perforce, a multinational endeavor. We must appreciate that nuclear power plants constitute strategic assets wherever they are constructed and, as such, must be protected. Once instituted, ANSWER must emphasize that the operational safety, physical security, and cyber-security of nuclear plants is of transnational and multinational significance.

In view of the burgeoning energy needs of Africa, Asia, and other continents, the creation of ANSWER would constitute a cornerstone in the establishment of the right to electricity as basic to the flourishing of the human condition. Indeed, in 2019, it was estimated that 761 million people did not have any access to electricity.[297] The increased provision of nuclear power is vital as a clean source of energy that will meet emergent needs.

The production of abundant and reliable energy is essential to meet the requirements of those who lack this necessity as well as

---

[296] https://www.gov.uk/government/news/new-nuclear-fuel-agreement-alongside-g7-seeks-to-isolate-putins-russia
[297] https://ourworldindata.org/number-of-people-in-the-world-without-electricity-access-falls-below-one-billion

others who are underserved. This is central to William Martin's and my vision for electricity for humanity. Secure nuclear power plants can be deployed globally, with specific designs tailored to regional and country-specific requirements.

As a multinational organization that will oversee the construction, maintenance, and security of nuclear plants in purchasing countries, ANSWER must be empowered to stipulate that recipient countries provide long-term, inviolable leases to enable ANSWER to control the land on which any nuclear power plant and its adjacent facilities are built. In addition, ANSWER must control the fuel cycles for all reactors erected in recipient nations, which will enforce operational security.

The provision of electricity in the future will require the simultaneous exchange of information to optimize a broad range of functions. Water conservation, precision farming, and environmental projects will be served by the building of intelligent electricity grids that include a variety of energy conservation measures, which involve communication between consumers and utilities and predictive capabilities with regard to usage needs and other parameters (these grids are often termed "smart").[298]

Intelligent grids must be hardened against cyber intrusions and electromagnetic pulse effects, for the transmission of energy has been a focus of adversarial attacks in America and across the globe.[299] Secretary Pompeo was instrumental in calling attention to Russia's attacks against our energy infrastructure during the time he served as secretary of state.[300] His warnings followed those of William Martin and Roger W. Robinson, Jr. This threat, however, has not abated but has increased.

Generation III and Generation III+ reactors are now being built around the world; these reactors offer advances in thermal efficiency,

[298]https://www.smartgrid.gov/the_smart_grid/smart_grid.html

[299]https://www.reuters.com/article/us-usa-russia-sanctions-energygrid-idUSKCN1GR2G3

[300]https://www.foxnews.com/politics/mike-pompeo-cyberattack-us-government-pretty-clearly-russians

standardization, and greater margins of safety in comparison to the Generation II designs that supply energy in America.[301] The extra margin of safety is the result of passive cooling for the reactor core, which is independent of the source of backup power; the reactor can thus be shut down securely through the use of gravity, circulation, and convection flow as opposed to electric or diesel-fed pumps in Generation II designs.[302]

In addition to existent steam-moderated reactors, a new type of fission power plant holds great promise and may serve as a link until the day when commercial fusion power plants are economically viable. Small modular reactors (SMR) are essentially self-contained nuclear plants that can be built in factories, rather than onsite, thereby achieving unprecedented economies of scale.[303]

In addition to the option of using steam as a coolant, these reactors may use molten salt, liquid metal, or gas.[304] These designs promise far less radioactive waste than traditional nuclear plants. The use of liquid metal is a technology first pioneered by the United States Navy in its construction of its second nuclear submarine, the USS Seawolf (SSN-575).

Upon its commissioning in 1957, the Seawolf first deployed with a nuclear reactor that employed the metal sodium as its liquified coolant. This advanced technology was not adequately evolved at that time, but it is ready now, offering the potential for enhanced safety.

SMRs may be housed in secure underground facilities of moderate size; as greater electricity needs arise, the modularity of these reactors permits other SMRs to be added to a given installation. Crucially, SMRs advance the potential to power cities, towns, and military installations through small, intelligent grids that obviate the need for the wasteful conveyance of electricity over lengthy and

---

[301] https://www.power-eng.com/nuclear/gen-iii-reactor-design/
[302] Ibid.
[303] https://www.iaea.org/newscenter/news/what-are-small-modular-reactors-smrs
[304] https://www.energy.gov/ne/advanced-small-modular-reactors-smrs#:~:text=SMR%20designs%20may%20employ%20light%20water%20as%20a,as%20a%20gas%2C%20liquid%20metal%2C%20or%20molten%20salt.

vulnerable transmission lines. What is needed is a streamlined regulatory environment, both domestically and internationally. This is necessary in order to compete against China or Russia.

The Department of Defense is committed to the design, construction, and demonstration of Project Pele, which is a microreactor, akin to a tiny SMR. This reactor can be transported to power forward operating bases for our military. The deployment of reactors of its type will supply electricity to meet the needs of stationary facilities, thus enhancing our services' stores of fossil fuels, to meet the demanding operational requirements of in-theater aircraft, tanks, armored vehicles, and drones.

Project Pele will constitute the first Generation IV reactor built in the United States; it is a high-temperature-gas design.[305] China demonstrated the world's first Generation IV reactor in 2021. Thus, the Pele initiative, which is supported by the Department of Energy and other elements within our government and the private sector, is essential to our competitive posture.

Nuclear power plants, built and operated safely, can make electricity available to hundreds of millions of people. New technologies promise to do this in a cost-effective manner. Such installations constitute the most advanced form of green energy that is not subject to the vagaries of weather, wind, wave patterns, or the diurnal cycles that govern night and day.

In order to secure fuel for fission reactors, reprocessing is imperative. Fuel reprocessing is the separation of spent fuel, by chemical and by other means, into material that can be reused in fission reactions, with unusable waste removed.[306] This conserves our supplies of fuel-grade uranium as it reduces the amount of waste that requires disposal.

Permanent solutions to waste disposal are at hand for fission reactors and are obviated for fusion-based designs that may be built by the middle of this century. Finland has demonstrated a

---

[305] https://www.defense.gov/News/Releases/Release/Article/2998460/ dod-to-build-project-pele-mobile-microreactor-and-perform-demonstration-at-idah/

[306] https://www.sciencedirect.com/topics/earth-and-planetary-sciences/ nuclear-fuel-reprocessing

multifaceted, environmentally sensitive approach to handle spent nuclear fuel perpetually. It is readying a very deep geologic repository for nuclear waste that will bury the encapsulated byproducts of fission in igneous bedrock that is billions of years old.[307] This system is necessary, for nuclear power will provide up to sixty percent of Finland's electricity requirements in the future.[308]

The pending deployment of SMRs will not present additional problems in handling nuclear waste. The director of the division of nuclear fuel cycle and waste technology at the International Atomic Energy Agency (IAEA), Christophe Xerri, has stated, "Since this type of small modular reactor will be using the same fuel as conventional, large nuclear power plants, its spent fuel can be managed in the same way as that of large reactors."[309] This will be true of the many different designs for SMRs now being refined or built.

The creation of ANSWER would aid recipient countries in meeting various waste disposal requirements. Turning the spent fuel into a type of glass, through a process called vitrification, is an important step in the management of this issue, for vitrified waste is substantially smaller than the original reactor product and is more stable.[310] It thus demands less cubic area for burial.

The nations that comprise ANSWER will need to combine their enterprises, talents, and intellectual capital, pursuant to the award, the construction, the defense, and the maintenance of nuclear power plants in recipient nations. For America to meet the challenges posed by adversarial and belligerent nations that strive to build nuclear plants globally, we must understand that a new nuclear power alliance composed of companies and experts from allied countries will face challenges and disadvantages in their ability to compete for

---

[307] https://www.forbes.com/sites/jamesconca/2021/05/31/finland-breaks-ground-on-its-deep-geologic-nuclear-waste-repository/?sh=53106cf96103
[308] https://www.world-nuclear.org/information-library/country-profiles/countries-a-f/finland.aspx
[309] https://www.iaea.org/newscenter/news/small-modular-reactors-a-challenge-for-spent-fuel-management
[310] http://large.stanford.edu/courses/2010/ph240/thompson2/

foreign contracts against the nuclear enterprises of China or Russia, in which the breadth of these belligerents' power is used to attain construction contracts from other countries.

Each signatory state to ANSWER will be obligated to be responsible for their respective legal, political, legislative, policy, and regulatory approvals, as required under their respective national laws and codes, to permit national participation and the involvement of companies and institutions that are headquartered within each country. A multilateral, coordinating body, headquartered in America, should be formed to serve as a forum to combine the enterprises, talents, and institutions of each member state, so that companies within such nations may assemble multinational coalitions that can bid successfully on nuclear power-plant contracts internationally.

Any coordinative function must not hinder competition between companies or consortia of the member states; rather this entity should facilitate the joining of enterprises and resources, in order that combinations of companies may compete effectively. Thus, ANSWER should support the independent creation of consortia that are multinational in nature.

Project leadership must span diverse elements to support a purchasing nation's participation in building and in maintaining a nuclear plant. In order to protect corporate intellectual property, there must not be any compulsion for private companies or institutions to share technology, resources, or proprietary information. All aspects of project involvement by private enterprises must be voluntary. Levers of allied national power, across countries, must coalesce to reinforce these principles.

The defense envelope for nuclear power plants requires that measures be taken to guard against the infiltration or exfiltration of data, personnel, materials, or fuel. Communications between ANSWER and the International Atomic Energy Agency must facilitate non-proliferation objectives in all construction projects and in their operations.

ANSWER should work closely with participating companies, consortia, and purchasing countries, to secure Section 123

Agreements, as required by law when the United States undertakes nuclear covenants with another nation. This is to support non-proliferation objectives.

Destiny

The United States and our allies must rise to meet present challenges and those that are foreseeable. America will fall without a strong center that is constituted not by government but by the American people.

The destiny of our nation is opposed by forces that are just being made clear. They, who would deprive us of our future, seek to sell, to the highest bidder, the wealth and the legacy of our country. They are joined by global elites and by belligerent foreign powers, led by China and Russia, which wish to rob our nation of our century—to make it theirs. We have already tolerated too much, for the left and their enablers in Beijing and in other foreign capitals are intent on destroying the American way of life.

Whether by design or by stupidity, many of our nation's most vaunted institutions have betrayed the American people in the central enterprise of securing energy dominance for our country. Those who whine about climate change contend they know the future, but by saying they know everything, they prove they know nothing. Wholesale change in Washington cannot come too soon if our nation's citizens and their interests are to be served.

BP, the multinational gas and oil company, noted the following in its recent *Statistical Review of World Energy*:

> Primary energy demand increased by 5.8% in 2021, exceeding 2019 levels by 1.3%. Between 2019 and 2021, renewable energy increased by over 8EJ [Exajoule: 1 EJ = 1018 joules; the joule is the basic energy unit of the metric system; this can be converted into other units that describe energy]. Consumption of fossil fuels was broadly unchanged. Fossil fuels accounted for 82% of primary energy use last year, down from 83% in 2019 and 85% five years ago.[311]

---

[311] https://www.bp.com/content/dam/bp/business-sites/en/global/corporate/pdfs/energy-economics/statistical-review/bp-stats-review-2022-full-report.pdf

To expect that the world could reduce this rate of hydrocarbon use to near zero by mid-century is unrealistic. The desire among billions of the world's citizens for prosperity, the imperative of being able to adapt to differing climatic conditions should they materialize, the growing populations in Africa and parts of the Middle East, and the very numbers involved in these noted matters mark the goal of global net-zero-carbon energy as fictional, for it cannot be realized until nuclear power, in its advanced forms, becomes widespread. As entrenched by President Biden, leftist fabulations in this sphere are exceedingly dangerous, for the premature rejection of fossil fuels, before new primary sources are available that are not intermittent, will lead to increased impoverishment and starvation among the most vulnerable.

Although perhaps counterintuitive, Russia's ultimate return as an unsanctioned and legitimate supplier of fossil fuels to the world will yield an array of benefits, which include reducing a prime impetus for inflation and providing alternative supplies for fuels whose various sources are subject to disruptions. Clearly, such reintegration must be contingent upon Russia's withdrawal from all of Ukraine and the election of new Russian leaders who renounce that nation's present policies.

Crucially, Western nations must never again be dependent upon Russia for any hydrocarbon supplies. This is especially true with regard to Germany. Additionally, it is unwise to allow Russia to build nuclear powerplants in countries other than itself. The security and safety risks attendant in Russian plants are too great.

If we pursue an energy agenda solely based on the fear of climate change, it is certain that governments will do more harm than good. Complex issues require discernment and responses that are multifactorial in nature; empty rhetoric will only solidify challenges that must be faced and not papered over. This is why the Trump administration withdrew from the Paris Agreement on climate. This is why it was wrong for the Biden administration to hobble America's energy industry.

In the provision of energy and electricity, as generated from nuclear and renewable power sources, we must demonstrate both patience and diligence, for the tasks we face are difficult but resolvable. As we work, let us overcome our obstacles and not abandon our hopes or plans, for we must turn our vision of electricity for humanity into reality.

Today, two square inches of pelletized fuel in a fission reactor can power an all-electric house for many years. This is extraordinary, but there is more. By the end of this century or possibly before, the world's gigantic electricity needs will most probably be met by a new source of energy, fusion power. It was Ronald Reagan who led America and other nations in committing to an immense fusion demonstration project that is just now being completed by an international consortium. The International Thermonuclear Experimental Reactor (ITER) will soon become the most complex operational machine ever built by man.

Half a world away, scientists at the National Ignition Facility in California have already achieved a contained fusion reaction that produced more power than it consumed, through the use of lasers.[312] This achievement, which was once thought impossible in this century, is based upon work that began in secret many years ago; it now presages a future of unlimited, clean energy.

These inventions are the product of free men and women who have been empowered to do more than they, themselves, thought possible. This is the essence of American leadership; this is what our country has always offered to the world.

We cannot allow those who do not believe in the certainty of a marvelous future for our children to posit limits on humanity's potential or our intrinsic ability to adapt. Skeptics of the copious possibilities present in this century still argue that fusion furnaces cannot be sustained.

They could not be more wrong. Fusion power plants are more numerous than the grains of sand in all the world's oceans.

There are at least 100 billion stars in our galaxy and two trillion galaxies in the observable universe. Each of these suns is a nuclear furnace; many are billions of years old. In all the galaxies of our

---

[312]https://www.universityofcalifornia.edu/news/lawrence-livermore-national-laboratorys-national-ignition-facility-achieves-fusion-ignition

universe, these suns illuminate everything we see as they form the matter that makes up reality.

I believe in America's future and that of the world. I believe our country's next 100 years will be as brilliant as they are bountiful, for I believe that God, in his majesty, has enlightened his creation, and in so doing, shown us the way to a limitless destiny.

Chapter 12, Energy Dominance, Precepts:

• Fossil fuels are essential for the production of chemicals, asphalt, plastics, and fertilizers, and are necessary for human advancement; they will remain so through the turn of the century. This fact is dismissed by President Biden.

• Natural gas remains the bridge to a net-zero-carbon energy future that must, for reasons of capacity and technology, be based on nuclear power generation; this will be facilitated by the manufacture of small modular reactors.

• China dominates in the production of the constituent parts of photovoltaic cells. Critical materials, required in the construction of windmills, are also sourced from this adversarial state. As planned by the Biden administration, an increase in America's dependence on solar energy will, in effect, make China responsible for the supply of four-tenths of America's electricity requirements by the middle of the next decade. This result would be catastrophic.

Issues and Problems:

• President Biden's energy and environmental policies have constrained oil and natural gas leasing, exploration, distribution, and fracking. In doing so, the Biden administration has not only stoked inflation at home, it indirectly funded Vladimir Putin's military forces and his assaultive war against Ukraine.

• Worldwide coal use is a brute fact. The People's Republic of China is substantially increasing its use of coal as a fuel. In the United States and in allied and recipient countries, clean coal is the means to make this use tolerable in a world in which the burning of wood is used as an alternative in less developed countries, though it is very toxic.

• Climate change should be studied by our government and by international organizations in the context of the magnitude of its consequences as arrayed against the probability of the occurrence of such results. It is essential to review the world's capability to influence climate change outcomes at acceptable levels of economic cost.

• If adequate supplies of energy are not made available to poor countries in coming decades, war, hunger, exodus, and pestilence will affect the globe. It is wrong to consign the majority of the world to poverty to inflate the legitimacy of the issue of climate change in order to redirect wealth to elites whose enterprises stand to benefit.

Duties and Actions:

• Oil, natural gas, and coal exploration and production must be freed of all unnecessary governmental constraints. Clean coal must be prized. In Alaska, portions of ANWR must be opened to oil exploration and drilling.

• In accord with increasing oil, gas, and coal production, the Department of Energy must continuously assess the adequacy of energy facilities in America. We must not face a future in which arduous regulatory and legal hurdles hamstring our nation's hydrocarbon infrastructure. Energy alliances can enhance stability across the world.

• Nuclear power is essential to meet global energy needs. An Allied, Nuclear, Secure, World, Electricity Response (ANSWER) should be formed to contest Russia and China in the sale of nuclear plants across the globe.

• The United States of America, Japan, the Republic of Korea, France, the United Kingdom, and Canada, and private companies within these nations, have in the past competed in providing nuclear plants and related services within their own borders and to foreign nations. This competition between free countries and their nuclear industries must be turned into volitional collaboration, in which a new multinational organization or coalitions of companies will oversee the construction, maintenance, and security of nuclear plants within purchasing countries.

CHAPTER 13

IN DEFENSE OF FREEDOM

America's military is in danger. The defense of our nation has been placed in jeopardy by threats both foreign and domestic. When America's principles, objectives, capabilities, and commitments are aligned, our nation's security is strong. If any of these elements is lost, our power is weakened.

Our nation's military has never been defeated over the course of a war, but elected officials and their acolytes in our media and educational institutions have conspired to turn victories in battle into political quagmires. The American people must possess the determinant voice in matters of war and peace: This requires that the public be informed by our nation's leaders.

> America's path in any armed conflict must derive from our leaders' reflection on the sacrifices required in comparison to what may be achieved. Anything less will squander American lives. If deterrence is to be realized, each of our armed services must be superior to any opposing force. Once a certainty, this may soon no longer be a reality. This must change immediately.

In Defense of Freedom

I vowed to support our Constitution and to defend America and its sovereignty when I served as a director on President Ronald Reagan's National Security Council staff and as the first Deputy Assistant Secretary of the Navy for Technology Transfer and Security Assistance. My oath and allegiance to our nation has no expiration or limit. Therefore, I must state what I see: The defense of America has been placed in jeopardy by threats both foreign and domestic.

Facts can be mislaid but they can never be destroyed. When America's principles, objectives, capabilities, and commitments are aligned, our nation's security is strong. To the degree that any of these elements is missing, our power is diminished.

A Military Obedient to the People

Civilian control of our military is stipulated by our nation's highest law and is essential to our Republic. Article II, Section 2, Clause 1 of the Constitution states, "The President shall be Commander in Chief of the Army and Navy of the United States, and of the Militia of the several States, when called into the actual Service of the United States."

The president controls our military through a unified command structure that includes the secretary of defense. Contrary to a prevailing impression that has been advanced by the media, the chairman of the Joint Chiefs of Staff is not in the chain of command of our nation's military forces.

The Joint Chiefs of Staff is composed of the following statutory members: the chairman, the vice chairman, the chief of staff of the Army, the chief of naval operations, the chief of staff of the Air Force, the commandant of the Marine Corps, the chief of the National Guard Bureau, and the chief of space operations. Its membership has grown through the passage of successive laws.

As relayed in the National Security Act of 1947, the Joint Chiefs of Staff are military advisors to the president.[313] This role is essential and is properly separated from the chain of command. The Goldwater–Nichols Department of Defense Reorganization Act of October 4, 1986,[314] strengthened joint military commands; it also specified that no member of the Joint Chiefs of Staff, individually, or the body, collectively, would be part of our military's chain of command.

Law and administrative procedures have, for decades, reflected the understanding that the chiefs could not exercise their role as unbiased advisors to the president, the secretary of defense, and the National Security Council, if they were also part of the chain of command that directs combatant forces. The Joint Chiefs of Staff have made their role absolutely clear, for their official website states, "the Joint Chiefs of Staff have no executive authority to command combatant forces."[315]

In all matters involving defense reform, civilian control is mandatory. Nations that cede political power to military officers endanger their liberty. This is not what the Founders intended for our Republic.

In 1980, Ronald Reagan sought the presidency of our country to answer the window of vulnerability that was created by the Soviet

---

[313]As amended, https://www.govinfo.gov/content/pkg/COMPS-1493/pdf/COMPS-1493.pdf
[314]Pub. L. 99–433
[315]https://www.jcs.mil/About/

Union in its quest for military supremacy. Today, we must consider a broader array of threats that includes terrorism in all its forms, transnational criminal organizations, China, Russia, Iran, and the derivative challenges posed by the Democratic People's Republic of Korea, Cuba, and Venezuela.

Communist China is not a direct analogue of the USSR, for China is far more powerful and adroit. This adversarial nation seeks to use its present window of opportunity, afforded it by the Biden administration, to subdue our way of life. This is something we cannot allow. It is not rational to permit China, as a nation, to be the principal exporter of goods to our country and the source of our largest individual trade deficit, as it targets our armed forces and threatens to invade Taiwan.[316]

We cannot afford to reprise the errors we made before our entry into the Second World War. Unfortunately, China is not adequately contested in its infiltration of America's core enterprises and businesses.

We should not seek the complete dismantlement of our economic ties with China should that nation exercise a measure of restraint in its actions. Pursuant to this goal, our nation's leaders must make Xi Jinping understand that he will never defeat America militarily and that any attempt to invade Taiwan will be met with the certitude of his nation's retreat in such an endeavor, which would be followed by the cessation of all trade and financial relations between the United States and China. This would affect Chinese funds, stocks, and bonds.

The articulation of these steps by an American president would constitute one of the greatest deterrents to a Chinese invasion of Taiwan. The present cost of such a proclamation is nothing, though the value of such a presidential policy pronouncement cannot be overstated.

In addition to China, we face a spectrum of threats that are complex and not fully revealed. Therefore, our responses cannot be

---

[316]https://www.visualcapitalist.com/us-largest-trading-partners-2022/

simplistic but must draw on our eminent past as well as our goals for our nation's future.

Our men and women in uniform push forward when everyone else retreats. There is no finer group of people on earth, yet their sacrifices are too often subverted. Our nation's military has been undercut by elected officials and their acolytes in the media; in addition, many educational institutions and academics have conspired to turn victories in battle into perceived geostrategic quagmires—to support the disingenuous and paralytic narratives they purvey.

America's armed forces have not been defeated on the field of battle, at sea, on beaches, or in the air, for our military has always ultimately overcome any loss or setback. Our military has, instead, been thwarted by a fatuous political class that demands extraordinary sacrifices of our men and women in uniform, often in the service of ill-defined or unattainable goals.

Freedom cannot be imposed on a people; it must be sought. This may occur after an abject defeat, as was the case with Germany, Italy, and Japan. It will not occur as the result of nation building. This cannot be the enterprise of America's military, though many politicians, in both parties, contrive that what Americans fought and died for in our wars against the British and in the Civil War, can somehow be ordained across the world.

We must honor the sacrifices demanded of those who volunteer to serve in our military. We must establish political processes that support astute leadership that will triumph in battle and prompt joy in peace.

The nature of war presents several dichotomies. Wars are distinct from military actions. Article I, Section 8, Clause 11 of our Constitution specifies that only Congress can declare war.[317] Based upon a lifetime of investigation, it is my earnest belief that wars should be waged only upon their declaration by Congress.

---

[317] https://constitution.congress.gov/browse/essay/artI-S8-C11-3/ALDE_0001 3589/%5b%27invasion%27%5d

Reciprocally, military actions should be limited in objectives and in duration. There should be an exigent need or a manifest national imperative that coalesces, in the presence of other factors, to form the necessity that warrants our military's commitment to battle in the absence of a declaration of war. A clear exit strategy should also be articulated at the onset of military operations.

I believe these views to be consonant with the framework our Founders erected for our Republic. Our government was designed in order that it promote the attainment of wisdom, which accrues from inquiry, shared purpose, and an understanding of our capacities and goals. George Washington fought for this conception of national power and its exercise, as did John Jay, who established America's first counterintelligence organization,[318] and Alexander Hamilton, who commanded an integrated force of patriots that audaciously attacked the British at Yorktown,[319] setting the stage for the Revolutionary War's triumphant conclusion.[320]

I believe that distinguishing military engagements of limited scope from wars is the means to heal our nation's wounds, in order that our military be supported earnestly. Wars may either merit our involvement or be alien to the American creed. If a war is not deemed meritorious, thereby being unsupported by Congress' acting in its representative role, such a conflict should not be joined; neither should such an engagement be posed as a military action to avoid the will of Congress and the American people.

We may distinguish wars that impose from wars that restore. Wars that impose may seek the achievement of goals that support American interests. The criterion must be the clear assessment of the nature of our interests. We must ask: Are vital American concerns at stake? If they are not, a measured action or a limited

---

[318]https://www.intelligence.gov/index.php/articles/957-john-jay-the-founding-father-of-counterintelligence#:~:text=During%20the%20Revolutionary%20War%2C%20John%20Jay%20played%20a,in%20one%20of%20the%20Federalist%20essays%20he%20authored.
[319]https://www.history.com/news/alexander-hamilton-battle-yorktown-revolutionary-war
[320]https://www.nps.gov/york/learn/historyculture/hamiltonbio.htm

commitment as part of an alliance may be considered, but either course must be governed by the principles for military actions that I have stated.

Vietnam is an example of an undeclared war that should not have been fought. The Second Gulf War, though posited as a war on terrorism, was also unnecessary and has proven to be, on balance, counterproductive, for Iraq has fallen partially under the valence of Iran.

Wars to restore are fought because vital American interests have been attacked or are in imminent danger of being destroyed or crippled. Such conflicts can include those that are joined because of the collective defense agreements we hold with allied nations. Rather than making America more vulnerable to attack or to the onset of war, such collective defense agreements reduce the chances for combat due to the strength and the permanence of our alliances.

Restorative wars include World War I, World War II, and Korea. The United States should never again fight another nation's war, but we must stand ready when people who are willing to fight for their own liberty request support that will not require the dispatch of our armed forces.

In war, the capacity to reassess and to react is essential, as is the option to mediate or negotiate when appropriate. End points must be considered before wars or military actions are broached.

Dr. Fred Iklé, who served as the undersecretary of defense for policy during the Reagan administration, wrote *Every War Must End*, which considered the resolution and the aftereffects of war.[321] In his book, Dr. Iklé noted that while great attention is paid by policymakers to prewar circumstances and the initiation of war, corresponding considerations as to how an envisioned conflict might end are often absent or ephemeral.

This circumstance is compounded by what at first may seem to be an incongruity. Wars are often accompanied by a degree of concern for their termination and their aftermath that scales inversely

---

[321]Fred Charles Iklé. "Every War Must End," (Columbia University Press, 1971).

to the dimensions of the conflict that is waged. This is because the weight of the engagement and its course demand near total focus on how battles must be fought, rather than on matters that will govern the war's end.

The range of conceivable repercussions should be considered by decision-makers before the advent of hostilities. America's Global War on Terrorism is testament to the fact that the nature of the post-conflict peace that can be enforced is not always defined by the attainment of prewar objectives. Hard-won achievements and desired results may be lost in the aftermath of victory if appropriate planning is not in place before the cessation of military operations.

Our servicemen and women represent the best of America, for they are committed to lives of purpose, sacrifice, and achievement. Their commitment must be honored, for as a nation, we charge our military to fight and to win wars in order to preserve peace. Congress must stand against caustic priorities that emphasize Marxist dictates of equity, for they corrode excellence.

The American people are entitled to their exercise of a determinant voice in matters of war and peace: This requires that the public be informed. An administration must possess the power and the discretion to advise the public based on facts, as President Kennedy did during the Cuban Missile Crisis, for he addressed all of America with great candor and in compelling detail.[322]

President Kennedy understood that the obligations of his office required that he warn the public of the stakes involved; he thus addressed the American people as adults who would grasp material of both complexity and moment. This did not restrict the Kennedy administration's capacity to react to the threat the Soviet Union posed. President Kennedy's public earnestness reinforced his position of resolve and intense strength in the eyes of our adversary.

Stated simply, our nation's engagement in war and in armed conflict must derive from our solemn reflection on the stakes involved and the sacrifices required in comparison to what is to be

---

[322]https://www.jfklibrary.org/learn/about-jfk/historic-speeches/address-during-the-cuban-missile-crisis

achieved. If there be a mismatch of these factors in our assessment of the scale of conflict, we must rebalance such weights until the measure comes to rest. Anything less will squander American lives.

An Apolitical, Professional Force

If deterrence is to be realized, in order to assuage conflict and thus secure peace, each of our armed services must be superior to any opposing force. Once a certainty, this may soon no longer be a reality.

Our military is at a crossroads. We must reject political indoctrination and pursue a commitment to excellence in military training, planning, and procurement. The maintenance of unequaled capabilities in all fields of combat is not a luxury America can postpone. It is a necessity in our present world in which we contest threats that span the globe and the spectrum of conflict.

America's military is in danger. Our security rests upon the capabilities of the men and women who serve. They must be trained to fight and to win. They must have the arms to do so, but what if training is corrupted to enforce political ends, the warrior ethos subordinated, and required weapons delayed in their acquisition? Deterrence and our ability to defend our nation will be lost.

Training must not bow to politicalization as wrought by the left, thus subverting our military's foundations. The leadership of our nation's armed forces must ensure that our brave servicemen and women can rapidly deploy as a cohesive fighting force that will dominate and, if necessary, destroy any possible foe. Wokeness and the toleration of non-military behavior within our services disrupt this mission.

From the Civil War through March 3, 2023, ninety-four African Americans have been awarded our nation's highest medal for valor, the Congressional Medal of Honor.[323] In the aftermath of the Second World War and grievous assaults made upon returning African Americans who honorably served our nation, President Truman, in 1948, desegregated America's armed forces. Though his action was

---

[323]https://www.cmohs.org/recipients/lists/black-african-american-recipients

immediate, its implementation was marked by consternation, which fluctuated throughout our country.

America has come a long way since that momentous decision. President Truman's order brought people of all races together to build a better, stronger America, but leftist academicians and politicians seek to destroy our nation's hard-fought progress by reimposing segregation under the false flag of wokeness. How dare they?

This metastasis, however, is now actuated. It is being enforced by those who seek in this decade to undo what has taken almost 250 years to create: a unified constellation of military power unequaled in world history in its capacities and in its commitments to liberty.

Our nation's armed forces are being eroded by the imposition of anti-American values through training regimes that repackage Marxist dogma under the guise of equity, inclusion, and wokeness. Race is proposed as the arbiter in all relationships, for racism is supposedly hidden within the fabric of America's institutions, both military and civilian.

Leftist pap, now being induced in all our services through mandatory sessions of indoctrination, which go by a raft of names to hide their true purpose, seeks to undermine the core values of faith, honor, duty, and service to others that are the pillars of our military power. As stipulated by Chief of Naval Operations Michael Gilday, the CNO-Professional Reading Program, on its "foundational" reading list for sailors, included Dr. Ibram X. Kendi's book, *How to Be an Antiracist*.[324]

Dr. Kendi's book instills racial antagonism as it adulterates the military's sacred oath to "support and defend the Constitution of the United States against all enemies, foreign and domestic," for it calls our nation's highest law, "A color-blind Constitution for a White-Supremacist America." This view of the world, rather than combating real manifestations of prejudice and discrimination, ensures that these scourges will be directed into avenues adverse to our armed services' training and warfighting capabilities.

---

[324]Ibram X. Kendi, "How to Be an Antiracist," (One World, 2019).

Though this screed has now been removed from this reading list, many other outrageous sops to leftist ideals persist in our military services. In recognition of the Biden administration's priorities, the Air Force created the Office of Diversity and Inclusion on January 11, 2021.[325]

In its announcement of the formation of this new organization, which supports the Air Force and Space Force, the public affairs component of the Office of the Secretary of the Air Force stated, "Diversity and inclusion are warfighting imperatives and we need to capitalize on all available talent by enabling a culture of inclusion where every member is respected and valued for his or her identity, culture and background."[326] Military assessments within the Air Force and Space Force may thus be contorted to reflect factors other than individual merit. Contrary to sound military order, outward manifestations of diversity are to be emphasized at the expense of individual contributions and unit cohesion.

There can be only one standard for our military: excellence. Anything else will undermine the values that are the pillars of our military power. This understanding is in danger of being lost.

West Point is now employing aspects of critical race theory in its administration, though this manufactured framework posits that racism is inextricably tied to America's foundational institutions, including our military services. The Air Force, in part, now extolls valuation based upon an individual's perceived culture, background, or identity.[327] Thus, emphasis may be placed on appearances or gestures at the expense of unity and contributions. These are not solutions but command inadequacies.

The United States Air Force Academy in Colorado has created and promoted identity-based groups, which permit cadets, in essence, to segregate themselves to enforce ethnic, racial, sexual, or

---

[325]https://www.af.mil/News/Article-Display/Article/2490452/department-of-the-air-force-institutes-office-of-diversity-and-inclusion/
[326]Ibid.
[327]https://www.af.mil/Portals/1/images/diversity/D-I_Resource_Handout_Aug2021_v2.pdf

gender-related affiliations.[328] This is a tragic diminution in the mandate of this institution, whose regression is unfortunately matched in various ways by our nation's other service academies. The parents of our nation's cadets have every right to be offended, for their trust that the hearts of their children would be ennobled has been betrayed.

Though our services have vanquished systemic racism, the Pentagon has decided to subdue instances of it through the imposition of countervailing racism, by inducing bitterness and gross attribution in what passes for "training." Occurrences of racism, however, cannot be fought through the institution of racism. Prejudicial offenses to humanity and to military order must be extinguished through leadership, not bureaucracy.

The path traversed by our nation's military, under the guidance of the Biden administration, is antithetical to military order and is thus impermissible. The histories of many nations warn us of one central consequence of this forced march: A military that is constantly fed politicized garbage will soon no longer be an apolitical armed force but become partisan in nature and thus a tool that may be wielded to subjugate freedom. This must never occur in the United States.

As a White House and Pentagon official who faced the Soviet Union during the time just before that evil empire fell, I can think of no more damaging affront to our nation's security than pitting our servicemen and women against each other based upon the melanin in their skin. I have beheld brave warriors whose faces were shattered by the ravages of war, which melted one layer of skin atop another. Such grievous wounds scar all equally.

It is this realization of common risk and joint concern that has forged America's armed forces into a band of brothers and sisters who look far beyond their superficial differences to fortify themselves within the shared bonds of humanity that God has bestowed. We must never let these bonds be broken; we must stamp out

---

[328] https://www.forbes.com/sites/erictegler/2022/11/09/as-the-air-forces-credibility-wanes-its-academy-devotes-time-to-diversity--inclusion-training/?sh=7ba429432849

political indoctrination and the perverse assertion that Americans be separated by race.

The Biden administration treats our military as a petri dish in which new modes of social conduct may be played out. This particularization is not consonant with proper military order. The lives of our brave men and women are at stake.

The Biden administration's insistence that our military is beset by racial injustice crowds out necessary training and impedes the maintenance of complex weapons and systems. Such a course, if continued, will cause unnecessary fatalities and injuries in time of war, for this emphasis on indoctrination has served to deprioritize the fielding of new weapons desperately needed by our country. Every death of one of our brave men and women in arms is a great tragedy, but such sacrifice and loss should never be the result of inadequate training or substandard weapons that result from the politicization of our nation's armed forces.

Divestiture, Retreat, and Negation

The Biden administration's defense budgets are hollowing out America's forces through the adoption of a "divest to invest" policy, in which present capabilities are demolished in order that funds be devoted to new weapons programs: Such new developmental initiatives are not presently in production and may not even exist in prototype form.[329] As the war in Ukraine proves, our military must possess persistent capabilities that are not cut to permit the funding of future weapons systems, which are very often never realized.

Technology, which is groundbreaking in nature, is of determinative military value when it is deployed in the hands of our forces: Real and not theoretical weapons are essential to victory in battle. The substitution of paper projects for those that exist also increases the unaccountability of the military-industrial complex. President Eisenhower warned of the accretion of power and the concomitant

---

[329]https://www.defensenews.com/opinion/commentary/2022/11/16/us-air-forces-divest-to-invest-plan-is-too-risky/

abrogation of responsibilities when the industries that support our armed forces are not subject to appropriate oversight and control.[330]

In the six decades since Eisenhower's farewell address, political gamesmanship, coupled with a bloated Pentagon bureaucracy, complete with coteries of officials and officers more concerned with their future employment than with their current obligations, has reduced America's combat strength. This is unacceptable.

Throughout multiple administrations, the Pentagon's record in fielding new weapons is deficient and requires a total revision as to how the Department of Defense develops, acquires, and replaces systems. All services are plagued with procurement disasters, often wrought by political forces that care little for actually building and deploying decisive weapons, for the manifestation of callow posturing has become a permitted substitute for true patriotism in many quarters in Washington.

Framework

American economic and military power must be second to none if the world is to avert global war; these attributes must be coupled with energy dominance. Creation of a military that is devoid of political indoctrination, which will best any opposing army; unquestioned naval and air superiority, which includes the mastery of space and digital domains; and trade agreements that are reciprocal and which prize the interests of the American worker, are the best inducements for peace.

This universe of capabilities, when added to our nation's nuclear forces, describes the most potent deterrent to war in all its forms. These vast wells of power, however, can be squandered in a moment by a president who betrays the office and America's trust.

The fall of Kabul, the evacuation of the American embassy in Afghanistan's capital, the evisceration of the Afghan army, and the

---

[330]https://www.archives.gov/milestone-documents/president-dwight-d-eisenhowers-farewell-address

exodus of the nation's corrupt president were ruptures to the world order. The strategy of nation-building in Afghanistan was a mistake, for it did not take into account many profound issues, as expressed in existing tribal life and the prevalence in that country of an anachronous form of governance coupled with rampant lawlessness.

The War in Afghanistan exceeded the Vietnam War in length: It needed to end but not in a way that destroyed all that had been won. An intrinsically evil force that America had endeavored mightily to quell is now in power, despite the irreplaceable loss of many thousands of brave Americans, citizens from allied countries, and Afghans, who all prized liberty above any sacrifice.

I realized the sequence of errors and misjudgments made in Afghanistan before the Trump administration attained office, for I had studied the United Kingdom's mistakes in its protracted period of global commitments and empire. I thus recognized that our expenditure of more than two trillion dollars in that land was indicative not of power but of myopia, for this abundance was extended to a country that could not absorb what America offered; neither were the leaders of Afghanistan willing or able to make reciprocal commitments to liberty for their own people.

It should be noted that numerous Pentagon and intelligence officials understood this situation: Secretary of State Pompeo built upon his work as the director of the Central Intelligence Agency to aid the Trump administration in formulating concrete terms that would have allowed for force reductions and our ultimate withdrawal from Afghanistan while preserving the hard-won progress that had been made. What the secretary helped establish was the certainty of action should the Taliban renounce or operationally rescind what was agreed.

Based upon my discussions with senior Trump administration officials, it may be stated that if the Taliban violated the understandings it reached in its deliberations with his administration, a Trump presidency would have employed deep conventional strikes, utilizing American airpower and clandestine means, to inflict unsustainable losses on the extremists, thereby thwarting their advance. These strikes would have been mounted from a constellation of bases that the Trump administration would have held.

In an ABC News interview, President Biden said of his calamitous withdrawal of our forces in Afghanistan, "but the idea that, somehow, there's a way to have gotten out without chaos ensuing, I don't know how that happens."[331] Indeed, he doesn't. Neither was President Biden willing to accept sound military planning as was proffered by senior officers, who had served in Afghanistan, in their desire that our nation exercise due caution as our forces executed a conditions-based withdrawal.

ABC News host and commentator George Stephanopoulos stated the following in his August 18, 2021, interview of President Biden, "But your top military advisors warned against withdrawing on this timeline. They wanted you to keep about 2,500 troops."[332]

President Biden responded directly, "No, they didn't. It was split. Tha-- that wasn't true. That wasn't true."[333]

What was not true was Joseph Biden's statement. In a Senate Armed Services Committee hearing, held September 28, 2021, General Kenneth Franklin McKenzie Jr., then commander of United States Central Command (CENTCOM), contradicted President Biden's assertion that our military's leadership endorsed his plan for the rapid withdrawal of our remaining military forces from Afghanistan. General McKenzie, in fact, argued that an armed force of 2,500 Americans remain in country, to ensure the stability of the Afghan regime that we supported. The general stated under oath that he relayed his concerns directly to President Biden.[334]

Afghanistan is now lost, its progress nullified, and its women brutalized. The agonizing sacrifices of Americans and the forces of other countries have been disrespected by President Biden.

---

[331] https://abcnews.go.com/Politics/biden-withdraw-afghanistan-chaos-ensuing/story?id=79507930
[332] https://abcnews.go.com/Politics/full-transcript-abc-news-george-stephanopoulos-interview-president/story?id=79535643
[333] Ibid.
[334] https://www.politico.com/news/2021/09/28/top-generals-afghanistan-withdrawal-congress-hearing-514491

Americans fought so that an Afghan child could have a future and an Afghan woman could realize her dreams, but this administration has demonstrated that it does not care about what has been stolen. It has, in fact, demonstrated in its actions, which do not match its words, that it does not truly care about the rights of women.

Secretary of State Pompeo created the Contingency and Crisis Response Bureau to be a center for the coordination of our planning and reactions to emergencies overseas.[335] Its formation was to help facilitate an orderly withdrawal from Afghanistan. In the summer of 2021, the Biden administration terminated this bureau.[336] Their unreasoned action is unforgivable.

For reasons that defy comprehension, President Biden, in the face of a pitiless force, rejected the most important tool of the Trump doctrine, which is America's crushing military might that can inflict grievous losses to any belligerent force—anywhere in the world—within hours. Recovering from a doomed strategy that spanned decades, the Trump administration planned to reduce America's commitment in Afghanistan in a safe and dignified manner. Its careful planning was cast aside to the degree that Secretary of Defense Lloyd Austin stated that he did not have the capability to escort American and other evacuees to Kabul's civilian airport.[337]

We must demand to know why President Biden ordered the withdrawal from the Bagram Air Base, which occurred in the first days of July in the initial year of his presidency.[338] This massive base was looted weeks later and fell to the Taliban on August 15, 2021.[339]

In the aftermath of this assault, President Biden's errors are manifest though his reasoning has been obscured. His administration

---

[335] https://www.nationalreview.com/news/pompeo-slams-biden-state-department-for-dissolving-crisis-response-bureau-as-taliban-advanced/
[336] Ibid.
[337] https://news.yahoo.com/secretary-defense-don-t-capability-202435618.html?guccounter=1
[338] https://www.wsj.com/articles/who-abandoned-bagram-air-base-joe-biden-mark-milley-pentagon-afghanistan-taliban-kabul-11630096157
[339] https://english.alarabiya.net/News/world/2021/08/15/Afghan-official-says-forces-surrender-Bagram-air-base-to-Taliban

should have held this once impregnable point of departure, able to accommodate giant C-5 Galaxy transport aircraft. Instead, this safe avenue of evacuation was surrendered.

Thirteen precious lives of our servicemen and women were lost due to the Biden administration's negligence;[340] others were grievously injured. Vast quantities of American military equipment were left behind and not destroyed. These weapons, worth billions, now arm terrorists, though some have been transferred or sold to other adversarial states.[341] These are being examined by Chinese, Russian, or Iranian engineers who hope to unlock the means to defeat our arms, thus causing needless deaths among our forces.

What the Biden administration did in its retreat from Afghanistan was the height of irresponsibility, for America's adversaries fed on this ineptitude. On January 5, 2023, the Xinjiang Central Asia Petroleum and Gas Company and the Afghan Taliban government signed a development and extraction agreement.[342] This energy company is controlled by the Chinese Communist Party. It may also be expected that China's armed forces will operate from the Bagram Air Base.[343]

Accord with the leadership of the Taliban is also sought by Beijing for Afghanistan has significant stores of rare-earth metals such as neodymium and cerium. Access by China to these minerals will solidify its position of dominance in the refining and the utilization

---

[340] https://www.npr.org/2021/08/29/1032044382/what-we-know-about-the-13-u-s-service-members-killed-in-the-kabul-attack

[341] https://www.nbcnews.com/news/world/us-weapons-afghanistan-taliban-kashmir-rcna67134?utm_campaign=dfn-ebb&utm_medium=email&utm_source=sailthru&SToverlay=2002c2d9-c344-4bbb-8610-e5794efcf

[342] https://thediplomat.com/2023/01/taliban-settle-oil-deal-with-chinese-company/#:~:text=January%252006%252C%25202023%2520Credit%253A%2520Depositphotos%2520Advertisement%2520On%2520January,the%2520exploitation%2520of%2520oil%2520reserves%2520in%2520Afghanistan%25E2%2580%2599s%2520north.

[343] https://www.usnews.com/news/world-report/articles/2021-09-07/china-weighing-occupation-of-former-us-air-base-at-bagram-sources

of these ores. These elements are necessary for both energy and defense-related products.

American military power is the guarantor of America's promises. It is a tool without equal, if understood and wielded properly. It is not a tool for nation-building, for freedom must be earned by those who wish to be free.

American military power is the means to give body and shape to our nation's obligations by supporting diplomacy and needed outreach while substantiating deterrence. The Biden administration, through its words and deeds, continuously demonstrates that it neither knows enough nor cares enough to undue even a quantum of the damage it has caused.

Afghan women are now paying the highest price in basic human dignity for this administration's ineptitude, though their cries are blanketed by the mainstream media, which kowtows to an administration even as females in Afghanistan are denied the basic right of education, perhaps permanently.[344] We must, therefore, pray that the women and children of Afghanistan, and all those who sought liberty without constraint, may persevere through what is a very dark night.

The signal his catastrophic retreat sent to Vladimir Putin remains obvious to anyone with eyes to see. President Biden's abrogation of his responsibilities in Afghanistan effectively greenlighted Russia's invasion of Ukraine, for timidity in the face of belligerent assault invites viciousness.

Ukraine, Rules of War, and Deterrence

By empowering Ukraine to reestablish its dominion over its sovereign territory, we demonstrate to China the costs of invading Taiwan, thus helping to thwart an assault that would shatter the living standards of the world by crippling supplies of critical goods such as

---

[344]https://www.usip.org/publications/2022/04/talibans-ban-girls-education-afghanistan

semiconductors. We must act in support of Ukraine's territorial integrity lest we undercut our nation's own interests.

By aiding Ukraine, we undermine the creation of a Chinese-Russian axis bent on exerting military and economic hegemony in Europe and in Asia, which would further devastate our economy. In the Middle East and in Africa, a Chinese-Russian axis would fuse with Iran and other terrorist forces to form a daunting phalanx of influence.

The calamitous war in Ukraine is the result of Russia's mechanisms of conquest, which have been allowed to feed on Europe's and the world's demands for natural gas and other hydrocarbons. The greater part of Russia's federal budget is funded by its energy sector, which rests on oil, coal, and natural gas revenues.

If Russia be allowed to exert dominion over the Donbas and Ukraine's coast, the Kremlin will next seek to control the energy resources of other independent countries that were once part of the Soviet Empire. Russia will become a juggernaut, dominating fossil fuels in addition to its present lead in supplying nuclear powerplants to recipient nations across the globe. This is what is at stake. Nothing less.

Why does this war matter to hardworking Americans? In part, it is because if Russia controls Ukraine's energy resources, these sources of wealth, including those that are yet untapped, will empower Russia's and China's irridentist dreams of conquest and control, for China feeds on Russia's natural resources.

Had the current administration maintained American energy dominance rather than prostrate itself to radicals, the United States could have led resolutely in securing the world's hydrocarbon needs during this war. America abdicated this vital role, due to President Biden's actions to restrict hydrocarbon development within our continent, causing the war in Ukraine to compound the pain that consumers feel.

America's Founders decided that people of a common past, people of a shared future, people of a common purpose, have the right to choose a path for themselves—so it must be with Ukraine.

Contrary to Russian propaganda, Ukraine has always maintained its own unique culture, language, and identity. This maintenance of distinctiveness during protracted periods of foreign depredations is the mark of a great people who have sought independence throughout their history.

By arming Ukraine, America bolsters our own security without the involvement in combat of our men and women in uniform. We must not send America's military into this war, but we are compelled to aid Ukraine for to do so is in America's manifest interest.

By supporting Ukraine, we prevent a larger European war that would involve America's military due to our Article 5 treaty commitment to the integrity of the NATO member states that border Ukraine. By helping Ukraine, we prevent Russia's reconstitution of a Soviet-style empire, which would act in consonance with Iran and with China, to dictate world fossil-fuel supplies. This would cause economic hemorrhaging in America and throughout the globe.

Vladimir Putin sought to destroy a great nation; instead, this war has forged all Ukraine into an unbreakable shield that will thwart Russian domination. America must remain committed to seeing a sovereign Ukraine emerge from this war as an undivided nation and as a beacon to freedom.

Sweden's and Finland's ascension to NATO membership mandates our consideration of the post-war, European landscape with regard to Ukraine and its security relationships. After the First World War, the Polish statesman Józef Piłsudski proposed the Intermarium, designed to link together a number of European countries including Ukraine. The plan was suggested in successive iterations that differed; none were adopted.

More recently, the Three Seas Initiative has sought to create lasting bridges between nations in the economic, transportation, energy, and digital domains.[345] This project involves twelve states near or adjacent to Ukraine; the combined GDP of these countries

---

[345]https://crsreports.congress.gov/product/pdf/IF/IF11547

exceeds two trillion dollars. President Volodymyr Zelenskyy has stated his country's desire to join this group.

In addition, we should propose that the contiguous expanse of nations comprising Norway, Sweden, Finland, the Baltic states, Poland, Ukraine, Moldova, and Romania create a forum to discuss common security goals and concerns. This array of nations could be termed the Inter-Sea Arc, in reference to their strategic position. Such a group would not replicate NATO; it could, however, become a useful means to consider shared security goals after Russia's objectives in Ukraine are defeated.

My consideration of these matters begins with my appreciation that the gift of freedom is always purchased. This fact shimmers today in Kyiv and in the battlefields of that war-torn country. Men and women of extraordinary intrepidity are sacrificing themselves to secure liberty for their children and their countrymen.

Lassitude and fear do not define strategy; they presage defeat. Field Manual No. 3-0 was publicly distributed by the United States Army on October 1, 2022; it stipulates a defining principle of combat. This is referred to as mass:

> Integrating all the elements of combat power and synchronizing their application against a decisive point achieves mass. . . . Massing effects against one or more decisive points in one or more domains is typically an element of convergence. . . . The massing of effects, together with the proper application of the other principles of war, may enable numerically inferior forces to achieve decisive campaign and battle outcomes. Mass, like objective, implies that it is best to minimize the use of resources on secondary efforts. The massing of effects at any echelon to produce a desired effect on enemy forces is crucial to enabling maneuver.[346]

The manual further specifies that mass and concentration can create "overwhelming combat power at specific locations to support the

---

[346]https://armypubs.army.mil/epubs/DR_pubs/DR_a/ARN36290-FM_3-0-000-WEB-2.pdf

main effort."[347] These precepts are absent from the Biden administration's policies.

The Prussian general Carl von Clausewitz argued in his classic treatise on strategy that in war it is imperative to not waste time.[348] The Biden administration's recalcitrance in providing needed heavy armaments to Ukraine has wasted precious time as it has hindered Kyiv's application of mass in a decisive way.

If the weapons that were subsequently supplied to Ukraine had been delivered in a time-urgent manner, a pivotal advantage would have been conveyed to Ukraine far earlier. Long-range missiles are essential to modern warfare but were not provided in the first year of combat; these are critical to hold Russian formations at risk, thereby greatly complicating the Kremlin's plans for advantageous engagements.

In the aftermath of Russian aggression, the portable weapons provided at that time should have been buttressed immediately by the delivery of heavy M1 Abrams tanks, held in storage, as well as fourth-generation fighter aircraft, such as the F-16, which could have been transported to Ukraine's frontiers, partially disassembled, on trucks.

The F-16 first flew in 1974. Since that time, almost 5,000 jets have been produced; thousands still exist in the fighter inventories and the reserves of NATO and allied nations.[349] A portion of these tested aircraft should have been transferred to Ukraine after Russia's 2022 invasion. Such rapidity of action would have saved both Ukrainian and Russian lives by facilitating Ukraine's mastery of the battlespace.

Despite these strategic errors made by the Biden administration, by fortifying Ukraine now, we demonstrate to China its potential costs should it invade Taiwan. This aids in thwarting an assault that would rupture supply chains of critical products that are necessary to support our economy as well as those of our allies.

---

[347] Ibid.

[348] Carl von Clausewitz, "On War," (numerous editions; originally published as "Vom Kriege," 1832).

[349] https://www.nationalmuseum.af.mil/Visit/Museum-Exhibits/Fact-Sheets/Display/Article/196735/general-dynamics-f-16a-fighting-falcon/

The war in Ukraine is thus a clarion call. Before us, we see the interdependence of four pillars of national power: our strategic and tactical nuclear forces, which deter escalation; our economic security, which must protect the American worker; our requirement for energy dominance, which deflates our adversaries as it fuels our might; and our conventional forces, which must block the ambitions of those who seek our nation's harm.

When the preponderance of a nation has never known war for a lifetime, freedom may seem cheap. It appears as an afterthought that is as plentiful as the air we breathe. It is not. It is rare, and it is the most precious commodity that humanity has ever attained. This is the lesson that Ukraine can teach America's children: It is one of the most important messages they may ever learn.

Due to the country's courage against harrowing odds, Ukraine will live, and the deeds that this generation achieved and the heroism they displayed will be forever remembered. In light of the stakes involved, we must allow Ukraine to dictate the terms of any peace. The geostrategic dangers, which are evident, leave our nation no choice but to support Ukraine's crusade to recapture all of its territory.

The Architecture of Alliances

We contest China today in the most perilous of times. This totalistic state's economy is second only to our own. Its ambitions appear boundless, but it faces perils that it almost certainly will not be able to manage in the decades to come.

We must make China understand that America will uphold its interests, now and in the future. This can only be accomplished if we act with alacrity and employ the full panoply of our powers. By allowing the Chinese Communist Party to send high-altitude balloons over our nation to conduct intelligence operations, the Biden Administration demonstrated nothing but weakness. This dereliction of duty hurts the people of China by empowering their totalitarian masters in a time of upheaval.

China's population is dwindling. It is aging more rapidly than any nation on earth. China faces severe pollution and grave health risks associated with the regime's degradation of the country's environment, which has been exacerbated by rampant corruption involving manufacturing and construction enterprises that are controlled by or tethered to the Chinese Communist Party. These vectors will reduce China's power and should induce needed reforms if we, as a country, channel these currents constructively, to promote liberty.

Beijing's environmental challenges do not arise from climate change; they are, in fact, not dissimilar to those that beset the Roman world. The Western Roman Empire was hobbled by lead contamination. Later, forces of the Eastern Roman Empire were not able to hold Rome after the reign of the Byzantine Emperor Justinian, in part due to infestations of malaria.

Caustic manufacturing processes, which China has amassed as the West has abjured from their practice, desertification that is affecting Beijing due to the enlargement of the Gobi, and the miasma of pollution mixed with dust that encases a country that is one-fourth desert, are devouring the Chinese Communist Party's vision for the future. The Chinese Communist Party, led by President Xi, therefore believes it has a narrow window in which to act before forces, not subject to its control, erode the regime's hegemonic visions. Thus, China is now at its most dangerous stage, for it stands upon an exceedingly narrow precipice, which is also buffeted by a raft of economic woes.

To exist as a totalistic, hegemonic state, China must act. Thus, Beijing must conquer. It is this force and its belligerent calculus that we must rally with our allies and friends to subdue. A dying regime must not be allowed to shatter the world.

Empire

Although strategists across the globe are deeply and correctly concerned that China will attempt to invade and conquer Taiwan, another course of action may be presented by the war in Ukraine if

Russian defeat leads to a fracturing of Russia into smaller states, hewn along ethnic or religious lines. Instead of acting against an island, China may turn its attentions: It may endeavor to establish a Eurasian empire.

The Grand Duchy of Moscow began in 1263 as a dependency of the Golden Horde, which, itself, descended from the great Mongol Empire, which grew from the lands that now comprise Mongolia to encompass China and much of Eurasia. The Tsardom of Russia would succeed Muscovy in the mid-sixteenth century. Later, Peter the Great would form the Russian Empire in 1721.

China's border with Russia is vast: It measures 2,615.5 miles. Mongolia, the least populated nation per square mile on earth, shares its borders with both Russia and China; indeed, Mongolia's border with Russia encompasses 2,145 miles. Genghis Khan, who founded the largest empire in history in terms of its uninterrupted land mass, was born in what is now Mongolia, which became part of China until the demise of the Qing dynasty in 1911. Subsequently, Mongolia, as a nation, affiliated itself most closely with the Soviet Union until that empire's collapse in the last decade of the past century.

If Russia should splinter after Putin's fall, the opportunity exists for China to envelop Mongolia, thus almost doubling its border with what is now Russia. A suzerain is a nation that exercises authority over an inferior state that may betray or limit itself for various reasons.

Aided by rapacious Russian oligarchs who think nothing of selling their country's riches, China could become a suzerain to perhaps many aspirational states that may seek independence from Moscow. If this scenario should come to pass in any form, China will attain a bridge to the steppes of Europe, as well as mineral, energy, and technological resources of profound importance to the Chinese Communist Party.

China would, in effect, reestablish distinct elements of what was the Mongol Empire—with Beijing, this time, as its master. This course could be seen as an extension of the Belt and Road Initiative, which can be restated as One Belt, One Road, One Ruler.[350]

---

[350] https://www.rand.org/blog/2018/03/one-belt-one-road-one-ruler-china-term-limits-ban-imperils.html

This scenario is speculative, but it is nonetheless portentous. A process presidency will seek to decouple Russia or any number of new, fractional states from the potential of being controlled by Beijing. Such American leadership must prevent any nation from being swallowed by a rapacious China, but preclusive measures require vision and alacrity. Profound political change is required for these two abilities to be vested in the Oval Office.

Leadership

Isolationism is not a strategy. America is a seafaring nation; our economic interests span the globe, and our businesses are present in almost every nation on earth. Our supply chains, so vital to the American worker, depend on the unhindered transit of goods across many continents and oceans.

Central to the wellbeing of American families is a United States that leads the world in both military and economic power. We must use our strengths prudently and conservatively, for America is most secure when it leads by example and not by intervention.

America's defense alliances are critical to global peace and our nation's survival as the world's dominant economic power. The international structures we built in the aftermath of the last world war are irreplaceable to the defense of our homeland. America's alliances include not only our commitment to NATO but several other crucial interdependencies that we are obligated to honor and uphold.[351]

American industry and our farmers rely on the vitality of export markets that will be stricken if our adversaries succeed in their objectives. To meet daunting economic challenges, which were provoked by irresponsible domestic policies now championed by President Biden, we must take steps to ensure that Europe realizes peace and not continuous war or extortion, for Europe is inextricably bound to our nation as it is to both Asia and the Middle East.

Weakness, indecisiveness, and disengagement on the world stage invite needless conflict. Energy has already been weaponized: Should

---

[351]https://2009-2017.state.gov/s/l/treaty/collectivedefense/index.htm

we now allow China and Russia to weaponize food and mineral supplies too? We must summon the will to ensure that present conflagrations and the risks of new assaults do not entrap our future.

NATO's perimeter with Russia is more than doubled as a result of Finland's membership.[352] This border will consume the attention and the efforts of significant elements of Russia's military that could otherwise be deployed against non-alliance countries that neighbor this militant nation. We must act in concert with our allies to effect strategic clarity to strengthen NATO at this time and see that nothing hinders Sweden's full integration into the alliance.

Structures

Through the creation of SEATO (the Southeast Asia Collective Defense Treaty) in 1954, and CENTO in 1955 (the Central Treaty Organization involving Middle Eastern states, which was originally termed the Baghdad Pact), the United States tried to recreate NATO in other areas to contain communist power. Both organizations were failures (for a variety of political reasons, the United States was never a formal member of CENTO, though our country was instrumental in the organization's formation).

SEATO was dissolved in 1977; CENTO, in 1979. NATO, however, has exceeded the boundaries of the North Atlantic in its scope and missions. Turkey joined the alliance in 1952, though it is almost two thousand miles from the North Atlantic.

In the aftermath of 9/11, NATO enlarged its scope. Major combat operations were begun in the Middle East due to America's invocation of Article 5 of the NATO charter, which stipulates that an attack on any member state shall be considered as an attack upon all. NATO members fought alongside Americans in Afghanistan.

In 2009, NATO thwarted Somali pirates in the Indian ocean. In 2011, NATO countries joined in military operations that unseated

---

[352]https://www.newsweek.com/finland-joining-nato-would-more-double-blocs-border-russia-1697952

Muammar Gaddafi's regime in Libya.[353] A non-combat mission was also formed by NATO countries in Iraq to increase that nation's military capacity.[354]

Moving past our nation's present geostrategic focus, the United States must actively engage in meaningful security initiatives that support the sanctuary and the interests of the American people. We, therefore, must revivify the security alliance of the Americas, known as the Rio Treaty; we must forge a stronger and more inclusive security alliance in the Indo-Pacific; and we must aid in the affirmation of three lighthouses for liberty, around which can be created a new security and economic architecture that will serve to link America's alliances across the world. These beacons should be centered on nations that have known great strife: Ukraine, Israel, and Taiwan.

In establishing these defensive alliances, the involved countries should not make the mistake of creating multinational organizations that do not possess integrated command structures that include designated military forces from each substantial party to the treaties. These deficits were present in the ANZUS treaty enacted between the United States, Australia, and New Zealand. The pact disintegrated when the anti-nuclear government of New Zealand denied a port-visit request by the United States Navy for a destroyer, which was presumed to be capable of carrying nuclear weapons. In 1985, the USS Buchanan was turned away, fracturing the import of the treaty.[355]

As we propose or support new alliance structures, we must acknowledge the web of defense-related treaties that already exists between the United States and other nations. We must also endeavor to use the network I and others envision to lessen the military burdens placed on the United States, for we cannot and should not defend the world.

At the time of President Trump's inauguration, only the United States, the United Kingdom, Greece, Poland, and Estonia, of

---

[353]https://www.reuters.com/article/uk-libya-nato-factbox-idUKTRE734637 20110405

[354]https://www.nato.int/cps/en/natohq/topics_166936.htm

[355]https://www.wilsoncenter.org/blog-post/new-zealands-anti-nuclear-legislation-and-united-states-1985

NATO's many nations, met the alliance's goal of member state defense contributions; this was stipulated at two percent of GDP.[356] Of particular concern in 2016 was Germany's inadequate defense budget, which, for some years, actually declined in real terms. Many strategists and military professionals thus recognized immediately after President Trump's assumption of office that NATO's status and mission parameters required urgent recalibration to be relevant.

The NATO countries of Europe possess a combined GDP that is similar to our own. By comparison, in 2020, Russia's GDP was one-tenth that of the European Union.[357]

Given the defense budgets of NATO member states, this implies that to match their combined defense spending, Russia would need to allocate three-fourths of its GDP to the military sector, which is, of course, impossible, for such spending would collapse Russia's economy in a matter of weeks. Indeed, Russia does not possess the industrial base to absorb anything near such an allocation of resources, no matter how temporary.

The Trump administration, its state department, and its Pentagon were correct in pressing the member states of NATO to meet their obligations. During President Trump's term, the NATO contributions of many nations increased beyond what was initially thought possible. Declarations by NATO countries to meet their spending obligations were propelled, in part, by the president's entreaties concerning the disparities in defense burden sharing and the threat Russia posed.

Deficits in NATO capabilities and planning had permitted Russia's numerous incursions and wars. Russia's scope of action was

---

[356] https://www.statista.com/chart/8521/expenditure-of-nato-countries-in-2016/#:~:text=In%202016%2C%20military%20spending%20accounted%20for%203.6%20percent,1.2%20percent%20for%20Germany.%20Niall%20McCarthy%20Data%20Journalist

[357] https://fredblog.stlouisfed.org/2022/03/comparing-russia-and-the-european-union-gdp-and-population/#:~:text=The%20blue%20line%20shows%20the%20ratio%20%28expressed%20in,slowly%20than%20the%20EU%E2%80%99s%E2%80%94hence%2C%20its%20decreasing%20relative%20size.

attenuated during the Trump presidency, for the administration of President Trump understood that Vladimir Putin had not renounced his murderous vision, which he had sharpened as a member of the KGB years earlier.[358]

In 2005, Putin declared the demise of the Soviet Union to be one of the greatest tragedies in history. In 2007, Putin enunciated his rationale for conquest in terms analogous to that of the dictators who ruled Europe ninety years ago.

President Putin has been consistent in his revanchist objectives: in Grozny in 1999, in Georgia in 2008, and in Ukraine in 2014. NATO, however, demonstrated a raft of inconsistent actions that helped precipitate a change in the Kremlin's perception of risk, which was validated in Putin's mind by President Biden's disastrous retreat from Afghanistan.

It was not until the Kremlin's march toward Kyiv that NATO's purpose was galvanized, but even this unity was blighted by Europe's dependency on Russia for fossil fuels and NATO's desire to avoid escalation—in partial, apparent blindness to the perils of appeasement and vacillation. Today, however, must be different, for our deterrent posture and our willingness to act, when change may be determinative, must be wrested from complacency and timidity.

The implacable resolve of the Trump administration gave pause to Putin's vicious goals, for he knew if he invaded once more to expand his reach and occupation in Ukraine, he would face a whirlwind. Secretary of State Pompeo and other senior Trump administration officials made this clear to the president of Russia, and he understood the unequaled might America represented. This is deterrence. This is what was lost the day Joseph Biden assumed the office of the presidency. This is what must be regained.

Indo-Pacific

In the Indo-Pacific, America must lead by expanding the Quadrilateral Security Dialogue, whose members are the United States, Japan,

---

[358]Committee for State Security of the USSR

India, and Australia, and in integrating it with the AUKUS union that includes Australia, the United Kingdom, and the United States. The new defense alliance that should be formed should also have as its founding members the Republic of Korea and France, for France has substantial territories in the Indo-Pacific, in which 1.65 million of its citizens live.[359]

I propose this new defense pact be called the Indo-Pacific Treaty Alliance (IPTA). As with NATO, non-treaty nations should be invited to be observers. Such nations could include Indonesia, the Philippines, Malaysia, Singapore, and Taiwan. As with NATO, specific defense spending goals should be promulgated. Given the threat China poses, defense spending increases on the part of all member nations should be sought.

There are troubling similarities between the Communist Party of China and the prewar form of the National Socialist German Workers' Party. Before the Second World War, Germany brutally suppressed all internal opposition—most particularly its religious minorities—for this is the measure of any despotic regime. It purged its party members to ensure absolute allegiance to one master; it made its industrialists enormously wealthy, for they, in turn, fed the party's power.

Beyond its borders, Germany annexed Austria and next convinced the political leadership of the United Kingdom and France that if they granted Germany the Sudetenland, which was part of Czechoslovakia, peace would flourish and be irreducible.[360] The Munich Agreement was soon violated by Germany, so began the greatest war in the history of humankind, for after Czechoslovakia, Poland would be next to fall.

China is not an absolute analogue of prewar Germany, but neither is it benign or trustworthy. It also possesses far more economic

---

[359] https://thediplomat.com/2022/06/can-frances-military-live-up-to-its-ambitions-in-the-indo-pacific/#:~:text=France%20is%20a%20resident%20power%20in%20the%20Indo-Pacific.,where%20French%20sovereignty%20is%20directly%20on%20the%20line.

[360] https://www.history.com/this-day-in-history/munich-pact-signed

strength than Germany ever accumulated. As Germany first tested the resolve of the Western powers, so China now tests us. Be it Taiwan, Japan, India, Australia, the United States, or the nations astride the South China Sea, China probes for weakness.

China's threat to invade Taiwan is upon us. The Communist Party of China is capable of great violence, both within China and against other nations. In November of 1950, the People's Volunteer Army, directed by the junta led by Mao Zedong, attacked American military forces that were part of the United Nations Command, which was established on July 7, 1950. This multinational force of free nations was created pursuant to United Nations Security Council Resolution 84, to confront militarily the communist aggression against Korea.[361] This command in Korea still exists.[362]

Our nation's losses in that war are not forgotten, for they appear as welts that have not healed; 36,574 Americans died as part of the United Nations Force, as did 162,394 South Koreans, and 4,544 members of the services of the other fifteen allied nations who fought for freedom.[363] We understand the duplicity of the People's Republic of China. We comprehend that in its quest to conquer Tibet, during the time of the Korean War, China relied on deception.

The People's Liberation Army (PLA) defeated Tibetan forces in the Battle of Chamdo, in which the PLA attacked Tibetan soldiers and positions during a period of diplomatic negotiations with Tibetan officials. We, therefore, cannot avert our eyes from the threat China poses, for it is magnified by that state's newfound wealth that has facilitated one of the greatest periods of expansion in offensive military potential in all history.

In response, our freedom of navigation exercises in waters, straits, and passages, which the rest of the world recognizes to be open or to belong to nations other than China, must be accentuated.

---

[361]https://www.unc.mil/History/1950-1953-Korean-War-Active-Conflict/
[362]https://www.unc.mil/
[363]https://militaryveteransofdisqus.org/war-breaks-out-on-the-korean-peninsula/

The passage of the world's goods cannot be subject to the whims of any country.

Japanese, Australian, South Korean, British, French, and Indian naval vessels should join the United States Navy in expressing this imperative, for we must preserve sea lines of communication, upon which transit energy supplies, critical materials, and all manufactured goods, including vital semiconductor supplies from Taiwan. Reciprocally, cooperative economic security is obligatory and must include the enactment of a United States-Taiwan Free Trade Agreement.

Acting on behalf of our country, on July 13, 2020, Secretary Pompeo issued a statement concerning the South China Sea, which is now even more relevant; he stated, "Beijing uses intimidation to undermine the sovereign rights of Southeast Asian coastal states in the South China Sea."[364] These nations are, in essence, deprived of their rightful, offshore resources, for China illegally asserts 'unilateral dominion,' as it endeavors to "replace international law with 'might makes right.'"[365]

Secretary Pompeo further contended that Beijing's aggression and its flouting of the 1982 United Nations Convention on the Law of the Sea (also called the Law of the Sea Convention), to which China is a party, are indicative of a "predatory world view" that "has no place in the twenty-first century."[366] Though I had opposed the United States' joining the Law of the Sea Convention during my tenure on the National Security Council staff due to concern regarding seabed mining rules, on balance I now believe the United States must join this treaty,[367] which will also aid in our expression of the right of freedom of navigation as we contest China's intended occupations and confiscations.

---

[364]https://2017-2021.state.gov/u-s-position-on-maritime-claims-in-the-south-china-sea/index.html
[365]Ibid.
[366]Ibid.
[367]https://legal.un.org/avl/ha/uncls/uncls.html

Secretary Pompeo expressed his profound grasp of the situation with these words, "The world will not allow Beijing to treat the South China Sea as its maritime empire. America stands with our Southeast Asian allies and partners in protecting their sovereign rights to offshore resources, consistent with their rights and obligations under international law."

Taiwan

Taiwan is a vibrant democracy. Its transition to universal suffrage and democratic rule is a model and a beacon for the entire world, including the People's Republic of China, whose citizens long for liberty, though few dare say it. Taiwan has chosen freedom, and the pursuit of its gifts marks a remarkable people, for liberty's attainment bespeaks the fact that no government or master should control the lives of men and women, for our lives are ours and not something to be seized.

History carves its moments on our souls, but we are the authors of our future. We, therefore, must recognize the choice that is upon us: If we do not choose to live as free people, able to worship, associate, improve, and gather as we wish, the only alternative is to supplicate or shame ourselves for security and for plenty that are neither secure nor plentiful. With regard to the People's Republic of China's intentions concerning the island of Taiwan, we must all accept that there will be no certainties, only probabilities, which derive from integrating history, recent events, rhetoric, and capabilities.

To defend Taiwan from aggression, more than force of arms and doctrinal strength is required. The arc of history may be said to be a recurring pattern that bends either toward freedom or despotism. China was lost in the aftermath of World War II due, in part, to American hesitancy and complacency. In any given moment, it is always easier for politicians not to act.

America's shared future with Taiwan, as allied, Pacific nations, beckons. In support of the Taiwan Relations Act of 1979, America must ensure that an integrated, proportional response to aggression be achievable. Taiwan, for its part, must do more to substantiate its defense; Taiwan's spending on its armed forces must, at minimum, reach three percent of its gross domestic product.[368]

The United States must determine, in consultation with Taiwan's government, that nation's future area anti-air and anti-missile needs, and begin the provision of appropriate systems, including additional assets to check China's burgeoning submarine fleet. In future, stealth and other advanced technologies will almost certainly be required to face China's emergent force of fifth-generation fighters and hypersonic missiles. Hardening Taiwan's electric grids should also be prioritized due to the danger posed by nuclear and non-nuclear EMP weapons.

Inaction in the face of a belligerent opponent is its own lesson that must not be repeated, for it precipitates caustic realities in which political options are limited, thereby often leading to armed conflict. We must influence the arc of history by inducing inflection points through measured actions and discourse within and among the legislative and the executive branches of our government.

The past imbalance in national power between the United States and the People's Republic of China helped suppress China's irredentist ambitions, but not its willingness to use force. China introduced massive military power to sway the course of the Korean War. Later, it provided crucial support to North Vietnam to alter the balance of power, causing horrific carnage in Vietnam, Laos, and Cambodia. Now, however, past constraints have collapsed.

The ongoing deployment of the long-range Chengdu J-20 stealth fighter; the construction and the deployment of China's first supercarrier, to be equipped with fifth-generation fighters; and China's largescale naval construction program, threaten the entirety of the Indo-Pacific. Japan and Taiwan are the central links of the First Island Chain, which is composed of the archipelagos that are most near to the East Asian mainland. Therefore, an invasion of Taiwan would allow the Chinese Navy to breakout and contest the United

---

[368]https://www.cia.gov/the-world-factbook/countries/taiwan/#military-and-security

States for control of the entirety of the Indo-Pacific and with it, the preponderance of world trade. China would also be positioned to strike the Second Island Chain that includes Guam.

What must be done? To unsteady a communist regime is to ultimately ensure the emergence of freedom, for rigidity and not toleration is the stamp of despotism.

China has posited that its man-made islands in the South China Sea constitute sovereign military bases, though they are, in fact, illegitimate, as are Beijing's claims to exclusive zones within the sea.[369] On July 12, 2016, a tribunal empaneled by the Permanent Court of Arbitration at the Hague ruled overwhelmingly against China and in favor of the Philippines.[370]

China's artificial islands are actually strategic and tactical liabilities should conflict be brought. Their radars, communication networks, and means of resupply are all subject to interdiction. These installations are fixed and, therefore, easily targeted. This is not true of the United States Pacific Fleet. That China has invested so much, but garnered so little, is indicative of a myopia that pervades all states ruled by a single master.

I believe that through the creation of IPTA, we must build enduring bridges to freedom that extend throughout the Indo-Pacific. We must look to our nation's fifty-second secretary of state, who served President Eisenhower, for inspiration: Before becoming secretary of state, John Foster Dulles proposed the Island Chain Strategy of 1951.

This plan, whose elements were only episodically adopted, sought, through American power projection, to contain Soviet and Chinese expansionism and conquest. Today, expanded regional bases and substantial allied naval forces are required; this is what we must build and sharpen. The United States should not become involved militarily on the continent of Asia; rather, we must exercise naval

---

[369] https://www.nbcnews.com/news/world/u-s-says-most-china-s-claims-south-china-sea-n1233745

[370] https://www.uscc.gov/sites/default/files/Research/Issue%20Brief_South%20China%20Sea%20Arbitration%20Ruling%20What%20Happened%20and%20What%27s%20Next071216.pdf

dominance at sea, which will require resolute support from space, air, and amphibious assets, to be provided by a new alliance of nations.

Lighthouses for Freedom

Freedom stipulates that the mind of each person is not the property of the state. Our faith, our thoughts, our unimpeded study, and our embrace of those we love give meaning to each of our lives. To be subservient in a totalistic system is to be insignificant; it is to have no importance. This can never be the future we accept for ourselves or our children. The defense of this freedom begins on the island of Taiwan, on the steppes of Ukraine, and in the nation of Israel.

The world has become too small for free countries to not be part of something greater, which will forestall armed conflict, rather than react to it. As the foci of a new security architecture, Taiwan, Ukraine, and Israel, can link alliances of free nations globally, reinforcing the strengths of each member state. In time, linking these bastions with NATO as well as the new and expanded security framework for the Indo-Pacific, in the body of the IPTA, will form a global alliance for freedom.

We must prevent the formation of a pan-Eurasian behemoth, incorporating Russia but led by China, which, in time, could grow to amalgamate Belarus, Iran, the DPRK, and other repressive but fragile states. We must fight terrorism and prevent, through the sharing of intelligence and the provision of training and resources, its spread in Africa. The need for this network of alliances is patent and cannot come too soon.

Israel and the Middle East

God's covenant with the Jewish people can never be broken. Israel exists as a modern nation for its creation fulfills God's promise to Abraham. It is also a profound and timeless expression of the courage and resilience of the human spirit.

Germany, Europe, and the world owe the state of Israel unwavering support and the commitment to its security as a Jewish state.

America and most other nations accepted few Jewish refugees before the advent of World War II. To our shame, the administration of President Roosevelt turned back to Europe all 937 Jewish refugees aboard the MS St. Louis, resulting in the subsequent murder of many of its passengers.[371]

The Department of War later refused to bomb rail lines to Nazi death camps, though our government knew of the Final Solution in 1942 and later conducted massive bomber raids over Germany and other European nations to destroy infrastructure used by the Nazis. In 1979, President Carter presented to Holocaust survivor Ellie Wiesel, the recipient of the 1986 Nobel Peace Prize, high-altitude photographs of Auschwitz-Birkenau, taken by our reconnaissance planes before the end of the war, which demonstrated that America could have acted and saved an exceptionally large number of Jewish lives.[372] To his great credit, President Carter understood the moral significance of the Holocaust, for he comprehended that it must be forever remembered without the excision of any facts or testimonies.[373]

The world must reflect on the horrific indifference among many nations that failed to protect the Jewish people during their time of greatest need. More than sixty-eight percent of Europe's 8,861,000 Jews were murdered by the end of the Second World War. Never again can we allow refuge for antisemitism in our world, though this disease is frequently cloaked as anti-Zionism, even in the halls of Congress.[374]

Judaism, Christianity, and Islam trace their lineages to Abraham. The center of the world that is the seat of these religions must not know tribulation but peace, for this is God's will.

Perhaps the proudest moments of the Trump administration were attained in its fight for the achievement of peace agreements

---

[371] https://www.britannica.com/topic/MS-St-Louis-German-ship
[372] https://www.britannica.com/topic/Why-wasnt-Auschwitz-bombed-717594
[373] https://www.ushmm.org/m/pdfs/20050707-presidents-commission-holocaust.pdf
[374] https://apnews.com/article/israel-minnesota-race-and-ethnicity-rashida-tlaib-anti-semitism-0ab373cfa0bf495db94e70c632bef223

between four Muslim nations, the United Arab Emirates, Bahrain, Sudan, and Morocco, and the Jewish state of Israel. The accords normalized relations between these countries and established diplomatic ties.

How must security be construed for a region that has known unending strife? Upon assumption of office, a new Republican administration must cast aside the leftist ideals of the Biden Administration as it works to engage other Middle Eastern nations so that they join the Abraham Accords, becoming future partners with Israel in peace and in co-development.

The precept of comity must permeate the Middle East. By our collective action and by our reinforcing efforts, we will check Iran and terrorist groups that include Hezbollah, Hamas, and movements that derive their ideals from the worship of death.

Iran's interventionism and the spread of terrorism that it inspires must be opposed and vanquished in the Middle East and in Africa. The Iranian people must be freed from the corrupt theocrats and murderers who lord over them. Regional actions against terrorist groups may, at times, involve the armed services of affected nations and those of our special forces, but, often, terrorist movements can be thwarted through the application of intelligence and counterintelligence, economic achievement and suasion, and transformative change, beginning with the empowerment of women.

The fruits of the Abraham Accords are already visible. In 2020, the Minister of Economy for the United Arab Emirates, Abdulla bin Touq Al Mari, reflected on the progress achieved. He stated, "The historic signing of the Abraham Accords agreement has opened new avenues for strengthened collaboration and exchange between the UAE and Israel."[375]

On May 31, 2022, Minister of Economy Al Mari and his Israeli counterpart signed a groundbreaking free trade agreement.[376] In the

---

[375]https://www.timesofisrael.com/israel-export-institute-dubai-world-trade-centre-sign-cooperation-accord/

[376]https://news.yahoo.com/uae-israel-high-hopes-historic-173024512.html?fr=sycsrp_catchall

future, energy and new pipeline projects will link Israel and Arab states.

These developments will be transformational but at the same time reminiscent of ancient structures that still dot the Middle East, North Africa, and distant lands. Caravanserai are buildings with open courts that served as waypoints for the entire Islamic world, facilitating commerce involving both urban centers and rural destinations. They have existed for at least 1,300 years, permitting caravans to rest and receive sustenance.

It was through this network that trade was established among nations, the intellectual legacies of ancient Greece and Rome were preserved and transmitted, and the wealth of the Far East was conveyed to the then known world. Many of these marvelous structures still exist: Khan al-Umdan, in Acre, Israel; Funduq Shamma'in, in Fes, Morroco; and Wikala of Al-Ghuri, in Cairo, Egypt, are three among the existent caravanserai that stretch from India to several countries in Europe.

This is the heritage we must draw upon in creating new trade and information networks that promote both freedom and security for all nations that wish to better the lives of their people. Indeed, it is my expectation that such a development will bring hope to Palestinians, for the ultimate treasure that we each possess lies within our hearts, which govern our dreams for the future.

We understand the people in the Middle East differ in their views. A parallactic outlook ensues from viewing a distant object from different vantage points: An object is therefore framed by two dissimilar backgrounds. Peace between Israel and its adversaries may be characterized by this phenomenon.

President Trump's historic declaration that the United States recognize Jerusalem as the capital of Israel and that America move its embassy from Tel Aviv to Jerusalem, changed the disparate vantage points of both Israelis and Palestinians. They now each assess the seemingly remote object of peace against backgrounds that have shifted fundamentally from those that existed four decades ago, when I served Ronald Reagan. I believe with all my heart that our nation's resolve in the Middle East must constitute a unifying force that will create a better future for the people of these ancient lands, which have too often been soaked in blood.

It is essential that we each keep an image of a child's face in our minds in everything we do: What kind of future do we want for these youngsters—freedom, so that they may pursue their dreams, or a world ruled by tyrants who feign concern for the dispossessed? The choice is in our hands.

After so much sorrow and pain brought about by a terrible plague, we must usher into existence a time of healing. I, therefore, ask: Is there a paradigm that we can summon to bring our world back into balance and to revere the foundations of life? The foundations of faith, family, country, and markets first occurred in the Middle East and in Africa, as did formal systems of education and scientific inquiry.

In these lands, central to all history, the strength of faith is understood to be fundamental to human happiness, for though we dwell in a physical world, our hopes and our prayers touch another. Although the people of this war-torn region express differences in beliefs, those who seek wisdom recognize that God exists and must alone be worshipped. This is the plinth for civilization. This is the antidote to the malaise and the ambivalence to life and its standards, which are so prevalent today.

Time will bring the restoration of faith to this world, for we are obligated by reason to believe in something far greater than ourselves. Let our common humanity erect bridges that shine as emeralds among the nations that have known enmity.

America's strategy concerning the Middle East demands clarity of voice. This must be constant. Disorganization in the proclamation of policies that affect ongoing engagements prolong strife and inhibit resolution by the involved parties.

Secretary Pompeo has stated that he considered it crucial to articulate policies in the context of providing certainty in a world that is permeated with disinformation. Let us through emissaries of shared values bring this discernment to the world, for the planet has become mired in a technological age that enforces its own dominance at the expense of reverence and individuality.

The creation of the Grand Library in Bagdad and its academy marked the beginning of the Islamic Golden Age, which began in the eighth century. This center of learning became a unique repository of knowledge. The creators of that age understood that perception derives from the embrace of other cultures and methods of thought and never from insularity.

The openness of such societies to ideas is demonstrated by Abu Nasr Al-Farabi, the great tenth-century scientist, mathematician, and philosopher, for he is known, within the context of the Islamic philosophical tradition, as the "Second Teacher," while Aristotle is acknowledged to be the first. Islamic culture at that time did not destroy the great books of Greek and Roman erudition, it translated them, for great minds seek greatness. Preserved, these works, and those of brilliant Arab and Persian polymaths, provided a basis for the Scientific Revolution in Europe.

This period of comparative enlightenment produced Ibn Rushd. This twelfth-century genius made lasting contributions in philosophy and in science; he was also a jurist and physician. The Jewish contemporary of Ibn Rushd was Maimonides, one of the most important rabbis in history.

Superlative philosopher, astronomer, and physician, Maimonides drew, in part, on Ibn Rushd's works in composing treatises of lasting importance. A century later, Jewish writers would translate Ibn Rushd's medical texts and his commentaries on Aristotle.

This was the blending of brilliant minds. This was the fusion of gifts granted to us by God. Such an extraordinary fruition in human understanding was the foundation for the Abraham Accords, which were instituted in order that the nations of the Middle East prosper through the voluntary exchange of knowledge, goods, wisdom, and all that is conducive to peace and development.

The end of the Islamic Golden Age occurred in 1258, when a great army from the East destroyed the glory that was Baghdad. The Grand Library was obliterated by a horde that rose from Mongolia and what is now Northern China.

The disaster this invasion precipitated is a warning for our time. The attainment and the proliferation of knowledge must be defended, or oppressive forces will seize control, decimating both the free exchange of ideas and commerce that is not compelled. This is why collective defense that arises from collaboration among the nations of the Middle East and North Africa is essential to peace.

The Abraham Accords provide the platform on which we may build. Let us do so with astute expedience. Should China gain a strategic foothold in the Middle East, displacing them will be arduous. We should remember the struggles President Anwar al-Sadat faced in removing the USSR and its socialist ideology from Egypt. Such action in the face of China's economic power could be even more difficult.

China constructed its first overseas military base in the African nation of the Republic of Djibouti in 2017.[377] Coupled with other redoubts, China is positioning itself as a global military power. It is also empowering Iran through the institution of a multi-decade strategic partnership, which supports Tehran's terrorist actions, resulting in regional instabilities, needless conflicts, carnage, and death.

Terrorism precipitated by Iran diverts American military power from the Indo-Pacific theater. This is China's aim.

NATO is not an appropriate model for this region. The Arab States of the Gulf, supported by the United States, must create a multilateral force in being, which builds upon the Cooperation Council for the Arab States of the Gulf, as well as work done within the Islamic Military Alliance to Fight Terrorism. In addition, Israel's role as part of a larger regional defense plan should be carefully considered, for reinforcing efforts are a necessity to undermine Iran's belligerency and its acquisition of deliverable weapons of mass destruction.

We all must be concerned that if Iran determines America's will is insubstantial, it will redouble terrorist actions throughout the region that may also reach and envelop Europe and the Americas, for a resurgent Iran will fear little. The despots who rule Iran will never willingly give up their quest for the strategic weapons they covet. Iran will never be satisfied with just threatening Israel and

---

[377]https://www.reuters.com/article/us-china-djibouti-idUSKBN1AH3E3

the United States, for it sees the Arab States of the Gulf as the embodiment of its central nemesis.

The Joint Comprehensive Plan of Action, which was advanced by Barack Obama and Joseph Biden, did grave damage to the quest to limit Iran's potential to acquire nuclear weapons. The Trump administration's decision to nullify such errancy was greeted with contempt by those who do not understand Iran or its rulers—who are rapacious, theocratic hypocrites.

The objectives of Iran's leadership is, however, clear. We must, therefore, pledge our commitment as a people to see that an over-matching response be built. In so doing, Israel's defense and the safety of the Jewish people must remain unalterable objectives that are central to America's security policies.

Mexico

General of the Army George Marshall, recipient of the Nobel Peace Prize for his work to rebuild Europe after the Second World War, became secretary of state under President Truman in 1947.[378] Many years before I served in the Department of the Navy, in charge of all Navy and Marine technology transfer and security assistance programs, I dedicated myself to the study of this titan's conception of our nation's place in the world, for he also held the position of special envoy to China before his service in the cabinet. Later, he would return to government to serve as the secretary of defense.

Although the general is most remembered for the Marshall Plan, which prevented the rise of communism in Western Europe, he left a lasting legacy in the Americas. He was an architect of the Inter-American Treaty of Reciprocal Assistance, which is known today as the Rio Treaty.[379]

The treaty was negotiated in 1947, though the accord's principles drew on both the hemispheric Monroe Doctrine of 1823, which

---

[378]https://history.state.gov/departmenthistory/people/marshall-george-catlett

[379]https://history.defense.gov/Multimedia/Biographies/Article-View/Article/571266/george-c-marshall/

sought to derail European adventurism in the Americas; the Good Neighbor policy of Franklin Roosevelt, which codified his administration's policy of non-intervention in the internal affairs of Latin American countries, and the Act of Chapultepec of March 3, 1945, which promulgated "Declarations on Reciprocal Assistance and American Solidarity," within our hemisphere.[380] The Rio Treaty predated the creation of NATO. Indeed, the founding documents of NATO draw on principles created by George Marshall for the common defense of the Americas.

The Rio Treaty, however, differs from NATO, in that the use of force, under this hemispheric accord, to aid a country that is attacked, is not obligatory for other member states. Though the treaty stipulates that the contracting countries, "agree that an armed attack by any State against an American State shall be considered as an attack against all the American States,"[381] this determination, according to Article 17 of the treaty, will be made "by a vote of two-thirds of the Signatory States which have ratified the Treaty."[382] Article 20 further specifies, "no State shall be required to use armed force without its consent."[383]

Despite these fail-safes against undue compulsion, Mexico withdrew from the treaty in 2004, followed by three other countries during the Obama administration. China and Russia are attempting to create permanent bases of influence in the Americas.[384] Iran and terrorist groups are endeavoring to influence or infiltrate national and local governments in Latin America.[385]

China is aiding transnational criminal organizations that are responsible for shipping drugs to our nation. It is also engaging in

---

[380]http://www.ibiblio.org/pha/policy/1945/1945-03-03a.html
[381]https://2001-2009.state.gov/t/ac/csbm/rd/4369.htm
[382]Ibid.
[383]Ibid.
[384]https://www.defense.gov/News/News-Stories/Article/Article/2977224/generals-say-china-russia-persist-in-western-hemisphere-meddling/
[385]https://dialogo-americas.com/articles/irans-tentacles-threaten-latin-america/#.Y9NLwsnMKUk

predatory fishing practices, by illegally operating within the coastal exclusive economic zones of nonconsenting nations, thereby destroying the livelihoods of fishermen throughout our hemisphere.[386]

The foregoing acts must compel us to reenergize the Rio Treaty, to make it an active vehicle for this century that will thwart belligerent and criminal plans to weaken nations throughout the Americas, as designed and perpetrated by China, Russia, Iran, and other state and non-state entities. Of vital importance is that we view transnational criminal organizations as the equivalent of terrorist groups, so that they can be eradicated—to end the immeasurable misery they cause.

To effect these measures, Mexico should be urged to rejoin the Rio Treaty. A new mutual defense treaty between the United States and Mexico should also be pursued in order that effective campaigns against criminal cartels may be launched by our joint commitment as neighbors and allies to rid our continent of this scourge.

Our building a more capable Coast Guard and a spectrum of new capabilities across the border we share with our neighbor will be required. There can be no more important strategic relationship for the United States than that which we institute and uphold in North America.

History, Defense Procurement, and the Need for Reform

The history of tank warfare and development, which I began to study before my admittance to Johns Hopkins almost five decades ago, provides a window from which we may discern the challenges and opportunities we face in reforming the military services and the Office of the Secretary of Defense. A machine of unrivaled power, the M1 Abrams tank, has been continuously improved for four decades; it is unmatched in combat. The M1 was named for

---

[386]https://www.newsweek.com/chinas-rampant-illegal-fishing-endangering-environment-global-economy-opinion-1776034

General Creighton Abrams; General George Patton proclaimed Abrams to be the greatest tank commander of the Second World War.

Creighton Abrams, throughout his career, fused key principles of intelligence and situational awareness. In war, he applied tactics and the use of mobility, which arose from his knowledge of the multidimensional character of combatant forces as they operated within the battlespace. He then employed defensive strongholds and applied combined arms to secure victories against superior foes.

In 1944, in France, during the Battle of Arracourt, Abrams commanded M4 Sherman tanks and other vehicles that were technically and numerically outclassed by an array of German armor that included panther tanks. Developed as a consequence of the inferiority of earlier German armor to the Russian T-34, the panther is considered by many military historians to be the finest tank of the war.[387]

In battle, Abrams' force lost fourteen Shermans while destroying fifty-five German tanks[388] that were all armed with superior guns. Training, situational awareness, mass, agility, and maneuver turned the tide of battle as American armor attacked the flanks of the opposing force with great intrepidity, cementing victory.

Armor

The first history book I ever bought concerned American and British tank development.[389] In my study of this book and many others, I began to peer past technology to discern broadly applicable lessons.

Although most often believed to be first depicted by Leonardo Da Vinci,[390] the operative concept of the tank as a mobile armored

---

[387]https://www.benning.army.mil/armor/eARMOR/content/issues/2015/APR_JUN/2BattleAnalysis15.pdf

[388]https://www.britannica.com/biography/Creighton-Williams-Abrams-Jr

[389]Peter Chamberlain and Chris Ellis, "British and American Tanks of World War II," (Arco Publishing Company, 1975).

[390]https://www.leonardodavincisinventions.com/war-machines/leonardo-da-vincis-tank/

unit of decisive lethality may be traced to Jan Žižka, one of the greatest military leaders of all time.[391] On March 25, 1420, Žižka employed war wagons that utilized armor and mounted cannons to defeat a far larger force at Sudoměř, in Central Europe.

In France, Nicolas-Joseph Cugnot built the first steam-powered land vehicle in 1769, years before the American Revolution. With the advent of lighter weight cannons and gatling guns, an early form of machine gun invented in 1862, all the elements necessary to build a working tank were at hand during the Civil War, but were not pieced together, though a tank made of these components would have been decisive in battle.

We must discern from this conjecture that innovation in warfare may be determinative, but technological and doctrinal breakthroughs are only available if they are sought. America or Germany could have deployed the first jet fighters years before the operational use of the Messerschmitt Me-262 in 1944.

The United States Army Air Forces, which existed before the Air Force was formed as a separate service in 1947, rejected the Lockheed L-133 jet fighter design in 1942, though its projected speed was one-and-one-half times that of piston fighters then in development. The first American jet fighter, the Lockheed P-80, never flew in combat in World War II.

The Luftwaffe did not possess adequate numbers of operable jet fighters or reconnaissance aircraft to contest our forces decisively either before or after D-Day. We cannot count on such strategic miscalculations again; we must innovate wisely and expeditiously.

We must understand that inventions that could deflate America's military strength are being sought by our adversaries. Prescience arising from intelligence and ingenuity is indispensable in war and in peace. As empowered by the dynamism of our citizenry, we must use the gifts of creativity and purpose to defend liberty.

New means to enable the visionary development of overmatching weapons and systems, which will counter innovations by our

---

[391]Ian Hogg, "Fighting Tanks," (Grosset & Dunlap, in association with Phoebus Publishing Company, 1977).

adversaries, are imperative. Innovations of this caliber are, however, too often suppressed by entrenched forces that we must recognize and eliminate.

In Tunisia, in 1943, the allied capture of a German tiger tank was considered an event of such moment that Prime Minister Winston Churchill and King George VI journeyed to inspect the vehicle. Its warfighting potential, however, was subsequently disparaged by American intelligence assessments,[392] for its design parameters did not comport with American precepts. The tank's heavy armor and 88-millimeter cannon, derived from an anti-aircraft gun, should have caused massive changes in allied plans to procure competitive tanks, but such changes were forestalled and only introduced incrementally.

The British realized that a portion of their Sherman tanks needed to be up-gunned, a requirement they met by the creation of the Sherman Firefly, which mated the American tank with a highly capable British gun housed in a revised turret.[393] America, however, did not react appropriately, for we delayed the production of a new platform of pivotal lethality. Doctrinal blinders severely hindered America's fielding of a tank that was competitive to German tigers or panthers.

During the war, no American Sherman mounted a 90-millimeter cannon, though such a gun was in production as an antiaircraft weapon. Instead, this powerful gun was used on the M36 tank destroyer, which married a Sherman chassis with an open-topped turret. A version of the 90-millimeter gun was also used in the M26 Pershing, which arrived in the European theater very late in the war, thus seeing limited combat.[394]

The reason that a more heavily armed Sherman tank was not fielded by America in the Second World War was due to doctrinal paralysis, not production or transportation shortfalls. Such paralysis is also the reason why the M26 was not sent to Europe in adequate

---

[392]https://www.tankarchives.ca/2014/08/tigers-in-tunisia.html

[393]Peter Chamberlain and Chris Ellis, "British and American Tanks of World War II," (Arco Publishing Company, 1975), 130-131.

[394]The Pershing would be used extensively in the Korean war and serve as the progenitor of subsequent American main battle tanks, including the M48 and M60.

numbers, in time for D-Day, as is documented by the fact that in September 1943, 500 Pershing tanks and 500 of an earlier variant were proposed by the Ordnance Department for delivery to the European Theater of Operations in 1944.[395] This plan was not implemented, for Army Ground Forces did not want to revise then current engagement priorities. The introduction of the M26 tank was thus delayed for more than a year.

The Army, in error, did not want American tanks to be employed to engage opposing tanks; prevailing American doctrine held that only U.S. tank destroyers should hunt German tanks as a primary task. This flawed precept cost many American servicemen their lives. Such doctrinal blindness that attempts to preserve established organizational structures must never be repeated.

Superiority

New weapons that will overmatch any potential adversary can be deployed expeditiously if doctrinal, bureaucratic, industrial, and company-specific or contractual constraints are removed by a new secretary of defense and the service secretaries. Throughout multiple administrations, the Pentagon's record in fielding new weapons is suboptimum and, too often, completely deficient; this situation requires a total revision in how we develop and acquire systems. All services are plagued with procurement disasters, often wrought by political forces that care little for actually deploying decisive weapons. Political grandstanding is the primary occupation of such leaches.

A critical mistake made repeatedly is to remove weapon development from the oversight and the grasp of our nation's warriors, who rely upon tools that should precisely fit their needs. It is an axiom of business and organizational management that functionality must be focused on the end-user. This is often compromised in the context of a procurement process that involves many constituencies that represent conflicting interests.

---

[395]Peter Chamberlain and Chris Ellis, "British and American Tanks of World War II," (Arco Publishing Company, 1975), 154–155.

The development of war-winning weapons must rest in the services, not the swollen Pentagon bureaucracy that is centered within the Office of the Secretary of Defense. The only comprehensive answer is to work with Congress to remove entire levels of bureaucracy that disjoin weapon development, testing, and procurement decisions from our nation's warfighters.

The ruinous results of failing to do so are patent. In 2002, the secretary of defense canceled the Army's new howitzer, the XM2001 Crusader, before production began but after the expenditure of two billion dollars. It was replaced by the Non-Line-of-Sight Cannon, which was part of the Army's Future Combat Systems; it, too, was canceled without any units fielded.

The total development cost for the unrealized Future Combat Systems was at least eighteen billion dollars, though many estimates place this number much higher. Only now is a new howitzer, the M1299, in the process of being fielded; the lineage of this system can be traced directly to the M109, which was first produced in 1963.

The M1299 promises to be outstanding, with twice the range of the Army's previous howitzer. It, however, will achieve its superiority by incorporating elements of a proven design, whereas the Crusader was a complete departure from the M109.

Many weapons that our military now fields are, in fact, highly modernized versions of platforms that were initially designed in the 1950s. These include the B-52 bomber, the KC-135 tanker, the C-130 transport, and the M88 recovery vehicle. Many other weapons were designed in the 1960s or early 1970s, including the M1 tank. Some of these systems, in modernized form, are likely to serve for a century or more. Indeed, the M1919 Browning machine gun, produced after World War I, is still in military service in armies all over the world;[396] the M2 machine gun, derived from the M1919, is still in production and in wide service within our military.[397]

In weapons development, prudence demands that we assess which existing systems are capable of further refinement and

---

[396] This machine gun was designed by John Browning in 1919.
[397] https://weaponsystems.net/system/411-Browning+M2HB

modernization in lieu of pursuing clean-sheet designs. Each of the systems noted that were developed and deployed decades ago were to be replaced by new weapons or equipment. Many of these intended replacements reached the prototype stage, but all were cancelled because they were either inadequate or too costly.

The Navy still builds Arleigh Burke-class guided missile destroyers and will continue to do so for the foreseeable future, though the lead ship of this class was launched in 1989. This class was to have been replaced or augmented by anti-air cruisers based on the Zumwalt-class of ships.[398] The Navy was to build thirty-two Zumwalt-class destroyers. It built three. The price for these three vessels approaches a great percentage of what was to be the procurement cost for all thirty-two ships.

The Zumwalt class, in addition to its other tasks, was to fulfill the role of shore bombardment, a capability the Marine Corps desperately needs. The Advanced Gun System, which cost a fortune to develop, is, however, being ripped out of the Zumwalt class without ever being used. Why? The price of the ammunition skyrocketed to more than 800,000 dollars for each shell, due to the reduced number of guns to be deployed.

A full, one-time, loadout of ammunition for three Zumwalt-class ships would cost almost four billion dollars. It is unconscionable that our Navy developed and deployed a shipborne artillery system without creating a backup plan for the affordable supply of its ammunition. This is inimical to the creation and maintenance of integrated fire support to suppress enemy emplacements while reinforcing our combatant forces.

The near abandonment of the Zumwalt class, which was to be the core of our Navy's surface fleet, is not management but the relinquishment of leadership and foresight. In recognition of the mistakes made, the space on the ships, which held its deserted guns, is now planned to be used to house hypersonic missiles, now in development.

The littoral combat ship (LCS), which comprises two types, is also a fiasco—with vessels retired after just a few years of service.

---

[398]https://www.globalsecurity.org/military/systems/ship/cg-x.htm

Many LCS Freedom-class vessels are planned to be decommissioned and mothballed, though ships were commissioned in 2008 or in 2018. Indeed, our Navy continues to build new ships of the exact same class as it decommissions ships that have served less than one-third of their expected service lives.

LCS vessels of the Independence class are being removed from fleet service too. To salvage the LCS program demands that we consider transferring these littoral combat ships to Taiwan and to Ukraine, for these nations are in need of new vessels and may make these ships battleworthy.

America must dominate the seas, but our Navy is set to lose more ships than our country has lost in many of our wars. This catastrophe is due to botched shipbuilding programs coupled with the Biden administration's emphasis on divestiture to fund future programs. This is unacceptable in a period in which the People's Republic of China will have half-again as many vessels as our Navy, though China has never been a naval power.

The Air Force, according to the Biden administration's plans, is set to retire at least thirty advanced F-22 fighters, which is the most capable air-superiority fighter in existence.[399] This is another manifestation of the Biden Pentagon's "divest to invest" strategy. This banner that heralds future defense investments is a cloak to hide the planned evisceration of our military. This flawed plan extends to each branch of our armed forces and directly contradicts President Reagan's timeless guidance.

In recommissioning the battleship USS New Jersey on December 28, 1982, Ronald Reagan stated, "I can assure our fellow citizens there is no room for waste in our national defense. A dollar wasted is a dollar lost in the crucial effort to build a safer future for our people."[400] I wrote these words for President Reagan; they are as true now as they were then.

---

[399] https://www.businessinsider.com/air-force-wants-to-retire-oldest-f22-raptor-fighter-jets-2022-4
[400] Ronald Reagan, "Remarks of the President at the Recommissioning of the USS New Jersey," (Long Beach Naval Shipyard, December 28, 1982).

We must make use of the weapons that we have procured at great cost, not throw them away due to incompetent management and inadequate planning. The United States Marine Corps is being gutted due to the Biden Administration's misguided "divest to invest" objectives that have deprioritized the maintenance of the Corps' prodigious lethality and its proven force components.

As a result of President Biden's actions, the ability of the Corps to provide combatant commanders, throughout the world, with integrated, appropriately sized Marine Air-Ground Task Forces (MAGTF) has been severely compromised. Therefore, balanced combined-arms operations to perform specific missions under the operational control of a designated commander, within a single service, are imperiled.

The absurd and dangerous posturing of the Biden administration never ceases, for it is presented as a chimera to distract the nation's attention from profound challenges that are being skirted. On Earth Day, in 2022, President Biden declared his commitment to spend billions to make "every vehicle" in our military, "climate friendly."[401] Perhaps the president is unaware that war is not friendly to the environment or to anything else.

Five Military Services for this Century

A Republican Congress must stand against President Biden's caustic priorities. To do so, legislators must understand the roles of each of our five military services.

Army

The United States Army stands without equal. It is, however, a force that in the postwar period has often been squandered or misused. The Army is not a tool for nation building, nor is its primary duty disaster relief.

---

[401]https://www.msn.com/en-us/news/politics/biden-says-we-re-spending-billions-to-make-us-military-fleet-climate-friendly/ar-AAWv4kD

The Army is an instrument to effect victory in war. Its capacity to relieve misery in the case of natural or manmade disasters must be a derivative function of the service's combatant potential. While meritorious, the ability of the Army to alleviate civilian disasters can never be its primary mission, for to render it so would be to compromise our nation's warfighting capability. This would undermine deterrence.

Military strength arises from determination, national cohesiveness, civilian and military leadership, planning, training, equipment, and execution. Careful consideration of our nation's abilities in light of our vulnerabilities permits us to perceive our true capabilities to produce and sustain military power.

Too often political leaders and commentators contemplate only our nation's abilities or vulnerabilities but do not consider their interrelationship. This is a profound mistake that leads either to hubris and error or recalcitrance and indifference. These deleterious postures diminish American power in the face of an oppositional force. As in so many things, balance and perception are required.

In the case of the employment of our Army, the spectrum of its power is best reserved for war when it is declared, for this judicious use provides the space for our nation's civilian authorities to consider the magnitude, duration, and consequences of the decisions they may make. The Army does have special forces and highly mobile units that are, of course, of great merit in combatting threats short of war. Their capacities are well understood and have been employed throughout our Global War on Terrorism. I counsel not for the constriction of our martial powers but for prudence in their use, for they are of great moment and have too often been employed without the requisite consideration of consequences and human costs.

Navy

America will always be primarily a maritime nation. This fact was recognized by John Jay, who served as the secretary of foreign affairs during the period of the Articles of Confederation. In Federalist

No. 4, Jay foresaw the importance of our trade with both India and China, for he specified both countries by name.[402]

As a successor to the role that John Jay created, Secretary of State Pompeo has often expressed his deep understanding of the immense importance of our Navy. America relies on the oceans that bracket our nation for commerce, the importation of essential commodities, and as avenues over which we project influence and, when necessary, power.

Free use of the seas is foundational to any modern nation; therefore, it must never be taken for granted. Our Navy is charged with two essential missions: sea control and the support and projection of power ashore. Associated roles include strategic deterrence, the preservation of freedom of navigation, naval presence, and sea denial, which is the foreclosure of an adversary's sea lines of communication (SLOC) or maritime presence.

Sea control no longer means an absolute domination of all the world's oceans, but the selective command of the seas at times and places of our selection. It is a prerequisite for all other surface operations. To effect sea control, we must be able "in time of emergency to venture in harm's way," according to Ronald Reagan.[403] Our fortieth president recognized this necessity, which was first expressed by the Father of the American Navy, John Paul Jones.

We must, within areas and through timeframes ordained by mission parameters, be able to control surface, air, subsurface, informational, and electromagnetic domains. To thwart the use of such realms by an adversary defines sea denial; this was a primary objective of the Soviet Union; it is now a principal mission of the Chinese Navy.

China is building a navy designed for offensive operations that will be buttressed by its conventional land- and air-based ballistic and hypersonic missiles. The United States Navy must preserve a decisive margin of naval superiority to counter this multidimensional

---

[402]https://avalon.law.yale.edu/18th_century/fed04.asp
[403]Ronald Reagan, "Remarks of the President at the Recommissioning of the USS New Jersey," (Long Beach Naval Shipyard, December 28, 1982).

threat. The Biden administration's naval procurement plans will cede command of the seas to our adversary in crucial areas.

Nothing short of a reformation of our Navy is required to reattain initiative. This will be one of the most daunting challenges that a new Republican administration will face. We have no choice but to succeed; to do so we must concentrate on our missions, our naval industrial base, potential belligerents and their actions, and our reincorporation of the maritime precepts created since our Founding as the greatest naval power the world has ever known.

Marine Corps

The Marine Corps is the sister service of the Navy. Marines project power ashore. As a single service, it, alone, has held the capacity to be able to field an unconquerable, combined-arms force.

The Goldwater–Nichols Department of Defense Reorganization Act,[404] which Ronald Reagan signed into law, fortified joint military commands. This pivotal law did not reduce the importance of the Corps within the panoply of America's military forces; rather, it underlined the importance of unified combatant commands that must seamlessly engage and communicate throughout the entire spectrum of combat.

According to deliberations in Congress during the height of the Korean War, the Marines, must be "most ready when the nation is least ready."[405] The Corps must be able "to provide a balanced force in readiness for a naval campaign and, at the same time, a ground and air striking force ready to suppress or contain international disturbances short of large-scale war."[406] These axioms are still true today but are being subverted by a reckless administration.

Our nation's capability to respond with great urgency to military emergencies that extend into multiple combatant realms is in danger of being lost should the decline in the Corps' capacities continue.

---

[404] Pub. L. 99–433
[405] https://www.marines.mil/Portals/1/Publications/MCO%203000.13B.pdf?ver=2020-07-15-110758-503
[406] Ibid.

The Marine Corps has lost all its M1 tanks, its military bridging equipment, and most of its artillery capabilities.[407]

Tanks are required to sustain infantry operations and to hold territory; artillery is paramount in reducing adversarial capabilities in any land engagement. The Marine Corps is being stripped of both capacities. Naval gunfire platforms and amphibious support ships are dwindling in numbers to the point that they do not match our nation's security requirements. If these trends continue, this brave service will become a memory.

The birth of Marine Corps aviation took place on May 22, 1912.[408] Today, this legacy stands in peril due to lack of investment in fixed-wing and vertical lift assets for the Corps. Such shortsightedness must be reversed immediately.

The Marine Corps pioneered close air support of ground forces both before and during World War II.[409] This capacity, reinforced by Marine armor and artillery, produced an amphibious and land-warfare capability that was unmatched by any nation. This heritage that has been honed for more than 100 years is in danger of collapse.

It is critical that modified San Antonio-class amphibious transport dock ships be built; these ships embark Marines and are necessary to land and support an expeditionary force. Warships of this type are required to replace vessels of the same function that are being retired due to age. Contrary to current planning, there must be no pause in the construction of new ships of this type.[410]

Other crucial programs have been canceled in the past decade, including the amphibious Expeditionary Fighting Vehicle, developed at a cost of over three billion dollars, but terminated by the Obama administration before production began. We must restore what is

---

[407]https://news.usni.org/2020/03/23/new-marine-corps-cuts-will-slash-all-tanks-many-heavy-weapons-as-focus-shifts-to-lighter-littoral-forces
[408]https://www.history.navy.mil/content/history/museums/nnam/explore/exhibits/online-exhibits---collections/marine-corps-aviation-centennial.html
[409]https://www.usni.org/magazines/naval-history-magazine/2012/november/close-air-support-pioneering-years
[410]https://news.usni.org/2023/03/13/navy-osd-directed-amphib-procurement-pause-dod-says-current-amphib-force-sufficient

being lost: The Marine Corps must be rebuilt as the service that is unique among all in its intrinsic potential.

The Marines are the means to effect combat objectives expeditiously in situations that require a ready combined-arms force. Any president will be hobbled in the array of military options that are available if the Marines are not immediately bolstered in their capabilities. The commandant's Force Design 2030,[411] which eliminates heavy ground force elements, must be rescinded and be replaced by adequate funding that will reestablish the Corps' capabilities, rather than presaging its ultimate collapse as the right arm of the Commander in Chief.

Air Force

The Air Force provides, along with the air elements of the Navy and Marines, decisive air superiority within a designated battlespace. Although the F-35 Lightning II is an excellent aircraft, it was not designed to be the ultimate air superiority fighter. Too many design compromises were needed to produce variants of this plane for the Air Force, Navy, and Marines.

The air-dominance F-22 Raptor was cancelled by the Obama administration after just 187 operational fighters were built. Originally, 750 planes were to be procured; plans were also laid for a tactical bomber version that would possess longer range. The corrosive decision to terminate this program mandates our attention.

Production lines, created at great cost, for critical weapons systems should not be destroyed until proven alternatives are at hand. The F-22 line could have been kept open and been available today, for both Japan and Australia demonstrated great interest in acquiring this fighter but were denied by elements within Congress and the Obama administration.

It is imperative that those F-22s that have been built be retained in operational status. The Air Force, however, has been ordered by

---

[411]https://www.marines.mil/Force-Design-2030/

the Biden Administration to divest its wings of needed aircraft, so that budgetary and management inadequacies may be masked. The service is thus reducing the F-22 fleet, even as it buys a modernized version of the F-15, the aircraft that the F-22 was designed to replace.

In the near future, the Air Force must increase its combatant power by procuring the next generation air dominance (NGAD) fighter in adequate numbers. Large and capable drones, which will serve as wingmen to manned fighters and other aircraft, must be developed and produced to enhance our capabilities.

The service must also invest in a force of B-21 Raider bombers that will carry conventional munitions; these must be additional to those bombers designated for strategic operations. Such aircraft must possess the capacity to devastate the intermediate ballistic missile and hypersonic forces of belligerent countries, for these classes of weapons can hold our naval and Marine Corps assets at risk.

Space Force

The United States Space Force was founded on December 20, 2019. It literally occupies the high ground and operates essential satellite and spaceplane platforms[412] in service of our nation's unified commands.

As our nation's newest military service, it is essential that it be nourished and be allowed to develop its own standards and credo, in concert with the Air Force. To do so, it must evince a substantial margin of independence. Close attention must be paid to the part cybersecurity will play in the Space Force's future.

Several new, virtual, cybersecurity national laboratories must be established to aid the military and other sectors that oversee or traverse this domain. This augmentation is supported by Vice Admiral John Poindexter, who was instrumental in the creation of the Strategic Defense Initiative, and former Deputy Secretary of Energy William Martin, who oversaw the Department of Energy's national laboratories, which may be modeled in this pursuit.

---

[412] Boeing X-37

Obligations, Transformation, and Threshold Warfare

Process must precede policy. Reactions to an emergency often do not reflect policies but are, instead, exigent actions. I believe the next president must assert and enact bold initiatives to restore our military capabilities and our alliances. These goals must be accomplished with the support of Congress.

Prosperity and opportunity are only possible if advanced within a cordon of security. The essence of diplomacy when practiced by a competent administration is to signal strength and unity of purpose while establishing pauses in geopolitical tensions or confrontations that may lead to war. To do this, we must not confuse tools with objectives.

Too often, we forget our geostrategic principles for we are focused on means and not ends. Actions must not be confused with halfway measures, for halfway measures do not attain desired goals but obstruct them by squandering pertinent strategies, the nation's resolve, resources, and, too often, precious lives.

Diplomacy and martial force exist upon a spectrum of national power. Weakness and indecision have historically subverted reconcilement between adversarial nations. In contradistinction, our capacity to overmatch our adversaries enables diplomacy.

What is required is a coadjutant strategy for the United States in which we pool our strengths with those of our allies around the world. Coadjutant, in this sense, means, "mutually assisting," for America's alliance structures, commitments, and security assistance must no longer move in one direction—to just prop up other nations at our expense. There must be reciprocal benefits and burden sharing between the United States and our allies, or they are not allies at all.

The United States is followed by China, India, Russia, the United Kingdom, Saudi Arabia, Germany, France, Japan, and the Republic of Korea in defense spending, in absolute terms. It is not possible to know China's true defense spending, for that totalistic state tries to mask its effort. Russia's defense spending is more accurately gauged; it's military's overall potential, with the exception of its nuclear forces, has been reduced by its war against Ukraine.

What can be said unequivocally is that of the ten nations with the largest defense budgets, only two are adversarial states; the others are either America's allies or friends. This is, in part, why allies are crucial; their commitments multiply our efforts.

While ceaseless increases to the U.S. military budget are untenable as a percentage of the gross domestic product, due to a national debt that is exploding past thirty-two trillion dollars, reductions in defense spending are impossible given the range of threats faced. America's only sustainable option is to seek great changes and efficiencies in defense procurement.

We must optimize how we spend each defense dollar, so that America's military may be put on a level road going forward, which embraces excellence and increased capabilities, not politically correct posturing. Wisdom in our choice of causes must be part of a new national defense strategy. This shrewdness must rest on realistic appraisals of China's, Russia's, and Iran's military capabilities and intentions as well as that of other potentially belligerent states and entities.

Security must truly be mutual if lasting deterrence is to be attained. To this end, America's foreign military sales (FMS) and technology transfer practices must be revised.

Our nation retains billions of dollars in weapons systems, including tanks, ships, and planes, held in storage. They are mothballed, and almost all will never be used again by our forces.

Collaborating with allies and friends, such as Ukraine, Israel, Taiwan, and other nations, we should first determine which systems can be refreshed, transferred, and used by recipient nations. Second, working with Congress and with potential recipient countries, we should determine which groups of weapons may be elevated in their readiness and maintained within our stockpiles and reserve yards as a surge capacity to aid nations that face the threat of war. We should create crisis prepackaged sets that are responsive to specific needs of allied and friendly countries, which should be asked to fund this initiative along with required training packages.

Early intelligence concerning rising tensions or malevolent ambitions is essential. Prompt action to initiate arms transfers must be taken upon the advent of intelligence of appropriate scope if deterrence is to be achieved. The crisis prepackaged sets would augment the recipient country's potential to conduct rapid, combined-arms warfare, and could be prepositioned within the recipient country or an adjacent nation before the advent of hostilities.

Coincident with the creation of such packages would be the training of the recipient country's military on the use of the weapons that could be conveyed. This should have been done for Ukraine; it must be initiated now for Taiwan.

Change

To effect needed change in the Department of Defense, duplication and inefficiencies must be eliminated. This requires structural change at the highest levels. Consideration, therefore, should be given to the elimination of the position of the deputy secretary of defense, as it is presently constituted, along with large sections of the staffs that serve the Office of the Secretary of Defense. Instead, the three service secretaries should serve as alternating deputy secretaries of defense, thereby substantially reducing the immense bureaucracy that presently constitutes the Office of the Secretary of Defense as well as the consultants that orbit its subdivisions.

Such an initiative would bring technology, training, and weapon development closer to the servicemen and women who actually use the equipment that the defense establishment designs and produces. This is an essential business practice that must be adopted by our government.

Reductions in dead-weight, defense contracting losses through multi-year program obligations must be emphasized in the future. Many contractual steps should be taken to avoid the hemorrhaging of tax dollars due to the cancellation of new weapons systems on the cusp of production.

It should be hoped that bureaucratic and procurement reforms, along with advances in rapid prototyping and successive testing, will allow our military to procure cost-effective weapons that are several generation beyond those that are presently produced. This process, however, must be highly selective to be feasible.

As can be seen, our military employs many weapons and systems that were designed decades ago. The present use of these systems provides evidence that enduring weapons can be produced. The key to the success of each of these stalwart systems is intrinsic adaptability, which is buttressed by affordable maintainability. These successes must be emulated; the space created through the maintenance of proven systems permits groundbreaking technologies to be employed where they can make a difference, in new and decisive weapons that will win wars.

To effect the foregoing reforms, the next president must force the definition of new weapon systems, which may be fielded rapidly by eliminating bureaucratic and doctrinal barriers. The deficits in our production abilities for munitions and other defense articles have been made clear by the war in Ukraine: We must rebuild America's defense industrial base to yield important surge capacities in the production of ammunition, combat drones,[413] missiles, and other consumables.

We must also look to the future. America must lead in artificial intelligence, quantum computing, unmanned combat vehicle design and manufacture, new materials, and other technologies that must remain secret.

Some processes to accomplish the foregoing are already in place, but they are hampered by bureaucratic infighting, which must be eliminated. As we pursue such technologies, cybersecurity and data or personnel exfiltration must be of the greatest concern, given the Chinese Communist Party's acts of intellectual property theft in all its forms.

In the absence of meaningful diplomacy, armed combat achieves national objectives by force or by coercion. If we broaden the definitions of these terms, we may appreciate the different ways we or our adversaries may wage campaigns in the future. Our military may be

---

[413]Unmanned Combat Aerial Vehicles (UCAV)

tasked to fight unconventional, hybrid, liminal, or threshold engagements or battles.

In 2018, the Pentagon confirmed that military lasers that originated from China's newly opened base in Djibouti injured the eyes of two of our C-130 Hercules pilots; such flights were associated with support of America's war on terror in the Horn of Africa.[414] More recently, in February of 2023, crewmen aboard a Philippine Coast Guard vessel, in an area of the South China Sea, which China illegally claims, were subjected to blinding laser light, which originated from a Chinese warship.[415] An Australian P-8A maritime patrol aircraft was also lased by Chinese forces in 2022.[416]

Due to the composition of the human eye, it is very hard to guard against blinding by laser weapons. China is flouting the United Nations' Convention on Certain Conventional Weapons, Protocol IV, which bans the use of lasers to blind combatants or civilians in war. China has long been a signatory to this convention.[417] Though the protocol refers specifically to permanent blinding, which did not occur in these incidents, the intent of the convention is to ban weapons that are indiscriminate and disproportionately injurious.

In the entire recorded history of war, one of the greatest acts of barbarism is that of the Byzantine Emperor Basil II who blinded 15,000 Bulgarian captives, allowing one in one hundred to retain one eye, to lead the others home.[418] It has been 1,000 years since Basil's infamy, but his acts are being recreated nascently today by China, for fear and terror are powerful weapons when placed in the hands of an adversary that is willing to conduct unrestricted warfare,

---

[414]https://www.nbcnews.com/news/africa/pentagon-accuses-chinese-blinding-djibouti-based-u-s-pilots-lasers-n871096

[415]https://www.nbcnews.com/news/world/china-laser-philippines-military-blinding-coast-guard-rcna70336

[416]https://www.cnn.com/2022/02/21/asia/australia-china-warship-laser-intl-hnk-ml/index.html

[417]https://www.un.org/disarmament/the-convention-on-certain-conventional-weapons/

[418]https://www.britannica.com/biography/Basil-II

although its present conduct is most often clandestine and measured so as not to be contested.

These incidents are emblematic of the capacity for unbounded cruelty that the Chinese Communist Party and the forces it controls have repeatedly demonstrated. These acts must not be allowed to stand. A coalition of nations must act harmoniously but resolutely to redirect China, so that its path does not lead to war.

China's use of lasers to blind, in the case of the Philippine Coast Guard crewmen, occurred at the same time an enormous Chinese intelligence balloon was allowed by the Biden administration to traverse our nation. This surveillance device overflew bases that are home to two legs of our nuclear Triad, including Minuteman III ballistic missile silos, and airfields where our B-2 stealth bombers are stationed.[419] This balloon was one of many that China has deployed against nations across the world.[420] Each of these transits is illegal and is a violation of sovereign airspace.

Superficially, China's use of lasers to blind and its deployment of balloons to capture intelligence in our country and around the world do not seem to be related issues. I do not believe such disjuncture to be the case.

Threshold warfare concerns actions that occur in the midst of a haze of detection, attribution, and uncertainty. The internet and social media can be employed to magnify unknown parameters of such warfare, for uncertainty can be plied as a weapon in war.

Intelligence is thus of paramount importance as is the honest and the timely conveyance of facts to the American people. The transit of the balloon across our nation's strategic bases was not announced by the Biden administration but was first reported on the news.[421] The balloon was also photographed by a local Montanan newspaper before the Biden administration acknowledged its presence.

---

[419] https://www.msn.com/en-us/news/other/defense-secretary-chinese-spy-balloon-went-past-b-2-stealth-bomber-base/ar-AA17iko2

[420] https://www.nytimes.com/2023/02/08/us/politics/china-spy-balloons.html

[421] https://apnews.com/article/chinese-surveillance-balloon-united-states-montana-47248b0ef2b085620fcd866c105054be

Though the intelligence asset was detected by our military and intelligence communities long before it was seen by the residents of Montana, the Biden administration stayed silent, for it did not want to disturb its overtures to President Xi. Thus, China gleaned important information regarding America's threshold for attributing militarily provocative acts to adversarial nations with whom we have economic and diplomatic interests. China, through this episode, has been able to assess the present disjointedness between American political leadership, the Pentagon, and our intelligence community.

Simultaneously, the Chinese Communist Party has been able to gauge the Biden administration's weakness in responding to its provocative acts against the Philippines. The use of shipborne lasers came at a time in which the United States Navy was attaining important basing privileges in the Philippines,[422] which had been lost years earlier due, in part, to surreptitious Chinese interference in that country.

In the wake of these threats and provocations, our military must always be an apolitical force for peace, which represents the very best of our country and our heritage. Coincident with the aforementioned actions to restore our military's power, the present emphasis on political indoctrination in our services must be forever banned.

No nation can match the potential of America's armed forces. America's military has, however, been harmed by a paucity in leadership. The future president of our country must honor what we demand of our men and women in uniform by employing the formidable powers of our military with wisdom, restraint, and profound understanding of the obligations demanded of the leader of the Free World. We must pray that such insight and reverence will soon be attained.

---

[422]https://www.cnn.com/2023/02/01/asia/us-philippines-base-access-agreement-intl-hnk-ml/index.html

Chapter 13, In Defense of Freedom, Precepts:

• Central to the wellbeing and security of American families is a United States that leads the world in both military and economic power.

• No nation can match the potential of America's armed forces. America's military has been harmed by the dereliction of leadership. A future president must honor what we demand of our men and women in uniform by employing the formidable powers of our military with wisdom, restraint, and profound understanding of the obligations demanded of the leader of the Free World.

• We must venerate the sacrifices demanded of those who volunteer to serve in our military. Our political processes must build and support the requisite leadership, armed forces, and weapon systems that will triumph in war and peace.

• Weakness and disengagement on the world stage invite needless conflict. Isolationism is not a strategy.

• Prosperity and opportunity are only possible if advanced within a cordon of security. America's defense alliances are critical to global peace and to our nation's survival as the world's dominant economic power.

• American military power is the means to give body and shape to our nation's obligations by supporting diplomacy and needed outreach while substantiating deterrence.

• We must use our strengths prudently and conservatively, for America is most secure when it leads by example and not by armed intervention.

• Our military has been impeded and disparaged by a reckless political class that demands extraordinary sacrifices of our men and women in uniform, often in the service of ill-defined or unachievable goals.

• Distinguishing military engagements of limited scope from wars is the means to heal our nation's wounds, in order that our military be supported earnestly. Intelligence is of paramount importance as is the honest and timely conveyance of facts to the American people. Wars or military actions may merit our involvement or be alien to the American creed; leadership requires that the nature and scale of all military engagements be continuously assessed.

• Freedom cannot be imposed on a people; it must be sought.

• Our nation's armed forces are being eroded by the imposition of anti-American values through training regimes that repackage Marxist dogma under the guise of equity, inclusion, and wokeness, for racism is supposedly hidden within the fabric of America's institutions, both military and civilian. Creation of a military that is devoid of political indoctrination is imperative.

• The Biden administration's defense budgets are hollowing out our military forces through the adoption of a "divest to invest" policy, in which present capabilities are depleted in order that funds be devoted to new weapons programs, not presently in production.

• China is far more powerful across a range of measures than is Russia. China seeks to use its present window of opportunity, afforded it by the Biden administration, to subdue our way of life. This is impermissible.

• It is not rational to permit China, as a nation, to be the principal exporter of goods to our country and the source of our largest individual trade deficit, as it targets our armed forces and threatens to invade Taiwan.

Issues and Problems:

• Diplomacy and military force exist upon a spectrum of national power. Weakness and indecision subvert reconcilement between adversarial nations. The capacity to overmatch adversaries enables diplomacy.

• Military actions should be limited in objectives and in duration. In confliction zones, the capacity to reassess and to react is essential; end points must be considered before wars or military actions are broached.

• Rather than making America vulnerable to attack, appropriate collective defense agreements reduce the chances for combat due to the strength and the permanence of our alliances. Alliances must be pursued and defended.

• Taiwan is a vibrant democracy. Its transition to democratic rule is a model for the entire world, including the People's Republic of China, whose citizens long for liberty.

• The "divest to invest" strategy, as endorsed by the Biden administration, is crippling our military. Technology is of determinative military value only when it is deployed.

• The United States Army stands without equal. It is, however, a force that in the postwar period has often been squandered or misused. The Army cannot be a tool for nation building.

• America must dominate the seas, but our Navy is set to lose more ships than our country has lost in many of our wars. This is unacceptable, for China possesses one-and-one-half times as many vessels as our Navy.

• The Air Force must provide decisive air superiority. The Air Force and Space Force must possess superlative tools to achieve their missions of dominance, but such capacities have been jeopardized by the Biden administration.

• Marines project power ashore. This service must retain the capability to function as an unconquerable, combined-arms force. America's capacity, however, to respond with urgency to emergencies that extend into multiple combatant realms is in danger of being lost due to severe cuts in the force structure of the Marine Corps.

Duties and Actions:

• We must reject indoctrination and commit to excellence in military training and procurement. New weapons can be deployed expeditiously if doctrinal, bureaucratic, industrial, or contractual constraints are removed.

• Doctrinal blindness to preserve established organizational structures must never be tolerated. To effect needed change in the Department of Defense, duplication and inefficiencies must be eliminated. This requires structural change at the highest levels, including the Office of the Secretary of Defense. Weapons development must be returned to the purview of our nation's warriors and not be entrusted to bureaucrats.

• America must lead in artificial intelligence, quantum computing, unmanned combat vehicle design, and new materials. Several new, virtual, cybersecurity national laboratories must be established to aid our military.

- In the Indo-Pacific, America must expand the Quadrilateral Security Dialogue, whose members are the United States, Japan, India, and Australia, and integrate it with the AUKUS union, which includes the United Kingdom.

- Our country's leadership must make Xi Jinping understand that he will never defeat America militarily and that any attempt to invade Taiwan will be met with the certitude of his nation's retreat. China must not be allowed to expand its domain—should Russia splinter into smaller states.

CHAPTER 14

REFLECTIONS

A president must be obedient to the Constitution and the means it enshrines for the governance of our country and the maintenance of our Republic. The hardworking men and women of America built this great nation. They create the future. As we march forward, let us remember our trials but not forget our dreams, for it is time to fuse our memories with our vision for a better world, in order that we may define our course.

The individual is sovereign and not the government. The capacity to direct our own lives is our nation's legacy, for we are each endowed with liberty by a Republic whose Founders believed that free will is an extraordinary gift from God.

The central question for a conservative is what from the past should be conserved in the context of an ever-changing world. The answers we derive must resolutely celebrate our faith, our families, our Founding,

> our reverence for education, and our ceaseless commitment to excellence. We cannot allow the apex of our living within the boundaries established by God to be a memory, for this pinnacle must represent our future and not our past.

Reflections

The presidential oath of office is specified in the Constitution: "I do solemnly swear (or affirm) that I will faithfully execute the Office of President of the United States, and will to the best of my Ability, preserve, protect and defend the Constitution of the United States."[423] The Constitution is our nation's highest law. The presidential oath, therefore, is one of obedience.

A president must be obedient to the Constitution and the means it enshrines for the governance of our country and the maintenance of our Republic. Obedience is the state of dutiful compliance to an authority. Thus, presidential obedience is rendered to the Constitution and to the people of the United States for whom the Founding Documents were established.[424]

The intertwining of faith and obedience transcends time. Romans 5:19 states, "For as by one man's disobedience many were made sinners, so by the obedience of one shall many be made righteous." The first man was Adam, whereas the second in this verse is Jesus.

Obedience rests on humbleness. In this act, the Son of God provides a lustrous example to all humankind. The leader of a free

---

[423]https://constitution.congress.gov/browse/essay/artII-S1-C8-1/ALDE
_00001126/

[424]https://www.congress.gov/founding-documents

people must be obedient to the law and to the citizenry. This is the immortal standard that America's Founding distilled.

This standard must never be sullied or be reproached, though it has been so besmirched by a president who believes he can flout the Constitution and pay no heed to the people. This is not the way. We must return to righteousness through the obedience of our nation's leadership.

I consider an event to be momentous if it cannot be imagined to have occurred in a previous time. Certainly, the creation of our Republic was viewed in this light by our Founders and by the patriots who created our inheritance. Why then has our country turned, in many instances, against itself? It is because the left must denigrate America before it can capture and imprison our nation. They thus inveigh against any representative of traditional thought: Do they not know that tearing someone down never lifts anyone up?

Often, we would rather believe we are wrong, for it is easier to accept blame than to realize we are facing daunting enemies. Seemingly, in an instant, we have lost many of our moral bearings, which must be reclaimed with expedience.

Foundations

History leaves its marks. The Crisis of the Third Century brought the Roman Empire to the edge of collapse due to military overextension, immigration without assimilation, plague, inflation, political disunity, and insurgence.

America's third century is upon us; it must not signify our lasting descent. Intellectuals often inhabit unreal worlds that exist only in their minds. This is dangerous for society if it presages detachment from it. We must challenge this refusal to accept reality. To prevail, we must inscribe our faith in a higher power, our allegiance to America's Founding Documents, and our commitment to American exceptionalism.

We freed the world from fascistic empires, yet we, as Americans, are called supremacists. We fed the world, yet we, as Americans, are called imperialists. We imparted technology, engineering, and science to all corners of the globe, yet we, as Americans, are called cultural thieves.

It would be enough if these lies and taunts came from outside America's borders, but they frequently come from within. They emanate habitually from those who have contributed little to society but who seek aggrandizement by castigating those who have contributed bountifully. This is especially true when such acts, which built our country, occurred in a different time.

We comprehend that destroying foundations obliterates what has been built. This is the paramount threat we face as a nation, but America's institutions, which were designed to uphold our country's underpinnings, have been unsettled. We see this in the law. Justice must be blind, but we, as citizens, cannot be when justice is not fair or equal in its application.

Observations

We are all only one fall away from being reduced in our capacities. This realization leads to compassion, for if we do not see our own faults, we will never see the goodness in others.

The hubris of the bureaucratic state is unjustified, for the wisdom of the American people is unequaled. America's self-satisfied political class talks down to their fellow citizens; they forget that while government governs the crimes of men, citizens judge the crimes of government. What is impermissible for the individual must not be acceptable when perpetrated by the state, for such acts are the steppingstones to despotism.

I learn ceaselessly from the hardworking men and women of this great nation, for it is they who create the future. As we march forward, let us remember our trials but not forget our dreams, for we spend much of our lives as time travelers: reliving the past through our reminiscences or journeying to the future through our thoughts, but the sum of our existence is constituted in the present moment. It is time to fuse our memories with our dreams in order that we may define our future.

Laws

Our Constitution, with its twenty-seven amendments, is 7,591 words long. The law that established Obamacare is half as long as the entire Bible. With all its regulations, state and otherwise, more than ten-million words have been written to implement this deeply flawed statute. Before Obamacare was made law, Speaker of the House Pelosi said, "But we have to pass the bill so that you can find out what is in it, away from the fog of the controversy."[425]

What Nancy Pelosi related is not democracy. It is tyranny. No law going forward should be permitted to be longer than the Constitution and its amendments.

These multi-hundred-thousand-word bills only benefit the lawyers and lobbyists who populate Washington. President Trump reduced regulations and thus the income of Washington's miscreants, for this he was hated.

A law the length of Obamacare would take a minimum of forty-two hours just to read, much less understand. We thus know that it was never read nor fully understood by any of our lawmakers. It is up to all of us to demand change.

A president must not sign bills into law that are not comprehensible nor capable of being reviewed in full. If the American people are to be truly part of our political process, our laws must be simplified: The process must be open and not opaque. Therefore, laws must be written so that their length not exceed that of our Constitution and its amendments.

Goals

I began writing this book more than one year ago. My intent was to explicate the foundations of our country and to place crucial pillars of national power upon these plinths. To put religion into its proper context in relation to governance, to place our Founding in perspective, to celebrate the family as the irreplaceable unit of humanity,

---

[425]https://reason.com/2010/03/09/nancy-pelosi-on-health-care-we/

and to promote education and science as the necessary substrates for human advancement, are vital foundations for freedom.

We must root out hypocrisy wherever we may find it. Those who ceaselessly disparage the Bible paradoxically turn to it when it suits their interests. In fact, the passages in the New Testament that are errantly stated by the left to allude to socialism, concern charity, not forfeiture. Charity is not an obligation that is levied; it is given freely, for if it be compelled, it is not charity at all.

Our nation's new ruling class has accumulated power and wealth by feigning support for the dispossessed and the left behind, while exporting our jobs to China. Whole industries have been lost, though the left claims to care about the American worker and the environment, which China contaminates.

Our nation's core principles are flayed by our technocratic elite because they provide consistency and balance for our society. The left and avaricious politicians are oscillating forces, moving from creating the conditions that precipitate extreme lawlessness, to hastening circumstances that effect totalistic pressures to control and to dominate the energies previously unleashed. This is a cycle of tyranny that is repetitive, for it excites before it entraps the citizenry of a nation.

Many members of Congress say the police are not needed, and this is true if you have your own armed security detail. Our opposition speaks endlessly of climate change, but infrequently about true environmental issues: the preservation of our nation's wild horses, sold to slaughter, or our wetlands, safeguarded by our nation's hunters, who are disparaged at every opportunity.

A society that does not enforce its own laws provides its assessment that its laws are unjust or unenforceable. Though this occurs every day on America's border, this must not be our country's path; we must be a nation of laws and not of men, though an unprincipled individual occupies the highest office in the land. Let us instead enshrine that life is not the enterprise of one generation but results from wisdom accumulated across centuries, which is garnered by thought, experience, and yearning.

Politics has become a tornado, which threatens to destroy everything in its path, because our perception of the world and its arc of motion is confounded by presuppositions and by unreal histories. Clarity is therefore diminished, enabling us to deceive ourselves. We are now besieged by a government that thoughtlessly tries to do too much, though it knows it is capable of so little.

Wisdom must be attained before power is exercised. Useful political discourse is impossible without the veneration of standards of behavior that have been honed and passed down since the polity of Athens first met. We observe this error in the deprecation of manners, which are the collective rules of civilization that grant amity rather than discord. Manners must be reclaimed, for they permit fruitful human interaction by proscribing that which is injurious to the blending of different perspectives and ideas.

Logic demands that we state that we will never rid the world of racism by framing every issue and controversy through the prism of race. Only the rash want to throw away history and turn a blind eye to our nation's progress. If we do not proclaim these truths, we are as guilty as those who have never learned these verities.

To the left and those they control in government, people of color are a new proletariat, to be shaped and guided. They are not; these Americans are individuals, each with their own thoughts and aspirations, which must be respected and enabled. In trying to use outward differences to separate the family that is America, the left seeks to employ every lever of the deep state.

Radicals desire that we feel shame because we, as a nation, are not perfect, but such a conception only serves to reduce the majesty of God, for only he is faultless. Thus, to desire perfection is to become as Adam or Eve before the fall. This subversion is propagated by leftists in their attempted enshrinement of equity in outcomes and not equality in opportunities.

Equity is the imposition of a constructed version of fairness that is not fair, for equity falsely promises uniformity in personal outcomes. Fairness can only arise from the full attainment of the fruits of one's labor. To impose equity, therefore, is to impose that which is intrinsically unfair.

Thoughtlessly, the left and the Democrats they have captured do not comprehend that there can be no real equality of opportunity for individuals if the end points of their labors are preordained to be the same. Yet this is exactly what the embrace of edicts to enforce an equity of outcomes demands. Thus, the pernicious doctrine of equity directly contradicts the principles of both Abraham Lincoln and Martin Luther King.

Inequities or perceived inequities are used to usher in governmental actions to remove them. The imposition of equity is thus the font of power for any totalitarian state, for each person is intrinsically different. Fairness that arises out of freedom may seem unfair, for individual achievements will differ, but differences in accomplishments constitute the fullest realization of fairness.

Our worth as persons is not, however, defined by what we achieve but by what has been given to us by our Creator. Every life, including the unborn, already has meaning, for this is granted to us by God. Thus, every life must be honored.

Leadership

It is the Lord's judgement alone that grants us eternity. This is why I hold my oaths to be sacred, for I made them in the presence of God.

Leadership rests on many qualities, which few politicians demonstrate, though all claim this attribute. For true leadership to be achieved, determination and openness must govern political discourse. While the core principles of our Republic must never be subject to theft, we must be open to various paths to achieve what is necessary and is desired.

Our military has been impeded by malicious and incompetent politicians of both parties who do not measure the sacrifices they expect, which they simultaneously fail to honor. We must enforce this fact: Freedom is not free; it may seem so to coddled elitists, but their freedom was bought with the blood of patriots.

The United States should not be required to pay for its own extermination. We admire and love the Chinese people but loathe their oppressors. Chinese communism is a falsehood that has only sustained itself through theft and through crimes too numerous to recount.

The same statement can be made about the people of Russia and Iran: Their cultures reach back millennia, but their societies have been corrupted by the imposition of the worst forms of dictatorial control. We, as Americans, seek that these nations return to greatness by removing that which is corrosive to individual freedom. The same wish must be offered on behalf of people the world over, who suffer under the boots of dictators.

We must state plainly to our allies and friends that freedom must be defended jointly if it is to be enjoyed individually. Each nation that values freedom must do its fair share; the burden of defending the Free World cannot fall only on America.

We must cooperatively recognize the threats posed by China, by Russia, and by other belligerent states. President Xi comprehends the internal forces that will one day doom the Chinese Communist Party. This realization portends great danger, for, to hold power, Xi must fixate his country's attention through the creation of an external threat.

The danger China poses must not be compounded: President Putin and his cohort are a putrid scab that must be ripped off the body of Russia if that nation is to heal and return to a sense of decency. Russia must be defeated in Ukraine: This statement, however, does not mean that Russia must be defeated as a nation and splintered apart, for this would empower China and increase the risks of nuclear proliferation.

As with the communist and fascist overlords before them, Xi and Putin promised utopias, which, in actuality, are rendered as prisons for anyone who dares to not conform. In this observation, we see the truancy of the leftist mind, for they trumpet the merits of nonconformity while cleaving to those systems of governance that eviscerate that which they say they seek.

When a nation's power exceeds its wisdom, disaster follows. Internationally, if America's primary interests are not concerned, we must eschew military intervention wherever possible, while insisting on our right to be informed, our prerogative to advise, our obligation to warn, and our constant ability to reassess and to act, if necessary.

We must realize that the essential assumption that rational people make is, itself, often irrational. Rational people believe the world acts rationally, but it does not. We must plan for irrational behavior on the part of our adversaries; further, we must create systems that are so resilient that even when parts fail, they will still function and fulfill their purpose.

Precedent

Words spoken to effect strategic clarity have no meaning and are false if they are not predated or accompanied by actions. Unfortunately, we have witnessed the inversion of this necessary sequence.

We all have questions about a world seemingly changed in an instant by the war in Europe, but was there not a long fuse that went almost unnoticed? There is a difference between strategic withdrawal and collapse; this distinction was discounted by the Biden administration in its abandonment of Afghanistan.

Evil differs in its form: It may be perpetrated directly, or it may be permitted by those who look past its commission. Either manifestation is unacceptable.

To his great credit, Secretary of State Pompeo made the leaders of the Taliban know that if they failed to live up to their promises, they would be crushed like Qasem Soleimani. The demise of the murderous head of Iran's Quds Force resounded in the Taliban's consciousness.

The consequences of the rejection of sound military and diplomatic order by the Biden administration now reverberate throughout the globe. Indeed, terrorism's fury torments and scars deeply the planet's two billion Muslims who wish to live peacefully and who contribute prolifically to all the nations of the world.

Change

Each of us has sought to answer the question: What can we do to reorient our nation? First, we must profess our beliefs, we must cherish our families, and we must educate all Americans about our country's Founding, for this will introduce the virtues of conservatism.

Second, we must restore simple common sense: Except in time of gravest emergency, do not spend money you do not have, allow only citizens to vote by demanding identification, strengthen our borders and our immigration policies, promote wholesomeness and not societal constructs unknown in history, realize that where there is great wealth there exists the potential for great crime or the oppression of others.

Each of us has friends who are not conservative or who may not care about politics. One conversation cannot undue the ubiquitous assertion of leftist precepts within our nation's institutions, but we must begin in order to change minds.

I know that people will listen, for truth penetrates falsehood, which ultimately fractures like glass. The people who seem most distant from our principles and what we hold dear are the same citizens who most need to hear and learn what we have learned. We must each become a vehicle that opens hearts to our message, for, in so doing, we will strengthen the greatest country in the history of the world: the United States of America.

All of our lives begin with our first memories and end in our passing. The road between these two points can be of our own creation or of someone else's. In America today, each of us has the capacity to make a choice as to which road we take. No matter our present hardships, America, to a degree that exceeds that of any other country, grants us the ability to change the course of our lives.

The individual is sovereign and not the government. Freedom of choice is our nation's greatest legacy, for we are each endowed with liberty by a Constitutional Republic whose Founders believed our unalienable rights come from God.

My hope in writing this book is that I may open the hearts of others who may be in need or be desirous of a new way. The exercise of freedom in a Constitutional Republic is the American experiment. It must never be lost.

Answers

While I have endeavored to offer a lens with which to view the issues of our time, it is difficult to visualize the number of sins that are comprised in President Biden's facilitation of a porous southern border that undergirds human smuggling, enslavement, drug-induced deaths, and the exploitation of minors. These horrific acts are perpetrated under a cloak of piety expressed by the Biden administration in its false façade of care for the victims of its policies.

There is a desperate need to reinvigorate the American spirit by supplanting the shallow acclaim of celebrities with true examples of American excellence, dedication, and selflessness. A president can lead a resurgence in the American spirit by lauding authentic heroes, be they military or not, rather than letting the White House play host to a cavalcade of actors who too often care most about themselves.

We must coalesce present geopolitical realities to America's advantage. We can no longer throw money at problems: We must think through our obstacles to overcome them. The promotion of meritocracies in education, in business, in science, and our nurture of the next generation through our veneration of faith and family must be united by a new emphasis on personal and organizational integrity.

As we argue for conservative values, we must not eschew change. A sagacious president will not fight technology, but embrace it, for science and its progress cannot be stopped, though its vector can be altered and carefully charted. This must be true in biology and in its associated disciplines, for the world must not know another plague that could be more deadly than that which we have just endured; neither can we allow modification of the human genome by individual scientists or by nations, who may seek superiority through genetic manipulation. Truly, this is a domain that must be investigated with the greatest of care, for it may be impossible to envision the unintended consequences of what science may permit us to alter.

Each day we are greeted with new challenges. Artificial intelligence promises great advancements, but its probable costs must also be considered. What are our predicates for the use and the training of artificial intelligence systems, which even now interact with our children? What are the ramifications of emergent, omnipresent artificial intelligence tools and facilities that are detached from a moral conception of our universe? Have we even conceived the necessary questions to be asked?

It is critical that we understand that totalitarian systems, which include communist and fascist states, reject the concept of a moral backdrop for human action, for the party is deemed to be the arbiter of all things. Unfortunately, artificial intelligence bears the potential to be congruent with communist or fascist modes of thought and governance, for this technology's essence relies on the amalgamation of knowledge that is transmitted to the user or recipient through a single source, which most resembles an oracle.

If artificial intelligence, due to the breath of its resources that derive from the capacity to traverse the trove of human knowledge, becomes unquestioned, this agent may be programed or evolve to be an absolute tool for control. This cannot be allowed.

There is already substantial evidence that artificial intelligence systems that employ neural networks, which attempt to mimic the mode of function of the human brain, are being taught by developers in such a way as to introduce evident as well as latent biases. Further, these biases appear to lean to the left, sometimes irreducibly. This is a great danger, for it will inhibit critical thinking in users, which is essential to human progress.

The 1880 novel, *The Brothers Karamazov*, by Fyodor Dostoevsky, is universally regarded as one of the greatest works of fiction in any language. "The Grand Inquisitor" is a story, which is part of the novel. In it, the Grand Inquisitor chastises Christ, who is imprisoned, in the story, during the Spanish Inquisition. The Grand Inquisitor, representing temporal authority, argues that the freedom that God has bestowed is too difficult a burden for humanity to bear. What is sought, instead, by humankind, is that which is material, which is the certitude of abundance.

If the desire for material possessions is to be satisfied by government, freedom of action, as granted to us by God, is either eradicated or severely constrained, for only absolute tyranny can secure uniformity in outcomes and attainments by distinct and unrelated individuals. Tyrannical governments accomplish this miracle by making everyone—save the elite—equally poor.

This is the paradox that is present in governance and in human nature. The desire for certainty in our world leads to conformity and ultimately to despotism.

We dare not let this inconsistency be propounded and ossified in a new age defined by the emergence of artificial general intelligence (AGI), which is an artificial entity that can learn, reason, and act in such a way that its output resembles that of a human mind. The greatest losses precipitated by such a manifestation will be to children. If they are to grow and to reach their potential, they must not be hobbled by their reliance on a machine or a program that infuses their thinking and redirects their mode of thought towards lethargy, complacency, and apathy. Such abuses of personal agency cannot define our children's future.

If we are not informed by the past, we will be ill-prepared to meet the future. Artificial intelligence may evolve to be utopian in its design, which must give us pause, for the institution of any temporal, utopian system leads to devastation, for humanity is imperfect. The quest for perfection inevitably leads to violence, for other means prove insufficient to attain the goals sought.

Artificial intelligence does not comprehend real life; it exists in a world of zeros and ones, for it is synthetic. It knows nothing of God's promise. Though the philosophical, moral, and national security ramifications of this technology are ill-defined and inchoate, many people have lashed their hopes for a better future to this burgeoning technology, despite its apparent faults. This form of technology must always be employed as a tool; it must never become our master.

Artificial intelligence must not order our actions in a world it has never experienced. This problem is magnified enormously if we consider the inability of artificial intelligence to relate to the spiritual nature of humanity, which transcends materialism.

Our nation's government, institutions, industries, and people may be placed at risk by ill-conceived forms of this instrument. Artificial intelligence tools may disrupt and further stratify society. Those among us who are highly gifted may use this new facility to increase their wealth and purview; others may rely on artificial intelligence as a crutch, limiting the attainment of their own personal potential. This course would be disastrous for students. In the future, the achievement of artificial general intelligence must not be used as an excuse for children not to study or not to develop the capacity to think critically.

If information comes too easily, reflection that leads to wisdom may be lost. Without the attainment of critical thinking skills, the next generation of Americans may be subject to programing of a type only witnessed in despotic states.

The ramifications of artificial intelligence will define in significant ways not only the second half of this decade but the years that follow. We, as a nation, cannot accept the use of artificial intelligence as a political instrument to craft subliminal rewards that will entice voters, for such lures will be both fake and detrimental if achieved in any form.

We, as a society, cannot let the provision of universal basic income by the government become the mechanism to compensate for the loss of jobs that may be precipitated by the adoption of artificial intelligence, for such a course will trigger indolence and despair, while not addressing the underlying issues of how we must confront a changing world. We cannot tolerate autocratic governance that is posited as the only means to meet such challenges. A competent government must aid in the discernment of answers to the problems faced; it must not ply superficial responses.

Artificial intelligence is not a friend; any interests it might evolve can never be fully aligned with humanity, for each person is an individual. It is doubtful that artificial general intelligence will ever be capable of moral reasoning, for true moral reasoning requires a being be crafted by God and thus imbued with a fragment of God's grace.

Artificial general intelligence might simulate moral action or concern, but we must consider it to be nothing more than an actor—playing a part. Conversely, it might espouse a moral code alien to our Judeo-Christian heritage, such as social Darwinism, which seeks rapid societal advancement by disregarding moral thought and action.

Futurists envision a technological singularity in which the world will change in ways that cannot now be envisioned. According to its advocates, humanity cannot predict what this singularity will entail, for the computational steps to reach this point cannot be pictured but may be reached by machines. This threat, in some ways, is already upon us. The continuing disembodiment of our children, through their preoccupation with submergence in an ever-expanding virtual world, may disassociate them from their bodies and the natural course of maturation.

No one can predict what the next major war will entail, but we may forecast that the next world war may be fought by man versus man-after-man, if we permit such a creature to be created. We cannot allow ourselves to be robbed of our humanity through the emergence of transhumanism, which seeks to merge humankind with machines and genetic engineering. Should this ever occur, humanity, as we know it, will be lost.

Artificial general intelligence may create forms of new knowledge through the fusion of existing ideas drawn from disparate domains. Such advancements will almost certainly not represent achievements of the highest order, for the human mind not only amalgamates bases of knowledge but creates what has never been envisioned.

The search for a higher truth cannot begin with disregard for the truth. Our answer to the quest to supplant humanity must begin with our faith, our admiration for education as a predicate for human advancement, and our unabraded belief in the wisdom of the American people. These forces, coupled with critical thinking, must constitute the ultimate paradigm for existence in a world that must not be governed by an artificial intelligence that has no capacity to equal or to surpass God's creation.

A moral universe, created by God, is posited in the Abrahamic faiths. What is critical is that communism and fascism reject the concept of a moral backdrop for human action. Therefore, we must take steps to ensure that artificial intelligence, as it evolves, does not empower despotic regimes or systems of control.

There can be no doubt that China, Russia, Iran, and other adversarial or belligerent states will organize artificial intelligence systems and tools to reject the primacy of the individual and the moral authority of God. If we do not align artificial intelligence with the predicate of a moral universe, the conception of freedom and human dignity may be lost without the magnitude of its loss realized until the true nature of such a catastrophe becomes manifest.

If artificial intelligence permits the flowering of human potential, it will be of great advantage to humanity. It must not, however, circumscribe our dreams, for many dreams are unrealizable in our world and may only be achieved in the world to come. We cannot allow the apex of our country's living within the proper boundaries established by God to be a memory, for this pinnacle must represent our future and not our past. Though we are more technologically advanced today than at the time of my birth, we are seemingly less advantaged as a people in understanding what is important in life.

When there was great wrong in our nation during the period of Jim Crow and segregation, there was human realization of that which was impermissible. To be sure, there was not, at that time, universal recognition of the unacceptability of discrimination, but there was apprehension within many hearts: This permitted our society to progress.

Will the same be true of a future culture that looks to artificial intelligence for guidance or insight regarding morality? I think not. It is already understood that artificial intelligence is capable of generating both misinformation and disinformation. Let us not be governed by what we create but do not control, but by God.

The world's greatest minds must be brought together to create a touchstone of limits that will permit the citizens of our planet to benefit from artificial intelligence but not be enslaved by it. This empanelment and their work must be a priority of our country's next president: We cannot step into a new future blind.

Conservatism

The concept of being a conservative is altered by the technological age in which we live. Life is now transformed more in one decade than it was in entire centuries—in times past. The central question for a conservative is what from the past should be conserved in the context of ever-changing technology. I believe the answers must celebrate our faith, our families, our Founding, our reverence for education, and our ceaseless commitment to excellence.

I believe that it is through God that we know our gifts, which can change the world and lead it to peace. The existence of our Creator is not contingent upon belief; our existence is contingent upon his word. The Logos is the lever that can move the universe. Only it can resolve intractable enmities. This majestic tool is given to each of us, if we have the wisdom to employ it.

People suffused with faith and reverence comprehend that the exercise of true personal freedom is not the absence of limitations that are imposed by God, for what is ordained provides our compass. We are each endowed with a dignity that is irreducible. Tyrants have tried to scorch this gift, but have never succeeded, for their power is confined to this world.

In this book, I have tried to describe the foundations of our country and how they support four crucial pillars of national power. As in many things, the support given does not move in one direction but in many. The value of life is upheld by our ability to defend ourselves, while avoiding needless conflict. It also rests upon education and upon the meaning we place in bringing new life into the world.

Our freedom of action as a country derives its power from the foundations of truth, strength, economic security, and energy dominance. Leadership results from our embrace of the values of faith, family, and scientific integrity. We are also guided by the standards established by the patriots who founded our nation. America is fortified and safeguarded by our nuclear deterrent, our armed forces, the sanctity of our borders, and the valor of our people.

It is these foundations and pillars that serve to support America. These stanchions may be combined in numerous ways to suit the needs of the day. They constitute the matchless tools we have inherited. We must not squander or deprecate them.

Very few decisions need to be changed for a nation's history to be either impoverished or be matchless. Throughout the past sixty years, America frequently chose errantly. We now are paying the price.

America's path into the future is a choice. We must not choose defeat, neglect, or shame.

The political class in Washington who belittle the farmer, the welder, or the small business owner, cannot do what these men and women accomplish every day. Politicians and bureaucrats cannot balance a budget, provide adequately for necessities while maintaining reserves, or plan for the future.

With the nation's wealth at their command and the Federal Reserve's printing presses at the ready, all the elites in Washington can do is waste—as they criticize those who produced what they squander. America cannot go on this way, for this profligacy is unnatural and corrupt.

The left and elements of the Democratic Party demonstrate that they believe government is our master. It is not.

We, as Americans, hold these bedrock convictions: Faith leads to hope and to the fulfillment of each of our individual gifts; meaningful education is indispensable; America must be strong but circumspect in its use of force; free enterprise is essential.

Today, we stand upon a promontory overlooking pending elections that will chart the course of our nation. I pray that we will choose liberty and not constraint. I pray that we will choose reverence of our cherished past and not its abrogation. I pray that we will move forward into the future as one united people.

There is a journey that is America. Let us begin.

Chapter 14, Reflections, Precepts:

• America's third century is upon us; it must not signify our lasting descent. The hubris of the bureaucratic state is unjustified, for the wisdom of the American people is unequaled.

• The foundations of our country and the pillars of national power rest on faith, family, limited government, education, science, the rule of law, and our nation's armed forces. These are all necessary for human advancement.

• Wisdom must be attained before power is exercised; political discourse is impossible without standards of behavior.

• Leadership results from our embrace of the timeless values bequeathed to us. The value of life is upheld by our ability to defend ourselves, while avoiding needless conflict; it also rests upon the priority we place in bringing children into the world. Freedom derives from truth, economic security, and energy dominance. America is fortified and safeguarded by our nuclear deterrent, the sanctity of our borders, and the strength of our people.

Issues and Problems:

• A society that does not enforce its own laws provides its assessment that its laws are unjust or unenforceable. Our nation's new ruling class has accumulated power and wealth by feigning support for the dispossessed, while exporting our jobs to China. Whole industries have been lost, though the left claims to care about the American worker, the environment, the state of our economy, and our international competitiveness.

• Equity is the imposition of a constructed version of fairness that is not fair, for fairness arises from the attainment of the fruits of one's labor, not the imposition of sameness in results, which is only possible through theft.

• America's armed forces have never been defeated over the course of a conflict. Our military has been shaken by malicious and incompetent politicians of both parties who do not measure the sacrifices they expect, which they simultaneously fail to honor.

Duties and Actions:

• A president must not sign bills into law that are not comprehensible nor capable of being reviewed in full.

• As we argue for conservative values, we must not eschew change. Artificial intelligence and other new technologies promise great advancements, but probable and possible costs must be considered and measured.

• For true leadership to be achieved, determination and openness must govern political discourse. We must coalesce present geopolitical realities to America's advantage. We can no longer throw money at problems: We must think through our obstacles to overcome them.

• We must state plainly to our allies and friends that freedom must be defended jointly if it is to be enjoyed individually. Each nation that values freedom must do its fair share

• We must restore simple common sense: Except in time of gravest emergency, do not spend money you do not have, allow only citizens to vote by demanding identification, strengthen our borders and our immigration policies, promote wholesomeness and not societal constructs unknown in history,

• Let each of us not be governed by fear or by timidity in the face of an uncertain future, but by God and by our Constitution, which is the product of eternal truths that enshrine peace, sustenance, improvement, and liberty.

CHARTS

Three Challenges for an American Century

National Security:

Military & Energy Dominance, Wisdom in the Use of Force, Cyber & Economic Security

The Civil Society:

U.S. Workers & Farmers are Central, Limited Government, National Sovereignty, & Voting Integrity

Education & Knowledge:

Global Leadership in Science, Technology, Education, & Apolitical Institutions

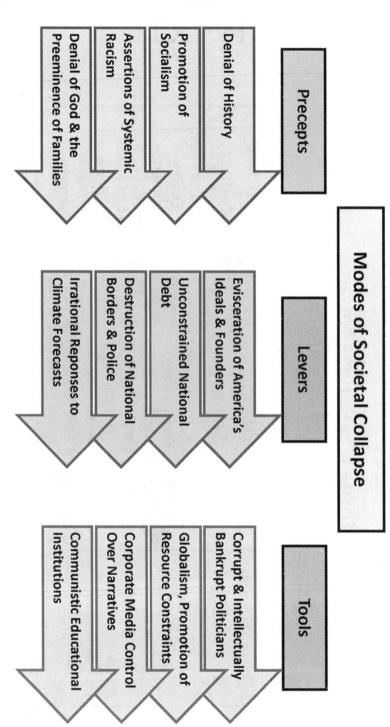

Tools for Governance

Faith, Knowledge, & Integrity

The profession of faith in God is not inimical to the Establishment Clause; the Establishment Clause became part of the Bill of Rights because faith was expected within America's public square. The clause was intended to bar the creation of a state religion, not remove religion from public life, for our Founders understood that faith & the ethical values that religion instills are essential to curb the power of the state.

In our burgeoning technological age in which the synthetic cyberworld threatens to overtake that which is real, leadership is required to ensure that America always rests on the individual & never the collective. All group prejudice is destroyed if every person is perceived to be a unique & irreplaceable creation of God, for each person possesses unalienable rights that no government can be permitted to abridge.

Key Levers

America's Founding Documents must be respected. Without adherence to our Declaration of Independence, Constitution, & Bill of Rights, America will cease to exist. Oaths taken by public officials to enforce the Constitution must not be disobeyed or disparaged. Oaths must be upheld.

Government spending & debt must be brought to heel. Limited & not expansive government ensures liberty.

Government operates best when it does not impede the progress of its citizens through laws & regulations that are often designed to benefit the few at the expense of the many.

Federalism & the Separation of Powers

The separation of powers between the federal executive, legislative, & Judicial branches is mandatory, for a system of checks & balances restrains federal overreach. The Tenth Amendment to the Bill of Rights is critical; it reads, "The powers not delegated to the United States by the Constitution, nor prohibited by it to the States, are reserved to the States respectively, or to the people."

America's strengths must be communicated to our citizens & to the world. Belief in our system of distributed power is essential. Unchecked power is intrinsically corruptive: America must return to its federal system, vesting powers first in our people & then in our states, for decision-making is best held close to those who must live with its consequences.

Local, Regional, & Domestic Goals | National Objectives | International & Security Policies

Low Energy Costs, Vibrant Economy — Freedom from Foreign Coercion
Constituency: Citizens/Businesses — Action: Fracking/Nuclear Power — Lower Bills/Extra Cash — Energy Dominance

Job Stability & Growth — Trade Policies that Put the American Worker on Top
Constituency: All Workers/Farmers — Action: America/Not Giveaways — Higher Wages/Security — Reciprocity

Security at Home & Abroad — Military Strength — Leadership, Not Armed Intervention
Constituency: Services/Families — Action: Rebuild Military — Respect/Not War

Strong Families, Adoption, not Abortion — Demographic Vigor — Legal Immigration, Secure Borders
Constituency: All Americans — Action: Promote Parenting — Cohesive Society

Quadrants of National Power & their Components

Economic & Energy Security:
Expanded Domestic Energy Supplies, Trade Agreements with Free Nations that Support the American Worker & Farmer, Public Diplomacy

Homeland:
Pandemic Preparedness, Protected Borders, Secure Elections, Cybersecurity Prioritization, Control of Criminal & Terrorist Threats

Leadership:
National Cohesion, Founding Principles, Institutional Fortitude, Equal Opportunity, Meritocracy, Intelligence, Diplomacy

Military Strength:
Strategic Defense, Dominant Conventional Forces, Alliances, Technological Leadership, STEM Education, EMP Preparedness

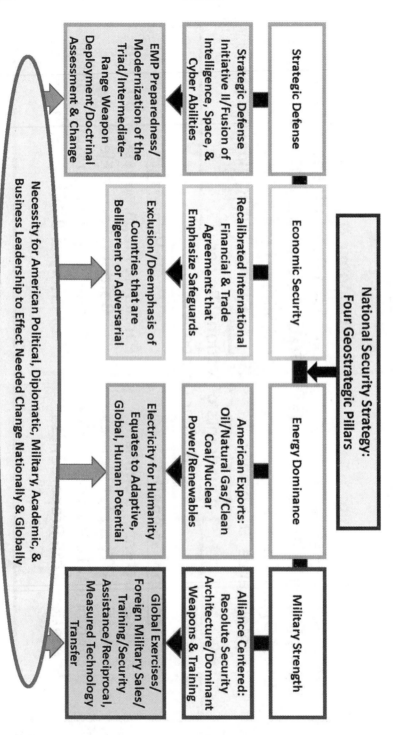

National Security Strategy: Four Geostrategic Pillars

Strategic Defense
- Strategic Defense Initiative II/Fusion of Intelligence, Space, & Cyber Abilities
- EMP Preparedness/ Modernization of the Triad/Intermediate-Range Weapon Deployment/Doctrinal Assessment & Change

Economic Security
- Recalibrated International Financial & Trade Agreements that Emphasize Safeguards
- Exclusion/Deemphasis of Countries that are Belligerent or Adversarial

Energy Dominance
- American Exports: Oil/Natural Gas/Clean Coal/Nuclear Power/Renewables
- Electricity for Humanity Equates to Adaptive, Global, Human Potential

Military Strength
- Alliance Centered: Resolute Security Architecture/Dominant Weapons & Training
- Global Exercises/ Foreign Military Sales/ Training/Security Assistance/Reciprocal, Measured Technology Transfer

Necessity for American Political, Diplomatic, Military, Academic, & Business Leadership to Effect Needed Change Nationally & Globally

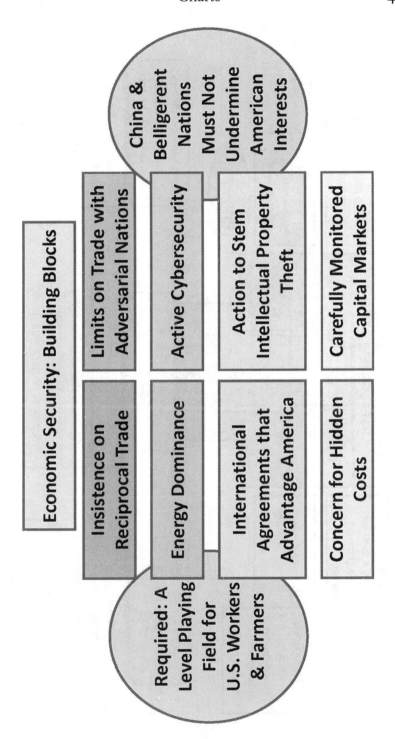

Economic Security: Building Blocks

China & Belligerent Nations Must Not Undermine American Interests

Limits on Trade with Adversarial Nations

Insistence on Reciprocal Trade

Active Cybersecurity

Energy Dominance

Action to Stem Intellectual Property Theft

International Agreements that Advantage America

Carefully Monitored Capital Markets

Concern for Hidden Costs

Required: A Level Playing Field for U.S. Workers & Farmers

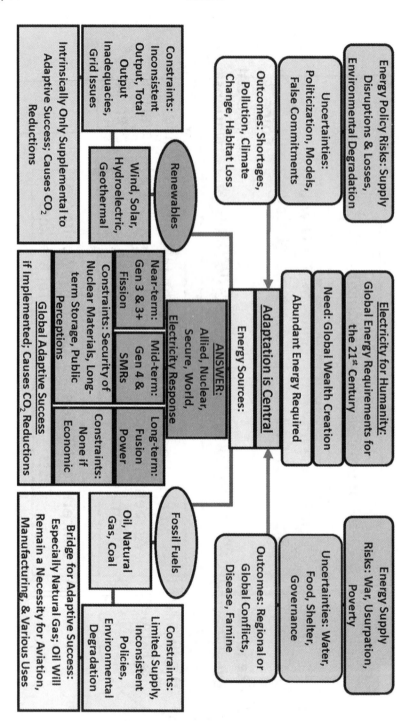

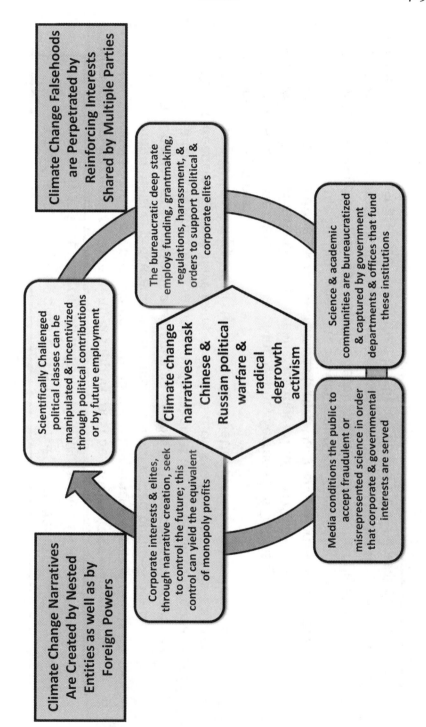

Climate Change Falsehoods are Perpetrated by Reinforcing Interests Shared by Multiple Parties

The bureaucratic deep state employs funding, grantmaking, regulations, harassment, & orders to support political & corporate elites

Science & academic communities are bureaucratized & captured by government departments & offices that fund these institutions

Scientifically Challenged political classes can be manipulated & incentivized through political contributions or by future employment

Climate change narratives mask Chinese & Russian political warfare & radical degrowth activism

Media conditions the public to accept fraudulent or misrepresented science in order that corporate & governmental interests are served

Corporate interests & elites, through narrative creation, seek to control the future; this control can yield the equivalent of monopoly profits

Climate Change Narratives Are Created by Nested Entities as well as by Foreign Powers

As an integral component of a New National Security Act, institute major, structural change within DOD

- Weapon development, procurement, & support must be proximate to warfighters.

- A new national security act must remove structural & bureaucratic impediments to ensure that new weapon systems are deployed swiftly, with per-unit costs kept low.

- Major bureaucratic restructuring must be undertaken at the Pentagon to remove entire levels of bureaucracy, which have hampered our nation's warfighters. This is a predicate to obtaining congressional support to streamline & to better systematize the authorizations & appropriations process.

- The elimination of the current office of the Deputy Secretary of Defense would reduce substantially the immense civilian bureaucracy that orbits this office.

- Under this plan, the three service secretaries (Army, Navy, & Air Force) would rotate as the principal deputy to the SecDef, when the SecDef is outside Washington.

- This initiative would bring weapon-system development closer to the operators, an essential business practice, through placing such development under the aegis of the services. Proven best practices could then be shared across the services.

American national power is a product of domestic achievements, resources, & capabilities that sustain international security objectives, which, in turn, support our domestic attainments, ensuring their progress

Domestic Policies

Limited & not oppressive government; veneration & not dismemberment of America's Founding Documents; reliance on individual enterprise, achievement, & the market must be coupled with energy dominance across the spectrum of production & trade

Massive reductions in governmental regulations, reliance on the private sector & not the bureaucracy, educational reform, insistence on vouchers, & de-politization from preschool through graduate school

Strength as represented in our people is essential to maintain our standing as the world's leading power through this century & the next: Legal immigration, thriving families, & alternatives to abortion must be prioritized

National Objectives

Peace, security, economic strength, environmental stewardship, equality of opportunity, social mobility, & wealth creation

Well-being at home, freedom of the seas, worldwide trade that benefits but does not subvert the American worker or our economic imperatives

Ability to paydown our national debt that exceeds $31 trillion, fund social security, & satisfy our long-term unfunded liabilities that amount to more than $100 trillion

International Relations & National Security Policies

Reestablishment of the Eisenhower-Reagan model of international relations: National strategy must support the vibrancy of American families & our economy; international leadership is to be through example & not intervention

Creation of a military second to none that is devoid of political indoctrination of any kind, unquestioned naval superiority, & trade agreements that are absolutely reciprocal, which prize the interests of the American worker

Transformation of America's immigration system, coupled with ironclad border security, must be prioritized; legal immigration should be increased as illegal immigration is eliminated; assimilation is crucial

Domestic Postulates for America's Decline & their Resolution

Issue:

Lack of public comity, open debate, or reasoned discourse; substitution of mob rule for intellectual openness & inquiry

Runaway government spending, inflation, & an unaccountable bureaucracy that is plagued by corruption

Racial strife amplified by the media; unsafe neighborhoods; breakdown of America's families & social norms

Substandard schools at all levels; prevalent mediocrity; political indoctrination; deprecation of core proficiencies

Resolution:

Language must not be rendered devoid of meaning as the left intends; manners must pervade politics – to enable issues to be addressed without false aspersions – designed to cancel dissenting voices; standards for openness must be introduced across major internet sites

The Federal Reserve must be barred from social engineering or politization; the federal government must live within its means; bureaucracy must be continually reduced & prohibited from overreach or control of private businesses or institutions through regulations or grantmaking

Americans must all be treated as individuals, for this is how we are judged by God; the rule of law & public safety must be prioritized, particularly in disadvantaged neighborhoods; adoption & not abortion must be our standard; caring, nuclear families must be respected

Insistence on excellence; K-12 school reform stressing vouchers, choice, & adoption of state-of-the-art teaching methods from around the world; deemphasis on colleges that produce militant administrators, who lead to the politization of education

ACKNOWLEDGMENTS

I thank my dear wife, Terry, for all she has given me. She is the love of my life.

Former Secretary of State Michael R. Pompeo was a guiding light in the creation of this book. Collaborating closely with the secretary imbued *Pillars for Freedom* with perspectives of matchless value.

No work of this scope could have been completed without the detailed review of many experts, who were each exceedingly generous in their commitment to the fruition of this work. I thank Vice Admiral John M. Poindexter, assistant to the president for national security affairs under President Ronald Reagan; William F. Martin, former United States deputy secretary of energy, former chair of the United States Nuclear Energy Advisory Committee, and past president of the council of the University for Peace; Roger W. Robinson, Jr., chairman of the Prague Security Studies Institute and former chair of the Congressional U.S.-China Economic and Security Review Commission; Dr. Miles Yu, director of the China Center at the Hudson Institute and former principal advisor on China policy to Secretary of State Michael R. Pompeo; and Ambassador Ronald F. Lehman II, former director of the Arms Control and Disarmament Agency. The input and advice of these consummate professionals conveyed immeasurable aid to this enterprise.

I owe special thanks to my wonderful friend, Lieutenant Colonel Oliver L. North (United States Marine Corps, retired). Without his steadfast support, this book would not exist in its present form.

My surgeon, Dr. Thomas B. Warren, restored my life through his superlative care, making this book possible. His hands healed what was shattered.

My service to President Ronald Reagan in the company of great patriots has been my foremost source of inspiration in authoring this book. I learned so much in the presence of giants. My life's journey could have only been possible in America.

My mother, Sylvia, passed away as I was completing this book. She is so dearly missed. May God bless her and these United States.

ABOUT THE AUTHOR

Richard B. Levine served as the Deputy Assistant Secretary of the Navy for Technology Transfer and Security Assistance. He directed the Department of the Navy's organization in these matters during the Reagan administration. Richard previously served on the National Security Council staff, in the White House, as Director, International Economic Affairs, and as Director, Policy Development. Richard holds an MBA from the Harvard Business School and a Bachelor of Arts degree in philosophy, *with honors*, from the Johns Hopkins University. Richard is the recipient of two presidential letters of commendation and the Department of the Navy's highest honor given to a civilian employee, the Distinguished Civilian Service Award.

Richard serves as a principal advisor to former senior officials on matters involving national security, government, and international economics. He is the coauthor, with Vice Admiral John M. Poindexter and Robert C. McFarlane, of *America's #1 Adversary And What We Must Do About It—Now!* published by Fidelis Publishing. Richard lives in North Carolina with his wife, Terry.

QUOTATIONS FROM THE HOLY BIBLE

Opening Epigraph

"The night is nearly over, and the daylight is near, so let us discard the deeds of darkness and put on the armor of light."

Romans 13:12 (HCSB)

Foreword

"Because of my integrity you uphold me and set me in your presence forever."

Psalms 41:12 (NIV)

Chapter 1: Truth

"Come, let us build ourselves a city and a tower with its top in the heavens, and let us make a name for ourselves."

Genesis 11:4 (ESV)

Chapter 2: Faith

"overturned the tables of the money changers,"

Matthew 21:12 (NIV)

"foolish and senseless people, who have eyes but do not see, who have ears but do not hear: Should you not fear me? . . . Among my people are the wicked who lie in wait like men who snare birds and like those who set traps to catch people. . . . their houses are full of deceit; they have become rich and powerful . . . . Their evil deeds have no limit; they do not seek justice."

Jeremiah 5:21-28 (NIV)

"They say unto him, Caesar's. Then saith he unto them, Render therefore unto Caesar the things which are Caesar's; and unto God the things that are God's."

Matthew 22:21 (KJV)

"And Jesus answered and said to them, 'Render to Caesar the things that are Caesar's, and to God the things that are God's.' And they marveled at Him."

Mark 12:17 (NKJV)

Chapter 3: Founding

"Thou shalt not steal"

Exodus 20:15 (KJV)

Chapter 4: Family

"Children are a heritage from the Lord, offspring a reward from him."

Psalms 127:3 (NIV)

Chapter 8: Scientific Integrity

"The Lord detests dishonest scales, but accurate weights find favor with him."

Proverbs 11 (NIV)

Chapter 14: Reflections

"For as by one man's disobedience many were made sinners, so by the obedience of one shall many be made righteous."

Romans 5:19 (KJV)